THEORY AND INTERPRETATION OF NARRATIVE
James Phelan, Peter J. Rabinowitz, and Robyn Warhol, Series Editors

Narrative Discourse
Authors and Narrators in Literature, Film, and Art

Patrick Colm Hogan

 THE OHIO STATE UNIVERSITY PRESS | COLUMBUS

Copyright © 2013 by The Ohio State University.
All rights reserved.

Library of Congress Cataloging-in-Publication Data
Hogan, Patrick Colm.
Narrative discourse : authors and narrators in literature, film, and art / Patrick Colm Hogan.
p. cm.—(Theory and interpretation of narrative)
Includes bibliographical references and index.
ISBN 978-0-8142-1209-7 (cloth : alk. paper)—ISBN 978-0-8142-9311-9 (cd)
1. Discourse analysis, Narrative. 2. Narration (Rhetoric) 3. Critical discourse analysis.
I. Title. II. Series: Theory and interpretation of narrative series.
P302.7.H643 2013
808'.036—dc23
2012038668

Cover design by Thao Thai
Text design by Juliet Williams
Type set in Gentium

∞ The paper used in this publication meets the minimum requirements of the American National Standard for Information Sciences—Permanence of Paper for Printed Library Materials. ANSI Z39.48-1992.

For my parents

Contents

List of Illustrations ix
Acknowledgments xi

Introduction Discourse Analysis and Narration 1

Chapter 1 Who Is Speaking to Whom:
The Communicative Discourse of Narrative Art 21

Chapter 2 Cross-Textual Implied Painters and Cinematic *Auteurs*:
Rabindranath Tagore's Paintings and Bimal Roy's *Madhumati* 64

Chapter 3 Authors, Implied and Implicated: Explaining Harriet
Beecher Stowe's *Uncle Tom's Cabin* and Kabir Khan's *New York* 113

Chapter 4 Narrative Reliability: Margaret Atwood's *Surfacing* 150

Chapter 5 Varieties of Multiple Narration (I):
Parallel Narrators in William Faulkner's
The Sound and the Fury and David Lynch's *Mulholland Drive* 183

Chapter 6 Varieties of Multiple Narration (II):
Embedded Narration, Focalization, and Collective Voicing in
Ngũgĩ wa Thiong'o's *Petals of Blood* and *Born of the Sun* by
Joseph Diescho (with Celeste Wallin) 222

Afterword A Note on Implied Readers and Narratees:
Mīrābāī's "Even if you break off, beloved, I would not" 251

Notes 259
Works Cited 276
Index 289

Illustrations

Figure 2.1.	Tagore, ink and watercolor.	69
Figure 2.2.	Tagore, ink.	72
Figure 2.3.	Tagore, ink and watercolor.	77
Figure 2.4.	Tagore, ink.	79
Figure 2.5.	Tagore, etched print.	81
Figure 2.6.	Tagore, ink.	84
Figure 2.7.	Tagore, ink.	85
Figure 2.8.	Tagore, ink and watercolor.	86
Figure 2.9.	Tagore, ink.	88
Figure 2.10.	Anand observes Madhumati from a distance.	104
Figure 2.11.	Anand and Madhumati look toward the distant village where they will go for a festival.	104
Figure 2.12.	Anand and Madhumati out of each other's line of sight.	105
Figure 2.13.	Anand and Madhumati invisible to each other.	105
Figure 2.14.	Anand disappearing into the fog.	106
Figure 2.15.	Madhumati engulfed in mist.	106
Figure 2.16.	The lovers emerge from the fog.	106

Figure 2.17.	Devendra is obscured by a white curtain as his past-life memory begins.	108
Figure 2.18.	Devendra's past-life memory is marked by extended superimposition.	108
Figure 2.19.	When Devendra fades from the screen, the white curtain passes in front of the memory of Madhumati.	108
Figure 2.20.	The return to the present is marked by the curtain obscuring Devendra's face.	108
Figure 2.21.	Madhumati's ghost has the same translucent quality (of superimposition) as Devendra's memories.	108
Figure 5.1.	The two forms of multiple narration. Embedding is marked by arrows.	185
Figure 5.2.	Opening jitterbug.	203
Figure 5.3.	Betty/Diane evidently winning the competition.	203
Figure 5.4.	Shot of Rita sleeping, after the Winkie's sequence.	207
Figure 5.5.	Camilla kisses another woman before Diane.	209
Figure 5.6.	But before the kiss, they check to make sure Diane is watching.	209
Figure 5.7.	Diane meets their eyes before the kiss.	209
Figure 5.8.	The decaying body of Diane Selwyn from the optimistic story.	212
Figure 5.9.	Diane, just before she wakes up in the pessimistic story.	212
Figure 5.10.	Diane turns with delight to the returned Camilla. Cut to Fig. 5.11.	215
Figure 5.11.	Camilla returns Diane's affectionate gaze. Cut to Fig. 5.12.	215
Figure 5.12.	Diane apparently continues to look toward Camilla. However, she becomes increasingly distressed. Cut to Fig. 5.13.	215
Figure 5.13.	Rather than Camilla, we find Diane apparently looking back at Diane.	215
Figure 5.14.	Highly unrealistic, highly theatrical scene of Diane's suicide.	217

Acknowledgments

PART OF chapter 1 appeared as "A Passion for Plot: Prolegomena to Affective Narratology," *symplokē* 18 (2011): 65–82. An earlier version of part of chapter 2 appeared as "Auteurs and Their Brains: Cognition and Creativity in the Cinema," *Visual Authorship: Creativity and Intentionality in Media (Northern Lights: Film and Media Studies Yearbook 2004)*, ed. Torben Grodal, Bente Larsen, and Iben Thorving Laursen (Copenhagen, Denmark: Museum Tusculanum Press, 2005), 67–86. An earlier version of another section from that chapter appeared as "Rabindranath Tagore, Implied Painter: On the Narratology of Visual Art," *South Asia: Journal of South Asian Studies* n.s. 35.1 (2012): 48–72. Part of chapter 3 appeared as "The Multiplicity of Implied Authors and the Complex Case of *Uncle Tom's Cabin*," *Narrative* 20.1 (2012): 25–42. I am grateful to the editors and publishers for permission to reprint. The University of Connecticut Small Grant Program funded indexing of this book.

Some ideas and analyses of the introduction and chapter 1 were presented at the Symposium on Discourse at the University of Connecticut in February 2009. A shortened version of part of chapter 3 was presented as a plenary talk at the conference "Storyworlds Across Media," June 2011, in Mainz, Germany. An earlier version of part of chapter 3 was presented as a keynote address at the International Society for the Study of Narrative Conference, April 2011, in St. Louis. Part of an earlier version of chapter 5 was presented as a plenary address at the 2011 conference of the Poetics and Linguistics Association in Windhoek, Namibia. In each case, I am grateful to the organizers—Bernard Grela, Marie-Laure Ryan, Jan-Noël Thon, Karl Renner, Emma Kafalenos, Erin McGlothlin, Michael Burke, and Sarala Krishnamurthy—for providing these opportunities and to the participants for their comments and questions. James Phelan provided painstaking comments on the discussion of implied authors and the treatment of Stowe, while Peter J. Rabinowitz, Robyn Warhol, and an anonymous reviewer for The Ohio State University Press proposed challenging revisions in scrupulous detail. The book certainly would not have been the same without their meticulous input.

I am grateful to Nilanjan Banerjee of Rabindra-Bhavana, Udaya Narayana Singh of Visva-Bharati University, and Andrew Robinson, editor of *The Art of Rabindranath Tagore,* regarding permission to reproduce images of Tagore's paintings.

I am grateful to Andrew Schelling and, particularly, Ira Raja for help in tracking down a text of the Mīrābāī poem discussed in the afterword.

It was, once again, a pleasure to work with Sandy Crooms and the rest of the editorial staff at The Ohio State University Press. I am grateful to Sandy for her great help throughout the process.

Introduction

Discourse Analysis and Narration

THERE ARE three main senses in which the phrase "discourse analysis" is used in literary study today. The first and fundamental sense is that of linguistics—the study of units of speech or writing above the level of the sentence. Alternatively, some writers characterize linguistic discourse analysis as the study of language in use (as Schiffrin, Tannen, and Hamilton point out in the introduction to their *Handbook of Discourse Analysis* [1]). Though different in emphasis, the two definitions largely converge. This fundamental usage encompasses the other two, that is, the analysis of narrative discourse and Critical Discourse Analysis.

Linguistic Discourse Analysis

Discourse analysis in the fundamental, linguistic sense has two main goals. One is to isolate rules or structures that guide the production and reception of speech or writing "beyond the sentence" (Schiffrin, Tannen, and Hamilton 1). The second is to interpret particular utterances or speech interactions, in part by reference to those rules or structures. The two common definitions of *linguistic discourse analysis* simply stress one or the other of these two goals.

Paul Grice's rules of conversational implicature provide an example. Grice influentially argued that, when engaged in conversation, people draw many nonlogical inferences from what the other speakers say. These are not illogical inferences. Indeed, they are quite rational. However, they are not governed by formal principles of inference. Rather, they are guided by looser principles of cooperation. Moreover, as speakers, people rely on these cooperative principles and they expect their listeners to draw nonlogical conclusions from what they say. One example of this sort of principle is the "Maxim of Relevance." People tailor their speech, and interpret other people's speech, as relevant to what is currently being discussed. Suppose Jones says, "I haven't seen Doe in a while." Smith replies, "He travels frequently." Jones is likely to infer that, in Smith's view, Doe is away on some sort of travel. However, that is not a strict logical implication of the statement, or of the conjunction of statements. It may be true that Jones has not seen Doe in a while, that Doe travels frequently, and that Smith knows Doe is in the local hospital. Smith may in principle have merely said something true that happened to occur to him—as he might have said, "The almanac predicts a wet summer." Jones tacitly assumes Smith did not do this, but observed the maxim of relevance and made a comment with bearing on the topic introduced by Jones.

Discourse analysts commonly distinguish types of discourse. They may then look for the same general kinds of pattern in these various types, while at the same time examining how those general kinds are manifest differently. One general kind of pattern is *coherence*—what makes a particular unit of discourse unified. Grice's principles of conversational implicature are in part a case of this. Grice focuses on a particular type of discourse, conversation. He then asks what makes a conversation cohere. The maxim of relevance is one part of the structure of coherence of conversational discourse.

Other recurring concerns in this "nomological" aspect of discourse are nicely illustrated by studies of politeness. Work on politeness addresses such issues as who can speak, when they can speak, what sort of vocabulary they can use, how they address others, and so forth. For example, it is generally impolite in contemporary American society for a high school student to address his or her teacher by first name, though the reverse is not impolite. This reference to "contemporary American society" indicates that nomological aspects of discourse analysis may be bound to particular cultures. They may also be cross-cultural. Presumably some principles along the lines of Grice's maxims are cross-cultural (see Stephen Levinson). Moreover, in the etiquette of address, a wide range of societies restrict forms of address based on social hierarchies.

However, that restriction need not take precisely the same form as it does in the United States today.

One type of discourse that is of interest to linguistic and related discourse analysts is narrative or storytelling.[1] As the first chapter will discuss, discourse analysts have taken considerable interest in narratives. These range from the daily anecdotes people share with friends, to people's description of symptoms for doctors, to the official summary of a department meeting, to literary works such as *Abhijñānaśākuntalam, The Odyssey,* or *War and Peace.* In order to make their subject matter more tractable, narrative discourse analysts often focus on subsets of narrative—such as patient narratives to their physicians or personal anecdotes in a particular group (see, for example, Mildorf). Literary critics and theorists who take up linguistic discourse analysis are unlikely to focus on anecdotes and related personal stories that are immediately functional in a pragmatic context and are recounted only a limited number of times within a small circle of acquaintants. Instead, they tend to be concerned with narratives that have had widespread emotional impact for a broad range of people. In other words, literary critics engaged in discourse analysis tend to be interested in verbal arts.

But there are two important qualifications here. First, some narrative discourse analysts may teach in literature departments, but may be more concerned with, say, patient stories about their symptoms than with Shakespeare. One might say that they are doing discourse analysis of cultural narratives, rather than literary narratives proper. Of course, to say that patient histories are not works of verbal art is not to say that there are no features of verbal art in those histories. There are. Indeed, that leads to the second important qualification. Many of the fundamental issues that concern discourse analysts of literary narrative are also issues in nonliterary narrative. Though it is important to distinguish the principles governing different types of narrative, it is also valuable to consider what all narratives have in common and what rules summarize those commonalities.

As already noted, discourse analysts often take up topics that recur across discourse types. These topics include the following: What makes a discourse cohere? Who is allowed to speak, when, to whom, and how? What sorts of vocabulary, what levels of diction, what forms of address are allowed? What information has to be filled in explicitly and what can be left for inference? and so on. In the case of narrative discourse, coherence is in part a matter of story structure. Thus it is in part resolved into subquestions, such as the following: What constitutes a story? When does a story begin? When does a story end? What are the genres of stories?

One of the most obvious recurring questions for narrative discourse analysis would include *Who speaks? Why does he or she do so? Who listens? Why do they listen?* These questions appear particularly pressing in verbal art, thus when the story is told not for pragmatic reasons, but for its intrinsic interest. This is perhaps clearest in conversational storytelling. As, for example, Liang Tao notes, the "organization of conversation is a turn-taking system" (see also Kitzinger). But telling a story violates the usual pattern of turn-taking. Thus it violates basic principles of who can speak for how long. That is fine, as long as the violation is justified. As William Labov put it, this is permissible so long as one "justifies the delivery of the narrative and the claim on social attention" by recounting something that is "tellable" (547). Tellability derives primarily from the emotional force (excitement, humor, suspense, etc.) of the narrative. In part this is a function of the story itself. But it is also a function of just how the story is told. Thus it concerns not only what information is given, but how much is given, when it is given, and how it is phrased.

Narrative Discourse Analysis

This leads to the second use of the phrase "discourse analysis"—the study of narrative discourse. In the theoretical study of narrative—that is, narratology—"discourse" is commonly used to refer to a subset of the concerns found in the linguistic discourse analysis of narrative. Specifically, within narratology, *discourse* is separated from *story*. As Shen explains, "*Story*, in simplest terms, is *what* is told whereas *discourse* refers to 'how' the story is transmitted" ("Story-Discourse" 566). That "how" crucially involves questions of who is speaking to whom, what information is conveyed, and so forth. To make the relevant distinction clear, one may refer to the large linguistic category of all suprasentential speech and writing as "linguistic discourse." In contrast, one may refer to the narratological counterpart of "story" as "narrative discourse."[2]

As the preceding points indicate, narrative discourse involves many of the same basic concerns as other forms of discourse. Moreover, literary and nonliterary forms of narrative—forms such as patient histories—have common features of both story formation and narrative discourse organization. This is what one would expect from a cognitive perspective. People generate stories using the same cognitive architecture whether they are in a doctor's office or a creative writing class. On the other hand, one would also expect that the cognitive processes at issue could be elaborated, embedded, integrated, varied, and otherwise rendered more complex in a heavily revised 500-page novel than in a spontaneous 500-word outline of one's shoulder problem.

Students of literature who have been reading to this point may wonder about something that has been left out of this discussion. Most literary critics spend most of their time talking about individual works. Sometimes they are concerned about, for example, genre patterns. But, on the whole, their interests tend much more toward the particularity of individual novels, plays, or poems, than toward what novels, plays, or poems have in common (not to mind what they share with medical complaints).

It was noted at the outset that linguistic discourse analysis has two main goals. One is, again, the isolation of broad patterns or, roughly, rules. The second is just what one would expect from the preoccupations of literary critics—the understanding of discursive particularity. If the former is, roughly, nomological, the latter is, roughly, hermeneutic. Literary study is, then, fully in keeping with linguistic discourse analysis in this respect. They both have two primary descriptive concerns.

It is perhaps less widely recognized by literary critics, however, that these two concerns are interrelated. First, interpretation contributes to rule-based explanation. Here it is useful to return to the example of conversational implicature. Jones says, "I haven't seen Doe in weeks," and Smith says, "He travels a lot." In and of itself, the conversation cannot contribute to the isolation of rules. Rather, rules explain the conversation *under an interpretation.* A discourse analyst interprets Smith as suggesting that Doe is away on a trip and that this is the reason Jones has not seen him. It is by way of this interpretation that a discourse analyst will take the conversation to instantiate the maxim of relevance.

The nomological part of discourse analysis also contributes to the interpretive part. This may not be obvious in cases such as conversation. That is because people have interiorized the rules of conversation and follow them automatically. In other cases, however, interpretive inferences may be guided and enhanced by the explicit formulation of patterns. Indeed, narrative—including literary narrative—provides striking cases of this.

To illustrate the point, it is useful to return to Labov. In an influential study treating inner-city oral narratives of personal experience, Labov isolated the following structure: abstract, orientation, complicating action, evaluation, resolution, and coda. An abstract is a brief summary of what is to follow. The orientation introduces the main characters, locating them in time and place. The complicating action presents the main events. It creates interest and tension. The evaluation involves commentary on the significance of the complicating action. The resolution is, of course, the conclusion of the complicating action. The coda "puts off any further questions about what happened or why it mattered" (as Norrick puts it [129]). Specifically, it is "a statement that returns the temporal setting to the present" (Labov 547). For example, it may indicate what happened to the main characters following the central action.

Labov isolated the structure using a very narrowly defined corpus of stories. Nonetheless, it seems clear that the structure is widespread, not only in personal anecdotes but in literary works. Consider, for example, the operation of abstract and orientation in works of narrative art. Films and novels often do not require an abstract in the text itself, since that is frequently given by reviews, advertisements, or a blurb on the back cover. With the leisure of hundreds of pages, the orientation may be delayed or spread out, dispersed over thousands or tens of thousands of words. On the other hand, the abstract and orientation may be much more straightforward also. A film may begin by showing pictures of the main characters (e.g., soldiers in a company), giving their names, and then presenting a scrolling text that outlines relevant history (e.g., about a particular battle in the Second World War).

This isolation of recurring structural components obviously illustrates nomological literary discourse analysis. The crucial point for purposes here is that this general pattern has consequences for interpretation. For instance, readers respond differently and make inferences differently when a story has an abstract and orientation and when it does not. Readers may tacitly recognize this. For example, they may have a vague sense of disorientation, or they may have a feeling of camaraderie with the speaker, who seems to be presupposing shared knowledge. In either case, the explicit (nomological) isolation of a recurring pattern helps critics to explore the implications of what otherwise would, in all likelihood, be an inarticulate feeling.

Consider, for example, Ernest Hemingway's "A Very Short Story."[3] It entirely lacks an abstract. It begins by, in effect, teasing the reader with the hints of an orientation. "One hot evening" has the effect of "Once upon a time." It sets out an arbitrary starting point. The geographical location "in Padua" could very easily lead one to expect a straightforward orientation—for example, "One hot evening in Padua, Rock Goodfellow, a lieutenant in the U.S. Marines, was seated on the roof of the military hospital with three other wounded, but recovering soldiers, and a nurse, Luzia Dellamore." But, in fact, the orientation breaks off after "Padua." Rather than being given any of this information, the reader is told simply that "they carried him up onto the roof." The reader does not know what the building is, who he is, why he is being carried. Subsequently, Luz is mentioned as if the reader already knows who she is.

Had there been an abstract, readers probably would have been led to expect something like a love story. Though war is obviously important in the narrative, the focus is on the couple and their desire to be married. The complicating action here would be anything preventing their marriage. There are, in effect, three complicating events—first, they are separated by his return to the front (their lack of documents and time for marriage are part of this complex separation); second, they are separated by his return to America; finally, they are separated by Luz's affair with the Italian major. This tripling of complications is obviously a recurring technique, though it is not part of Labov's model. The first and second complications are in principle temporary. The third leads to the resolution, since it determines that they will never be married. There is a brief evaluation just before this resolution. In recounting a story of a narrow escape from a vicious beast, an oral storyteller might stress the danger by saying something like "It was the biggest, meanest-looking dog I ever saw." Along the same lines, Hemingway has the curious evaluative statement "she had never known Italians before," which, in context, may suggest virility and skill in sexual performance or charm in courtship. The final paragraph of the story gives a coda, telling what happened to the two characters after the events of the main story.

Recognizing this structure does not lead directly to any interpretive conclusions. However, it does organize the story in such a way as to make certain aspects of the work salient, and thus important for interpretation. First, the lack of orientation makes both characters somewhat anonymous. The reader never has a sense of just how well they know one another and, indeed, may suspect that they do not know one another much better than the reader knows them. They are brought together by circumstances in a context where they would feel lonely and vulnerable. This is likely to provoke feelings of emotional dependency. The reader sees the same scenario two other times in the story. First, there is the relationship of Luz and the major. Clearly, Luz does not know the major well enough to realize that he will not marry her. She was drawn to him in part because the place was "lonely and rainy" during winter. Similarly, the soldier does not know the salesgirl well enough to have any sense that she might have a venereal disease. It is as if the characters too suffer from a lack of orienting introduction to each other.

The lack of an abstract has similar resonances. Luz herself indicates that she expects to be married "absolutely unexpectedly." My students at least find the sudden introduction of gonorrhea at the end of the story to be so unexpected as to constitute a shock. The reader's lack of a sense of what will happen is paralleled by that of the characters. The point is clearer if one imagines a similar story by a religious moralist, entitled, say, "The Wages of Sin," or an abstract that made reference to how men and women learn the wickedness of fornication only through pain.

We might extend these interpretive points further. Perhaps the story suggests that these particular people did not know one another well. But it may also suggest that this lack of knowledge, with its false certainty and dubious expectations, is an inevitable condition of human relations. It may suggest that, to put it somewhat crudely, abstracts and orientations are part of stories, but not part of life. Perhaps when the soldier and Luz were together on the roof, alone, they were really as much of a mystery to one another as they were to readers—even though they believed that they understood one another and were beginning to have a clear sense of the future.

Finally, there is the evaluation. Again, the story would have quite a different impact if it began by suggesting that the abomination of unchastity leads to Godly retribution. This could be part of an abstract. But it would also clearly have an evaluative function. It is important that there is no culminating, moral evaluation in the story, nothing to make this pathetic series of events sensible. That is in keeping with its location in the miserable, pointless First World War. The story does not have any place for a divine plan or other context that gives the pain of these individuals any redeeming value.

At the same time, it does have one hint of evaluation—the peculiar ethnic comment about Italians. Depending on how one interprets it, one may find this comment objectionable. My guess is that readers will be more inclined to find it objectionable to the degree that they interpret it as referring specifically to sexual skill (and, perhaps even more, to physical endowments). In other words, I imagine that most readers would find it less objectionable to the degree that they interpret it as a matter of cultural practices relating to courtship. There is also the issue of the degree to which they attribute the belief to Hemingway, as opposed to one or both of the characters. In any case, these interpretive points become more salient by reference to the nomological structure isolated by Labov.

The Politics of Narration: Critical Discourse Analysis

The comment about Italians in Hemingway's story points to a further aspect of literary study. For literary critics, one set of recurring and important concerns is normative. Critics care not only about what a work means but also about what it does. Indeed, a great deal of the preceding discussion concerns what effects Hemingway's lack of an orientation, abstract, and overall evaluation, is likely to have on readers. That examination of effects is sometimes explored purely descriptively (as in certain sorts of empirical reader-response study). But it is probably more often considered evaluatively, in systematic judgments that go well beyond the sorts of internal comments isolated by Labov. In other words, literary critics are frequently concerned with specific sorts of literary effects. These effects tend to fall into two large categories—ethico-political, on the one hand, and aesthetic, on the other. Ethico-political effects would include, for example, the tendency of a story to foster ethnic stereotyping. The comment about Italians might prompt concerns of this sort. Aesthetic effects address the emotional consequences of a work—for example, the effect of eliminating the orientation on a reader's engagement with the story. If well done, the absence of orientation could enhance curiosity (as Sternberg would put it). However, if done badly, it could simply confuse the reader.

The reference to ethico-political evaluation leads to the final use of the phrase "discourse analysis." Again, narrative discourse analysis focuses on a particular type of discourse within the larger field of linguistic discourse analysis. What is called "Critical Discourse Analysis," in contrast, focuses on a particular function of discourse—its consequences for political and social structures, specifically those that have an ethical component and are therefore open to ethical evaluation.

Since most Critical Discourse analysts would probably not characterize their approach in terms of ethics, it is worth elaborating on the point. A wide range of political and social practices—for example, driving on the right or left side of the road—are ethically neutral. Critical Discourse analysts are not usually interested in the effects of discourse on these practices. They are, rather, interested in the ways in which discourse has an impact on, say, ethnic or sexual minorities or the prosecution of wars. Here, too, they are not concerned primarily with technical matters (e.g., which terrain is more advantageous for the government's campaign). Rather, they tend to be concerned with the ethical valence of the various policies. Of course, not everyone would identify ethical concerns in the same way. As a rough approximation, one might say that Critical Discourse analysts are concerned with the ways in which discourses operate to produce or sustain unmerited hierarchies in the distribution of goods and services in society.

Critical Discourse Analysis is, of course, attentive to individual works. Indeed, it prominently features the interpretation of individual works. However, it locates that interpretation within a larger, roughly nomological context. Thus, in keeping with discourse analysis generally, Critical Discourse analysts are concerned with, for example, the rules governing who can speak about what, when they can do so, and how. However, they are concerned about this in a particular manner. They pay close attention to the ways in which constraints on who can speak are simultaneously ways in which power is established or exercised; the degree to which what one can say serves to constrain how one thinks—or does not think—about alternative social structures, particularly structures that would alter relations of power; the manner in which forms of address and the practical consequences of address (e.g., in commands or appeals) orient action in politically consequential ways. In connection with this, drawing particularly on the work of Michel Foucault, Critical Discourse analysts tend to be concerned with the ways in which discourse is institutionally situated. Thus they may attend to the power relations of a particular institutional structure (e.g., a hospital), exploring how such power relations are intertwined with discursive relations (e.g., those defined by the discourse of medicine).

Here, too, the general theory has interpretive consequences. For example, when one approaches Hemingway's story from this perspective, one immediately sees that the relations of lovers, including their discursive interrelation, is mediated by institutions. First the hospital, then the church, then the army constrain what they can say to one another, when they can speak, how they can communicate, and what effects that communication can have. The late delivery of all Luz's letters, after the armistice, is a striking case, as are the restrictions preventing their profession of wedding vows. Clearly, all these cases are inseparable from relations of authority and power.

Discourse Analysis and Narrative Art

It should be clear that these three senses of discourse are different, but also related. Linguistic discourse analysis provides the general context for the other two. The analysis of narrative discourse and Critical Discourse Analysis are interrelated as well. Hierarchies of power bear on storytelling, both in terms of what stories are told and in terms of how those stories are shaped in narrative discourse. Conversely, narratives themselves regularly concern relations of power, most obviously in their represented events or story line, but also in the relations of authority, irony, reliability, and knowledge developed in narrative discourse.

The focus of the present book is on narrative discourse analysis, specifically on the analysis of literary and cinematic discourse, and to a lesser extent painting. Thus the following chapters will examine such topics as the nature of the narrator and the function of the implied author. However, this exploration of literary narrative discourse will take place largely within the broader field of linguistic discourse analysis.[4] Indeed, the discussion will assume the continuity between literary narrative and other forms of narrative production and reception. More generally, it will follow the presumption of linguistic discourse analysis—as well as cognitive science—that the cognitive processes at work in the production and reception of literary narrative are not and, indeed, cannot be fundamentally different from the cognitive processes at work in the production and reception of other, more ordinary and ephemeral forms of narrative discourse. Literary narrative may involve unusually complex interrelations of such processes, or distinctive forms of interaction and elaboration. But the cognitive structures at issue and the operations in which they engage are necessarily of the same sort. For this reason, the effort of the following pages will always be to explain the principles of narrative discourse in terms of a well-established cognitive architecture. Ideally, this will involve refining knowledge of narrative principles by reference to cognitive architecture and expanding comprehension of cognitive architecture by reference to narrative principles.

More exactly, the first goal of the following chapters is to isolate some of the unrecognized principles governing narrative discourse—for example, with respect to the embedding of narrators or concerning the isolation of points at which narration is unreliable. In the last fifty years, narratology has advanced enormously, isolating important patterns in stories and in narrative discourse. But that hardly means that the research is complete. My hope is that the following pages advance nomological understanding of literary narrative discourse.

A second goal is to explore the ways in which this nomological part has interpretive consequences. Thus each chapter includes not only general theoretical discussion but also practical interpretations. Indeed, my hope is to show in each case that the hermeneutic and nomological analyses contribute valuably to one another.

The book has a third goal as well, though considerations of length have prevented its full development in the following chapters. This goal is to suggest how a nomological understanding of discourse and discourse-based interpretations of particular works may connect with ethico-political concerns of the sort treated by Critical Discourse analysts. In part for this reason, most of the works examined in the following pages are directly political.

Probably the main way in which literary narrative bears on political thought and action is not abstractly conceptual, but concretely motivational. It is a matter of emotion. This leads to one of the main ways in which the approach to narrative discourse in the present book differs from that of most linguistic discourse analysts and Critical Discourse Analysis. In the following chapters, recent research on emotion is of particular importance. Indeed, the accounts of the narrator, implied author, and other aspects of narrative discourse make repeated reference to emotion. This is not to say that no one has treated emotion and narrative. Narrative theorists have been interested in emotion since Aristotle. Moreover, topics such as empathy have been central in some recent discussions of literature (see, for example, Keen's very valuable book on the subject). However, there has been relatively little work drawing on recent emotion research to examine topics that are not in themselves straightforwardly emotional (such as empathy). Despite this, one may argue that emotional processes are ubiquitous both in story construction (governing the organization of cross-culturally recurring genres[5]) and in the operation of discourse. This is not to say that narrative discourse is entirely a matter of emotion. As will be discussed in the first chapter, the composition and reception of literary narratives involve complex processes that are only in part affective. But that affective part is crucial, for it governs the motivations of authors and readers, as well as narrators, narratees, and characters, and the relations among these (e.g., the reader's relation to the narrator). Indeed, it even guides perception and more seemingly abstract inferences. It would be going too far to label the methodology of this book "affective discourse analysis." However, the following chapters do aim to show the great importance of emotion research for all forms of discourse analysis.

Overview of the Following Chapters

The first chapter begins by outlining the main components of narrative discourse as these are commonly understood today—the real author, the implied author, the narrator, and so on. The chapter then takes these components in turn, focusing primarily on who speaks and who is spoken to. It reformulates the relation between the author and the implied author, seeking to resolve some problems that have arisen with respect to this division. Specifically, the chapter distinguishes different varieties of authorial intent, stressing the importance of receptive and implicit intent. In connection with this, drawing on work in cognitive science, it develops an account of cognitive processing that bears directly on implied authorship and literary interpretation. The chapter goes on to distinguish varieties of narrator, to argue for the centrality of emotion in understanding focalization (roughly, the restriction of third-person narration to a character), to consider the ways in which the implied reader is as much a motivational (thus emotional) structure as a cognitive one, and to examine the role of the critic in relation to real readers. In order to illustrate these points, the chapter turns repeatedly to "A Very Short Story."

The second chapter takes up the idea of the implied author more systematically. Following the general account from the first chapter, it considers the degree to which the notion of an implied author may be applied to painting. It takes as a starting point some enigmas in two paintings by Rabindranath Tagore. It goes on to argue that these enigmas are open to partial resolution by drawing on principles and ideas from a range of Tagore's works. This suggests that, beyond the implied author or implied painter of a particular work, one is well advised to consider the implied author or painter across a series or canon of works—indeed, the implied creator, when the canon spans different types of work (such as literature and painting). This "cross-textual implied creator" does not substitute for the implied author of an individual work. However, it provides one important context for interpreting that implied author and that individual work. Moreover, it does not render the work unequivocal. Rather, like any other context, this one alters the *profile of ambiguity* of the work—the range of interpretations the work sustains and the different degrees to which it sustains them. In some cases this context may even enhance rather than reduce ambiguity.

Indeed, the importance of ambiguity is one of the main reasons that I chose to treat painting in the book, particularly in the context of a study grounded in cognitive and affective science. In his book *Inner Vision: An Exploration of Art and the Brain*, the prominent neuroscientist of art Semir Zeki has a brilliant discussion of Vermeer. His focus in that discussion is on the way in which the impact of Vermeer's paintings results from their ambiguity. Though Zeki does not put it this way, the ambiguity he is discussing concerns precisely the narrative implied by the necessarily isolated moment depicted in the painting. The ambiguity of visual art is significant in itself. It is also significant in its implications for the cross-textual interpretation of a creator's work. As discussed in the second chapter, Tagore in effect enhances the ambiguity of his paintings by not giving them titles, largely avoiding standard iconography and other factors. At the same time, however, these paintings are embedded in an extensive authorial canon, including more readily interpretable verbal narratives. These factors make Tagore's paintings particularly suitable for an examination of cross-textual implied authorship and ambiguity. In addition, those paintings, while highly regarded, have received very little interpretive attention.

The idea of cross-textual implied authorship is related to a concept that has been important in film studies—that of the *auteur* or authorial force behind a set of films. The second part of this chapter concerns the difficulties of extending the idea of implied authorship to cinema. Despite auteurist theory, film poses a challenge for any account of implied authorship, due to the diversity of creative input that results in a film. After treating this issue theoretically, the chapter turns to a concrete case—the great Indian filmmaker Bimal Roy. The chapter explores some recurring techniques in Roy's work and their development in his 1958 film, *Madhumati*.

The third chapter goes in the opposite direction from the second. Rather than addressing larger units of understanding and interpretation, it considers smaller units. Specifically, drawing on cognitive and emotional research, it argues that one may distinguish the overarching implied author as an explanatory principle that gives the work a degree of coherence. However, the same cognitive and emotional research suggests that this broad coherence will not be maintained with perfect consistency. Rather, one would expect there to be local variations, not only in narration but in implied authorship as well. These local variants or "implicated authors" may derive from different, context-sensitive models or associations and may have very different, even directly contradictory emotional and thematic consequences. The chapter explores this idea in Harriet Beecher Stowe's controversial *Uncle Tom's Cabin,* arguing that the different political interpretations of the novel reflect some of the diversity in implicated authorship.

The chapter ends by returning to implied authorship in cinema. It considers different sorts of implied authorial inconsistency in film, focusing in particular on the creation of multiple implied audiences and the way implied authors may implicitly misdirect members of one implied audience. The chapter goes on to distinguish different types of cinematic narrator and their relation to implied and implicated authors. It concludes by discussing an extreme example of potential authorial incoherence—Kabir Khan's film *New York,* in which the status of the entire conclusion of the film is questionable.

The discussion of Khan's film leads to the issue of narrator unreliability, which is taken up in chapter 4. This chapter distinguishes three levels at which readers respond to the problem of narrator reliability. The most basic level is largely emotional and a matter of trusting or not trusting the narrator. The intermediate level is triggered by distrust at the basic level. This intermediate level involves the application of heuristic cognitive structures that serve to guide the adjudication of information supplied by the narrator. At the most abstract level, the reader engages in a highly effortful elaboration of the evidence for or against particular conclusions regarding the story as it may be inferred from the unreliable narration. To explore and illustrate these considerations, the chapter takes up Margaret Atwood's novel *Surfacing.* This novel is told in the voice of a character who repeatedly misunderstands her own memories, confusing and misattributing them, and who, in connection with an (apparently) incipient emotional collapse, comes to remember having had an abortion.

The fifth and sixth chapters consider cases of multiple narration. Atwood's novel has a single, individual narrator. However, many works have parallel narrators (the topic of chapter 5) or embedded or group narrators (the topics of chapter 6). Parallel narrators are individual or group narrators who do not embed one another. An embedded narrator is simply a narrator whose telling of a story is included in the story told by another narrator. A group narrator is a collective rather than an individual.

Works with parallel personified narrators are fairly common.[6] These narrators usually offer different, and sometimes incompatible, accounts of the storyworld. Even when they agree on the storyworld, the emotional or thematic implications of their versions may differ. One task of interpretation involves evaluating these variations. In order to consider some aspects of that process, this chapter takes up William Faulkner's *The Sound and the Fury*. Unlike parallel personified narration, parallel nonpersonified narration is rare. Though the interpretation of parallel personified narration is complex, it is a process directly comparable to the interpretation of single narration, treating for example some of the same issues regarding reliability in much the same way. However, parallel nonpersonified narration is far more difficult. As a result, it tends to be far more equivocal than other types of work, in terms of theme, emotion, and even story. Indeed, it is difficult to interpret such narration without reconstruing one or both of the parallel narrators as personified. The point is illustrated by David Lynch's *Mulholland Drive*.

The final chapter turns, first, to the embedding of narrators. It also takes up associated topics in focalization. Thus the chapter considers what sorts of narrator may appear at what level of embedding, how an embedded narrator's or focalizer's knowledge or perspective may be altered by the embedding narrator, and related issues. In order to explore these topics, the chapter turns to Ngũgĩ wa Thiong'o's *Petals of Blood*, a national allegory of independent Kenya told in the form of a detective story and framed, in part, as a written testimony.

Some of the narrational complexity in Ngũgĩ's novel derives from the way it treats group experience and expression. The discussion of *Petals of Blood* leads to an outline of several types of group narration. This introduces a final issue of narrative multiplicity—the relation among narrating and narrated consciousnesses. In order to explore this topic, the chapter examines *Born of the Son* by Joseph Diescho (with Celeste Wallin), a novel about the developing political consciousness of a rural Namibian man who goes to work in the South African mines during the Apartheid period.[7] Diescho (with Wallin) is careful in limiting the narrator's access to the consciousnesses of characters other than the protagonist. However, there are moments when the focalization of the novel, with its limited access to other minds, is violated. This often produces a focalization equivalent of group narration—group focalization. The moments have an isolable pattern that is related to both the thematic point and the emotional force of the novel. As a result, the novel suggests a more finegrained "access hierarchy" for a narrator's knowledge about character minds, leading beyond the traditional limited/omniscient division.

The final chapter is followed by a very brief afterword. Chapter 1 outlines both the "productive" and "receptive" elements of discourse—

thus implied authors and narrators (the productive elements), on the one hand, and implied readers and narratees (the receptive elements), on the other. As should be clear from the preceding outline, the remaining chapters cover a range of issues bearing on the productive elements, separately and in relation to one another. Broadly speaking, chapters 2 and 3 focus on implied authors; chapters 5 and 6 focus on narrators; and chapter 4, on reliability, examines a key aspect of the relation between the two. Thus the receptive part of narration is largely bypassed in the book. The purpose of the afterword is to suggest that the receptive part is highly complex and does not simply mirror the productive part, as one might initially imagine. Through an examination of a poem by the important Indian poet Mīrābāī (early sixteenth century), the afterword seeks to point out some of what differentiates the analysis of narratees and implied readers from the analysis of narrators and implied authors. It thereby points toward future work in discourse analysis.

Discourse, Interpretation, and the Purposes of Fictional Narrative

Before turning to the overview of discourse, it is important to set out two sets of presuppositions that underlie much of the following analysis. The first set concerns the purposes readers have in approaching works of art—principally, fictional narratives. These purposes guide what critics do with narratological principles, including how they use them for interpretation. They also guide how real authors understand and respond to their creations. The second set of presuppositions concerns the nature of interpretation and meaning in literary works, specifically the ambiguity of such works.

As to the purposes of reading, one may say that, first, and most fundamentally, for any representation, readers (as well as audience members for films, viewers of representational paintings, and so on) are concerned with what is represented. In standard narratological terms, readers wish to reconstruct the story. One may borrow a term from hermeneutic theory and refer to this as "understanding." The most obvious function of discourse is to enable—but also to selectively constrain—understanding of the story.

Both the enabling and selective inhibition relate to the second concern that drives representative art. That is emotion. Here, one may distinguish the emotions of the story from the emotions of the discourse.

Emotions of the story involve such things as readers' empathy with characters' suffering. There are different types of discourse emotions. The most obvious discourse emotions, such as suspense, relate to plot. (Plot is the manifestation of story in discourse. This includes what the reader is told when—for example, if the identity of a murderer is revealed early or withheld until the end.) But there are discourse emotions, such as trust in a narrator's reliability, that relate to narration as well. (Narration, in this context, is the part of discourse bearing on who speaks to whom.) The experience of emotions in relation to story or discourse is "response." The examination of such emotions is "response analysis." Such analysis may focus on real readers or on the normative implied reader (a concept examined in chapter 1). The following pages are concerned almost entirely with the latter.

The final concern driving readers' engagement with a representational work may be called "theme." Theme is, roughly, any norm—particularly an ethical or political norm—that carries over from the narrative to the real world. People tend to think of themes as sentence-length statements. However, the establishment of a character as an ideal or the development of a complex criticism of patriarchal society counts as a theme in this sense, even though it would be impossible to encompass in a single sentence. Taking up another term from hermeneutic theory, but somewhat changing its definition, one may use "explication" to refer to inferences concerning the themes of a work.

Given this account of understanding, response analysis, and explication, one may give a technical definition of "interpretation." Interpretation is any inference regarding a feature of a narrative that contributes to understanding, response, or explication. Conversely, one may consider any isolable feature of a narrative to be interpretable insofar as it falls into one of the following categories: 1) elements with consequences for the reconstruction of the story, 2) elements with emotional consequences (for story, plot, or narration), or 3) elements with thematic consequences. Insofar as a feature does not fall into one of these categories, one may say that it has not been selected by the implied author, but occurs incidentally. (For example, verbal stress patterns may be selected for aesthetic reasons by poets, but such features are unlikely to be relevant in a work of prose fiction.)

A main focus of the following pages is the relation between narrative discourse analysis and interpretation—specifically, how one relies on aspects of discourse to infer the storyworld, the implied authorial themes, and the normative emotions of the work.[8] This leads to two important issues. First, there is the nature of interpretive standards. That will be addressed in connection with the implied author in chapter 1. Second, there is the related issue of interpretive multiplicity or the ambiguity of literary works. It is important to say a few words about this before going on.

There seems to be widespread agreement that interpretation should not be seen as entirely constrained nor as entirely free, but as "limited" (as, for example, Umberto Eco put it). The point is reasonable, but excessively vague. In order to overcome this vagueness, one might conceive of interpretation on the model of a mathematical function. Along the x-axis there are different possible interpretations—representational, thematic, or emotive. Along the y-axis there is the plausibility of any given interpretation. The most likely interpretations are those with the highest value on the y-axis; the least likely interpretations are those with the lowest value on the y-axis. An absolutely unequivocal utterance would be a single point at 100 (or whatever number is used to mark certainty). There would be no line because the likelihood of all other interpretations would be zero. In contrast, an absolutely ambiguous utterance would be graphed with a single horizontal line very close to the x-axis. This is because all interpretations would be equally likely, which is to say, they would all have a nearly (but not quite) zero likelihood.

Suppose I get out a pack of gum, take a piece, and then turn to my wife and say, "Want a piece of gum?" One might say that the ambiguity function for this utterance is pretty close to a single point. In contrast, suppose I deliver a lecture on narratology in a place where many audience members' grasp of English is not firm. After the talk, I imprudently ask someone, "Well, what did you think?" He replies "Hmm" and nods. His response is highly ambiguous—indeed, virtually a flat line.

When people talk about interpretation and meaning, they often appear to be looking for a simple point ambiguity function, like that found in the offer of gum. In other words, they seem to underestimate ambiguity. When people criticize the idea of validity in interpretation, they appear to overestimate ambiguity; they seem to act as if the ambiguity function is a flat horizontal line, as if literary works were like the "Hmm" from my imaginary audience member. In fact, neither is true. For any work, there is always a range of possible interpretations—a *profile of ambiguity*.[9] What differs from work to work is the gradient of plausibility. Some works present fairly steep and relatively narrow curves. In other words, the number of plausible interpretations is limited and sharply distinct from surrounding possibilities. This occurs, for example, when it is not clear whether a work is ironic or not. One curve represents the straight interpretation; another represents the ironic interpretation. We might refer to works of this sort as having *discrete ambiguity*. Other works present much more gradual slopes, such that there is a wider range of plausible interpretation and a much less sharp distinction between more and less plausible alternatives. We might refer to the ambiguity of such works as relatively *continuous*.

Most often, when interpreting a work, critics are interested in isolating what they take to be the best supported meaning. This is certainly a legitimate, indeed important project. However, another interpretive task is outlining the work's profile of ambiguity. The following analyses will be concerned with both tasks, specifically as they are bound up with discourse.

Chapter 1

Who Is Speaking to Whom

The Communicative Discourse of Narrative Art

*N*ARRATIVE APPEARS in a range of contexts and forms. In many cases, stories are told only once or twice because they concern events of interest to the speaker and perhaps the addressee, but to relatively few people beyond that. In other cases, stories may have greater general appeal and may be repeated by a range of tellers to a range of addressees because of their humor, pathos, or other engaging qualities. Narratives of verbal art are, prototypically, works that are widely disseminated beyond their initial teller and his or her associates to a broad and various audience. In keeping with this, they are recounted for their emotional and thematic impact, not for their direct relevance to some current situation. In line with these purposes, a narrative of verbal art is likely to have been rehearsed and revised, made more thematically nuanced and more emotionally powerful as the author generated and evaluated details of the story and ways of telling it. This is particularly clear in written narratives or literature (as opposed to orature). As a result, both what is told in literary narratives and how it is told tend to become increasingly complex. But that complexity is not random. It is the product of the human mind and human social interaction. Thus it follows the general principles that guide human cognitive processing, human emotional response, human interaction, and so on. It is the purpose of the present chapter to outline some basic components of this complexity in the case of narrative discourse.

As already noted, within narratology, "story" refers to the events recounted in a narrative, events as they, so to speak, "really" occurred. "Discourse," in contrast, refers to the way in which they are told. As Seymour Chatman puts it, "In simple terms, the story is the *what* in a narrative that is depicted, discourse the *how*" (*Story* 19). In David Herman's words, it is "the difference between the chronological series of events recounted . . . and the manner in which those events are organized in the recounting" (*Story* 214).

Discourse may be divided into two broad categories. The first concerns who speaks to whom. The second concerns what is said. The former is sometimes termed "narrational," but that is somewhat misleading, as it may suggest only the operation of narrators and narratees. It is perhaps better referred to as the "communicative" part of discourse. The other part of discourse—thus, what is communicated—is often referred to as "plot," but is perhaps better thought of as the "representational" component.[1] This and the following chapters are concerned specifically with the communicative part of discourse, though of course the two parts overlap, and one cannot discuss who speaks to whom in a particular case without also talking about what is said. In Jakobson's terms, who speaks to whom is a matter of a sender relaying a message to a receiver (see 66). But, in narrative discourse, who speaks to whom is somewhat more complicated than the division between sender and receiver may suggest.

The Basic Components of Narrative Discourse

Though there is certainly disagreement about parts of the structure, narratologists generally see the communicative part of narrative discourse as involving the following basic components:

Real Author [Implied Author [Narrator [Focalizer [story [embedded discourse [embedded story]]]][2] Narratee] Implied Reader] Real Reader

The real author is, of course, the flesh-and-blood person who composed the narrative. The real reader is any given flesh-and-blood person who reads the narrative. The real author and the real reader are commonly seen as being "outside" the text. This is marked by the fact that they are outside the square brackets. Thus the outermost square brackets in some sense mark the bounds of the text, or perhaps more properly the textual world. The implied author and the implied reader are, then, commonly understood as part of the textual world (rather than the real world) in the sense that they may be inferred (at least primarily) from what is given in the text. (The following discussion will complicate and, in significant ways, alter this standard characterization.)

There has been considerable controversy over just what an implied author is and whether such a thing exists. Some writers see the implied author as just what a reader construes from a text. For example, Bal writes that "the implied author is the result of the investigations of the meaning of a text, and not the source of that meaning" (18). But this would seem more appropriately termed an "inferred author,"[3] as Chatman points out (*Coming* 77). "Implied" suggests a norm that defines the validity or invalidity of readers' inferences—what Bal tacitly presupposes when she refers to investigating "the meaning of a text."

In keeping with the suggestions of the word "implied," it is common to see the implied author as a complex of norms. Thus the implied author is often understood as the standard against which one may judge the reliability of narrators. But then there is controversy over whether those norms are to be understood as "anthropomorphic," or more accurately whether they are to be understood as tied to a person or as somehow purely textual. Put differently, there is controversy over whether linking norms to an author, in whatever form, simply reintroduces an intentional fallacy. Moreover, if one opts for "tied to a person," then one faces the further problem of distinguishing the implied author from the real author. Some writers, such as James Phelan, see the implied author as "a streamlined version of the real author, an actual or purported subset of the real author's capacities, traits, attitudes, beliefs, values, and other properties" (*Living* 45). Other writers see the implied author as an idealized version of the real author (see, for example, Dan Shen's summary of Xiangjun She's work [172]).

The following section will present an argument for a close relation between the implied author and the real author. The distinction between them will be drawn not in terms of personal traits, but in terms of types of intent. A crucial part of that intent is the author's understanding of his or her readership—which leads to the implied reader.

In any act of communication, the speaker has a certain conception of the addressee. Clearly, in literary works with any sort of success, the real author does not envision his or her real readers.[4] Those readers are necessarily too numerous and diverse. But he or she does tacitly assume that the reader will have certain sensitivities, certain capacities, certain sorts of knowledge. At minimum, the author conceives of a reader who will be able to follow the story, detect ironies, infer thematic concerns, and so forth. Put in terms of the model thus far, the author writes for a reader who will be able to infer the implied author. Just as the implied author is (primarily) an implication of the text, the implied reader is (primarily) an implication of the text. Implied readership is most obviously marked by anything that provides evidence for inferring the implied author. However, it is also marked by such communicative strategies as providing or not providing background information and highlighting or not highlighting important points. In, for example, explaining (or not explaining) a historical event, a text may suggest something about the implied reader and about (the implied author's) expectations regarding that reader's knowledge.

The implied reader and the implied author should not be taken as defined in all details. The implied author presumably involves a great deal of indeterminacy. Likewise, real readers may adhere to the norms of the implied reader but still maintain considerable leeway in just how they understand and respond to a given text. For example, a given story may present a narrator as unreliable. Suppose the character is a politician who makes certain campaign promises. Suppose he or she is defeated in the election so that no one ever finds out exactly what he or she would do in office. The implied author may indicate that the reader should not simply believe the campaign promises. He or she should expect that often the character would not follow through on the promises if elected. But there may be indeterminacy for the implied author as to whether the politician would follow through on any of the promises and, if so, which ones. Readers may adhere to the norms of the implied reader and still disagree among themselves on this issue. Indeed, this is one of those points where the difference between the implied author and the real author becomes clear as well. Specifically, the real author may have an opinion on this issue, which is not necessarily more valid than that of any other reader. Of course, to say that a particular aspect of the implied author/implied reader is indeterminate is not necessarily to say that the textual evidence for all alternatives is equal. Here, as elsewhere, there is a profile of ambiguity.

The next level of communicative discourse is that of the narrator and narratee. The narrator is the voice telling the story. Narratologists distinguish different sorts of narrator. For example, the narrator may be "homodiegetic," thus part of the story, or "heterodiegetic," thus not part of the story (see Abbott "Narration" for this and other ways of categorizing narrators). The narrator also may be unreliable or reliable and, related to this, he or she may be treated with or without irony. Irony is commonly understood as a certain sort of discrepancy between the implied author and the narrator. A standard example is Jonathan Swift's "A Modest Proposal." In that work, the speaker (equivalent to the narrator) suggests that the problem of Irish poverty may be solved in part by using Irish babies for food. The speaker proposes the idea with apparent seriousness. However, based in part on the assumption that no English person of the time would seriously advocate cannibalism, and based on the common association of cannibalism with barbarism, one infers an attitude different from that of the narrator, an attitude that is critical of British policies in Ireland—so critical, indeed, as to view those policies as barbaric. That inferred attitude is held by the implied author, and it is relative to that implied author that one judges the text ironic. One does not need to read any other works by the real author (e.g., letters, a diary) to learn that he was not an advocate of cannibalism.

The narrator is, so to speak, on the cusp of the storyworld.[5] As the names indicate, the heterodiegetic narrator is just outside the story. The homodiegetic narrator is inside the story, or rather inside a story. In this way, the narrator may be part of the represented storyworld or not—or both, if the narrator appears in a frame story but not in the embedded (perhaps main) story.

The narratee is the addressee counterpart to the narrator, just as the real reader is the counterpart of the real author and the implied reader is the counterpart of the implied author. On the other hand, there are some significant differences among the three. As already noted, the real reader is not in fact addressed by the real author, who cannot possibly envision even a fraction of his or her readers. Moreover, the implied reader is perhaps not so much an addressee for the implied author as a set of sensitivities that allow accurate construction of the implied author, or of the story as guided by the implied author as a norm. In contrast, the narratee is the addressee of the narrator. One important role of the narratee comes when a homodiegetic narrator tells versions of an embedded story to more than one narratee, thereby revealing different aspects of the embedded events and of his or her own character through differences among the tellings (or between one such telling and information about the event gleaned from elsewhere).[6] On the other hand, one may infer implicit narratees as well. As will be considered in more detail below, it is sometimes possible to infer a narratee from the information or attitudes presupposed by a narrator. In this way, the narratee too is marginal to the represented story. Like the narrator, he or she may be represented or only implied by the representation.

While the narrator and the narratee may be part of the represented discourse, they are part of the communicative discourse as well. This is not precisely the case for the focalizer. The focalizer is located more squarely within the storyworld. Moreover, the focalizer does not directly communicate story representations with anyone. The focalizer is still important for discourse and is appropriately studied within discourse analysis because the focalizing function is part of the selection and organization of information. Specifically, the focalizer is the center of consciousness that orients the narrator's treatment of the storyworld. (There may be more than one focalizer, of course. But the same points hold for multiple focalization.) For example, the narrator may report only the information that bears on the condition of the focalizer. In a war, for example, the narrator may leave aside information on the battle except insofar as it has an impact on the focalizer (usually the protagonist). Going further, the narrator may report information only insofar as it is actually available to the focalizer, representing the focalizer's psychological states, but not those of anyone else.

We might briefly consider where these components fit within an interpretation of Hemingway's "A Very Short Story."[7] The real author is obviously Hemingway. An interpretation focusing on the real author would pay attention to the sources of the story in Hemingway's own life. It would be a case of biographical criticism. The implied author is a bit more complex. Indeed, this case suggests that implied authorship may be understood at different levels—a point explored in the following chapters. The simplest is at the level of this story alone. But there is also at least the level of the book. This possibility is complicated by critical disagreement as to whether *In Our Time* (which includes "A Very Short Story") should be considered a collection or something more like a novel (see Moddelmog for the second view; for discussion, see Barloon). There are several differences these levels might make. In this story considered alone, it is difficult to ascertain much of any attitude toward war in general or toward the First World War in particular. However, a more broadly construed implied author may contextualize the story in such a way as to make it less about relations between men and women generally and more about men and women in wartime. (For example, Barloon notes that the book "invites a question . . .—to what extent is *In Our Time* about the Great War, or war generally?" [5].)

In any case, the narrator here seems very close to the implied author (and, indeed, to the real author, as a number of critics have stressed [see, for example, Scholes *Semiotics* 121-26]). On the other hand, there are points at which the two are not identical, points at which the reader needs to infer an implied authorial view beyond what is stated by the narrator. Take, for example, the statement that "they agreed he should go home to get a job." The verb "agree" can mean either "formally accept" or "genuinely share the conviction." After being convicted of misconduct, Jones might "agree" to apologize to his opponent, but that does not mean that he genuinely shares the conviction that he should apologize. Similarly, here, the decision about the soldier returning home alone may suggest genuinely shared conviction or formal acceptance only. The narrator leaves the phrase ambiguous. Contrast, for example, "*After some disagreement* they agreed *to her recommendation that* he should go home to get a job." One might begin to construct an implied author who understands the phrase in the sense of formal acceptance only, thus an implied author whose views go beyond what is stated by the narrator. Note that this does not say they *contradict* the narrator. We often think that there is a narrator/implied author difference only in cases of contradiction. The point of choosing an example such as this is in part to indicate that the differences may be more subtle.

More strikingly, the subsequent elaboration—"It was understood," and so on—could mean that the two were of one mind on the issue. However, it could also mean that the dominant partner made it a tacit condition for the marriage. The reader gets some idea that the implied author may have the latter in mind after reading that the restrictions were entirely on the soldier, not on Luz. The suggestion, then, may be that Luz made it understood. Moreover, the restrictions are very extreme. The understanding is, first, that he will not drink. That seems fair and prudent. But it is not followed by, say, "and she would try to be brave." Rather, it is followed by the rather difficult restriction that he would not "see his friends." Though a bit extreme, it may be plausible in the context of giving up alcohol, if his friends were drinking buddies. But the extremity of the requirement is indicated by the extension of his isolation to include "anyone in the States." In connection with this, we might infer an implied author for whom Luz is being overly demanding and even somewhat authoritarian (especially given her later behavior). Indeed, the exact phrasing of the sentence is even more extreme than just indicated. The precise statement is, "It was understood he would not drink, and he did not want to see his friends or anyone in the States." He could hardly *want* to condemn himself to solitary confinement. But the "understanding" goes so far as to govern not only his behavior, but even his emotional attitudes.

The issue of focalization in the story is complicated. Probably the simplest account makes this a case of dual focalization where the narrator alternates between Luz and the soldier.[8] However, there is clearly a stronger orientation toward the soldier, since the reader is given some information about him that Luz does not have, but, it seems, no information about Luz that he does not have. In keeping with this, Scholes has demonstrated that the story translates easily into first-person narration from the soldier's point of view (substituting "I" for "he"), but not from Luz's point of view (substituting "I" for "Luz" or "she"). This bias in focalization may suggest a preference on the part of the implied author.

Most readers would probably say that there is no narratee in this work. However, there seems to be a narratee in the same sense that there is a (heterodiegetic) narrator. There are hints of this narratee from the information that the narrator presupposes, but that is clearly not presupposed for the implied reader. In other words, one can isolate a narratee through its difference from the implied reader. The introduction noted that "A Very Short Story" does not include an "orientation" explaining who the soldier and Luz are. Indeed, the reader is never given the soldier's name. The phrasing from the start suggests that the addressee is supposed to know who "he" is and who "they" are. It seems clear that that addressee is not the implied reader because no reader, not even an "ideal" reader (e.g., in the Structuralist sense [see Eagleton 121]), could know who the soldier is at the beginning of the narrative. The addressee, then, is a narratee—a heterodiegetic narratee. The narratee presumably shares the narrator's interest in the soldier prior to the beginning of the story. Indeed, the fact that the soldier is always referred to by a pronoun, while Luz is identified by name, suggests that this narrative may be viewed as implicitly part of a larger discourse. The topic of that larger discourse would not be Luz, but the unnamed (because familiar and unmistakable) soldier.

The implied reader is, again, different from the narratee. However, this implied reader is able to piece together the story background from the clues in the text. Thus he or she can arrive at the information already familiar to the narratee. The implied reader is also able to sense the ironic distance between the implied author and the narrator, drawing out the implications of such phrases as "It was understood." Arguably, the implied reader is more closely aligned with the soldier than with

Luz—to use Murray Smith's term for increased "access to the actions, thoughts, and feelings" of a character (220). This is what one would expect, given that the focalization of the text is biased in that direction. But it does not follow that one needs to have an allegiance with the soldier (again, drawing on Murray Smith's distinction). The implied reader follows interpretive norms. Thus the implied reader *understands* the attitudes and evaluations of the implied author. But there is no requirement of *sharing or not sharing* those attitudes and evaluations. Put differently, a real reader can be mistaken about an implied author's compassion for a character. For example, in my view, it would be mistaken to say that the implied author lacks sympathy for Luz. But a real reader cannot be spoken of as mistaken in his or her own compassion for a character. Thus I cannot say that a student is mistaken if he or she has no sympathy for Luz.

As the last point makes clear, the real reader of the story will differ from the implied reader in many ways. Most simply, the real reader is free to fill in or imagine indeterminate details as he or she wishes. More significantly, as just indicated, he or she can reject the attitudes and evaluations of the implied author (and the real author). The real reader can even decide to reject more fundamental aspects of the implied reader. He or she may decide that one part of the work is a fair representation of male–female relations, but that another part is guided by patriarchal ideology. In connection with this, real readers sometimes contradict the apparently clear determination of the story, saying things such as "No, Luz would never do that. She must have done . . . instead." This does not, I believe, violate principles of the narrative as long as the reader realizes that he or she is contradicting the implied reader and implied author. (Needless to say, the reader does not have to formulate this realization in these technical terms.) On the other hand, a reader may fail to correctly infer the implied author and implied reader, or, more simply, the story. So it is indeed possible for real readers to be mistaken. Indeed, real readers usually are mistaken to some degree. Thus this model of narrative discourse suggests that there is genuine freedom of reader imagination and response in that readers are free to reject even the straightforward formulation of story elements. But that does not mean that there is no issue of getting things right or wrong. While there are, again, many indeterminacies, there are also aspects of the story that are indicated by the discourse with greater or lesser certainty.

Leaving aside a few theoretical ideas (e.g., the "profile of ambiguity") and elaboration, the preceding outline is largely consistent with common views in mainstream narratology. However, there are difficulties that arise in connection with each of the preceding components. Moreover, there are aspects of narrative discourse that are not captured by this analytic. The remainder of this chapter will go through the components in greater detail reformulating them in response to some of these problems.

Real Author/Implied Author

Perhaps the most obvious question about the idea of the implied author concerns whether it is simply redundant. Isn't the implied author covered by the real author? In one sense, the answer to this question is "Yes." The implied author must, in some way, be the result of the goals and interests of the real author as he or she puts together the narrative. For example, if there is irony in a work, this is presumably because the real author put the work together in such a way that there is some untrustworthiness of the narrator. However, there is another sense in which the answer to this question is "No." It is not necessarily the case that the untrustworthiness of the narrator is untrustworthiness relative to the real author himself or herself. In other words, there may actually be a difference, indeed an opposition between the real author and the implied author.

Consider the following variation on the case of Jonathan Swift. Imagine another author, call him Jonathan Sloe, a politician who is trying to appeal to a group of voters who are concerned about Irish poverty and object strongly to British policies. Sloe writes his "Modest Proposal" in which he recommends eating Irish babies. The irony is clear. Anyone reading or hearing the piece would grasp its irony immediately. They would rightly infer that the implied author is harshly critical of British policies in Ireland. But, in fact, Sloe wholly supports those policies. Sloe's own feelings do not affect the irony of his pamphlet. However pro-British he may be, he has put together a treatise that is ironic and in which *the author implied by the text* is opposed to British policy.

As this indicates, the role of the implied author is easiest to isolate when a real author has written insincerely. One could give a technical definition of insincerity in terms of distance between the implied author and the real author, just as one can give a technical definition of irony in terms of distance between the narrator and the implied author. Indeed, generally, these distinctions become consequential to the degree that there are differences. It is important to distinguish the implied author from the narrator to the extent that the implied author establishes a norm from which the narrator deviates. When the narrator adheres to the norms of the implied author, the distinction is not terribly consequential.

Indeed, there seems to be a general principle here. Readers seem to distinguish narrator/implied author/real author only to the degree that they diverge. Moreover, such readers judge them to diverge *only when given reason to believe that they diverge*.[9] In other words, a basic principle of discursive interpretation is that *the default assumption is congruence of narrator, implied author, and real author.* Moreover, even when there is incongruence (thus irony or insincerity), readers generally assume this is limited to the points where there is evidence of divergence. Thus one may say that inference to incongruence is *motivated* and *localized*.

"Congruence" seems to be the appropriate term here rather than "identity" for the technical reason that the narrator may be spoken of as asserting certain situations or events to be facts, whereas, for many of those situations or events, the real author is asserting only that they are part of the story. On the other hand, the implied author is also usually making some claims about the real world. In this way, the implied author may be understood as always theoretically different from the narrator in part because he or she can make claims about the real world and not merely about the storyworld.

The difference between claims about the fictional world and claims about the real world is important in a number of areas, including understanding the relation between the implied author and the real author. For example, it seems that one only counts a work as insincere to the extent that it suggests certain implied authorial claims about the real world that the real author does not hold to be true. If there is a discrepancy between the implied author and the real author in a claim confined to the fictional world, readers would most likely consider that unintentional and thus some sort of flaw in technique rather than insincerity.[10]

Consider again Hemingway's story. One might first look at a claim that is particular to the fictional world—for example, the claim that Luz wrote a Dear John letter to the soldier. Obviously, the narrator communicates this. There is no indication in the text that the implied author has a different idea (i.e., that the narrator is unreliable on this). Suppose, however, it was discovered that, in Hemingway's view, the letter was made up by the soldier. Since there is no indication of this in the story, most readers would probably consider it a flaw in the execution.

In contrast, the story suggests that attachment deprivation or loneliness can drive people (perhaps women particularly) into imprudent attachment relations. It also suggests that anger at attachment rejection can lead people (perhaps particularly men) into imprudent sexual relations. If it turned out that Hemingway did not believe either of these things about the real world (perhaps he just thought readers would like these ideas), readers might be inclined to see some sort of insincerity in the narrative.

If one were to try to isolate objective rules here—following the example of Rabinowitz[11]—one would probably come up with something along the following lines. A real author may be judged sincere or insincere for any implied authorial claim about the real world. These claims need not be articulated explicitly. Rather, unless there is specific reason to believe otherwise, one generally assumes that the real author is claiming truth for general causal principles, for ethical norms, and for explanations and evaluations of actual events, as well as some particulars bearing on actual events (e.g., when a fictional film about an actual war massacre suggests that superior officers were aware of the massacre).[12] "Reason to believe otherwise" would include, for example, genre conventions (e.g., those of fantasy) that allow for the changes in physical, psychological, historical, or other principles.

As just indicated, the Hemingway story provides an example of general causal principles—in this case, general psychological causal principles (perhaps gender-based). But some readers may have been inclined to question the extent to which such psychological generalizations could really justify a judgment of insincerity (if it turned out that Hemingway did not believe them). It certainly does not seem to be as strong a case as that of Jonathan Sloe, with his misleading implications of anti-imperialism. In connection with this, one would probably have to hierarchize these components. It is probably the case that, on the whole, readers consider discrepancies in ethical/political principles or judgments to be more insincere than discrepancies in ethically and politically neutral facts or empirical generalizations. Readers also seem to be more inclined to label an author insincere if he or she gains materially by the discrepancy, as in Sloe's case. To capture this, one would need to further qualify the rule.

On the other hand, all of this may suggest that a very different approach is in order. In judgments of insincerity, people are probably not guided by objective rules at all. Rather, such "rules" approximate something else—feelings and the cognitive developments that are connected with those feelings. Specifically, a reader has an emotional response to a story. Part of that emotional response is to fictional aspects of the story. But part of that response bears on the real world. This is manifest most significantly in one's attitude toward the world after one finishes reading the fiction and resumes daily life. That attitude may involve one's judgment of political policies, one's understanding of other cultures, one's view of historical events, one's expectations about romance, or many other matters.

In this context, a plausible hypothesis is that readers tacitly judge a real author's sincerity by reference to their own emotional response to the real world, as that is affected by the narrative at issue. In other words, readers tacitly react to certain aspects of the work as if they were claimed true about the real world in ways that those readers care about. Those reactions guide readers in evaluating the author's sincerity. Specifically, one judges an author to be insincere—or, rather, condemns an author for being insincere—to the degree that one feels one has been misled by the author on some issue of emotional significance.

However one understands the nature of insincerity, the very possibility of real authorial insincerity leads back to the more general issue of the relation between the implied author and the real author. On the one hand, the possibility of insincerity indicates that the implied author is not simply the real author. On the other hand, it also indicates that they cannot be entirely different. If they were entirely different, one would not judge the real author by reference to the implied author at all. Moreover, there are cases where knowledge about the real author has consequences for one's understanding of the implied author. For example, suppose Jonathan Sloe is a well-known imperialist politician. He publishes his "Modest Proposal" in the context of many anti-Irish speeches and votes. Readers would certainly take this into account in interpreting the work. Readers would probably not conclude that he is really advocating cannibalism. However, readers may infer that the implied author is trying to create mirth by dehumanizing the Irish.

These points are related to the disagreement among narratologists regarding the nature of the implied author.[13] As Nünning notes ("Implied Author" 240), there is a conflict between the view of the implied author as "a construct inferred and assembled by the reader" (Rimmon-Kenan 87) and the view of the implied author as "a streamlined version of the real author" (Phelan *Living* 45). The preceding discussion has already pointed out a problem with too close an identification of real and implied authors. There are cases in which the implied author is directly opposed to the real author. It might seem that this leads to the reader-response version of the implied author. It is certainly true that the implied author has existence only as imagined by readers. But the issue is whether the implied author is wholly constructed by readers or, so to speak, reconstructed by them. The difference is that, in the case of "reconstruction," there is a norm, a possibility of getting the implied author right or wrong. This leads back to the connection with the real author, since the real author would seem to be the obvious place where that norm could be defined. Moreover, the example of a publicly anti-Irish Sloe suggests that readers do commonly understand the implied author in relation to the real author. In certain contexts, a change in one's understanding of the real author produces a change in one's understanding of the implied author. But still the possibility of insincerity indicates that the implied author cannot simply be the real author, even part of the real author.

To complicate matters even further, there is a longstanding tradition in literary study that the author's self-conscious ideas about a work—even the most sincere ideas—have no special status among possible interpretations. If the author's interpretation of his or her work is not necessarily valid, then it would seem that the real author cannot stand as a norm for the implied author or anything else. At the same time, some theorists (e.g., E. D. Hirsch) have maintained that the only reasonable norm for interpretation is authorial intent, while Knapp and Michaels have gone so far as to maintain that we always interpret for authorial intent no matter what we think we are doing.

These problems may be at least partially resolved by refining ideas about authorial intent and the processes involved in meaning. The crucial, fundamental distinction here is between "productive" and "receptive" meaning. Most people have probably had the experience of saying something that they thought would be clever or funny, but that sounded crude or silly once actually uttered. Sometimes, one is able to sense this before committing the faux pas. In that case, one does something like hearing the words in one's mind before actually saying them. These are instances of a conflict between one's own productive and receptive meanings. More complicated cases of this come in revising something one has written. When I revise a book chapter, I am often trying to align my productive and receptive meanings, my sense of what I want to say and my sense of what I am likely to be understood as saying. In fact, my revision may go further. As I experience my text receptively, I may see connections and implications that I had missed initially. I may reject some of those, and elaborate on others. I may also change my mind about some of my initial ideas. In this way, one may distinguish my initial productive intent from my subsequent, receptive intent.

This simple division provides a way of speaking about real authors and implied authors more clearly and with greater explanatory rigor. Specifically, the implied author may be understood normatively as the final receptive meaning of the real author, the receptive meaning of the author when he or she feels satisfied that the work is complete or "right."[14] This has several beneficial consequences.[15]

First, it indicates that the meaning is indeed understood from a reader's point of view. However, it does not thereby avoid norms (thus the possibility of saying that a particular interpretation is inaccurate), since it makes one particular receptive or reader-based meaning the standard. Indeed, this form of authorial intent preserves the central cases of determinacy that almost everyone sees as relevant. For example, critics generally believe that interpretations of a text should be confined to the meanings of words at the time the text was produced. Within most reader-oriented approaches, there is no reason for the reader not to bring in current meanings (e.g., twenty-first-century meanings when reading a medieval tale). From the perspective of authorial receptive intent, however, then-current word meanings are crucial. At the same time, however, this account largely filters out idiosyncratic meanings, such as personal associations that may have led an author to choose a particular word or image when producing the text initially.

In keeping with these points, this account has the advantage of giving particular importance to the text of the literary work. Various sorts of information will be significant and consequential for the receptive intent of the author, thus for the implied author. These would include what the author assumes to be common knowledge, including common knowledge about his or her own political views (as in the case of a publicly imperialist Sloe). But the bulk of the relevant information is almost certain to derive from the sentences that compose the narrative, from the utterance itself. In this way, it still makes sense to take the "implied author" as implied by the text—though it is now necessary to qualify that as "primarily" or "largely," not wholly. Moreover, this allows one to conclude that some interpretations are warranted by the text and others are not—again, with the proviso that interpretation cannot be a matter of "the text alone," even if it is primarily a matter of the text.

It is also worth noting that this division does provide a place for biographical criticism. Biographical criticism would have particular relevance for the productive intent of the work. Specifically, it is perhaps the best way to isolate the causal antecedents of productive intent (e.g., in idiosyncratic associations). In this way, it is valuable for the comprehension of literary "making," the psychology of creation, the particular generative processes of individual writers, and other topics. It is usually not as important to the interpretation of the literary work, since its focus tends to be on aspects of an author's experience that were not public and thus not part of his or her receptive intent. On the other hand, it may be interpretively relevant insofar as it informs the reader of parts of the author's life that were public but have been forgotten. Again, such public aspects of an author's life may bear on the implied author.

In relation to this, such a receptive account also helps to filter out the author's self-conscious statements about his or her meanings. In other words, it helps to explain and avoid the "intentional fallacy." It might at first seem that authors must have direct introspective access to the reasons why a particular work feels right, thus why they receptively accept a particular revision as the completed work or final version. But, in fact, people are fairly bad at isolating such reasons for their feelings and evaluations. Even for some fairly simple responses, one's stated reasons are often more akin to rationalizations.[16] The problem becomes much worse for a highly complex behavior such as literary creation and evaluation. Consider the far simpler operation of forming regular plurals in English. Whenever an English speaker hears or utters a regular plural, he or she follows a rule. Thus any English speaker can fill in the plural of "gerb"—one gerb, two ___—even though he or she has never heard of a word "gerb." However, if asked what the rule is, he or she is almost certain to get it wrong. He or she has self-consciously learned an orthographic rule—"add *s*." This rule is therefore available to working memory. However, he or she processes English utterances by a more complex rule. Specifically, in regular English plurals, one adds [s] after unvoiced nonsibilants (as in cat/cats), [z] after voiced nonsibilants (as in dog/dogs or gerb/gerbs—spelled "s," but pronounced [z]), and [əz] after sibilants (as in bush/bushes—spelled "es," but pronounced [əz]).[17] How likely is it that an author can formulate the reasons governing his or her receptive satisfaction with an entire novel when he or she probably cannot even formulate the reasons governing his or her receptive satisfaction with the plural "gerbs" or even "dogs"? Thus a receptive intent account of implied authorship fits well with current accounts of cognitive processing in such a way as to avoid the intentional fallacy.[18, 19]

Narrator and Narratee

In some ways, the situation with the narrator and narratee is much simpler, since there is no issue of a real person. But in some ways the issue is more complex for the same reason. The narrator and the narratee are part of the communicative discourse structure. But, of course, they are not actually communicating with one another. They are a fiction. How such fictional entities function to mimic communication is clear enough when both are overt. But things are much less clear when one or both are implicit, as in "A Very Short Story."

To address these issues, one must first consider the basic function of a narrator. Perhaps here too it is helpful to compare the narrator with the author—not only the implied author, but the real author. Of course, the real author exists as a person in the material world and the narrator does not. But that is not functionally relevant here. From the perspective of the reader, the narrator, the implied author, and the real author are imagined people. Readers, of course, know that narrators are not real. But in order to respond to a narrator (e.g., to trust or distrust him or her), readers need to imagine him or her as a person. Thus the key difference here is not that authors are real and narrators are not. There has to be some other difference, a difference that is relevant to the response of readers—including the normative response of the implied reader.

As a first approximation, one might say that the basic function of a narrator is to report the story, to represent (or misrepresent) a storyworld that is in some way separate from the narrator's representation of it. The author, rather, creates the story, defines a storyworld that is not separate from his or her definition. The narrator chooses what to say about what happens in the storyworld. In contrast, the author chooses what actually does happen in the storyworld.

As it turns out, things are slightly more complicated than this suggests. Authors often assert that their characters act independently, take over the story, force the author to follow a certain path. As Mey puts it, "Authors frequently complain that their personae assume independent lives and voices, and that the plot starts to develop by an inner logic of its own, with the author as a bemused spectator on the sidelines, following the antics of his or her creatures and chronicling them as best he or she can" (794). This has a certain point and, indeed, complicates the relation between the author and the narrator. It is therefore worth considering in greater detail.

Once the author has imagined the personality and circumstances of a character, his or her normal cognitive processes will produce a relatively automatic anticipation of that character's action. Again, when people create fiction, they use ordinary cognitive architecture. This architecture includes structures and processes for anticipating one's own and other people's actions. I know Smith; I have a sense of how he acts in various situations. I am thinking about asking him to observe my teaching and write a letter of recommendation. I try to imagine how Smith would respond to my class, how this would affect a letter, and so forth. Note that the entire (evolutionary) function of such imagination is lost if I simply make up Smith's response to suit my preferences. Indeed, that is precisely the difference between such hypothetical imagination and fantasy.[20] Rather, the imagination has to be constrained by my understanding of Smith. In order to proceed with adequate speed, particularly in pressing circumstances, imaginations of this sort have to be more or less automatic as well (i.e., they are not usually or primarily matters of effortful calculation). For that, the understanding and familiarity must be largely implicit—based, for example, on memories that I do not inspect self-consciously, but that give me an implicit sense of how Smith would act.[21] It is also important to stress that my understanding of Smith and my inferences about his likely behavior are both open to dispute. Thus it may be quite reasonable for someone to tell me that I am, say, crazy to trust Smith with a teaching evaluation.

It seems extremely likely that this is just what occurs with real authors and fictional characters. Authors create a character by imagining traits, a history, interests, and current conditions. These are partially considered self-consciously and partially remain implicit. Moreover, they are bound up with complexes of authorial memories. These memories need not concern the character's (fictional) history, but may bear on other, real or fictional individuals who are parallel to the character in some way. Such memories are almost entirely un-self-conscious.[22] Those imagined properties and conditions, along with the associated, un-self-conscious memories, produce the sort of semimechanical trajectories of character action that one finds in everyday hypothetical imagination (as in the case of Smith observing my class).

By this analysis, there are two sets of inputs to the imagination of character trajectories. One set is textual—including the character's traits and conditions. But the second set derives from an author's or reader's own memories. Those memories will, of course, differ. As such, various readers may imagine the arc of a character's actions differently. Often, readers' imaginations will be vague enough to fit with authorial imaginations. However, sometimes they will contradict authorial imaginations. When this contradiction results from divergence in noncharacter memories, it seems there is no reason to believe that the author is necessarily correct or normative. Indeed, in some cases one may say that, given what is known about the character from the text, the author's imagination is less plausible than a given reader's imagination. In other words, many people have the intuitive sense that readers can reasonably criticize an author's character development—saying, for example, "Oh, Mr. Gallstone would never have accepted a bribe to marry Lucinda—at least not such a small one" or "The screenwriter and director simply don't understand Lucinda. She would certainly have boarded the boat for Buenos Aires, at least after she found her evil stepmother's letter to Gallstone." This analysis suggests one way in which such statements can indeed have force, and why it is possible for authors to misunderstand their characters. Character trajectories are a function of the characters' own histories and conditions, supplemented by the author's memories. Those memories, used tacitly as models for the characters, may be biased or otherwise misleading.

Here, it is possible to treat the functional relation between narrators and authors more precisely. First, there is a crucial similarity. Both authors and narrators to a certain extent represent a storyworld that is beyond their control. In other words, authors also to some extent report—rather than choose—what their characters do in imagined trajectories.[23]

But authors do choose the conditions of the storyworld, select from the possible character trajectories, and fill in further details that are undefined by the initial conditions and trajectories. In contrast, the narrator is the witness and communicator of the trajectories produced by authorial imagination. But, of course, the narrator may be—usually is—more than this as well. Specifically, as communicator, the narrator manipulates that information.

There is, presumably, certain information that the implied author takes to be crucial for the reader. There are two primary ways in which that information may be manipulated—through the *sequence* and *manner* in which it is given. Thus some piece of information may be given early or late in a narrative, directly or by implication, and so forth. The narrator may be understood as the speaker who determines this sequence and manner of the communication, with the caveat that the narrator may be trustworthy or untrustworthy. If the narrator is untrustworthy, then the relevant information must still be communicated, but it must be communicated, not only indirectly, but, so to speak, inadvertently relative to the narrator. (This issue will be considered in chapter 4.) Note that the narrator can be unreliable precisely because the narrator is not the author. If the author changes the story, then the story is actually different. If the narrator changes the story, then that is a misrepresentation. Even in cases where the author misunderstands his or her characters, that misunderstanding affects one's evaluation of the story, not one's interpretation. In the preceding hypothetical narrative, for example, Gallstone did accept the derisory bribe in the storyworld, however inconsistent that is with his character.

Many narratologists take the fundamental division of narrators to be that between those who are within the story and those who are outside the story. This is certainly important. However, it does not seem to be the most crucial for one's understanding of communicative discourse. Rather, a different, if partially related, distinction seems to be the essential one. Specifically, one question arises immediately when one speaks of a narrator describing a trajectory—is there really an agent there who can be spoken of as doing such describing? Clearly, there is such an agent in the case of a first-person narrator. However, one may wonder what sense it makes to speak of such an agent in the case of a third-person narration. The issue here does not seem to be one of whether the narrator is inside the story or not. Rather, the issue seems to be whether the narrator is the sort of entity one would think of as making choices, selecting the order and manner of information. In other words, the difference seems to be between whether the narrator is *personified* or *nonpersonified*.[24]

Of course, if there is a narrator, then there is some choice, some selection. However, that choice is not invariably accompanied by an imaginative objectification or *constitution* of the narrator, to use the Phenomenological term. (Constitution is the mental integration of information to form an object of thought—as when one synthesizes different glimpses of, say, a chair to form an image of that chair.) Put differently, narration implies a constituting subjectivity, but it need not involve any self-objectification of that subjectivity—thus the presentation of any physical or psychological attributions, even the minimal attribution contained in the personal pronoun "I."[25]

Generally, it is easy to envision a personified narrator as selecting information, phrasing it in a certain way, and so forth. Indeed, an author's imagination of personified narrators is just like his or her imagination of characters. The author both explicitly and implicitly envisions properties, histories, interests, and circumstances for the narrator. The author's mind tacitly associates these with memories and allows imagination to produce behaviors and circumstances for the narrator—in this case, behaviors of storytelling. Thus what the personified narrator says or writes is the result of imaginatively generated trajectories of the same sort that one finds in the story itself.

Indeed, the narratee fits here as well. The narratee is, fundamentally, the addressee for the narrator. The function of the narratee, however, is somewhat different from that of the narrator. The narratee does not operate so much as an independent agent. Rather, he or she operates as a sort of regulative principle for what information the narrator has to provide, what sort of rhetorical techniques he or she has to use, and so forth. In other words, speakers always aim at some sort of audience. A speaker cannot communicate everything about any topic. He or she assumes certain sorts of knowledge. Moreover, a speaker does not adopt the same rhetorical strategies with everyone, since a speaker does not assume that everyone begins with the same prejudices or emotional propensities. The narratee is the imagined guide for the narrator's information and rhetoric.

In this sense, the narratee is embedded within the imagination of the narrator. This is just what one would expect, since this is the way people speak. People formulate descriptions, adopt a certain tone, press certain judgments for a particular addressee as they imagine him or her. In keeping with this, one's imagined trajectories of communicative behavior routinely embed "theory of mind" ideas, which is to say, simulations of other people's imaginations of speakers and addressees (sometimes along with some more self-conscious inferences).[26] Suppose I know that Professor Jones, an academic advisor, will be speaking with Ms. Smith about satisfying her mathematics and science requirements. In imagining how the conversation will go, I implicitly take into account what Jones believes about Smith and vice versa. I will imagine the conversation differently if I know that Jones believes Smith is unmathematical, if Jones believes that Smith is considering a major in physics, and so on. It is important to note that part of this simulation is emotional. I imagine Jones's emotional attitude to Smith as well as his conception of her. For example, I may imagine that Jones likes Smith and genuinely wants to help her plan out the best course of study for her future, or that he finds her an irritating pest.

Again, people's usual imaginative practices carry over to literary imagination. This occurs most clearly when authors simulate characters.[27] For example, Hemingway embeds Luz's understanding of the soldier in her speech to him, just as he embeds her emotional response to the major—not only romantic interest, but trust—in her response to him. The former embedding comes out clearly in her letter to the soldier. She "finally wrote to the States that theirs had only been a boy and girl affair," and so on. The first sentence indicates that Luz is envisioning him as young, immature, inexperienced. She makes the same statement about herself, since she refers to them as a "boy" and "girl" respectively. But it is clear that, at least since her relationship with the major, she considers herself to be an adult, a woman, whereas—in her imagination— he is still a boy. This embedded imagination continues throughout the rest of the letter, as when she writes that "he would probably not be able to understand," as if his level of intellectual maturity is too low. On the other hand, it is difficult to say if one should fully believe Luz's expression of her imagination. One might, rather, infer that she has a more complex, tacit imagination of the soldier, but has developed a self-conscious idea of his immaturity as a rationalization of her actions. In other words, one might interpret her imaginations as both ambivalent and ambiguous.

In the middle of the letter, there is an indication of Luz's imagination of the major. But it too is an indication that is rhetorically oriented toward a particular audience. It is an indication aimed at the understanding of the soldier. Specifically, she writes that her engagement was "absolutely unexpected." The suggestion here is that she did not envision the major as a possible spouse until he proposed to her. Clearly, this is not a claim one can trust. Rather, it is a claim made to affect the soldier's imagination of Luz and thereby to guide his subsequent response to her. The idea is that he would not imagine she had in any way anticipated any of this.[28] This, in turn, suggests a much more complex imagination of the soldier than is overtly expressed in the letter. He is not merely a naïve youth who will grow to see the wisdom of her decision. He is, rather, a potential accuser. He is also someone for whom she still has some feelings, so that she cares about his potential accusations.

The case of Luz illustrates some of the ways in which authors imagine characters imagining addressees—including imaginations of those addressees' imaginations—thereby embedding levels of simulation. As usual, the same principles hold for narrators and narratees. Indeed, in her letter, Luz is an embedded narrator. This leads to several points.

First, recognizing Luz's role as an embedded narrator imagining the soldier shows an ambiguity in the notion of a narratee. Within the story, the soldier is actually not a narratee, but a real reader. The narratee is, most importantly, the addressee imagined by the narrator. Ordinarily narratees are not developed in enough detail for this to be an issue. In keeping with the general principles governing narrators and authors, one assumes a congruence of readers and narratees within stories unless one is given reason to distinguish them. But one may be given such a reason—sometimes in embedded narrations, such as Luz's letter.

This example also leads back to the issue of personification. It is clear that behind this personified narrator (Luz), there is a nonpersonified narrator, the narrator of the entire story. The point appears to be generalizable. In other words, the point holds not only for such localized, embedded narrations, but for larger personified narrations as well. This would be in keeping with Nielsen's view that "behind every homodiegetic narrator is a 'nonpersonified voice' of the fiction and that sometimes the homodiegetic narrator gives way to this voice" (as Phelan and Booth ["Narrator" 391] put it; see Nielsen).[29] Perhaps more importantly, it is also in keeping with the Phenomenological understanding of constituting subjectivity as necessarily underlying constituted subjectivity (as well as the Lacanian idea of a subjectivity underlying the ego and the cognitive view of a self as underlying any self-concept). Of course, here too there is a general presumption of default congruence. Nonetheless, there is always a possibility of incongruence.

Needless to say, this does not solve all problems about the nature of narrators. Most obviously, it leaves the task of understanding the nonpersonified narrator. Indeed, the preceding discussion leads to positing a nonpersonified narratee with this nonpersonified narrator, which intensifies the difficulty. In the case of Hemingway's story, one may envision the soldier as embedded within the imagination of Luz in writing her letter. That is parallel to what one does in ordinary life. But how does one embed a nonpersonified narratee in a nonpersonified narrator? That does not seem parallel to anything one does in ordinary life, since people at least seem to imagine only personified speakers, themselves simulating only personified addressees.

In fact, the issue of the nonpersonified narratee might be fairly easily resolved. People do alter their speech and writing for fairly amorphous addressees—such as particular individuals whom they do not know, or groups (e.g., one may write a report for an archive without any sense of who might read it, but one still tries to give necessary information, not to give unnecessary information, and so on). As long as one has a personified narrator, a nonpersonified narratee may not be a problem.

But what about that nonpersonified narrator? It might at first appear that such an entity is not even possible. But literary works clearly do incorporate nonpersonified narrators, with embedded nonpersonified narratees. One sees this, for example, in presumptions about knowledge. The point is obvious at the start of Hemingway's story, as already noted. But it continues all the way to the end, when the addressee is tacitly expected to know that the soldier was in Chicago.[30] Again, the implied author has organized everything so that real readers are able to infer this. But the information is not foregrounded in the way it would ordinarily be if the addressee were not already familiar with the soldier and his hometown. Thus there is a clear discrepancy between whoever is speaking and the implied author, since the latter recognizes that the reader does not have such prior familiarity.

For a cognitive account, one primary way of resolving such a dilemma is isolating a real-world situation in which people engage in a process of understanding or imagining a nonpersonified narrator. In fact, people frequently engage in understanding or responding to such a situation along these lines—when they overhear conversations, specifically conversations in which the speaker is telling a third-person narrative. The general relation between everyday overhearing and one's response to literature has been developed by Richard Gerrig and Deborah Prentice in their concept of the reader as a "side participant" ("Notes"). However, it does not seem that narratologists have recognized the relation of such overhearing to the understanding or imagination of a nonpersonified narrator (and embedded, nonpersonified narratee). This is somewhat surprising, given that many overheard conversations are genuinely nonpersonified in the sense that, other than what one gathers from his or her speech, one does not know anything about the speaker beyond his or her being a person (perhaps in a particular location). Rather, one begins with a fairly minimal sense of this being a speaker, a speaker who has some addressee in mind. From here, one is able to follow what the person says more or less well (despite the fact that there is no implied author checking this narrator for communicative problems).

If there is in fact continuity between overhearing, on the one hand, and understanding a nonpersonified narrator, on the other, this indicates that the nonpersonified narrator is, in principle, a full person.

Again, as far as one's explicit knowledge goes, he or she is simply a voice—hence the label "nonpersonified." But he or she is a voice that is tacitly imagined as part of a communicative scenario, thus a voice that has knowledge and motivation—even though one does not initially know much about what these are, as in real cases of side participation or overhearing.

The preceding analyses have considered the nonpersonified narrator only from the reader's perspective. Again, this is the crucial perspective, since it includes the receptive intent of the author. However, it is worth turning briefly to the perspective of the author as creator. The author can generate a nonpersonified narrator's voice in many different ways. One way is by simulating an overheard conversation. However, that is probably very rare. It seems more likely that authors unreflectively take up an emotional orientation, presumptions about narratee knowledge, a vocabulary, and so forth, through the priming of a range of narrative models stored in memory. (Priming involves partially but not fully activating some mental content or process, which is to say activating it below the threshold of self-conscious awareness.) These models, drawn from a range of precursor works, may guide the production of the narrator's voice without the author reflecting self-consciously on them. Of course, the effects of these different imaginations and memories are not all the same. Thus there are different degrees and kinds of influence. What is crucial overall is that the author probably does not have a developed character self-consciously in mind. As a result, his or her relation to the nonpersonified narrator's voice is comparable to one of overhearing.

More generally, people do things like this when they shift into, say, a regional dialect (e.g., a Boston accent) or imitate technical speech (say, deconstructive vocabulary) for comic effect. They are taking up the voice of a narrator—one distinct from the "author" (themselves)—a narrator who is clearly following principles of some sort, even though the speakers do not really know anything about the "personality" of that voice. In other words, the speakers are, in effect, adopting the voice of a nonpersonified narrator.

In the case of literature, of course, the assumption of a voice is far more prolonged. Throughout its extended development, the assumption of that voice is repeatedly subjected to the constraint, organization, and direction of the implied author. This in effect makes the production—or at least revision—of such a nonpersonified voice in fiction into something even more like a case of overhearing or side participation. Specifically, the author has to receptively respond to the narrator's voice in such a way that it consistently unfolds the story in an appropriate way (i.e., in a way appropriate to the experience that the author wishes to produce or feels is right for a particular work). This is necessarily a process of (tacitly) understanding a nonpersonified narrator's knowledge, interests, imagination of a narratee, and so forth.

In isolating the operation of the nonpersonified narrator and nonpersonified narratee in Hemingway's "Very Short Story," the preceding discussion considered how one may infer some beliefs of the narrator about the knowledge of the narratee. But there are important issues surrounding the narrator's own knowledge (as narratologists have stressed), as well as his or her interests. It is important to consider some of these in the context of focalization.

Before going on, however, we might note the expansion of part of the diagram of narrative discourse. That diagram now includes the following:

Real Author [Implied Author [Nonpersonified Narrator {Personified Narrator {Focalizer} Personified Narratee} Nonpersonified Narratee] Implied Reader] Real Reader

Again, the nonpersonified narrator is often congruent with the implied author, and the personified narrator is often congruent with the nonpersonified narrator. But this does not mean that the status of all these discourse agents is the same. Personified narrators and narratees, as well as focalizers, are optional elements of a fiction. By the preceding analysis, there is always a narrator and a narratee,[31] even if they are congruent with the implied author and the implied reader.[32] This is because there is always some manipulation (at least selection and phrasing) of information from a storyworld. That manipulation is a function of the narrator oriented toward a narratee. Finally, there is a difference in degree of story embedment between the nonpersonified narrator and narratee, on the one hand, and the personified narrator and narratee, on the other, just as there is a difference in narrative or textual embedment between the real author and reader, on the one hand, and the implied author and reader, on the other. (Roughly, square brackets indicate implication by the text, thus embedment within communicative discourse, while curly brackets mark representation in the text, thus embedment in a storyworld.)

Focalization and Topicalization

As is well known, Gérard Genette distinguished focalizers from narrators. The narrator is the "agent who produces a narrative" (Herman "Glossary" 280). Focalization, in contrast, "denotes the perspectival restriction and orientation of narrative information relative to somebody's (usually, a character's) perception, imagination, knowledge, or point of view. . . . Hence, focalization theory covers the various means of regulating, selecting, and channeling narrative information" (Jahn "Focalization" 173).

"Perspectival" is the key word here. It indicates the relation of the narrator to some point of view on which that narrator focuses his or her attention. For example, narrators sometimes confine their narration to what a particular character experiences or thinks. Suppose a story includes the following lines: "Jones was feeling apprehensive. Smith seemed preoccupied and distant all morning. Jones walked out of the office, worried about what Smith might be thinking." Jones is not the narrator. But the perspective of the narrative is at least quite close to that of Jones. The narrator reports what Jones sees, thinks, and feels. The narrator does not report what Smith sees, thinks, and feels—except insofar as these are inferred by Jones. Jones is, then, the focalizer.

Genette distinguished three types of focalization. The first is "zero-focalization." In this case, there is no focalizer. The narrator relates events and scenes without any filter from a character in the story. The second is "internal focalization," which restricts the narrator to the experiences (perceptual, imaginative, etc.) of one or more characters. The third is "external focalization," where the narrator does not have access to inner thoughts, but reports only external facts about the storyworld insofar as these are available to the focalizer.

Mieke Bal and others have criticized this distinction, arguing, for example, that "even typical 'non-focalized' passages are rarely entirely free of point of view" (Jahn "Focalization" 101). Jahn cites an example from James Michener's *Hawaii* as an example. The passage begins, "Across a million years, down more than ten million years [the island] existed silently in the unknown sea" (qtd. in Jahn "Focalization" 97). Jahn's point is that even this small piece of narration involves selection. It is not simply a part of a statement of everything. Thus it is focalized.

But this seems problematic. If "focalization" becomes so broad that it encompasses all forms of selection, then it has ceased to serve its initial theoretical functions, both explanatory and descriptive. Perhaps this is a point where it is valuable to return to an older distinction, that between omniscient and limited narration. It is true that focalization is not identical with limited narration and that the isolation of focalization is an important advance in narrative theory. However, that does not mean that the omniscient/limited distinction should simply be discarded. It addresses something different from focalization—and perhaps, when adequately refined, it may help clarify focalization and the issue of zero focalization.

As seen in the preceding section, when one speaks of a narrator, even a nonpersonified narrator, one is not speaking of a mechanism or an abstract principle, but tacitly simulating a human or humanlike agent. That humanlike agent—as one simulates him or her—should have certain properties. The properties do not have to be precisely the same as those that characterize real humans. But they should presumably be of the same general sort. Humans gain information about the world through sensory perception, thus without direct access to other minds. Moreover, human perception is limited spatially and temporally. If one takes a narrator to be humanlike, one may assume that he or she has some way of gaining knowledge about the world. That way may be limited to sensory perception or it may not. It also may or may not be spatially or temporally limited.

This already begins to solve some of the problems. One could use the phrase "internal focalization" to refer to cases where the narrator's knowledge of the storyworld is not confined to sensory perception but is focalized by one or more characters. One may use the phrase "external focalization" to refer to cases where the narrator's knowledge is confined to sensory perception, and is also focalized by one or more characters. Cases of the latter sort are fairly common in film. For example, a romantic comedy may involve dozens of characters. But it may show only scenes where one of the lovers is present. If one is given no internal thoughts of these characters (e.g., through voice-overs), then one is probably dealing with an external focalization.

But what about "zero focalization"? That does not seem to be a matter of limited knowledge. Indeed, that is presumably why Genette's distinction has intuitive appeal. On the other hand, it seems clear that, even if some narrators know everything, no narrators *say* everything. In this way, there is some limitation. Of course, if one defines every form of limitation as a form of focalization, then this means there is focalization. However, if one wishes to keep the sharpness of the concept, one should probably confine use of the term "focalization" to characters (or characterlike components) in a story. In that case, it seems clear that passages such as Michener's are not focalized. But how then does one describe their limitation?

In fact, this problem is already in effect solved. Again, if one spontaneously simulates narrators as humanlike, one tacitly understands their minds as having the same sorts of structures that human minds have. Human minds include not only knowledge—perception, memory, language, inferential capacities, and so on (thus the omniscient/limited distinction). They also include emotion. Without emotion, one would not speak or listen, direct one's attention to one thing rather than another, select some information as being of interest and ignore other information. Zero-focalization, then, is a situation in which there is a narrator with emotions—emotions that lead him or her to select certain facts of the storyworld and not others—but whose reports are not focalized to any character in the story.[33]

What about cases such as *The Great Gatsby,* where there is a homodiegetic narrator, Nick Carraway, who focuses a great deal of his attention on another character, Gatsby? In other words, Gatsby is in some sense a "focus of interest" for the narrator. But it is clear that the narrator is not in any sense confined to Gatsby. This arises as a possible issue due primarily to an accidental coincidence of terms—"focus" and "focalizer." There seems to be no focalizer in *Gatsby* other than the personified narrator, Nick. But what is the status of Gatsby, then? Though not a focalizer, he is not simply a character at the same level as the others. One might say that Gatsby is the protagonist of the novel, since much of the plot is organized around his goals and their possible fulfillment. But this does not suggest his relation to the narrator.

Borrowing (and altering) a term from linguistics, one may refer to Gatsby and similar characters as *topicalizers.* Topicalizers guide narrative development, but do not constrain narration. Put differently, they have intrinsic interest for a narrator. In other words, the narrator attends to one set of characters because their attitudes, perceptions, ideas, and so on, have instrumental significance for other characters. Thus the villain may be important because he or she has an impact on the hero. In contrast, the narrator attends to another set of characters because they are significant on their own. Thus the hero's ideas and attitudes are valued in their own right as productive of narrative trajectories. In consequence, the hero is commonly topicalized.

Focalizers are often topicalizers, but they need not be. They are clearly of interest to the narrator. But their interest is perspectival. As such, the focalizer's ideas, attitudes, and so forth, may or may not drive the story line.

In addition to differentiating focalization from topicalization, the preceding analysis suggests the possibility that focalization may come in two varieties. Given that narrators select according to interest and preference, it may be that focalization—internal or external—is not always a matter of limitation in knowledge. It may equally be a matter of limitation in interest. In other words, one may distinguish between epistemic and affective focalization. This may, in turn, have interpretive implications regarding a narrator's emotion-based encoding sensitivities. For example, suppose there is a love story with dual focalization on the lovers. One may consider asymmetries in the selection of information for the two focalizers, exploring these in both epistemic and affective contexts. This may have social and political consequences insofar as such asymmetries relate to gender or other social hierarchies.

Here it is valuable to return once again to Hemingway. The precise nature and degree of the narrator's epistemic limitations, if any, are not entirely clear. However, there are suggestions that he or she has internal access to characters. For example, he or she reports that the patients "all liked Luz" and that Luz and the soldier both "felt as though they were married." Moreover, the narrator knows that the major never married Luz, "in the spring, or any other time." (Though stated in the past tense, the narrator's claim presumably covers the all possible story time. To avoid this suggestion, Hemingway could have written something like "The major did not marry her in the spring. Eventually, they broke off the engagement.") Though ambiguity remains, these points suggest that the narrator may not have epistemic limits. Whatever limits he or she has, then, are presumably affective.

In part, this limitation is the result of the topicalization of the narrative to the lovers—just what one would expect in any romantic narrative. But it goes beyond topicalization. The internal access we have to others is very limited. For example, we know merely that the patients liked Luz—a very general attitude. In contrast, we know that as the soldier "walked back along the halls he thought of Luz in his bed." This is a much more specific internal access. It is also far less ambiguous (i.e., it is far more difficult to understand this as inference). It therefore suggests internal affective focalization.

Here, the issue arises as to whether there is internal affective focalization on both characters or on only one. The narrative seems ambiguous on this score. As already noted, it is possible to read the narrative as having only a single focalization on the soldier (recall Scholes's point about rewriting the work in first person). But it is not necessary to read the story that way. Indeed, as already noted, there are points at which we seem to have internal access to both Luz and the soldier. At the same time, however, those moments may be reinterpreted as inferences based on overt statements. For example, they presumably both *said* that they felt as though they were married. Overall, then, single focalization seems more likely. Nonetheless, a profile of ambiguity remains. This is almost certainly consequential—to both one's interpretations and one's emotional responses.

More exactly, even at points where there seem to be clear indications of two focalizers, there are discrepancies between the two. These discrepancies may be construed epistemically. But they are probably best understood as affectively motivated. For example, at times, an apparent focalization on Luz shifts to a focalization on the soldier. Consider the opening of the fourth paragraph, "Luz wrote him many letters." This seems to involve a clear epistemic limitation. It is something known, first of all and for some time exclusively, to Luz. But the sentence continues— "Luz wrote him many letters that he never got until after the armistice. Fifteen came in a bunch to the front and he sorted them by dates and read them all straight through." Retrospectively, one can see the opening of the sentence as focalized by the soldier, as he infers the unobserved process of writing. Either way, the crucial matter here is not knowledge of facts. It is affective orientation. Indeed, the focalization here is doubly affective, for the narration is guided by the narrator's emotional interest in the specifically emotional perspective of the focalizer. When readers go on to learn about Luz's feelings, reported in the letters, they do so in a context where the (emotionally saturated) reading presence of the soldier has been rendered salient. This at least makes possible an affective focalization on the soldier, even if the soldier's own affective topicalization is on Luz.

The point is clearer when Hemingway repeats the technique later. He begins a sentence by treating Luz's affair with an Italian major, apparently focalizing her, but then continues the sentence with a Dear John letter ("and finally wrote to the States that theirs had only been a boy and girl affair"). Here, again, there is an epistemic shift. What seems at first to be focalization on Luz becomes—or is revealed to have been— focalization on the soldier; the reader is told, not what Luz knows alone, but what the soldier knows through her report and perhaps his inferences from her report. More importantly, this has emotional significance. As readers receive the rest of the letter implicitly filtered through the soldier's reading, it is difficult not to be aware of and affected by the soldier's anger and resentment. The light-hearted "she expected, absolutely unexpectedly, to be married" feels insensitive; the use of "boy" appears belittling, and the explanation that she "believed in him absolutely" seems patronizing. Presumably the epistemic content of the letter is equally available to Luz and the soldier.[34] The focalization, then, is more a matter of emotion than of knowledge.[35]

On the other hand, this is not to say that this affective focalization is absolute and determinative. First of all, one need not read the story as having a single focalization. Indeed, it is possible to read the story as concerning information shared by the lovers—Luz tells the soldier that the hospital administrators are "glad to let her" stay on night duty; the soldier tells Luz that he thinks of her in his bed as he walks back along the halls at night. In this respect, focalization on either lover would give information about both. Only at the end does the reader get information that is not shared—in keeping with their emotional alienation. First there is the report that Luz and the major do not get married, perhaps known only to Luz. Then there is the final sentence reporting the soldier's affair with the sales girl and his gonorrhea, presumably known only to the soldier. Of course, even this is not entirely clear, since the second sentence of the final paragraph is ambiguous. The narrator explains that "Luz never got an answer to the letter to Chicago about it." It is not clear what "it" is. "It" may refer to the initial engagement. In that case, there is only one letter and only Luz knows that the marriage does not occur. However, "it" may also refer to the fact that the marriage did not take place. In that case, there were two letters, and the soldier did know about the ending of the engagement, thereby allowing single focalization on the soldier.

In any case, the work's profile of ambiguity extends to narration. That ambiguity is not only a matter of aspects of the storyworld. It bears on the nature of the work's focalization.

Indeed, even an affective focalization of the story on the soldier embeds an affective topicalization of Luz. Specifically, the soldier's own affective focus is on the feelings and plans of Luz—her story, in effect. This leaves both the focalization and the topicalization available for interpretation and reader response—one as a "surface affective focalization"; the other as an "embedded affective topicalization." For example, many readers undoubtedly suspect that the soldier's affair with the salesgirl is not an expression of lust, but something more like revenge, an attack aimed at Luz, even if it is never communicated to her. Perhaps more significantly, there is sympathy in the narrator's treatment of Luz's abandonment by the major and a lingering sense of attachment that highlights her loneliness after the soldier leaves. That, in turn, may complicate the understanding of the gender ideology of the work (thus the Critical Discourse Analysis of the work). This topic will come up again in relation to real readers and critics.

The Implied Reader, Sahṛdayas, and Gaps

As already indicated, the implied reader is parallel to the implied author. Indeed, one could see the implied reader, first of all, as a version of the implied author. (The afterword will show that the implied author–implied reader relation is more complex than this indicates, but the generalization is a useful starting point.) The implied reader is, in this sense, a receptive attitude that may be adopted by real readers in keeping with the receptive intention of the author. Put differently, when one studies literature and learns how to read more competently (to use Culler's term [see *Structuralist* 113–30 and "Competence"]), one of the things one learns is how to approximate the experience of an implied reader/implied author. Fundamentally, this involves such things as encoding certain features of a text, drawing particular sorts of inference, paying attention to certain aspects of a work, and asking particular kinds of questions.

To examine this process more fully, one needs to consider some of the cognitive operations involved in reading and understanding/response. Like authors, readers tacitly encode and process some features of texts but not others. In part, this encoding is enabled by attentional orientation. Cognitive structures, such as scripts and prototypes, partially guide attentional orientation as well as the processing of encoded information (a point stressed by Herman; see chapter 3 of *Story*).

Imagine, for example, that Jones is watching a crime drama. One character is eating at an Indian restaurant, consuming delectable-seeming dum aloo and lamb saag. Having begun his slimming program that morning, Jones is famished after three meals of celery and radishes. He stares longingly at the steaming cubes of meat smothered in delicate, creamy spinach, the crumbling, crimson bits of potato, the crisp papadum (which, when it breaks, makes a sound like kisses). Someone enters and murders the character at his dinner (at least he died happy). But

Jones never lifts his eyes from the plate and thus does not know the identity of the murderer. As a result, he never understands the tension or the tragedy of the rest of the story, in which an innocent man is framed for the murder. In this case, he has failed to orient his attention properly, which is to say, he has deviated from the norm of the implied reader (or implied viewer) with respect to attention.

A less crude example might be the following. In watching detective stories, one general principle readers acquire is to pay attention to—thus encode and store—any distinguishing features of any characters. One character may have a tendency to use a certain phrase (e.g., "you know"). Another may sometimes make a particular nervous gesture (e.g., rubbing his nose). A third may drag his foot ever so slightly when he walks. It would be easy to ignore these features, particularly if they are not foregrounded. (If the filmmaker cuts to a close-up of a character's nose when he rubs it in a nervous gesture, then one does not have to be paying particular attention to encode it.) But, having seen a number of detective stories, one learns that these are just the sorts of clue that may be important later in the story. One learns, furthermore, that the clues are likely to be covered up. This leads to more complex forms of attention—roughly, attention to absence (which is extremely difficult to maintain). If the criminal drags his foot slightly, then one should become more suspicious of any suspect who only sits or stands—but never walks—when the detective is present (and the viewer sees him or her).

The implied reader is, first of all, the norm (established by the implied author) that involves this sort of encoding and processing. But that is, so to speak, the mechanical part of the implied reader. The implied reader, like the implied author, also imagines and feels. As, for example, Roman Ingarden stressed, readers "concretize" what they read. Readers fill things in perceptually, and emotionally. Readers do not simply rely on the basic statements of a text. They expand and particularize. They imagine how a character feels at a particular moment, they tacitly envision what he or she looks like, and so on. Like the encoding of a text, this is only in part a matter of self-conscious reflection. For example, one may not realize that one has imagined a character's appearance until one sees a movie version and says, "That's not at all the way I pictured Gallstone." Here as elsewhere this imagination is probably the result of a confluence of memories, a network of past perceptions that results in one's tacitly assuming certain features. The same point holds for the simulation of character emotions.

Moreover, readers not only imagine appearances and simulate emotions, they experience emotions themselves. This is obviously true of real readers. But it is also true for implied readers. Stowe creates her portrait of Tom in *Uncle Tom's Cabin* in order to produce compassion. That compassionate response is part of the implied reader. Of course a real reader may have any number of responses. He or she may find the portrait maudlin and be repulsed; he or she may delight in the suffering of someone else; he or she may be bored and indifferent. But the norm established by the text is one of compassion. Again, that norm does not mean that the real reader must actually feel what the implied reader feels. It means that the real reader should understand that there is a particular normative emotion. Moreover, it means that there is some failure when the real reader does not experience the same emotion as the implied reader. The failure may be in the reader or in the text.

Leaving aside the case where the fault is in the text, it is worth considering what is going on with the implied reader with respect to emotional response. Clearly, actual emotional response is not simply a matter of inference or encoding. Again, a reader may perfectly understand that Tom is supposed to inspire compassion, and yet not feel compassion. Compassion in these cases is the result of two primary factors. First, there is the imaginative effort to simulate the experiences of the character. I might know that Stowe wishes me to empathize with Tom, but I may simply fail to simulate Tom's condition. Second, there is the complex of emotional memories that are cyclically activated by and, in turn, guide the further development of such empathy—such as memories of physical pain or discrimination.

This leads to a particularly interesting and complex feature of the implied reader. The implied reader has such memories. When the real author judges that the work has the right receptive impact—that is, when he or she is satisfied with the work as an implied author—he or she tacitly assumes that the reader will experience a range of emotional memories and that these will enable his or her emotional response to the work. Without those memories, the real reader will not be able to take up the emotional role of the implied reader. For example, when portraying someone suffering, an author tacitly assumes that readers will have their own memories of suffering that will contribute to their emotional response.

Of course, the particular memories of real readers are necessarily different. In keeping with this, one may distinguish a relatively fixed part of the implied reader. This part involves, among other things, encoding, attentional orientation, and cognitive structures (such as scripts) that guide processing. Of course, this is not entirely fixed. But there seems to be relative uniformity here. In contrast, there is a more significantly variable part as well—memories and what follows from memories, including concretization. This variable part of the implied reader suggests, for example, why certain works are more likely to inspire an intense response at one age, but not at another. Some works rely on emotional memories that are most intense when one is young. Others rely on emotional memories that develop significantly only in later life.

On the other hand, to say that particular emotional memories and concretizations are variable is not to say that there are no commonalities. Indeed, the very possibility of the implied authorial response presupposes such commonality. In order to understand this, it is necessary to consider emotional response to fiction more fully.

First of all, to some extent, genuinely personal memories are not wholly idiosyncratic. For example, virtually everyone has experienced some sort of attachment loss and virtually everyone has experienced fear, anger, and sadness in connection with that loss. The precise proportion of those emotions may be different, and that may affect individual responses to a story treating attachment loss. However, it is not the case that one's personal emotional memories all treat wholly individual types of experience.

Moreover, in treating emotional response in relation to emotional memories, I have been tacitly relying on the work of the great tenth-century Sanskrit theorist Abhinavagupta, along with more recent cognitive developments of his ideas.[36] Abhinavagupta stressed that these memories are drawn not only from personal life but from literature—and, one might add, other aspects of culture—as well. In this sense, the memories presupposed by the implied author (for the implied reader) may also concern more directly common experiences. Crucially, they include a partially shared body of literature. This is part of the reason why lack of familiarity with a literary tradition may inhibit one's ability to respond emotionally to works in that tradition.

In keeping with Sanskrit poetic theory generally, Abhinavagupta took up the term "sahṛdaya"—explained as one who enters "into identity with the heart of the poet" (Gnoli xlivn; more technically, one might say "the implied poet"). He used this term to refer to the reader who has the appropriate cognitive orientation and emotional experience, both literary and personal, and who makes the right effort in responding to the literary work. One could in principle take the implied reader to be a sahṛdaya. However, it is perhaps more useful to interpret the implied reader more minimally. Thus one might say that the implied reader correctly understands the storyworld, thematic concerns, and normative emotions of the work. The sahṛdaya, in contrast, feels the appropriate emotions in response to the work.

There are two things to say about the idea of appropriate emotions. First, these are related to the receptive response of the implied author. However, they are not necessarily determined by that receptive response. Just as one can reasonably complain that an author misunderstood his or her own characters, one can reasonably complain that an author has responded inappropriately to his or her storyworld. Thus the sahṛdaya is a sort of "ideal reader" in the sense that he or she is emotionally sensitive to the concerns of the implied author. (This usage obviously takes up a term used by earlier narratologists, such as Prince [see "Introduction"], while giving it a somewhat different meaning.) But his or her responses need not necessarily coincide with those of the implied author. Second, the necessary variability in individual emotional experience means that a range of responses may manifest emotional sensitivity. In other words, there is a, so to speak, *profile of ambivalence* in the sahṛdaya, with different readers fulfilling the function of the sahṛdaya somewhat differently. At the same time, the notion of a sahṛdaya suggests that there are norms. For example, regarding an antislavery novel, one may say that anger over the treatment of slaves, compassion for the slaves, disgust over collaboration with slave-owners and other responses are all part of the normative profile of ambivalence and different real readers may fulfill the role of sahṛdaya in feeling one or the other more strongly. However, most readers would probably be inclined to say that a response of complete indifference or of Schadenfreude at the slaves' suffering would fall outside the norms defined by the sahṛdaya.

Up to this point, the analysis has focused primarily on spontaneous processes that may or may not reach conscious awareness. But readers also engage in self-conscious, effortful processes. This is important because readers' processing of works is not straightforward, unproblematic, and uniform. It is often marked by bafflement, questions, reconsiderations. Moreover, that is not merely incidental. Such responses are a central part of one's understanding of literature; the communicative discourse of literature does not occur without it.[37]

Drawing on Wolfgang Iser's terminology, one may say that reading or viewing processes encounter *gaps,* points at which one's spontaneous processing falters. Typically, this is due to a contradiction in or lack related to information or emotion. The real reader must then consider this contradiction or lack in relation to the implied reader/implied author. Specifically, he or she must determine whether the contradiction or lack is his or her own (i.e., whether it lies in the real reader), whether it is a matter of the implied reader (the case Iser had in mind), or whether it is a matter of the real author (thus some sort of error or flaw). It is worth considering each of these.

An informational contradiction or lack in the reader is probably the simplest case. For example, many readers of Hemingway's story simply do not know what "arditi" refers to. Thus they come upon a reference to "arditi" and experience a contradiction between the implied reader assumed by the implied author (an implied reader who understands the reference) and their own knowledge. This gives rise to working-memory-based reflection. In this case, the problem is readily resolved by simply looking up the reference.

An emotional contradiction or lack is more complex. There is an emotional lack when one's experience simply does not give one the emotional responsiveness to react appropriately to a particular feature of a narrative. For example, I recently read Jhumpa Lahiri's *The Namesake*. Lahiri treats the experience of a woman in labor. The manner in which the section is developed indicates to me that it is supposed to be highly emotional. However, I am largely emotionally indifferent to the passage. This suggests some sort of fault. Either Lahiri has failed to communicate the emotion of the scene adequately, or I am lacking in sensitivity to the events, due in part to an absence of emotional memories. Given the response of others to the novel, I am forced to conclude that the emotional lack is in me and the force of the section is different for women and men who have been more intimately involved with giving birth.[38]

In other cases, informational or emotional contradictions may be attributed to the real author. There are many ways in which this may be the case. It is valuable to distinguish two. The first is a flaw in knowledge or craft on the part of the author. This bears on the aesthetic value of the work. The second is a broader, ideological contradiction, thus the sort of gap stressed by Marxist writers such as Althusser and Balibar (*symptomatic invisibility*; see, for example, 25–27) or Macherey (*incompleteness*; see, for example, 130–35). This sort of gap bears on the political or ethical value of the work.

Instances of the first sort include cases where one would say that an author misunderstood his own character. An example may be found in

Born of the Sun by Joseph Diescho (with Celeste Wallin). This novel concerns a Kavango man, Muronga, who travels from his village in Namibia to work in the South African mines. Diescho (with Wallin) makes a great deal of Muronga's belief that airplanes are birds. This leads him to fear that he will be eaten by them and to believe that he is inside a bird when he boards a plane. Some readers may not question this. However, the sequence seems obtrusively implausible. First, Muronga is fully familiar with cars, carts, trucks, and trains. Thus he has some concept of man-made vehicles; he does not believe, for example, that trucks are some sort of elephant. Second, Muronga maintains his belief that it is a bird even after he boards and travels in a plane. These contradictions lead me as a reader to conclude that Diescho (with Wallin) has failed in the imagination of Muronga's capacities for inference and understanding. As such, there is a flaw in the imagination of the character, which is to say, an aesthetic flaw in the novel.

In reflecting on the characterization in this way, I am confining myself to the text. However, one might also expand consideration beyond the text to, for example, the suggested inferential and imaginative capacities of illiterate African villagers. In this context, one might infer that, despite general political commitments and sympathies, Diescho (with Wallin) has been guided by an ideologically consequential misunderstanding of such villagers. Thus the gap is not only aesthetic, but also ideological.

For most students of literature, the most interesting and significant gaps in a literary work are not to be found in the inadequacies of the reader or the author. They are, rather, internal to the text itself. They are part of the experience of the implied reader. As such, they are moments where the text provokes hermeneutic reflection. This is broadly the sort of gap that Iser had in mind. As he explains, gaps give rise to a "frustration of expectations" that "blocks the flow of sentences" such that "we are led off in unexpected directions" and "bring into play our own faculty for establishing connections" (279–80). The reflection provoked by a gap may concern character motivation, the causes of a particular event, the nature of social relations within the fictional society, or a wide range of other topics. In this way, they affect one's precise construal of the story from the discourse, as well as one's emotional response to that story. No less important, such moments of reflective consideration often bear on the thematic concerns of a literary work, thus the ethical implications of the work for one's daily life or its political implications for one's social relations.

There are numerous gaps in the Hemingway story. One of the most obvious is the entire development of the marriage of Luz and the major. On first reading, I suspect most readers imagine that Luz's engagement with the major was fixed. However, the phrasing is equivocal. The narrator says that the major courted Luz and Luz writes in the letter that "she expected . . . to be married in the spring." Readers are actually given contradictory clues here. The word "expected" suggests that there has not been a formal engagement. However, the reference to a particular time for the wedding suggests that there has been such an engagement, since the time of the wedding would hardly be determined before the couple decided to get married at all. One can resolve this by interpreting the sentence to mean that they were definitely getting married, but that the uncertainty (indicated by the word, "expected") only concerned the precise timing. On the other hand, this is qualified by the fact that the marriage never took place. There is, of course, no logical contradiction between a fixed engagement and no subsequent marriage. However, the latter does bear on one's reflective interpretation and one may conclude that there never was a formal engagement. Perhaps Luz falsely inferred that they would marry, or perhaps they spoke informally about it, but never went through the formal process—for example, issuing the marriage banns mentioned earlier in the story.

The gap is not inconsequential. Thematically, it points toward a sort of contradiction in engagement and marriage themselves. On the one hand, marriage suggests equality of the partners—such equality that they can even be spoken of as, in some sense, "one." But the real human relations of the couple almost always involve some degree of inequality or dominance. That inequality renders the union unstable. Indeed, in this story, the dominated partner apparently overestimates the stability of the relationship in both cases. In keeping with this, the dominant partner ends that relationship—Luz breaks things off with the soldier, and the major ends his relationship with Luz. Moreover, the inequality is itself unstable. When Luz is thrown over by the major, it may be that she writes to the soldier about it. In another gap, the reader is not told what she wrote (if she did write). But he or she might reflectively infer that Luz expressed penitence over her action, perhaps even hinting at a reconciliation. If so, she is no longer the dominant one in the relationship. As newly dominant, the soldier now forecloses the possibility of reestablishing his relationship with Luz, first by not responding to her letter and second by choosing a new partner.

It is important to note that gaps may be emotional rather than informational. Oliver Hirschbiegel's film *Der Untergang* provides numerous examples. The film concerns Hitler's last days and often portrays Hitler and his associates as much more normal and human than one would expect. Contradictions arise between the film's cultivation of empathy with some of the characters and most viewers' prior emotional attitude toward the historical figures they represent. Goebbels is perhaps the most striking instance. Goebbels had a central role in some of the most unspeakable acts of brutality in human history. Yet the film portrays him as a man with tender familial attachments and, most importantly, with a love for and devotion to Hitler that outweigh any self-interest. In contrast with some other prominent Nazi leaders, he remains committed to Hitler even when it is clear that defeat is imminent. The film portrays that loyalty as admirable, even though it is loyalty to perhaps the worst mass-murderer in history.

For many viewers, this portrayal is likely to generate a contradiction with their prior emotional response to Goebbels as a historical figure. As such, it produces a gap, something incompatible and unreconciled, that requires reflective consideration. In this case, the norm for this reflection is not entirely clear. One could view the film as partially rehabilitating some Nazi figures. Elsewhere in the film, there is a benevolent physician, also based on a historical figure, who could be cited as evidence for this view. My inclination, however, is to take the implied author/implied reader as simply assuming that nothing about Nazism should or could be rehabilitated. The thematic project is, rather, twofold. First, it is to suggest that even the worst atrocities committed by people are still committed by people. The Nazis were human, however much one would like to deny it. They were not some sort of mutants with no relation to people today. Thus we cannot so easily segregate their crimes from actions we ourselves undertake. Second, the film points to some of the reasons for these atrocities. It may or may not be accurate in the case of Goebbels, and that is not insignificant. But the point, I take it, is not to exculpate him. It is, rather, to indicate that one cause of a complete obliviousness to the cruelty of one's actions—actions that, in the case of Goebbels, extend even to murdering all his children—can result from one's complete emotional subordination to another person, a subordination in which all one's motivations and understandings come to rest on the motivations and understandings of that other person.

The Real Reader and the Critic

The consideration of gaps and reflection clearly leads to both the real reader and the critic. The real reader, after all, is the one who engages in reflection, even if it is reflection that in part seeks to ascertain the norm of the implied reader—though it may also be reflection that evaluates the author or the real reader himself or herself. The critic, in turn, is the one who systematizes and elaborates the interpretive inferences, as well as the aesthetical and ethical evaluations, produced by reflection. Indeed, these are probably the central functions of the real reader and the critic, insofar as they are of general interest.

Nonetheless, there still are a few things that it is worth adding about both the real reader and the critic. First, it is important to stress once again that the norm provided by the implied reader is a norm of comprehension, not of actual response. Most critics would probably be inclined to say that a reader does not understand a work if he or she mistakes the implied reader—for example, if he or she sees *Der Untergang* as representing loyalty in a bad light, thus preferring the Nazi leaders who abandoned Hitler. However, readers are entirely free to diverge from the implied reader emotionally—or even inferentially, insofar as this bears on character autonomy and related matters. In other words, there is no need for viewers of *Der Untergang* to sympathize with Goebbels or even to understand his behavior as driven by loyalty (rather than, say, an inability to think of any way to save himself). The same points hold for the sahṛdaya. Readers may recognize and reject the emotional sensitivities assumed by the implied author. (As this phrasing suggests, one might think of such a rejection as denying the implied author's assumptions about the ideally sensitive reader, rather than rejecting such an ideal itself. For example, one might say that a truly sensitive viewer would not sympathize with a mass murderer such as Goebbels, no matter what the film's implied author may assume.)

Indeed, in recent decades, feminist and other politically engaged theorists have often advocated that a reader should be "resistant." In terms of the present analysis, one could say that such a reader would not adopt the position of the implied reader, but would oppose it in certain key respects. Like response generally, such resistance can either be spontaneous or self-conscious. For example, sometimes theorists and critics suggest that women, directly as a result of being women, are resistant readers for patriarchal texts. This indicates that women will spontaneously reject the adoption of the implied reader's ideas or attitudes insofar as these are guided by patriarchal ideology. In contrast, some critics would accept the basic Marxist view that class (or sex) origin does not determine class (or sex) stance. In other words, one's membership in a certain group does not determine one's attitude toward social issues concerning that group. Rather, a stance must be cultivated. In this respect, one might say that feminist resistance is a reflective opposition to the implied reader.

The culmination of reflective analysis is found in the systematic interpretive and evaluative practices of critics, in particular theoretically oriented critics. Critics set out to do two things. First, they examine and articulate features of a work to which readers respond un-self-consciously, features that readers encode and process, but do not formulate explicitly.[39] In this way, critics are parallel to linguists, who describe and explain the features of speech spontaneously produced and unself-consciously understood by speakers and hearers of a language. But critics go beyond this also. They seek to isolate features of the work in order to change spontaneous readings, in order to produce either further encoding on the part of readers or different processing. In connection with this, critics often seek to make gaps salient in order to produce further reflection on the part of readers. These critical undertakings may contribute to the development of readers' experiences of a work (e.g., their response to its emotional force), their interpretive comprehension of the story or its thematic concerns, their evaluative judgment of its aesthetic or political/ethical value, even their acceptance of or resistance to the norms of the implied reader.

In summary, it is possible to give a more complete version of the diagram presented earlier for the communicative part of discourse:

Real Author [Implied Author, guided by partially "autonomous" imagined agents [Nonpersonified Narrator {Personified Narrator {Focalizer {Topicalizer}} Personified Narratee} Nonpersonified Narratee] Implied Reader/Sahṛdaya] Real Reader/Critic

Chapter 2

Cross-Textual Implied Painters and Cinematic *Auteurs*

Rabindranath Tagore's Paintings and
Bimal Roy's *Madhumati*

*T*HE PRECEDING discussion of discourse is, of course, far from exhaustive. There is a great deal more to say about each of its components. This chapter and the next take up some complications and extensions of implied authorship. Specifically, the present chapter examines the consequences of bringing the idea of implied authorship into the analysis of works in two other media—painting and cinema. As with other aspects of discourse, one would expect the idea of an implied author to have consequences outside its original domain of narrative fiction. However, critics and theorists rarely extend the concept beyond novels and short stories. That is unfortunate, because a broader application should complicate and enhance the theoretical understanding of the implied author (and other aspects of discourse) while simultaneously deepening comprehension of and response to nonliterary works. In other words, such an extension should challenge and improve ideas in both areas.

This chapter first takes up the relevance of narratological discourse analysis for painting.[1,2] Focusing on some of Rabindranath Tagore's work, it considers such theoretical issues as what an implied painter may be and what relation the implied painter may have to a narrator in painting. In connection with this, it explores the consequences of "implied paintership" for interpreting Tagore's famously enigmatic works. These paintings have been widely admired, but infrequently analyzed, and, it seems, rarely understood. Many years ago, Asok Mitra pointed out that the center of Tagore's creative work shifted to painting in his later years. For this reason, it is crucial to understand Tagore's paintings if one wishes to gain an understanding of Tagore. Moreover, Mitra maintained that Tagore is "one of the greatest painters we shall ever have" (62). Thus, understanding his painting is intrinsically important as well.

One of the main conclusions of the first part of this chapter is that there is a level of interpretive relevance, thus cognitive unity or patterning, above the individual work—the level of an author's or painter's canon. Thus, just as one may refer to the implied author of an individual text, one may also refer to the "cross-textual implied author" of a body of works. This concept is obviously closely related to the idea of a film "auteur."[3] On the one hand, this link with auteurism confirms the significance of the cross-textual implied author. On the other hand, there are well-known problems with the idea of a film auteur. These arise primarily due to the highly collaborative nature of film production. The second half of the chapter examines some of these problems. It begins with a discussion of how the receptive account of authorial intent resolves some of the more obvious dilemmas about auteurism. Nonetheless, difficulties remain. These lead to a partial reformulation of the idea of a cross-textual implied author and, indeed, a partial reunderstanding of authorial receptive intent.

Painting as a Challenge to Narrative Discourse Analysis

The differences between painting and verbal narrative appear so obvious and extensive that one may ask whether they should even be compared. What can be learned by bringing together such disparate phenomena? In fact, there are considerable continuities between verbal narrative and representational painting. Moreover, they are continuities that fit well with narratological concerns. But there are, of course, crucial differences as well. The similarities indicate the possibilities for extending discourse analysis to paintings. The differences suggest the possibilities for altering and developing discourse analysis through this extension.

REPRESENTATIONAL PAINTING AS NARRATIVE DISCOURSE

For present purposes, the most fundamental connection between verbal and visual art is that representational works imply a represented world. Viewers do not simply see that represented world directly. They construe it by processing the information given on the canvas. In short, there is a discourse and an inferred world—perhaps not a story in the restricted, prototypical sense, but something at least parallel to a storyworld. Moreover, the purposes of this construal are the same as in verbal art—emotional response and thematic reflection.

A wide range of examples could be cited to illustrate these points. Obviously didactic works come to mind, such as Picasso's *Guernica* or Goya's *Third of May*. These are clearly painted to inspire aversive emotions in viewers—horror, anger, disgust, fear—and to connect those aversive emotions with a normative/thematic condemnation of the violence they represent. The entire range of devotional paintings and sculptures fits here as well—Christian depictions of Jesus's crucifixion, Hindu paintings of Rāma or Kṛṣṇa, and so on. These foster feelings of devotion (*bhakti*, in the Hindu lexicon) and thematically suggest the divinity, as well as the humanity, of their subjects.

Of course, the thematic point of a painting is not always entirely clear or open to formulation in precise, unequivocal terms. Perhaps it is never so, except in the crudest instances of propaganda. But that too only means that it is like literature.

Needless to say, not all works of visual art have thematic implications. But, if they do not have thematic implications, then their *raison d'être* derives from something else—emotional effect. Here, too, the emotional effect is of two sorts. The first relates to the storyworld. I see a lover touching his beloved—say, a couple kissing in a painting by Chagall—and, as a result of emotional memories or facial mirroring,[4] I feel some of their joy. The second is related to the discourse. In part, this is a matter of "narration," for example, the visual perspective—is the subject close or distant, facing toward or away from the viewer, seen from above or below? It is also in part a matter of how much information one is given, thus, roughly, the plot: Does the painting suggest events that preceded or will follow? To what extent are these unequivocal, and to what extent will any tension (or suspense) aroused by the work remain unresolved?[5]

Of course, there is still the issue of narrative as a sequence of causally linked events. After all, representational art is not necessarily storytelling art. Indeed, narrative painting proper—in the sense of painting that sets out to represent even two or three episodes from a story—is clearly not the most ordinary form of painting (though it is not as rare as one might initially believe).[6] On the other hand, the paintings mentioned above are clearly embedded in narratives. *Guernica* and *The Third of May* depict moments from larger historical stories of violence. The point is obviously crucial for their thematic import. If the pain in *Guernica* simply arose, then disappeared, with no cause or consequence, it would be confusing rather than damnable. If there were no story of fascist bombardment, there would be nothing to condemn. The point holds no less for the emotional impact of a work. The initial emotional force of a particular painting or sculpture may derive from a facial expression or bodily posture. But as one reflects on the work, one must be able to elaborate on it imaginatively, bringing it into connection with a wider range of precedents and consequences. The point holds no less obviously for the depictions of Jesus crucified, or paintings of Kṛṣṇa and Rādhā, which suggest their surrounding stories.

Needless to say, not all such surrounding stories are elaborated and particularized. In some cases, narrative reconstruction is more general and prototypical. But it is still there. For example, it may seem that one does not engage in narrative elaboration around a work such as Chagall's *The Birthday*. But in fact one does, even if one is not self-consciously aware of it. Viewers so readily integrate the episode into a prototypical romantic narrative and a prototypical set of birthday events that they may not even notice they have done so.

In this respect, paintings are very similar to lyric poems. Lyric poems often represent junctural moments in implicit narratives.[7] A junctural moment is a moment of particular emotional intensity associated with a change in a character's pursuit of goals (e.g., when lovers are separated). It seems that moments of particular emotional intensity are often isolated for representation in paintings.[8] Moreover, these frequently do seem to be narrative junctures—as in the cases of the crucifixion, or the dance of Kṛṣṇa and his beloved gopī devotees.[9]

In these respects, then, visual art is well-suited for comparison with verbal art in terms of the components and operation of discourse. There are some clear and significant continuities across the two, continuities that are illuminated by narratological concepts. But, of course, this does not mean that there are not striking differences as well.

Perhaps the most significant difference between works of visual art and works of verbal art, even lyric poems—the difference stressed by Lessing—is that paintings and sculptures are so severely limited in the time frame of explicit information. A lyric poem may focus on lovers' leave-taking. It may not even tell the reader anything outside the time of that leave-taking. But it can at least spread across the minutes of that separation. A painting or sculpture is usually confined to an almost extensionless point in time. Of course, it may give much more information about that single moment. But it remains confined to the moment nonetheless. The result is not simply a loss of information, but often a loss of specifically *disambiguating* information. Moments may be embedded in many narratives. The differences in those narratives entail different understandings of the moment itself, different thematic implications, different emotional responses. Consider a photograph of people crying outside a church. One's understanding and response are likely to change if one assumes it is after a funeral but is then told it is after a wedding.[10]

TWO PAINTINGS BY TAGORE

To work out these implications of ambiguity in visual art, it is helpful to consider concrete cases. In some ways, Tagore's paintings are particularly well suited to this task. In 1932, Joseph Southall wrote that "Tagore's drawings constrain us to pause and ask ourselves anew, what is the purpose of drawing, of painting, of art generally?"[11] One reason for Southall's question is that Tagore was generally very nondirective in orienting the viewer's interpretation of his works. He did not title his paintings, rarely dated them, and did not generally rely on standard stories, such as that of Kṛṣṇa and his gopīs. In considering Tagore's paintings, a critic is likely to become acutely aware of just how important titles and shared topical allusions are.[12] Knowing the story of Jesus, in the case of Michelangelo's *Pietà*, or having the title *Guernica* and the date of the painting, in the case of Picasso's work, are crucial for understanding the depiction, explicating the thematic concerns, and emotionally responding to these works. Looking at Tagore's art tends to highlight the ambiguity of individual paintings. At the same time, it may suggest ways to expand the understanding of individual works and further enrich the conception of discourse.

The first piece to consider is plate 9 from Robinson[13] (Fig. 2.1). It is an ink and watercolor work in black and shades of tan. The background, covering the top third of the paper, is a landscape, a horizon with foliage and hills. In the foreground, occupying the bottom two-thirds of the paper, there are nine figures. Though one or two may be female, these figures appear largely male. Immediately behind them is a black surface. The heads of the figures are just below the ground level of the landscape.

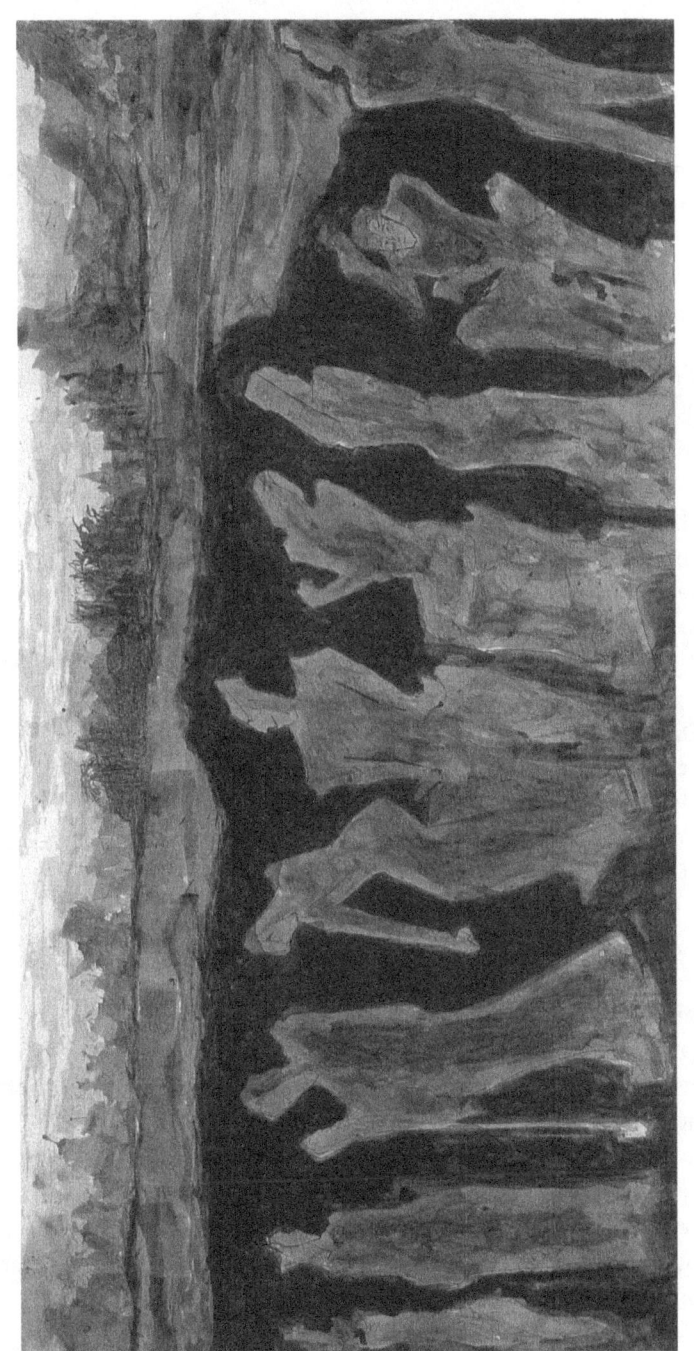

Figure 2.1. Tagore, ink and watercolor.

This suggests either a cliff or some sort of a tunnel. Most of the figures are faceless; many are turned away from the viewer. Figure three (from the left) seems to be walking with a staff. Figure four seems to be sitting down or getting up, perhaps with difficulty. Figure six is tensing away from the central figure (figure five). The central figure (five) is also the highest, giving him an apparent position of authority. He sits with his hands on his thighs, his legs spread, looking in the direction of figures three and four. The smile on his relatively clear face does not appear benevolent. Figure eight, the lowest, also has a clear face. He is concentrating on his work, which seems to involve hammering.

A careful description of the picture suggests a few things. There may be some sort of hierarchy here. There is a dominant figure who is not working and who appears to have a rather unempathic attitude toward the other figures. The face of figure eight is likely to draw a viewer's attention and interest. But his facial expression does not seem to have much emotional force. Indeed, figure six may be the most emotionally communicative. But it is difficult to say precisely what his apparently tensed muscles and withdrawal express—or even if they are genuinely tensed muscles and withdrawal. To complicate matters further, the seated figures seem to blend with blocks on which they are sitting as if they are not people at all but statues.

Different titles or stories would help to disambiguate this work. But there is no title (say, "Johannesburg," suggesting South African gold mines) or story. Thus the picture remains disturbingly ambiguous. But that does not imply that one can make nothing of it. The figures are not, say, lovers; the place is not a battlefield. The painting allows a number of interpretations and a number of emotional responses. But some are normatively excluded. Moreover, of those that are not excluded, some seem more likely than others.

As indicated in the introduction, works of art—both verbal and visual—are all to some extent ambiguous. That ambiguity may involve a limited range of closely related and highly plausible interpretations, a broad range of interpretations with low plausibility, or some other configuration. Again, each work has a *profile of ambiguity* rather than a strict, unequivocal meaning. Indeed, some of the effects of artworks rely on just that ambiguity. My own engagement with plate 9 (Fig. 2.1) is in part a matter of the way my mind runs through the different alternative construals of the figures, their relations and possible actions.

On the other hand, this does not mean that ambiguity is a good in itself. In fact, generally, when viewing paintings, viewers engage in strategies to reduce ambiguity. After all, when it becomes too great, ambiguity ceases to be intriguing and becomes simply disorienting. Most of these strategies involve embedding the work in a larger, relatively well-established set of meanings, usually linguistic or semilinguistic. Again, titles and well-known stories come to mind. The stories may be signaled by various sorts of allusion or by iconography (e.g., in Indian tradition, blue skin and a flute indicate Kṛṣṇa).

Another obvious alternative is symbolism (cf. Wolf 432). This operates most straightforwardly when the symbols are already socially established and fairly clear. For example, the use of a halo to represent a saint or Buddha is immediately identifiable. Such a symbol is, in fact, virtually linguistic since it has been assigned a conventional meaning. Interpretation of putative symbolism that does not rely on established convention is more problematic. The lack of disambiguating information in Tagore's paintings has led a number of critics to rely on symbolism. But, as Robinson rightly remarks, the results are questionable (56).

Two concepts that seem potentially more appropriate for interpreting paintings are metaphor and *dhvani*. Dhvani, or "suggestion," is a fundamental concept of Sanskrit literary theory. It refers to the associative network that surrounds a word, image, event, or any other topic. That associative network includes emotional memories and therefore it is a crucial component in producing *rasa* (usually translated as "sentiment"), the emotional response to a work of art (see Bharatamuni for the foundational discussion). The difficulty with both metaphor and dhvani (including rasadhvani, dhvani that produces rasa) is that these are as ambiguous as the rest of the work. It seems very likely that the cavelike area in Tagore's painting has metaphorical resonances. One can begin to suggest what some of those resonances might be (e.g., burial). But one needs a better sense of the painting as a whole before one can infer which possible metaphorical meanings are plausible and which are not—or even just what their target might be, what any metaphor might apply to (e.g., just what might be buried).

Here, it is useful to consider a second work, plate 156 (Fig. 2.2), an ink drawing of six women. The background is black, suggesting a night sky. The foreground is black and white, suggesting the ground at night. The women are all seated on the ground. Each is clothed in an apparently single piece of cloth. Figures one, two, four, and five have their heads uncovered. The colors of their clothes are also similar. Figures one and four have a sort of batik print. Figures two and five have a blackened red garment.

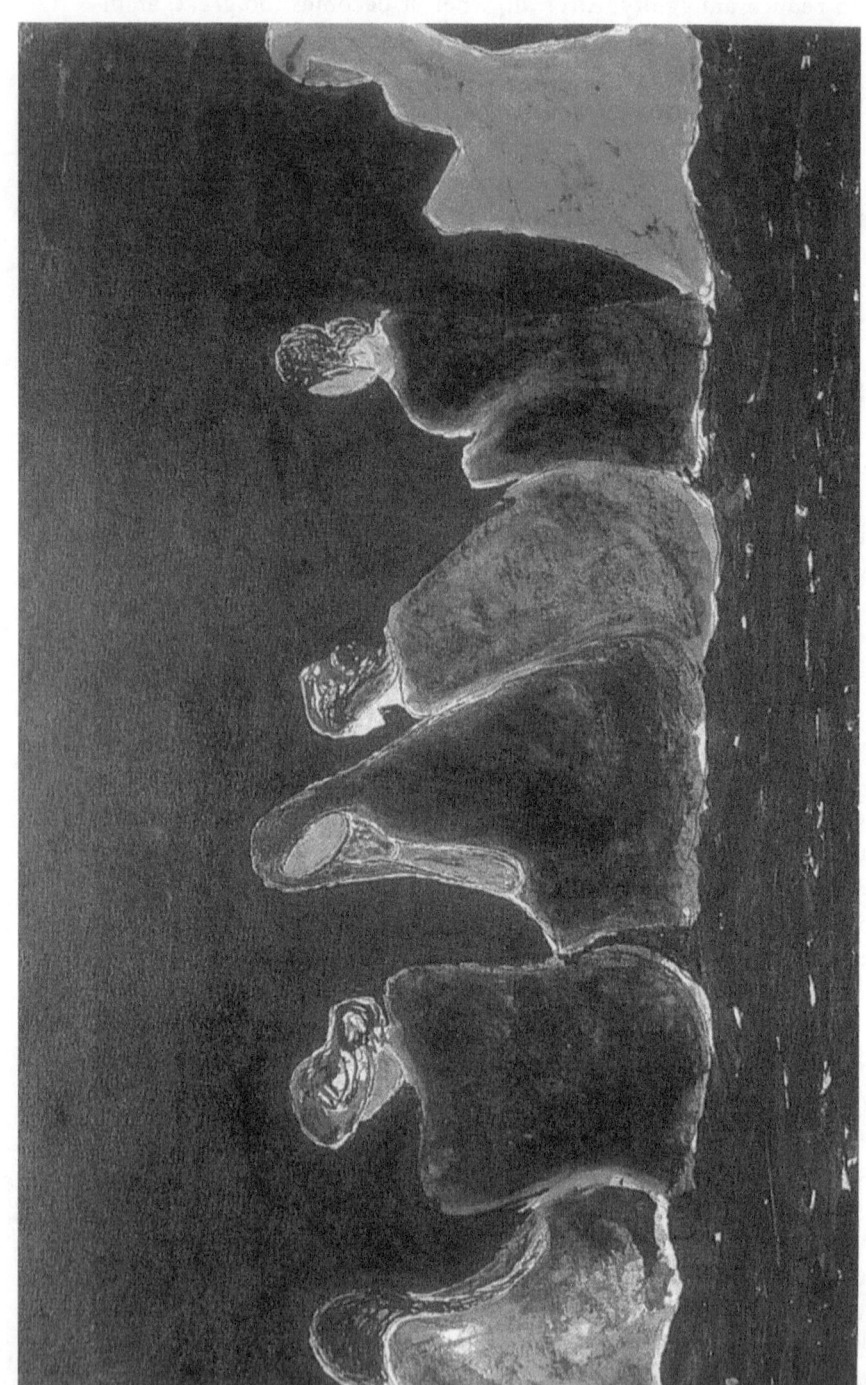

Figure 2.2. Tagore, ink.

Figures three and six stand out from the rest. They have their heads covered. Moreover, their clothing is distinctive. Figure three is in dark blue; figure six is in a bright rose and red. These figures are also placed highest on the paper. Figure six is further differentiated by the fact that her skin is noticeably darker than that of the other women. More significantly, figure three is the only one who is facing the viewer. The other five women are turned away.

Figure three draws particular attention. She rests her head in her hand in a gesture that seems sorrowful. But there is no face beneath her head covering, just a tan oval. So, here again, one encounters ambiguity or at least uncertainty. This woman is not precisely central (the number of figures being even). But she is approximately centered and is, very slightly, the highest on the paper, the tip of her head rising just above that of figure six. She is thus roughly parallel to the central figure in the first work (plate 9/Fig. 2.1). But the differences are striking. While the central man is genuinely central, the "central" woman is not. While the central man sits erect and angular, the woman gently curves downward. While the central man smiles as he looks at the others (who may be in pain), the woman presents the viewer with no face, but a sorrowful gesture.

Moreover, as already noted, the figure to the right of the central man seemed to be pulling away painfully. In contrast, the woman to the right of the focal female figure is actually leaning toward her, pressing her shoulder against the focal figure's back. The relation between the contiguous male figures seems to suggest fear. In contrast, the relation between the contiguous female figures seems to suggest warmth, attachment.

One may begin to get a sense here that plate 9 (Fig. 2.1) is, narratively and thematically, a painting about a world of hierarchy and mutual isolation, largely a world of men. It is also about labor, as suggested by the man with the hammer. In contrast, plate 156 (Fig. 2.2) suggests mutual connection, but also sorrow, in a group of women. This fits with a broader sense of Tagore as an author. His stories, poems, plays, and novels recur continually to the condition of women in India, to their constraints and trials. Thus one would expect to find these concerns once more in his paintings. As Satyajit Ray wrote, in painting, Tagore's "special field remained the study of women" (13).

One recurring motif in Tagore's treatment of women was their physical confinement within the home, their constraint to live in the inner rooms, away from light and life.[14] Once one remembers this, the blank darkness of the background in plate 156 (Fig. 2.2) takes on new resonances. The background for the men is the open horizon of the world. Even if they have sunk themselves in some sort of tunnel, the light is there, available to them. The women face only an impenetrable wall of black.

Of course, none of this entirely disambiguates either work. However, it begins to give the viewer a sense of what their thematic concerns are, as well as their implied narratives. The story of the men, it seems, concerns pride in social hierarchy—perhaps even Schadenfreude—and interpersonal fear in the public world; the story of the women, it seems, concerns attachment and sorrow in the home.

CROSS-TEXTUAL IMPLIED AUTHORS, MOTIFS, AND OTHER COMPLICATIONS OF VISUAL DISCOURSE

These feelings and themes will be considered again below, along with other aspects of the second work particularly. For now, it is valuable to isolate a few implications of the analysis thus far. The first and most crucial involves the scope of evidence cited in the preceding interpretations. Most obviously, the preceding analysis took up recurring issues in Tagore's writing and painting. This may seem to suggest a return to the real, biographical author and a rejection of the implied author, but it does not. It is very different to look at Tagore's other works for disambiguating information and to look at, say, his private family life.[15] In effect, when looking at Tagore's other works, one is appealing to the implied authorship of those works and assuming a certain degree of continuity across that implied authorship. In this way, it is an extension of the idea of implied authorship to an entire canon of works. This may be referred to as *cross-textual implied authorship.*[16]

The second implication of the preceding analysis is related. Indeed, it is the converse or "objective" side of the continuity in (subjective) implied authorship. The preceding examination of Tagore's two pieces drew on recurring features in order to group the two works together. For example, both involve a planar composition of figures forming a single line parallel to the viewing space. This is in part a feature of the storyworld, since the men and women are arranged in that formation in the represented world. But it is also a discursive feature because it relies on a particular point of view given in the discourse. In this way, it is a recurring complex of interrelated storyworld features and discourse features. One may refer to recurring complexes of features—from the storyworld, the discourse, or both—as *motifs*. Motifs may be of particular significance for interpretation, especially in cases where a work is highly ambiguous, as in Tagore's paintings.

The mention of point of view brings up a further feature of paintings that is important and requires development before it is possible to continue with Tagore's art. The precise point of view on the subject of a painting, like the precise choice of words in a text, is that of a narrator. Here it is important to draw a couple of distinctions. First, it is valuable to distinguish perceptual from verbal (or, perhaps, semantic) narrators. Films may have both, though they always have perceptual narrators. Literary works have only verbal narrators. What about paintings? It may seem that paintings have only perceptual (specifically, visual) narrators. But things are more complicated. First, there are ways in which a work of visual art may suggest narratorial commentary through visual means. In other words, there are often suggestions that a visual image has been organized verbally, that it is not purely perceptual, but gives the viewer a perception designed in relation to speech. The use of well-established symbols, such as halos, provides a case of this sort. Put simply, a viewer of, say, Jesus would not actually see a halo. The halo is, therefore, a narratorial comment, rather than a narratorial perception.

More commonly, a work of visual art may use some amount of text. This occurs most obviously in titles. One's default assumption about titles tends to be that they are the product of the implied author. But viewers can and do interpret titles ironically. That fact alone suggests that titles are best understood as spoken by a narrator, since they can be evaluated relative to an implied authorial standard.

TAGORE'S NARRATION: THREE CAPTIONS

It is now possible to return to Tagore. Though he did not use titles, Tagore did sometimes include sentences with his paintings (see Robinson 71). These are much more evidently and consistently equivocal than titles, much more complex in their relation to the paintings. Yet, as such, they serve to highlight some of the issues surrounding the relation of titles to narrative voice, including the issue of irony.

The first problem with Tagore's sentences is that it is not entirely clear what their status is. They undoubtedly represent some sort of voice commenting on the paintings. But the precise status of that voice is not self-evident. Tagore decided that it would be valuable to pair some paintings with sentences when they were published in *Chitralipi*. Thus he made a judgment that the sentences should bear on viewers' response to the works, at least in that context. However, just how they should bear on one's response is far from obvious. For example, though the sentences are paired with individual paintings, they sometimes seem to bear on a larger set of works and to provide a broad context for the viewer's emotional or thematic orientation, rather than a particular interpretive orientation. More generally, they rarely seem to be parts of the painting in the way that a title is part of the painting. Rather, they seem more like the sort of commentary a painter might give when asked about his or her work in an interview. Indeed, these sentences sometimes even point toward Tagore's inability to articulate what he experiences when faced with his own paintings.

A good instance of this concerns plate 12 (Fig. 2.3). This ink and watercolor work is a portrait of a woman's face, blotchy and darkened, wrapped in a black chador. Her expression involves a subdued sadness, like that in so many of Tagore's portraits of women. The quality of the emotion suggests an enduring condition, not an acute episode. She looks off to her right, without turning her head. It is as if she is avoiding a potentially confrontational meeting of eyes. But at the same time, she is not signaling submission, for she does not turn her face or head down.

Tagore's sentence for this painting is "The phantoms of faces come unbidden into my vacant hours" (Robinson 202). The simple fact that this refers to faces (plural) suggests that the comment is more general than this particular painting. More importantly, the reference to "unbidden" indicates that the appearance of the faces is not something in the artist's self-reflective control. Indeed, it is not something that Tagore himself can fully explain or evaluate. Here, there is the peculiar situation that the apparent narrator converges with the real author and both are distinct from the implied author. They are not distinct by irony, however. Rather, they are distinct by ignorance. Recall that the implied author is, so to speak, the real author's receptive intent, his or her experience of the work as a reader—or, in this case, his or her experience of the painting as a viewer. That implied painter judges that the painting is somehow "right," that it produces the desired effect. But this does not mean that the real author can articulate precisely why or how such an effect comes about or even precisely what that effect is. Indeed, typically the real author cannot do this. The point is particularly obvious in an author's or painter's commentary on his or her work. Such commentary commonly arises in a creator's post facto pronouncements about a

Figure 2.3. Tagore, ink and watercolor.

work. Those pronouncements are often taken as untrustworthy. Tagore's sentences here point toward that commentatorial unreliability. At a theoretical level, what is perhaps most striking here is that this real authorial unreliability with respect to implied authorship is directly parallel to the well-known unreliability of narrators.

In other cases, the sentences suggest a post facto attempt to interpret the principles that guided implied authorial judgments at the time of the painting. In principle, these might provide a broader context, particularly some elements of a story. There is an example of this in plate 151 (Fig. 2.4). This is a red and black ink drawing. In the middle, there is a couple in profile, facing left. The faces of the figures are outlined in white against the black background (a recurring technique in Tagore, as several critics have noted [see Robinson 61]). To some extent, this recalls photographic "edge lighting," where the contour of a figure is more brightly illuminated than the rest of the figure. Among other things, this technique allows the viewer to see the figures distinctly while at the same time placing them in near total darkness, which usually hints at either threat or intimacy. The man's features are sharply angular with straight lines and right angles. The woman's features are more curved. She wears a chador over her head. He wears a shawl over his shoulders. Neither face is strongly expressive, but the slight elevation of the pupil in the woman's eye may hint at wateriness, and her lips seem less tight than those of the man. Thus there may be a hint of sorrow in her face that is absent from that of the man. The background is primarily black. But the left third of the work has an irregular column of red. It is easy to see this as either dawn or sunset.

Tagore's sentence for this painting is "The day's gains and losses are lost to their sight when they gaze at an unrevealed promise gleaming out from the dark" (Robinson 208). Here, one is tempted to say that Tagore has just not done a very good job of interpreting his own painting. The sentence seems to suggest a certain amount of hope. But it is not clear that the two people are experiencing any hope. On the other hand, the sentence is so obscure that it is difficult to say if it really does suggest hope. The couple forgets not only temporary "losses," but also temporary "gains." There is something "gleaming out of the dark," but it is also "unrevealed." Viewers would probably be inclined to identify a "promise gleaming out from the dark" as dawn. But why would dawn be contrasted with the day's gains and losses? That contrast suggests that the glow is sunset—but then why is sunset a promise? These apparent inconsistencies seem to indicate that the author/narrator here is not reliable.

Figure 2.4. Tagore, ink.

There is the same lack of knowledge as in the previous painting, but this time the accompanying sentence in effect denies that lack of knowledge. The painting is hauntingly beautiful, but opaque. Tagore's narratorial comment does not render it less opaque.

A related example may be found in plate 79 (Fig. 2.5). The sentence reads, "The eyes seeking for the enigma of things explore the boundless nothing" (Robinson 205). This black and white etched print presents a seated woman beneath a black sky and beside or above the swirling currents of a river. She is turned away from the viewer, staring, it seems, into the black void. The figure forms a soft arc, which is a recurring motif in Tagore's depictions of women. The caption is as obscure as the work itself. Both suggest some sort of sorrow. But the statement provides few clues as to the nature of the sorrow. Indeed, one almost wonders if the author is making fun of the viewer here, saying, in effect, "You want profound meaning—here's some." In other words, the caption may be ironic. But it seems unlikely that it is simply suggesting the opposite, as irony sometimes does. Rather, the unreliability is primarily a matter of concealing information, "underreading," as James Phelan would put it (see "Rhetoric/Ethics"). The sentence indicates that the woman is searching for an answer to some question. But to say that the question concerns "the enigma of things" is only to render it more enigmatic. It may contribute to the sense of sadness. But that sadness remains vague, if nonetheless affecting.

A peculiar feature of the drawing is that the woman's breast is lighter than her clothing, as is her face and the exposed part of her neck. The slight hint of an areola at the end of the breast may suggest that it is uncovered. If so, this may give some indication of the precise nature of her suffering. To explore this further, however, one must turn again to the cross-textual implied author and the recurring motifs in Tagore's work. Indeed, these are precisely what one needs to consider in further exploring plate 156 (Fig. 2.2).

THE GRIEVING WOMAN

As already noted, according to Satyajit Ray, the condition of women was of preeminent importance in Tagore's painting. Ray was not the first to notice this. In his valuable study of Tagore as a painter, the eminent novelist Mulk Raj Anand wrote that "Always there were echoes of the silences of women before the patriarch" (60) and "The pathos" of

Figure 2.5. Tagore, etched print.

Tagore's characteristic "oval faced woman came back again and again" (74).[17] Ray and Anand were, of course, referring to the paintings. But both were also familiar with Tagore's literary works. In the terms introduced above, they were making reference to recurring motivic and thematic concerns of Tagore as a cross-textual implied author (or, more broadly, cross-textual implied creator).

As Ray and Anand indicate, the condition of women is one of the most persistent topics in Tagore's literary works. Yet, it is arguably overshadowed and to some extent encompassed by another concern—attachment, the bonding that most prominently characterizes the relations of parents and small children.[18] In Tagore's work, the tragedies of women are, more often than not, the tragedies of broken attachments—frequently the attachments of romantic love, but also attachments to parents or children.

Unsurprisingly, then, Tagore's narratives often treat attachments that are shattered. This destruction is frequently the result of social identities, dividing people by nation, race, sex, or caste; but the cause may also be more personal, as in the scapegoating of someone who is vulnerable. In keeping with this, perhaps the most prominent emotions in Tagore's work are those that involve attachments—romantic love (or śṛṅgāra, in rasa theory) and parent-child love (vātsalya)—along with empathy. Indeed, empathy is already associated with attachment, since attachment tends to focus one's attention on and intensify one's sensitivity to the emotions of the person one loves.[19]

In the context of Tagore's recurring concerns, it is useful to return to plate 79 (Fig. 2.5), the woman by the river. Even the mention of love makes one realize immediately that the most common significance of a representation of this sort involves romantic love. The "enigma" would then appear to concern the beloved; the "boundless nothing" would be his or her absence. But, on reflection, this does not seem right. Except for the swirls of the river, the piece does not seem to convey passion (e.g., in the woman's posture). The breast may seem to sway the interpretation. But the woman does not appear to be in a condition of specifically sexual undress.

Suppose, then, that one considers the etching to address some other form of attachment. One might in that case imagine that the bare breast refers to the nurturance of a child—a child who is absent, perhaps dead or unborn. Of course, here too there is not much in the way of evidence. Either interpretation is plausible.

This leads back to the cross-textual implied painter. There are recurring motifs in Tagore's paintings that point toward enduring representational, emotional, and thematic concerns. One of these motifs is the smooth arc of the seated woman, an arc rendered even more salient by its contrast with the angular bodies of men.

A striking case of this sort is plate 4 (Fig. 2.6). This ink drawing in orange and black depicts a woman curved into a rocking-chair shape (perhaps in a rocking chair). There is the soft arc from legs to shoulders. In this case the woman leans forward. Her face is black, the features outlined in ochre. One aspect of the piece is particularly anomalous. A swath of black begins at the woman's head, suggesting a lock of hair. But it ends in flattened breast with a clear nipple. The woman stares down at her lap and seems to be smiling. There is nothing to suggest eroticism. Perhaps one should envision a child below the arm of the chair.

Another work seems to point toward related concerns. This is plate 162 (Fig. 2.7), an ink on paper drawing. This work presents only the woman's upper body. For this reason, one cannot directly link it with the arcing seated figures. But the woman leans over, about to rest her head on her hand, balled into a fist. Her eyes are nearly closed; her face is blackened. Though she seems to be wearing her scarf and shawl, her breast is bare. The resonance is, again, more maternal than sexual. The fist may suggest anger. The face could communicate exhaustion or despair. One thing seems clear from the fisted arm—the woman is not holding a child.

The suggestions drawn from the preceding paintings appear to be confirmed by plate 145 (Fig. 2.8). Here there is another seated young woman. An arc curves around from her legs to her neck. Her head bends forward. She rests her cheek on the head of a child at her breast.

Narratively, then, these works point toward some relation of mother and child. This does not mean that they are unambiguous. They remain ambiguous. But, considered together, they suggest variations on a story, along with an associated set of emotions—prominently, sorrow for lost attachment or a shared feeling of warmth in attachment.

All this allows a reconsideration of plate 156 (Fig. 2.2). Having looked at these other works, one cannot help noticing that the central figure is seated and partially curved forward, tilting her head, leaning against her hand (recall plate 162/Fig. 2.7). Now something about the second figure from the left becomes noticeable. She has her left arm raised as if she is cradling something. Here, too, then, there is the dhvani of maternal attachment (figure two) and maternal loss or separation (figure three). Indeed, on inspection, it is clear that one could interpret figures one and five as preoccupied with something in their laps as well.

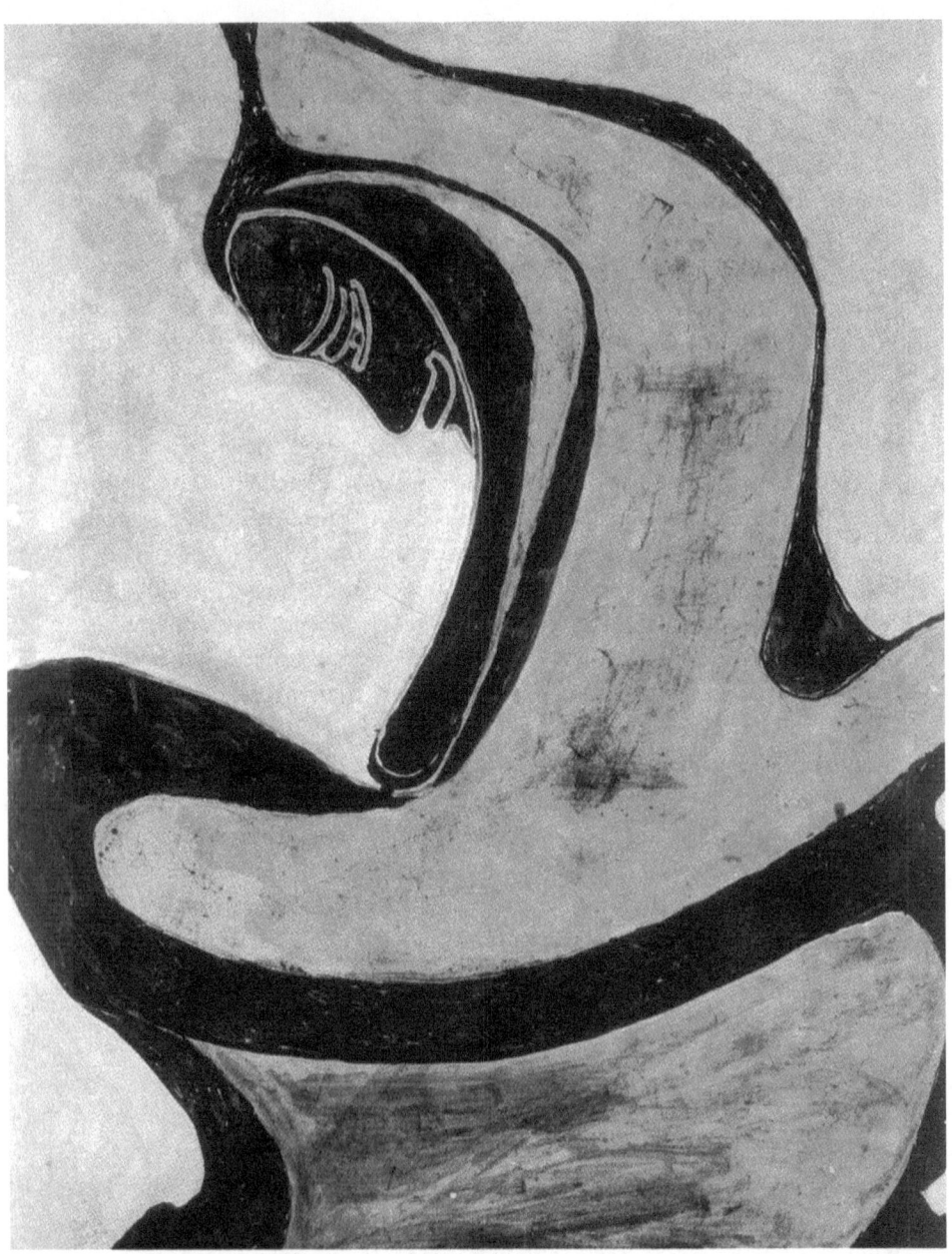
Figure 2.6. Tagore, ink.

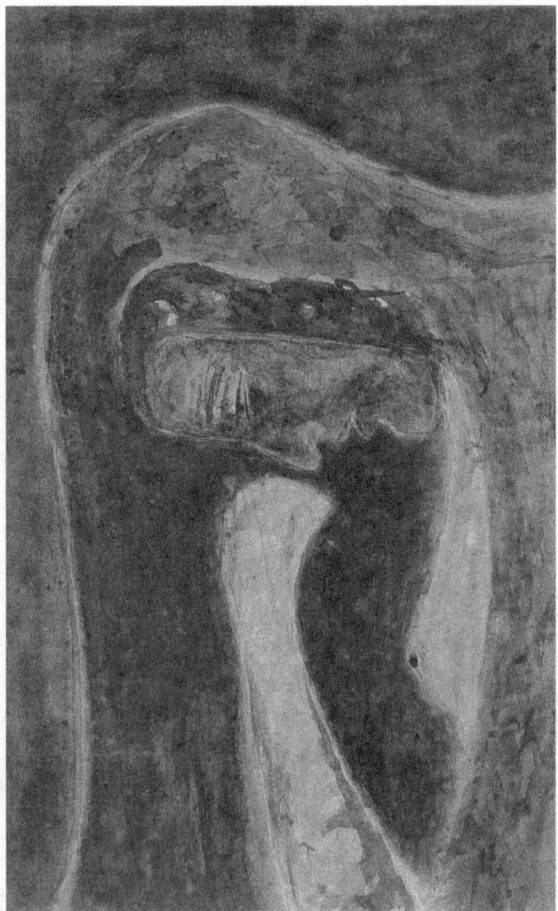

Figure 2.7. Tagore, ink.

The overall "narrative" dhvani, or suggestion, of the piece, then, is one of maternal loss. The central, focal figure appears to be suffering the absence of the child that preoccupies at least some of the other women in the painting.[20] This does not at all eliminate the ambiguity of the work. The viewer does not know the precise nature of the loss (e.g., has a child died, or has the woman been unable to conceive?). Moreover, the loss remains only one of the possible interpretations of the represented world. On the other hand, the integration of the work into the

Figure 2.8. Tagore, ink and watercolor.

receptive intent of the cross-textual implied author foregrounds this possible meaning, giving it a more prominent place in the work's profile of ambiguity. Moreover, that integration reacts back on one's encoding and explanation of details of the work, altering what one notices about the figures and how one understands them. It also bears on one's emotional response to the work, one's sense of the third figure's pensive sorrow and the intimacy of the third and fourth figures—an intimacy that is qualified by the fourth figure's apparently positive, perhaps even enthusiastic interest in something to her left, such as a child in the lap of the second figure.

Needless to say, these points bear on the thematic implications of the paintings as well. Unsurprisingly, ambiguities arise there too. For example, the work may hint at a criticism of the relation between motherhood and family status. At the same time, one might wonder if the paintings suggest that women find fulfillment only in giving birth and raising children. Certainly, the two works considered at the outset now seem to contrast male labor—perhaps the creative labor of sculpture—with the female labor of reproduction. (The two possibly female figures in plate 9/Fig. 2.1—numbers two and seven—are motionless and uninvolved observers, in contrast with the apparently male figures.) Anand maintains that, at least in some of Tagore's pictures, "The feminine principle" is "asserted in the Mother and Child" (61). However, in the context of Tagore's other works, it seems much more likely that he is suggesting the central importance of attachment in human life. The contrast with the men, in that case, is not primarily one of reproduction versus production. It is, rather, a contrast between relations of hierarchy and relations of attachment, or even violence and nurturance. Note, for example, that one male figure hammers between his legs, at precisely the place where the women cradle their children.

Moreover, as Anand noted, other works by Tagore are highly critical of patriarchy and its effects on individual women. Indeed, this is connected with another potentially troublesome feature of plate 156 (Fig. 2.2)—the facelessness of the central figure. Tagore used this motif elsewhere, at least at times to suggest the anonymous labors of women, concealed within the house, unacknowledged and unrewarded. This may be seen in plate 157 (Fig. 2.9). In this ink on paper drawing a seated man looks on as a faceless woman serves him.

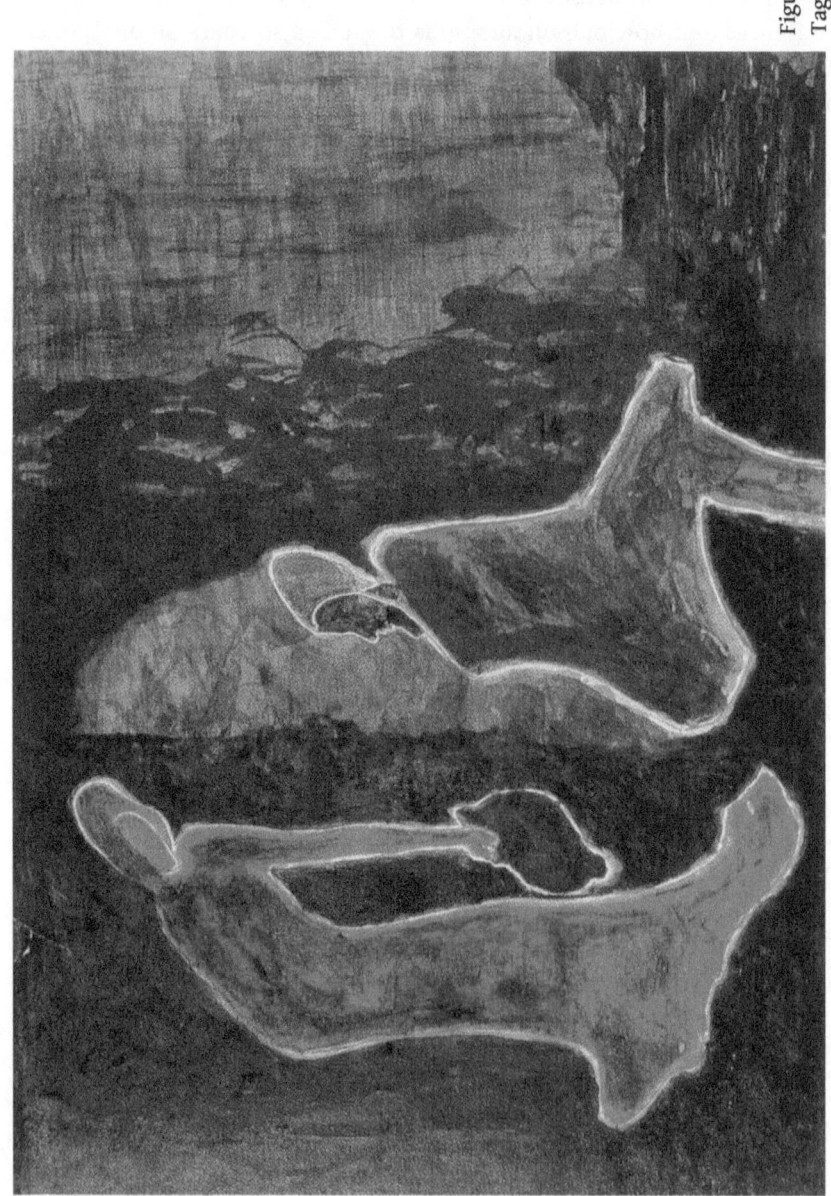

Figure 2.9. Tagore, ink.

Film as a Challenge to the Cross-Textual Implied Author

In contrast with mainstream narratological studies of the implied author, the idea of an individual creator's canonical reach has been quite important in film studies. As David Bordwell points out, "a body of work linked by an authorial signature encourages viewers to read each film as a chapter of an oeuvre." Auteur studies stress the "consistency of an authorial signature," including "recognizably recurring devices," such as "camera technique" and "narrational qualities" (*Narration* 211). In many ways, the recognition of such canonical reach means that the idea of a film auteur converges with the idea of a cross-textual implied author. However, the idea of an auteur is notoriously difficult to spell out in theoretical terms—perhaps even more difficult than the idea of an implied author. The remainder of this chapter concerns two things. On the one hand, it considers the ways in which the preceding analyses can clarify the understanding of a film auteur. At the same time, it considers how the idea of a film auteur may expand and modify the idea of a cross-textual implied author.

AUTEURISM AND RECEPTIVE INTENT

For many decades, auteurism has been central to the study of film. Film criticism, histories of film, film retrospectives, and film courses in universities all routinely recur to the director as a central organizing principle. Though critics can and do shape discussions of film in other ways, they regularly view the director as the crucial individual behind a film. This presupposition often pervades discussions, not only of particular films, but of periods, movements, stylistic developments, and, in some cases, technical innovations. Even writers who reject auteurism as a theoretical concept are often drawn unwittingly into auteurist ways of speaking and thinking.

Yet, there are notorious theoretical problems with auteurism. The problems may be organized under two broad questions. First, who is an auteur? More exactly, is there only one, and is it always and only the director? Second, what is an auteur? More exactly, just what makes someone an auteur, whether he or she is a director or someone else, and what properties does one find in films that manifest the operation of such an auteur?

Classical auteurism is fundamentally a doctrine with three component principles. First, there is a guiding intentionality for a film. Second, intentionality not only defines films singly but produces a patterned coherence across films; in other words, the unit of an auteur's intentionality is not the individual work, or not the individual work alone, but the oeuvre. Finally, the guiding intentionality of both individual films and sets of films is that of the director.

The problems with auteurism are obvious as soon as one spells out these premises. Most obviously, the decisions made about a film are not made by one person. They are made by many people, at different times, in different ways. The point turns up even within auteurism itself. Thus Virginia Wright Wexman explains the general consensus that "directors are . . . the crucial creative force" (9) behind films. However, she also notes that producers, writers, editors, cinematographers, production designers, and stars have been "put forward as significant authors" (8). In contrast, consider literary works. It is virtually impossible to imagine someone arguing that the true creative force behind a poem or a novel is the publisher, the typesetter, or the copy editor.

The difficulty here is straightforward. There are many aspects of film, and many people are involved in the creation of a film.[21] The different people make contributions in varying degrees. Of course, this is in some ways true of anything. To a certain extent, editors really do contribute to novels. They may suggest revisions of phrasing; they may urge that particular sections be cut or elaborated. However, the degree to which editors contribute to novels is, in most cases, very limited. In film, things are different. To get a comparable situation in a novel, one person would write the basic plot, someone else do the dialogues, someone else do the descriptions of scenes (perhaps one person describing the light, another describing the organization of the objects, a third revising everything for point of view); a further contributor might provide accounts of how the dialogue is delivered (e.g., inserting adverbs such as "sadly" or "with an accusatory tone"), and so on. If novels were created in this way, how could one possibly decide that any single person is the crucial creative force? As Harvey points out, it is very difficult "to assign value"—for example, normative value for interpretation—"to the various players active in the 'supply chain'" (81; for some examples, see 83).

There is a way in which this problem is straightforwardly solved by the preceding account of implied authorship in terms of receptive intent. One might say that it does not really matter who produces the various components of the film. The crucial thing is that there is a unifying reception. Suppose that the lighting director sets the lights one way, then another, then another. The director chooses the manner he or she prefers. The costume designer presents various sketches, of which the director chooses what he or she deems best, and so on. In each case, the director makes his or her decision, thus organizing the entire work under his or her receptive intent.

But this clearly will not suffice. For example, Notaro (citing work by other researchers) discusses how people create new artistic works simply by selecting from templates offered by software programs (88). When faced with such a work, one is likely to take the intent of the "selector" as a guiding norm for interpretation. But interpretation in those cases is likely to be very limited.

For example, suppose little Sally uses a program and produces an artwork with a cut-and-paste drawing of a little girl, a cut-and-paste heart, and a cut-and-paste woman. She then hands the printout to her mother and says, "Happy Mother's Day, Mommy!" Most people will interpret the artwork according to her receptive intent. Sally presumably receptively intended to express her love of her mother. The original, productive intent of the drawing of the girl may have involved representing a particular person unknown to Sally. The original, productive intent of the drawing of the heart may have been to guide the design of candy pieces. These productive intentions are irrelevant. They are normatively overruled by the receptive intent of the artist, Sally.

To this point, the account of receptive intent works well enough. But now a problem arises. Perhaps the little girl has blonde hair and Sally has black hair. Is that an interpretable detail? Does it suggest some self-image problem on Sally's part? Maybe the mother is wearing an apron, but Sally's mother rarely cooks and never wears an apron. Is this a subtle (thematic) suggestion that Sally would love her mother more if she spent more time in the kitchen? In both cases, the answer is "probably not." There are two issues. The first is whether Sally encoded (roughly, noticed) these features of the images. The second is whether she had alternative choices. In other words, viewers are more likely to say that these features are interpretable if Sally receptively encoded these features and if she chose them over other available images with different features. (Actually, things are more complicated, since she could have had choices of, say, blonde and black-haired girls, but preferred the clothes or posture or height of the blonde girl. But it is possible to leave aside these complications aside, since they are merely extensions of the same basic issue.)

Similar points hold for film, though without the same interpretive preference that one may have in the case of Sally. Imagine a very thematically oriented cinematographer and a very aesthetically oriented director. The director tells the cinematographer to set up the shots for a particular scene. Imagine further that the screenplay has a thematic concern with the way people are metaphorically blind to one another, continually misunderstanding each other. The cinematographer has the idea of echoing that theme by having a number of shots with interpositions[22] or partial occlusions, something set between the camera and the focal person, partially blocking or distorting the audience's vision of him or her. Thus the cinematographer may choose to shoot part of a scene through a window or with a curtain fluttering before one of the characters. The director may heartily approve of the shots. But, for the director, the important point is that they are visually interesting; he or she does not even notice that they have thematic resonances. Indeed, one could imagine an even more extreme case where the director is concerned only with whether the viewer can recognize the characters and understand the action. After that, he or she is happy to let the cinematographer do whatever he or she pleases. One can also envision the reverse. In this case, the cinematographer sets up different ways of shooting a scene. In one case, it is difficult to get the right angle, so he or she suggests shooting through a window. In another case, a curtain happens to keep fluttering before the actress as the scene is being rehearsed. In both cases, the thematic resonances strike the director and he or she chooses the partially occlusive shots, though the occlusions were never intended (for any reason) by the cinematographer. Finally, one can imagine a scenario in which the director explains his or her thematic and aesthetic concerns to the cinematographer, who comes up with the idea of partially occlusive shots.

These film examples are not entirely fanciful. Guru Dutt's films seem to use interpositions with unusual frequency. It is difficult to tell who exactly is responsible for this. The obvious choices are Dutt and his usual cinematographer, V. K. Murthy.[23] Thus the frequency of interposition may have been Dutt's self-conscious directorial plan, or it may have resulted from Murthy's unself-conscious aesthetic preference and Dutt's relative indifference, or something else.

In contrast, there are some prominent uses of interposition in Bimal Roy's film *Prem Patra*. In that case, the film involves a thematic concern with perception, treating literal and metaphorical blindness. It probably alludes to the Vedāntic idea of illusion, with its common image of illusion as a veil, thus a form of interposition or occlusion. A usage of this sort is part of Roy's more general tendency to design his cinematography in such a way as to echo his thematic and emotional concerns. This design necessarily takes different forms in different films. Thus it is not always a matter of interposition. For example, in *Sujata* it is more bound up with staging in depth.[24] Roy's responsibility is clearer here as this tendency appears with different cinematographers (Kamal Bose for *Sujata* and Dilip Gupta for *Prem Patra*).

The question, then, is how should one interpret these different cases? For example, if the cinematographer and the director have different understandings of a shot, what establishes the interpretive norm? If the cinematographer set up the shots for thematic reasons while the director selected them for aesthetic reasons, does that mean that only the aesthetic reasons are interpretively relevant?

In fact, this is not a real problem. It is only a problem if one assumes that one intention must have some sort of ontological status that makes it definitive. But that is not the case. A particular intention becomes definitive only when one names it as being definitive, only when one *stipulates* it.[25] Put more simply, there is no right answer to the question "What is the meaning of these shots?" or "What is the norm governing the interpretation of these shots?" There are only the questions "What is the profile of ambiguity for these shots in the receptive intention of the cinematographer?"; "What is the profile of ambiguity for these shots in the receptive intention of the director?"; and so on. (Note that the intentional subjects here are not confined to people involved in selecting the shots. One can equally ask, "What is the profile of ambiguity for these shots in most viewers seeing the film for the first time?" or "What is the profile of ambiguity for these shots for such-and-such a director or cinematographer who was influenced by this film?")

On the other hand, this still leaves a problem. It is important to recognize the multiplicity of norms available in any given work, the various profiles of ambiguity. But, in any case, critics want to be able to interpret the work. Part of the advantage of being able to embed a work in a canon is that it allows further insight into the work as a whole. By embedding Tagore's painting of six women in his canon, one gains a greater sense of the representational, emotive, and thematic concerns of the painting. This advantage seems to be lost if one cannot necessarily locate a film in the directorial canon and draw on recurring patterns of that canon for interpretation. In other words, it seems that, far from supporting the idea of a cross-textual implied author, film (despite auteurism) may partially undermine it.

THE PRODUCTION PROCESS AND VARIETIES OF INTENT

At this point, one might feel that it is best to discard auteurism. But that would throw the baby out with the bathwater. The preceding discussion not only suggests problems with auteurism. It also suggests the importance of clearly and explicitly formulating the interpretive norms for a work. In particular cases, that may crucially involve embedding the work in a canon. One key point is that the canon need not always be the same. This is true even with a single author. One may first embed Tagore's painting of six women in the canon of his paintings and subsequently embed it in the larger canon of his creative representations (including literature). The problem with cinema is that there are many intents—and thus canons—that could in principle be stipulated as establishing norms for the interpretation of a particular film (the canon of the director, that of the producer, that of the cinematographer, etc.).

In order to get a better sense of how to respond to these difficulties, it is necessary to return to the nature of film production. Such an examination shows that the production and selection process is more complex than indicated earlier. As already noted, film production proceeds in stages. But what was left out earlier was that at each stage there are multiple forms of feedback, thus multiple forms of productive and receptive intent. In connection with this, one needs to distinguish at least three components of creation, whether one is speaking of films, novels, or anything else. First, there are broad structures that guide creation; second, there are ways of developing and instantiating those structures; third, there are procedures for evaluating and selecting from developments and instantiations. When an author writes a play, these various functions are all fulfilled by the same person in almost all cases. Thus the playwright decides on the general structure (e.g., a romantic tragedy), begins to work out specifics (e.g., that the lovers will be from rival families that include violent youths), tries out different possibilities (e.g., regarding whether one of the youths is killed and, if so, which one), chooses among them, revising in light of receptive response (e.g., scratching "There's a lamp in that room; who lit it?" in order to substitute "What light through yonder window breaks?")—and so on, often through multiple cycles.

Now and then, an editor might intervene, taking up a small part of selection (e.g., suggesting that a particular section should be cut) or even generating a local specification (e.g., proposing some particular phrase for a piece of dialogue). But these contributions are, again, very limited in most cases.

What, then, about film? Clearly, these three tasks may be distributed across different individuals in a film. That is what makes auteurism questionable. However, merely characterizing these tasks as separated may be overly simple. What is most obviously the case in film is that many of the specific possible instantiations of general structures are produced by different individuals. In other words, the multiplicity in film is, most crucially, a matter of the second component of creation. One might, then, revise the first principle of classical auteurism along the following lines. There is—or, at least, may be—a guiding intentionality in films, the auteur. That auteur defines the broad structures for the film, not only in general, but in particular areas as well. Thus the auteur sets out the structures for set design, lighting, music, and other areas. He or she assigns individuals (including himself or herself) to specify and develop those structures—thus to specify and develop his or her guidelines for set design, lighting, music, or whatever. Those individuals then generate instantiations, from which the auteur selects just what will appear in the film. Moreover, this occurs in multiple sequences of feedback. The auteur gives broad structures to the set designer, who returns with sketches. This allows the auteur, not only to choose from among alternatives, but to suggest particular changes, to reformulate the general structures that he or she established initially, and so on.

It will not have escaped the notice of any reader that the preceding revision of auteurism is quite consistent with the notion that the auteur is the director. After all, the director commonly articulates general structures for the set designer, the actors and actresses, and the cinematographer. Moreover, in some cases, the director himself or herself undertakes that specification as well—acting, directing photography, composing the music. These points seem to at least partially salvage auteurism. There is a guiding creative force for a film in that there is someone who sets the general structures for the components of the film, assigns subordinates to work out the particulars, gives instructions for revising those particulars, and finally selects the instantiations of those structures.

But here two further problems arise. First, the director does not monopolize the first and third stages of creativity. Indeed, general structures may be established at different points by different individuals, and tasks are divided in different ways by different people. A producer may set a particular task for a screenwriter and choose a star. He or she may determine certain aspects of the development of the film (e.g., insisting on specific sorts of special effects). The screenwriter certainly establishes structures for the director. Even if the director revises the script, he or she is still instantiating and developing the script's main organizing principles and trajectory. In this way, the director is like the set designer or the director of photography. They too instantiate structures drawn from the script and the producer; they too generate structures that they expect subordinates to instantiate and develop.

The second problem is that the generation of broad structures and the selection of instantiations need not involve any crucial creative work. Suppose Jones determines that he or she will put together an anthology on auteurism, then assigns different topics to different authors. As the authors submit their papers, Jones makes suggestions for revision, finally accepting the papers when he or she feels that they are ready for inclusion. In this case, Jones has established the general principles; he or she has engaged in cycles of feedback; he or she has selected the specifications. But no one would wish to assign a great deal of credit to Jones for the creativity of the work composing the volume. Jones may be congratulated for a fine collection, but no one would say that Jones is responsible for the new insights or theories provided by the essays, nor would anyone make Jones's receptive intention the interpretive norm for understanding those essays.

This all appears to work rather strongly against auteurism. Indeed, the example of the anthology seems devastating. It seems to indicate that the director is really not all that important. But only a slight change in the example shows that this is not necessarily true. Suppose that Jones is an experimental psychologist. He or she determines that several sorts of empirical study are crucial for understanding auteurism. He or she decides what those studies are and assigns them to technicians in his or her lab. Jones is involved at each stage in the design, execution, and evaluation of these studies. The interpretation of the findings is guided, in each case, by the framework Jones has provided. The studies are then written up by the subordinates and included in Jones's anthology. In this case, I imagine most people would be quite willing to credit Jones with the overall creativity and insight of the volume.

What, then, does all this suggest about auteurism? In the example of the collection of research writings, the degree to which the editor or director of research is the crucial creative force is clearly an empirical matter. One determines it by looking at the specifics of the collection and at its history. Though somewhat banal, the same point holds for the director—or, for that matter, the producer, cinematographer, editor, or star. The degree to which a director may be credited with (or blamed for) the creation of a film is an empirical matter. Moreover, as the preceding sentence indicates, this is not an absolute, but a relative attribution, a matter of degree. Indeed, it is possible to acknowledge that creativity is distributed, while still retaining a version of auteurism. All that is strictly necessary to preserve some form of auteurism is that individual (e.g., directorial) creativity be discernible. As a result, the second principle of classical auteurism becomes crucial, for the obvious way of discerning a director's, producer's, or other agent's contribution to a film is to abstract from the set of films to which he or she contributed. In other words, this account emphasizes the oeuvre—or, rather, multiple oeuvres.

More exactly, classical auteurism is, so to speak, "maximal." It asserts a single guiding intentionality and it does so a priori. It is possible to substitute for this a more plausible "minimal auteurism,"[26] which revises the three principles of classical auteurism in the following way. First, it is possible to discern one or more guiding intentionalities in a film. In itself, this revision is not particularly novel. For example, Richard Dyer adopts a "model . . . of multiple authorship (with varying degrees of hierarchy and control) in specific determining economic and technological circumstances" (187). Berys Gaut has defended a multiple authorship view through arguments that partially overlap and partially complement the preceding discussion.

But it is not enough to point out that there are often several intentionalities in a film. One needs to have a sense of the process through which these intentionalities are interrelated. That process may be roughly defined by the three recursive subprocesses outlined above. The precise ways in which these subprocesses are themselves particularized (what is done by the producer, director, cinematographer, and so on) will vary from film to film. Understanding individual cases should have both interpretive and theoretical consequences. As to the latter, it should allow one to define the nature and varieties of authorial control more precisely. For example, it should help to explain how a work may be the product of conflict among various authors, as discussed by Gaut. Conversely, it should help to clarify how there may be varying degrees of "global authorship," as treated by Paisley Livingston.

The second, and in some ways most important, principle of minimal auteurism is that authorial intentionalities are expressed or enacted not only in individual films, but in sets of films on which a given auteur works in a particular capacity (e.g., as director), thus canons. Indeed, the patterns that manifest intentionalities are often discernible only by reference to the authorial canon. Thus, in studying an auteur—for example, a director—one must usually place the film in the context of that director's other works. One then tries to discern a pattern across those works—more precisely, a *distinctive* pattern, a pattern that is not found across, say, the producer's or screenwriter's works. Insofar as the features of the particular film conform to that distinctive pattern, one may with some confidence attribute those features to the director as auteur. Indeed, one may *explain* them by reference to the auteur.

It is important to note that one's understanding of patterns should not be too narrow. If one looks at the cinematography of Bimal Roy's films, one may not see significant, recurring features. For example, occlusive shots or staging in depth recur, but not, it seems, very prominently. This may make it appear as if Roy's cinematography does not involve cross-textual authorial patterns. However, many of his films involve a coordination of theme and stylistic technique. Again, there is prominent staging in depth in *Sujata,* his film about Untouchability (there, staging in depth gives concrete form to the physical isolation of Untouchables). There is some striking interposition or interference with vision in *Prem Patra,* his film about literal and metaphorical blindness. There is an enveloping of figures in mist and the visually similar superimposition of present and past images in *Madhubuti,* a film about memory and forgetting. These cases do not most importantly share directly perceivable stylistic properties. Rather, they manifest a recurring principle—the coordination of theme and style—that guides the production and receptive selection of such properties.

As to the third principle of minimal auteurism, it seems that, in general, the most consequential auteur is likely to be the director. However, in the majority of films, the director will not be the only auteur. Moreover, there will be films in which the producer, screenwriter, or someone else is the most consequential. In all cases, the issue is empirical.

Cinema, then, complicates the idea of the cross-textual implied author. It leads one to recognize that the initial production of the work is not rendered irrelevant due to receptive intent. Specifically, initial production has consequences for whose intention one considers important and in what degree. Nonetheless, receptive intent remains interpretively definitive (depending on the stipulated interpretive target). An implied author—or implied auteur—still establishes interpretive norms by receptively judging the work (or some section of a work) complete. On the other hand, in the case of a film, there may be more than one implied auteur and those different implied auteurs may yield different interpretations of the work or features within the work (as when an interposition has thematic implications for an implied auteur/cinematographer, but only aesthetic implications for an implied auteur/director). At the same time, the case of film demonstrates all the more clearly the importance of the cross-textual implied author. Specifically, it indicates that the canon of a creator is key for separating out at least some of what applies to which potential auteur (director, producer, screenwriter, and so on) for any given film.

BIMAL ROY'S *MADHUMATI*

Clearly, there is not space here to cover the entire range of any filmmaker's work. Nor is there space to cover all the implied auteurs in any single film. However, it is important to illustrate auteurial patterning, at least briefly.

Bimal Roy was one of the major filmmakers in the classic period of Hindi cinema from the 1940s to the early 1960s. Roy's works show a number of recurrent, "auteurial" features, not only in style, but in narrative and theme as well. First, his films often treat very precisely isolated but also broadly human personal problems—for example, the misunderstandings that repeatedly vitiate human relationships, because one's experience of other peoples' actions is limited and biased. Commonly, these problems manifest themselves in the possible or actual separation of two people who have some attachment relation to one another (either romantic or parental/filial). Second, he recurrently locates these problems in the context of some important social or political issue—for example, caste hierarchization. Third, he often develops this problem and its consequences in relation to Vedāntic principles, thus early Hindu ideas of illusion, suffering, rebirth, spiritual liberation, and so on. In this way, he tends to give the problem a broader scope and greater, so to speak, ontological significance—for example, by connecting human misunderstandings with "māyā," or the illusions of material existence. The second and third recurring features give rise to a fourth. Specifically, the spiritual concerns in part respond to the political problems, as when Vedāntic monism suggests the falsity of caste hierarchization. This integration of Vedāntic concerns into politics forms a central thematic preoccupation in a number of Roy's films.[27] Finally and, for present purposes, most importantly, Ray develops those thematic concerns not only through the story, but through visual and aural elements of narration—or style—as well.

As to the final point, as already noted, Roy has a sort of generative principle according to which the visual and sound patterns should contribute to the thematic concerns of the work. They do this both emotionally and interpretively. The emotional impact tends to be, so to speak, implicit. In other words, Roy does not need to draw the viewer's self-conscious attention to the relevant narrational features for him or her to respond to those features emotionally. That is because the emotional impact of these features tends to derive from the way they depict the storyworld. In contrast, their interpretive effects may require that the techniques themselves become to some extent salient.

There are two obvious ways in which a technique may be rendered salient. The first is through increased frequency. When repeated above some threshold, a particular device may become obtrusive. To take a simple example, frequent tight close-ups of hands may, at a certain point, lead viewers to notice that there are many tight close-ups of hands. The second obvious way of producing saliency is through a single shot that is somehow "intensified" so as to draw the viewer's self-conscious attention. This may occur in different ways. For example, a filmmaker may intensify a shot simply by extending its duration. Thus a single close-up of hands may become noticeable if it is sustained for a long time. Alternatively, a filmmaker may enhance the distinctiveness of a shot by a contrast in the normal lighting for the rest of the film or a contrast in the use of color (an obvious case would be a shift from black and white to color or the reverse). An intensified shot or sequence of this sort may serve as a sort of signal to the viewer to attend to a particular technique. Once such a signal has occurred, other instances of the device may become more salient even if they are not particularly frequent, enduring, or even contrastive.

Of course, there is another way in which recurring patterns of significance may become salient to a viewer—more precisely, to a critic. That is through the distinctive recurrence of a device in an authorial canon. The fact that Roy uses theme-style connections in some works serves to draw attentional focus to possible theme-style links in other works. Moreover, there is some overlap across works in the stylistic techniques he uses and in some of their metaphysical resonances. These techniques include staging in depth, blocked line-of-sight staging (in which characters visible to the viewer are not visible to one another), nonface close-ups (e.g., close-ups of hands), and some form of figural occlusion relative to the viewer (i.e., some interference with the viewer's sight of a character). The last is particularly interesting and occurs in different varieties, from interposition of various sorts—prominently aperture, sheer medium (e.g., a curtain), and latticework interposition—to "enclosure" (e.g., in fog) to superimposition of film images. There is also some overlap across Roy's films in what might be called "metatechniques," that is, means of rendering interpretable techniques more salient. Specifically, in at least a couple of films, he uses a "signal" shot or sequence to cue the viewer's sensitivity to a particular technique.

The basic story of *Madhumati* (1958) concerns an engineer, Devendra, who is trying to meet his wife (Radha) at a train station, but ends up spending the night in a strange mansion. On entering the mansion, he finds himself filled with memories, apparently from an earlier birth. In a flashback, the viewer witnesses the story of Anand (Devendra in an earlier life) and Madhumati. Madhumati is the daughter of the former raja of the place, who has been displaced and impoverished by the new raja and the "company" (the characters use the English word), a timber enterprise. Madhumati and Anand fall in love, but Madhumati is abducted by the new raja. She commits suicide in order to avoid rape. Anand exposes the landlord and then joins her in suicide. In the end, it is revealed that Anand and Madhumati have been reborn and are now united as husband and wife.[28]

The means by which Anand exposes the landlord are somewhat surprising. He meets a young woman, Madhavi, who is physically indistinguishable from Madhumati. However, there is a systematic change. Madhumati was a village girl who did folk dances in actual village celebrations. Madhavi is a city girl who does folk dance as part of an artistic revival of traditional customs. Inspired by Madhavi's appearance, Anand devises a plan to make the new raja confess his crimes.

The discussion of the old raja, the new raja, and the "company" alone would suggest some of Roy's thematic concerns here, particularly to members of an audience watching the film slightly over a decade after Indian independence. The old raja suggests Indian self-rule; the new raja suggests the British—or, in this case, those Indians who collaborated with the British; and the "company" calls to mind the East India Company, the initial agency of British colonialism in India, commonly referred to simply as "the company." These links are enhanced by the fact that the new regime is associated with extensive corruption (on the notorious corruption of the early East India Company, see Wolpert 188–89; the problem continued past Company rule and well into India's independence). In a standard allegorical pattern, Madhumati is traditional India, or perhaps the traditional culture of India, and two men fight over her.[29] Somewhat surprisingly, she dies—but then the traditional culture she represents is revived in an artistic and learned form (through Madhavi). That revival of traditional culture inspires a rejection of the colonial rule (manifest here in Anand's exposure of the new raja). This points fairly accurately toward what happens in nationalist movements. As traditional culture is threatened by the colonizer, nationalists seek out that traditional culture to develop in national arts.[30] The end of the film points to the new, independent India. This is manifest not only in the rebirth and reunion of the couple, but in the birth of their child—a standard image of the new nation.[31]

Turning back to the list of recurring patterns in Roy's work, one may wonder just what personal problem is being treated here. The whole narrative is organized by Devendra's worry over being reunited with his wife and his sense of being haunted by a past that he does not fully understand. The course of the narrative involves working through that past. The literal problem may be seen as a sort of haunting by a ghost, particularly after Madhumati dies and begins to call to him and even appear to him. But this would hardly be a common human problem of the sort Roy typically addresses. Rather, there is a hint that the recurring human problem is the interference of memory with current life and current human relations.

In keeping with Roy's usual practices, this personal concern is carried into the politics of the film. Specifically, the traumatic memories that trouble Devendra are the traumatic history that troubles modern India. Indeed, for viewers who do not believe in reincarnation, the point fits India better than it fits Devendra, since history was uncontroversially an experience of people in another lifetime. Moreover, patriots in effect often did commit suicide in fighting against the unjust rule of their country.

In connection with both the personal and national problems, the problems of memory and history, the film seems to urge remembering the past without thereby becoming emotionally distorted by it. Devendra achieves a sort of peace by remembering his traumatic past. When he forgets the past, he is anxious. But remembering the past does not inspire anger or resentment, as one might have feared. Rather, it enhances his joy in the present.

The metaphysics of the film are more straightforward here than in the other films. The story explicitly treats reincarnation and, thus, karma. The main idea of karma is that the desires of previous lives carry over into new births.[32] Specifically, souls continually return to the material world, the world of illusion, with all its attendant suffering, because they have not overcome the desires of previous lives. These desires include not only lust or greed, but also the desire for revenge (in anger), the desire for status (in envy), and so on. The desires have their effects through memory traces or *saṁskāras* (see, for example, Patañjali). This does not mean that the film is necessarily advocating an actual belief in reincarnation. It may or may not be doing so. The crucial point is that the desires associated with memory are a cause of being drawn back into painful illusions. As such, they inhibit one's ability to achieve *mokṣa* or freedom, with its associated sense of peace.

The metaphysics of the film clearly bear on the personal problem, since Devendra is troubled by the *saṁskāras* of his previous traumatic experiences. He only overcomes the anxiety produced by those experiences when he works through the memories, accepts them, and realizes that he now has what he desired all along. He and Madhumati/Rādhā are now united. These points may be extended to the politics of the film, where "freedom" has national rather than personal implications. The nation too is troubled by saṁskāras; it too needs to recognize that it has achieved the union which it was previously denied (i.e., the union of India), and so on.

The film addresses these thematic concerns through several narrational and stylistic means. First, Roy sometimes uses staging in depth to separate the lovers. This is unlike the staging in depth that he uses in *Sujata,* as it does not suggest alienation or prohibition. Indeed, the lovers clearly respond with joy to even their distant presence. Moreover, the location of the staging in depth is different. It is not separation across indoor spaces (e.g., between rooms), but outside, in large natural settings of water and mountains (see Fig. 2.10). Thematically, the lovers' joyful response even to distant connections in nature may suggest—and, indeed, inspire—joy in the land of India with its national links across great distances. This suggestion and inspiration are enhanced by the cinematography (an aspect of narration) that conveys a close connection between the lovers and that land stolen from its rightful raja. Related to this, Madhumati repeatedly leads Anand to distant places, barely visible across the mountains and valleys (see Fig. 2.11). As one might expect from the thematic concerns, these are historically and culturally

Figure 2.10. Anand observes Madhumati from a distance.

Figure 2.11. Anand and Madhumati look toward the distant village where they will go for a festival.

significant places. One is the plateau and cave where her ancestors are monumentalized and the family deity is worshiped. Another is the local village, where the traditional songs and dances are performed. A third is her home, where she lives with her father, the deposed raja. The significance of these places for the cultural heritage of the new Indian nation need hardly be spelled out.

Another technique used by Roy is blocked line-of-sight staging. Roy repeatedly makes Anand and/or Madhumati visible to the viewer, but invisible to one another (see Figs. 2.12 and 2.13). They shift positions, one becoming visible to the other, then disappearing, and so on. There may be a hint here of Roy's recurring Vedāntic concern with illusion and ignorance. Alternatively, it may merely suggest the nature of memory, the way that memory may be elusive. One tries to remember the past, but often fails. Moreover, a memory can appeal to someone without fully revealing itself. These connections are no less relevant in the case of partially remembered history than in the case of partially remembered personal experience.

Another way of expressing this aspect of memory or history would be to say that the past calls to one or one hears a voice from the past. This relates to a more unique feature of this film. Roy pays much more attention to sound in this work than seems to have been typical in his other films. Often, one lover will hear the other before seeing him or her. Indeed, Anand's initial introduction to Madhumati is by way of a song that he hears in the distance. Thus the voice signals presence, even as the visual relation is often troubled by lack of recognition or immersion in māyā.

Figure 2.12. Anand and Madhumati out of each other's line of sight.

Figure 2.13. Anand and Madhumati invisible to each other.

In connection with this last point, Roy often interweaves signals of auditory presence with another recurring technique—that of an enveloping occlusion. Again and again, the lovers are obscured in masses of white (see Figs. 2.14, 2.15, and 2.16). In some cases, this is the foam of rushing waters. That most often isolates the figures, rather than enveloping and concealing them. More frequently and more significantly, one or both lovers are swallowed up in billowing clouds of mountain fog. Repeatedly, they disappear in or appear out of a white, misty expanse—though, again, a voice often penetrates the haze even when no image is visible. The parallels here with fading and reappearing memory seem straightforward. The same point holds for history, which is often spoken of as hidden by the mists of time.

In the context of Roy's works, the connection of this concealing mist with illusion may seem, at first, self-evident. However, the watery whiteness of the fog and the river are not wholly negative. The suggestions of the technique are more complex and ambivalent. This becomes apparent if one contrasts the mist and water with the more obvious way of engulfing and concealing figures—darkness. In opposition to the more stereotypically frightening image of dark night, the engulfing white may even suggest a sense of monistic unity. Indeed, the fading of the two lovers into the mountain fog (see Fig. 2.16) particularly may point toward monism in identifying the lovers with the encompassing and undifferentiated world of nature, thus the material aspect of the absolute. (In the Vedāntic school of Absolute Monism, there are two aspects of reality—nature and spirit. These are ultimately identical. But, viewed from different angles, the Absolute appears as one or the other [see, for example,

Figure 2.14. Anand disappearing into the fog.

Figure 2.15. Madhumati engulfed in mist.

Figure 2.16. The lovers emerge from the fog.

Pandit 66].) This identity of the lovers with nature is an important motif elsewhere in Roy's work. In *Sujata* it contributes to the political use of monism in criticizing Untouchability. In both *Sujata* and *Madhumati*, the lovers—the women especially—are closely identified with nature. In the case of Madhumati, this further associates her with the nation, which is not only a population and a government, but also a land.

All these techniques are repeated with enough frequency to become salient. However, Roy also includes a pivotal "signal" sequence. Moreover, he includes it at perhaps *the* crucial point of transition in the discourse. Specifically, there is a moment when Devendra suddenly realizes that he is recalling a past life. A series of memories comes flooding into his mind. This is introduced by a curtain covering his face, followed by a number of superimpositions that represent the past; those images from the past are themselves occluded in turn by the white curtain (see Figs. 2.17–2.20). The sequence is striking in context and certainly calls attention to itself. This signal quality has implications for viewers'—particularly critics'—reception of the rest of the film. Specifically, the partial obscuring of Devendra's face in the white images should help sensitize viewers to the obscuring clouds of white in the film. It also suggests the association of those clouds with memory.

This use of superimposition to treat Devendra's past life is thematically resonant in several ways. First, it points toward a sort of paradox about memory and history. On the one hand, memories represent the past. But at the same time their effects are wholly in the present. Moreover, in the present, they have an illusionlike status. This is all nicely suggested by the ghostlike superimpositions, where images from the past obscure Devendra's face—and, presumably, his vision—in the present. Indeed, when Madhumati's ghost appears later in the film, she is superimposed with the same partial transparency as in this sequence of memories (see Fig. 2.21). Thus, once again, salient and distinctive techniques in the film suggest the complex thematic interweaving of the personal, the political, and the metaphysical, which is so characteristic of Roy's work.

In short, there are interpretively consequential, recurrent auteurial patterns in Roy's work, as there are in Tagore's. However, in Roy's case, the patterns are more complex. Specifically, both Tagore and Roy have enduring thematic concerns. But, in Roy's case, there is a complex of motivic relations among personal, political, and metaphysical ideas along with discursive devices bearing on those ideas. Moreover, these relations are broadly consistent, but not precisely identical from film to film. To

Figure 2.17. Devendra is obscured by a white curtain as his past-life memory begins.

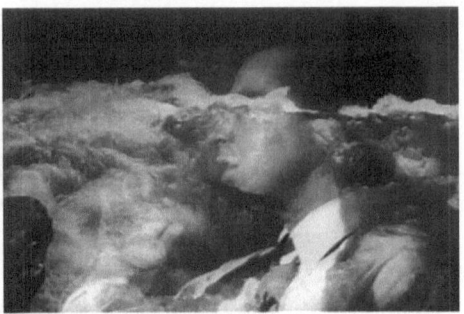

Figure 2.18. Devendra's past-life memory is marked by extended superimposition.

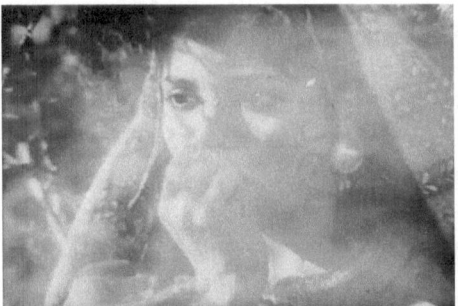

Figure 2.19. When Devendra fades from the screen, the white curtain passes in front of the memory of Madhumati.

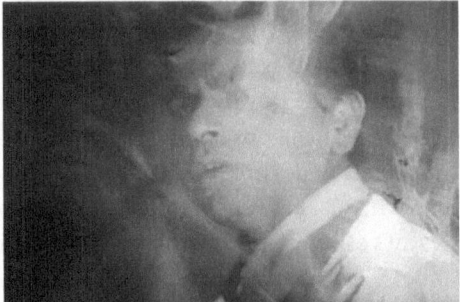

Figure 2.20. The return to the present is marked by the curtain obscuring Devendra's face.

Figure 2.21. Madhumati's ghost has the same translucent quality (of superimposition) as Devendra's memories.

make a terminological distinction, the motivic parallels were not based on *fixed symbolic correlations* but rather on *generative principles*. Thus, in *Sujata*, Roy draws on the metaphysical identity of spirit and nature to oppose caste, whereas in *Madhumati* he draws on the same model to personify the nation and to address the problem of remembering a traumatic history. Similarly, there are different sorts of figural occlusion in *Prem Patra* and *Madhumati*, and these are used somewhat differently. In both cases, they are related to māyā, but the occlusions in *Prem Patra* are wholly negative, wholly a matter of ignorance (or avidya, a succumbing to māyā). In contrast, in *Madhumati*, the māyā-like clouds simultaneously suggest the nondifference claimed by Absolute Monism. In this way, Roy begins with a set of concerns, models, and techniques that he interrelates in different ways in order to address distinct problems (e.g., caste or national history). The result is different from the recurring correlation of a particular visual pattern and a particular thematic issue (such as the curving posture of a woman and concern about childbearing).

Of course, if one looked at different topics in Tagore's work, and a wider range of his work, one would certainly find such generative principles there as well. Indeed, even in the cases just considered, it is really a difference of degree, not of kind. Even Tagore's gently curving women are not identical with one another, and they differ in whether they have or lack children. Thus these figures too have a degree of generativity. Conversely, there are undoubtedly more nearly fixed patterns in Roy's work as well. (In addition, it is important to say that generativity is not in and of itself artistically superior to fixed correlations.) In any case, the point is not that Roy is somehow unique. In fact, the point is the precise opposite. These sorts of patterns—both fixed and generative—recur in all authors. They are what give the critical idea of a cross-textual implied author or auteur its interpretive value.

Conclusion

An examination of visual art in relation to narratological discourse analysis leads to several enhancements of the preceding account of discourse. First, and most significantly, it is necessary to recognize the importance of cross-textual implied authorship, separating the implied author of the entire oeuvre from the implied authors of specific works, as well as the real, biographical author. (If one wishes to stress the implied author of a particular text, one may refer to the *textual implied author.*) In correlation with this, it is also important to distinguish "motifs," recurring discourse features and/or story elements. The recognition of motifs and cross-textual implied authorship may contribute to one's understanding of the represented world and the thematic concerns of a work.[33] They may also play a role in criticism that operates to enhance or modulate emotional response. These points hold for both literature and painting.

Rabindranath Tagore's paintings are particularly well suited for exploration via narratological discourse analysis, due in part to their great ambiguity. As such, they highlight something that is true of all works, but is not always so obvious. First, these paintings forcefully convey how a work involves not a single expressive meaning but rather a receptive profile of ambiguity. That ambiguity is sometimes enhanced by narratorial texts (such as titles) or post facto commentaries by the painter. Those texts and commentaries manifest various sorts of unreliability and irony. In Tagore's case, one's sense of this profile of ambiguity changes as one locates his works in the various levels of receptive intent defined by the implied painter and implied author. Recurring narrative, emotional, and thematic commitments—here, recurring concerns bearing on attachment relations—suggest possible inferences about the depicted world while simultaneously altering one's encoding of the paintings themselves (e.g., leading one to notice the lifted left arm of the second figure in plate 156/Fig. 2.2).[34] Recurring motifs also suggest that some thematic interpretations are less plausible than they might have seemed initially, while others are more plausible. In connection with this, the paintings indicate that the study of narrative discourse may contribute to the theory and criticism of visual art, just as the study of visual art may contribute to the theory and practice of narrative discourse analysis. Moreover, both sorts of study may enhance the sense that Tagore's paintings are not only aesthetically affecting and interpretively rich, but valuable sources for theoretical reflection as well.

In film studies, an idea similar to that of an implied canonical author was developed in auteur theory. However, there have been many problems explaining just what an auteur is and how auteurist continuities operate across films in a particular oeuvre. These problems are partially solved by the idea of receptive, implied authorial intent. However, further problems arise immediately.

First, receptive intent seems definitive only when the same person is responsible for the productive intent. That is often not the case in film (e.g., the cinematographer may produce the camerawork that the director merely approves). Second, there may not even be a single receptive intent for a film. In any case, there are embedded receptive intents (e.g., the director approves the cinematographer's selection of an option proposed by a camera operator). Third, even if there is a "culminating" receptive intent (e.g., even if the director receptively approves all contributions), that intent may have encoded selections only minimally. For example, the director may approve the lighting based only on the clarity of visual information while the lighting director established the lighting for its emotional effects as well.

But, in fact, none of this undermines the idea of an auteur or a cross-textual implied author. Rather, it expands the concept to different possible auteurs and makes the precise distribution of intentions in any given case an empirical question. It also foregrounds the degree to which implied authorial interpretations are a matter not simply of patterns across an author's canon but of at least partially distinctive patterns.[35] More exactly, the arguments against auteurism suggest that there may be many implied authors in any given film. One understands, interprets, and appreciates those authors by reference to different canons—one for the director, one for the cinematographer, and one for each of the other individuals involved in the production of the work—again, insofar as these canons involve distinctive properties. As to a film as a whole, the director does remain the most prominent candidate for an encompassing receptive implied intent. This is particularly true for directors with great autonomy relative to producers, expertise in various aspects of film production (e.g., cinematography), involvement in the script (most obviously as author of an original script), and in general greater integration into the various processes that converge to make the film.

Differences in auteurial function may be understood in terms of three components of film production—the definition of broad guiding principles, the particularization of those guidelines, and the evaluation and selection of resulting particulars. This threefold pattern recurs at various levels in the production of a work. For example, the first component ranges from a large vision for the film as a whole to guidelines about lighting for a particular shot. Moreover, the various contributors to a film engage in cycles of guidance, particularization, evaluative feedback with a change in guidance, further particularization, partial selection, and so forth. Here, too, the director is the one who most obviously makes the fullest evaluative and selective decisions. He or she is, in the usual case, most fully involved in establishing guidelines as well. In some cases, he or she may even be deeply involved with particularizations.

Finally, the case of Bimal Roy reveals some of the possible complexities in auteurial canonical patterns. These patterns need not only be a matter of relatively fixed, recurring correlations between storyworld patterns, thematic or emotional concerns, and discourse techniques. They may also be a matter of more diverse, generative principles. These principles may produce a variety of mappings from diverse models and techniques onto various story interests and thematic issues. In Tagore, there was a connection between women in a particular postural orientation, the emotion of grief, the loss of children (in the storyworld), and a thematic concern with the burdens placed on women in an inegalitarian society. In Roy, metaphysical ideas were brought to bear on a more diverse set of personal and political themes through a range of narrational and stylistic techniques. Rather than a fixed linkage, there was a looser generative principle requiring that the metaphysics address the personal and political dilemmas and that a few highlighted visual and/or aural techniques contribute to developing or illustrating the thematic points of the work and enhancing its emotional effects.

Chapter 3

Authors, Implied and Implicated

Explaining Harriet Beecher Stowe's *Uncle Tom's Cabin* and Kabir Khan's *New York*

THE PRECEDING CHAPTER was concerned with continuities in the implied author, not only at the level of the individual work, but at the level of the canon. The present chapter argues that the unity or consistency of implied authorial intent is greatly overestimated. Recent accounts of cognitive architecture predict that, rather than a single, consistent authorial or implied authorial intent, there are partially contradictory ideas and attitudes. These partial contradictions affect not only theme and emotional response, but even some story elements. This is not to say that there is no unity in a narrative. There are certainly strong tendencies toward continuity within most works. But there are various sorts of discontinuity and even contradiction as well.

Authorial Self-Understanding

The first chapter stressed that an author does not have direct, introspective access to the principles guiding his or her decisions. Thus all English speakers are able to judge correct and incorrect regular plurals. But only those with some knowledge of linguistics are able to state the rule governing such judgments. Of course, the limitations of self-knowledge should not be overstated. Clearly, authors do know some things about why they produced and accepted certain sentences, certain plot developments, certain narrative voices, and so on. The point is particularly clear in the case of self-consciously political literature. Before going on to consider the diversity of authorial response, then, it is important to briefly reconsider authorial self-understanding.

Again, an author wants to produce a certain sort of effect, a certain sort of response in his or her readers. He or she develops the plot, alters the narrative voice, revises the phrasing, and so forth, until he or she produces, in implicit, imaginative simulation of the reader's response, the effect that he or she desires. That simulated effect may be accompanied by explicit, self-conscious goals. For example, Stowe wished to oppose the Fugitive Slave Act. This was a self-conscious purpose and she could almost certainly have articulated some of her implied authorial reasons—for authorial intrusions, for characterization, and so forth—by reference to that goal.

On the other hand, her introspective access was only partial. After all, even in the most apparently overt cases—for instance, in direct arguments against the Fugitive Slave Act—Stowe's implied authorial decisions were embedded in a complex of ideas, feelings, and imaginations that all contributed to her sense that a particular passage produced the "right" effect. One might say that her *explicit reason* for a particular argument was itself embedded in a more complex set of *mental causes*.[1] It was the entire set of mental causes that gave rise to the decisions involved in producing, revising, and accepting the passage at issue.

Indeed, even authorial reasons are somewhat more complex than this suggests, since reasons need not be explicit or self-conscious. A mental cause is whatever gives rise to a certain behavior or action. One may understand a reason, in contrast, as a justified motivation in context. In this usage, the reason must be a genuine motivation (i.e., it does not include rationalizations). Thus it must be part of the mental causality. At the same time, it must provide a rationale for the action. That rationale may be prudential or ethical or something else. But it should cohere with some contextually relevant aim. In relation to narrative discourse and authorship, reasons are those mental causes that bear on receptive, thus implied authorial, intent, with their guiding aim of producing a certain effect on the reader.

Authors are self-conscious about some reasons for their decisions, but only some. Thus one may distinguish between a self-consciously thematized part of the implied author's reasons and a part that is not self-consciously thematized. Reasons of the former sort are usually open to fairly clear articulation. Indeed, they may even have been articulated in the literary work. This articulation may occur through an "authorial intrusion," where the voice of the author and the voice of the narrator are (temporarily) conflated, or through "authorial ventriloquism," where a character becomes (temporarily) the voice of the author.[2] A more attenuated form of authorial ventriloquism occurs in what might be called "authorial mirroring." In this case, one or several characters manifest the normative emotional orientation of an implied author, particularly characters witnessing the relevant event (as opposed to characters directly involved in those events). As Suzanne Keen puts it, "Many novelists call up empathy as a representational goal by mirroring it within their texts" by "present[ing] empathetic connections between characters" (121). This is a technique used repeatedly by Stowe, who, for example, has characters witness a scene of familial separation and weep, thereby expressing the implied author's emotional response and helping to guide that of the reader.

Within the unthematized part of an implied author's reasons, one may distinguish genuine vagueness from recurring features that suggest governing principles. Implied authorial reasons of the former sort are imprecise, not fully specifiable. They may fall within a certain range of possibilities. But, in many cases, it is difficult to say if any particular articulation is correct within that range. This is not accidental. It is, rather, a key feature of receptive intent, bound up with the profile of ambiguity.

At the same time, not all specifiable reasons are self-conscious for an author. The articulation of reasons sometimes requires knowledge that the author simply did not have. With adequate knowledge, however, it may be possible to articulate principles governing these patterns, thus reasons. These may be referred to as "theoretically specifiable," though unthematized, reasons. Here it is useful to return to the example of English pluralization. Regular English pluralization is not vague. It is rule-governed. However, most speakers require special knowledge to be able to articulate the relevant rule. In the case of authors, similar points hold for, say, reasons governing human emotional response, which may require knowledge of human emotion systems before they may be adequately formulated.

These complexities are, in fact, part of the rationale for literary criticism. One task of a critic is, roughly, isolating reasons for the choices made by an author. The mental causes that bear on the initial creation of a work are all to be found in the real author. In part, authorial biography serves to set out some of those mental causes (e.g., in describing the personal acquaintances of the author who contributed their idiosyncrasies to his or her characters). But the reasons for authorial choices operate most importantly at the level of the implied author. Sometimes those reasons are genuinely vague and lead to ambiguity. Sometimes those reasons are explicit. But often they are implicit and require inference and articulation, frequently with the help of knowledge unavailable to the author.

Implicated Authors

The preceding chapters have tacitly presupposed that there is a single implied author for a literary work. In a sense, there is only one implied author for a particular work taken as a whole, the textual implied author. Indeed, in a sense the unity of a work is a function of the unity of the implied author. At some point, an author makes a judgment regarding his or her receptive response to a work—the judgment that the work is finished. That judgment of completeness defines any global unity the work may have.[3] Whatever the author had in mind when writing a particular passage, choosing this word or that, devising one or another plot element—all that is now superseded by the final evaluative response. That final response is, in some degree, singular. Moreover, it undoubtedly includes cognitive and affective elements that are relatively constant across the course of the work.

Yet, even in a final reading, the simulative, receptive experience of a work is temporally extended. As such, it necessarily involves shifting attentional foci, different interests, variable inferences. If one takes seriously what is known about human cognitive architecture, one has no choice but to conclude that there is great multiplicity in implied authorship throughout the course of an extended work. Specifically, as contexts shift, different elements will become salient. In consequence, different cognitive structures and affective orientations will become active. Those changing structures and orientations produce sometimes radically different understandings and may develop into very different evaluative responses on the part of the author/reader.[4] One result of these shifting contexts and cognitive activities is that the implied author, even if relatively consistent at the global level and consistent within each separate context, is unlikely to be fully or ideally consistent across all those contexts. Instead, it is likely that local implied authors will be partially inconsistent with others, while some will form themselves into patterns of coherence.

For example, one well-known study showed that people tended to support military intervention in a hypothetical political crisis when presented with a fictional event that was framed to activate the model of World War II. However, test subjects were likely to oppose military intervention, given identical relevant facts, when the fictional event was presented in such a way as to activate the model of the Vietnam War (e.g., in having refugees leave by train in the first case and by boat in the second case).[5] These sorts of shifting contexts occur regularly in novels and other creative products. Indeed, precisely these circumstances could arise for an author in the course of writing a novel—circumstances that prime (i.e., partially activate) models of World War II in some places and the Vietnam War in other places. In such a novel, one could very well find an explicit thematic statement that is pro-intervention (based on the tacit activation of a World War II model). But, even a few pages later, one may find a case that is implicitly anti-interventionist (based on the tacit activation of a Vietnam War model).

Indeed, things are even more complicated. Most importantly, there are other influences on one's judgments beyond exemplary models. One of the most frequent is simply common beliefs or common emotions. One often, so to speak, believes that one believes something or feels something because one has heard that so many other people believe or feel it. Such an "asserted belief" or "asserted emotion" may be entirely at odds with one's actual "operational beliefs" and "operational emotions," which guide one's thought and behavior—including one's creation of literary narratives.

At this point, it would be good to have a terminological distinction in order to help keep these differences clear. I will continue to use "implied author" for the explanatory coherence that governs a larger work. But it is necessary to distinguish that global explanatory coherence from the more local receptive intentions. I will refer to the latter as "implicated authors." Thus it is possible to say that any given work has one globally implied author, but many locally implicated authors.[6]

It is important to note that a degree of diversity in the implied author has been suggested by some critics and theorists, if usually without cognitive development and without a systematic treatment of varieties of intent. For example, Susan Lanser has rightly commented that one should not "assume that a text has a singular, coherent implied author" and that "implied authors can be—and perhaps more often are—multiple personalities" ("(Im)plying"). Booth himself notes that "The flesh-and-blood author is already full of conflicts" and that "many voices are present in every published work" ("Is There" 125)—though, in the terms presented here, Booth seems to have in mind a multiplicity in expressive rather than receptive intent.[7]

A crucial point here is that explicit, thematized reasons, given in authorial intrusions or authorial ventriloquism, are, as such, only (locally) implicated authorial ideas or attitudes. The fact that they are explicit does not give them special status in determining (more global) implied authorial meanings. Indeed, it seems rather that concrete, narrative representations are the crucial part of literary work, not the authorial statements.[8] As such, one's interpretations should give greater weight to the former than the latter. This is most obvious when the statements appear to be concessions to a particular audience, such as government censors, or restatements of commonplaces (that authors may simply believe that they believe).

More complex and interesting cases occur when the contradictions among implicated authors are not a matter of explicit statement versus implicit narrative development, but of one implicit narrative development versus another implicit narrative development. These cases are at the center of interpretation and are crucial to understanding the implied author. In part, the task of interpretation is a matter of isolating these discrepancies, these divisions and contradictions. But that is not the entire task of interpretation. The task of interpretation is equally a matter of ascertaining just what it is that underlies those contradictions and connects them.

In most cases, such "reconciliation" will be a matter of finding some principle that governs the contradiction. For example, in the case of the hypothetical prowar/antiwar novel, it would be a matter of isolating different historical models for military intervention—Germany and Vietnam. Note that, in this case, the contradiction remains. Some sections of the novel are still prowar and others are still antiwar. But interpretation has been able to account for the contradiction by reference to the models.

This does not mean that the implied author equally favors all the mutually contradictory options. He or she may have clear preferences without thereby entirely eliminating ambivalence. Indeed, this is just what one would expect, given the general operation of the human mind. People like to think of themselves as consistent and univocal in their beliefs and attitudes. However, people are usually ambivalent, even if the ambivalence may be more or less strongly weighted toward one option.

Of course, people are in some cases aware of or at least sensitive to their own ambivalence. This tends to occur when the different options are more equally balanced. When an author thematizes his or her ambivalence, this produces what might be called a "dialectical" work. A dialectical work is a work in which different emotional attitudes, different political or ethical positions, or other sorts of contradictory options are developed in such a way as to highlight their relative advantages and disadvantages. This occurs most obviously in works where the different positions are articulated explicitly, often by way of characters who may even engage in literal debate. However, it may also occur implicitly or by a combination of implicit and explicit representations.

In some cases, apparent contradictions may be bound up with the simulated readership. It is often important to recognize the degree to which an implicated author is bound to an implicated reader. Again, implied authors are defined by a receptive simulation of readers. In consequence, there are implicated, local readers as well as implicated, local authors. Divergence across implicated readers may occur serially or simultaneously. For example, Stowe clearly envisions both Northern whites and Southern whites reading her book (with perhaps a smattering of free blacks as well, though blacks are clearly not her main simulated audience). To some extent, her goals with respect to different white readerships are the same. Specifically, she wishes to cultivate self-criticism in both Northern and Southern whites while simultaneously appealing to their compassionate inclinations. However, she does not equally simulate all audiences at all times. When writing about the Bird family in Ohio, she is appealing primarily to the humane impulses of Northerners. When writing about Ophelia, she is first of all addressing antislavery New Englanders. When representing Mr. Shelby, she may be trying to provoke greater self-criticism among the more liberal segment of Southern whites.[9]

Conflicts among implicated authors also often involve some social ideology. The obvious case of this occurs when an author explicitly states some criticism of dominant ideology, but goes on to manifest dominant ideology in his or her narrative and characterization. For example, an author might affirm feminist views in authorial intrusions, while simultaneously portraying female characters in stereotypical ways or tacitly endorsing patriarchal social structures through his or her guidance of readers' expectations and preferences in the emplotment of events. This sort of discrepancy is a central concern in Marxist and related forms of ideological critique (e.g., feminist ideological critique), though it is not usually framed in narratological terms.

In some ways the more interesting case occurs in the opposite direction. Then, the author explicitly asserts some dominant ideological position. However, his or her representation of actual conditions and events contradicts that assertion. This is the case of repeating standard beliefs, as mentioned above. For example, an author might overtly state that a particular national war was a noble venture. But he or she might go on to present the concrete development of the war as degraded, cruel, and cowardly. Again, one's usual inclination is simply to accept the overt statements as the view of the implied author—and they are part of that view. However, the concrete development of the story is usually far more consequential.

This has been recognized in the Marxist tradition. Specifically, Georg Lukács argued that the self-conscious political "tendency" of an author does not necessarily determine the political orientation of his or her "portrayal" of society in a literary work. Citing Engels, he considers the example of Balzac—"his conscious intention was to glorify the declining class of the French *ancien régime,* but in actual fact he was 'compelled to go against his own class sympathies and political prejudices,' and present a correct and exhaustive picture of the society of his time. His 'tendency' thus stood in contradiction with his portrayal" (40). In keeping with this—and in keeping with the general possibility of ideological critique—an author's observation and imagination are not wholly constrained by his or her ideological predispositions.

Consider race or gender. An author has certain self-conscious beliefs about race or gender. He or she also imagines characters. Perhaps he or she begins with racial or gender types. But as he or she develops these characters—imagining their inner lives, for example, or drawing on characteristics of real people—they become increasingly individuated. As such, the stereotyping will tend to become less pronounced, in keeping with the general cognitive tendency for particular information to suppress generalizations (see Holland and colleagues 215). The result may be a set of characters who do not fit the stereotypes—even though the author may continue to assert those stereotypes explicitly.

Before continuing on to specific cases, it is worth making one final point about contradiction. Sometimes an author will have a sense of the contradictions he or she is expressing. Even if he or she has not fully recognized and formulated the problem, he or she may have a more or less vague feeling that something is not quite right. (Such a feeling is obviously in keeping with the operation of authorial receptive intent and evaluation.) This feeling often gives rise to forms of explicit or implicit elaboration in which the author seeks to reconcile possible difficulties in the ideas or emotions of the text. Such elaborations are, of course, encompassed by the implied author's final judgment of the work. Nonetheless, they often have the status of rationalizations and may diverge considerably from the patterns a critic may be able to isolate.

The Many Implicated Authors of *Uncle Tom's Cabin*

Uncle Tom's Cabin is, as Leslie Fiedler once remarked, "an astonishingly various and complex book" (*Love* 264). It is a sign of that complexity that it includes a good deal of discontinuity across its implicated authors. To a great extent, these are straightforward contradictions between overt general statement and particular narrative depiction. An obvious case of this is the view that Africans are not industrious—a view explicitly stated, but not borne out by the African characters. A more nuanced case concerns the putatively "childlike" quality of Africans. The comments about African lack of industry seem incidental to the work's purposes. In contrast, the view of Africans as children—equally contradicted by actual depictions—seems more important in implied authorial reasons.

Readers familiar with criticism of the novel will recognize that these points are closely related to debates about the work's politics and ideology. Some critics have condemned the novel, stressing its racialist comments. Others have praised its cultivation of sympathy, its real political effects,[10] and its feminist sensibilities. As Tawil puts it, "Perhaps the most enduring problem in Stowe criticism over the past several decades has been to find a way to analyze her most famous novel's assault on the practice of slavery, and at the same time to come up with some satisfying account of its particular brand of racialism" (154).

A common solution is to see the novel as manifesting "romantic racialism," in which racial differences are asserted, but in a nondemeaning way (see Frederickson; see also Otter). There is certainly an element of this in parts of Stowe's novel. In other words, this view does appear to have been held, self-consciously, by one or more implicated authors of the work.

The same point holds for Tawil's account of the novel's racialism. Tawil engages in a painstaking analysis, arguing that Stowe's racial ideology attributes to "the Negro" a highly imitative and malleable nature. There are some weaknesses in Tawil's analysis. For example, it is not clear that an ability to mimic (which characterizes some of the black characters) is the same thing as a susceptibility to influence. Indeed, self-conscious mimicry seems to suggest a degree of control over the imitation that is incompatible with malleability. More significantly, it is not clear that Tawil has gotten hold of the precise property at issue. It does not seem that Africans are centrally malleable in the novel. Rather, in certain contexts, the implied author understands Africans according to a childhood model. That model includes a propensity toward mimicry as well as some degree of malleability—or, put more positively, openness to change and development. (This model will be considered further below.) Nonetheless, it seems clear that Tawil is partially correct. He has isolated an aspect of implicated authorship in the novel—though only one such aspect.[11]

Early treatments of Stowe tended to be much less nuanced than those just mentioned. Referring to such interpretations, Cindy Weinstein laments that they "hermeneutically contained" the novel, creating "a critical paradigm in which Stowe can only be trapped or transcendent" (6). But even the more subtle, recent readings have something of this effect. A more complex, differentiated understanding of the implied author and implicated authors may help to preserve the insights of these discussions while avoiding the tendency toward reductive binarism.

A SIMPLE CONTRADICTION OF IMPLICATED AUTHORS

As just noted, one straightforward contradiction in the text involves the commonplace that Africans are not enterprising. In an apparent authorial intrusion, the narrator explains that Africans "are not naturally daring and enterprising" (108). In the following paragraph, the narrator elaborates on the point, claiming that "the African" is "naturally patient, timid, and unenterprising" (108). Later, St. Clare, often a ventriloquized voice of the implicated author, says that Africans need to be given "an idea of that industry and energy which is necessary to form them into men" (358). The idea is a commonplace of American racist ideology. Like much ideology bearing on group identities, it can be expressed in more or less demeaning terms. The more demeaning version is that "blacks are lazy." Stowe's narrator presents the same idea in the less overtly derisive form of "unenterprising." The difference is related to the explicit model of Africans as children (discussed below). Seeing Africans as children has a modulating effect on such racist attributions, since children may be educated and thus outgrow these putative inclinations.

What one finds here, then, is the implicated author expressing an ideological commonplace, modulated by a common model of Africans as children. This is what one would expect from a certain sort of liberal white attitude toward Africans.[12] But Stowe's novel communicates a much more complex attitude, for her representation of Africans—and, indeed, Europeans—seems entirely contradictory with this view. There are at least two ways in which one could construe "enterprising" or having "industry." The first is the simple pursuit of accumulating wealth. The second involves a broader sense of self-advancement and advancement of one's family, community, or society.

First consider the monetary construal. It is true that Africans are not generally presented in the novel as seeking to accumulate wealth. At the same time, Europeans are not generally presented that way. The whites who are represented as "enterprising" in this sense fall into a small number of categories, all of which are despicable. One character of this sort is Haley. Haley is the epitome of rational profit maximization. He is not particularly cruel to his slaves, but his treatment of them is guided entirely by the calculation of what will make them most salable. Stowe's implicit model here seems to be that of a machine, as Haley lacks natural life (Haley is "alive to nothing but trade and profit" [39]). The other obvious character of this accumulative sort is Legree. In contrast with Haley, Legree treats his slaves with consummate cruelty, exacting every drop of productive labor from them. In economic terms, the difference between them is that Haley profits by trade whereas Legree profits by production. Their different treatments of slaves and their different sorts of accumulative industry are the result of their different locations in the economy. Stowe's model for the productive sector, thus Legree, is explicit—he is Satan and his plantation is Hell.[13]

Before going on to the other, and more significant, sense of "enterprising," it is worth remarking on something about these two models. They are in part models explicitly or implicitly employed for Africans in white American racist ideology. The case of Satan is particularly clear. Blacks were commonly assimilated to devils in white racist ideology. Stowe reverses that standard characterization, which was based in part on the supposed blackness of devils. For Stowe, the proper application of the model is moral, not physical. While she draws many parallels between the slave-owning planter and Satan, the crucial one is that both are the antithesis of the moral ideal.

The more implicit mechanical model is no less significant to the themes of the novel. Of course, the machinelike nature of the capitalist had been a commonplace since at least the beginning of the Romantic movement (see, for example, Schiller). But it is particularly germane here because it represents Haley as a more or less feelingless object. This unfeeling quality is particularly stressed in connection with attachment relations, as when Mr. Shelby remarks that Haley would "sell his own mother at a good percentage" (39). Of course, within the system of slavery, it was precisely Africans who were treated as feelingless things, who would be untouched by the sale of mothers—or husbands or children (Stowe has characters repeat this view, which she clearly condemns; see 197). Moreover, Legree's attitude toward his slaves is precisely an attitude toward machinery. Its entire function is to produce. It is only right for such machinery to be used up in production (this being Legree's view of slaves [386–87]). After all, what is the point of saving and protecting your equipment? Thus, in this case too, Stowe is taking up a model that has operated against Africans and in the service of slavery (as shown by Legree). However, she is reversing it to apply to whites involved in the slave system.

But, of course, this is not the primary sense in which the implicated authors of Stowe's text are using words such as "enterprising" and "industry." When St. Clare speaks of training Africans in industry, he is suggesting that they need training for self-improvement or self-advancement, both individual and collective. But this simply does not fit the characterization of Africans elsewhere in the novel. For instance, in terms of advancing one's family, there could be no more striking case of such a commitment than Eliza escaping with Harry. Indeed, the characterization of African enterprise is quite general. A lovely instance is found in Dinah, the St. Clares' cook. Much to Ophelia's dismay, she shows the careless disregard for structure that was so celebrated in the romantic cult of genius. The results of her efforts are also in keeping with romantic accounts of genius. Her dinners are, St. Clare avers, "sublime" (241). Some readers may be inclined to take this as ironic. But there is nothing in the text to suggest this. Rather, it is important to take St. Clare's comment entirely seriously, as both an antiracist and antisexist claim. Clearly, a dinner does not have the enduring quality of a painting or a poem. But, Stowe suggests, cooking can manifest the same sort of aesthetic brilliance and creativity. Within the astonishingly narrow confines of possible self-cultivation, Dinah has manifested the very highest form of artistic industry.

The two characters who are most obviously relevant here, however, are Tom and George. Both are, in fact, remarkable for their industry and enterprise. For example, when Tom comes to the St. Clare home, he is struck by "the wasteful expenditure of the establishment." In contrast, St. Clare is "struck with [Tom's] soundness of mind and good business capacity" and ultimately "all the marketing and providing for the family were intrusted to" Tom (230). Indeed, subsequently, Ophelia explicitly characterizes Tom as "industrious" (369). Similarly, once George is free, he "devote[s] all his leisure time to self-cultivation" (487), eventually going to a university (491) and committing himself to work in Liberia (494).[14]

There are two particular incidents that stand out with these characters. With George, it is his youthful invention of "a machine for the cleaning of the hemp, which, considering the education and circumstances of the inventor, displayed quite as much mechanical genius as Whitney's cotton-gin" (13). This is industriousness of the highest order—or, rather, the highest order within the economic system. George here shows a keen devotion to advancing himself and the firm where he is employed.

Tom shows an even greater degree of industriousness toward the self-advancement of Africans. Despite the common use of the phrase "an Uncle Tom," Tom is deeply committed to the freedom of Africans.[15] This is shown by the culminating commitment of his life. He devotes himself fully to the protection of Emmeline and Cassy. He literally allows himself to be tortured to death, but he will not betray them and thus prevent them from escaping a life of slavery. If this is not properly spoken of as "enterprising," then it is a form of striving for social betterment that is elevated above enterprise and industry.

Here it is worth returning to the conceptual domains and models drawn on by Stowe. It is no accident that George exhibits his enterprising nature in a positive way by inventing a machine. This stands in direct contrast with the machinelike nature of the slave-trader Haley and the reduction of Africans to machines by Legree and other planters. It is not a metaphor, but a literal statement that contradicts the racist models that were pervasive at the time. The case of Tom is even more striking. If Legree represents the worst sort of striving, Tom represents the best. Just as Legree is metaphorically assimilated to Satan, one central model for Tom, noted by many critics, is Jesus (see, for example, Gilmore 72, Karcher 207, and Tompkins 138). Indeed, his death has liberatory consequences beyond Cassy and Emmeline, for it inspires young George Shelby to free all his slaves (see 498–500).

Finally, Stowe is careful to indicate that this is not simply a fictional idealization. The final chapter of the book includes a series of real cases, testimonies to the industry and enterprise of real Africans and people of mixed African and European ancestry (see 508–9). She also stresses that her characters are to a great extent based on real people (Stowe explains that she herself "or her friends have observed characters the counterpart of almost all that are here introduced" [500]). Moreover, George's invention is itself based on a real case (13n.).

Thus, it seems clear that the great weight of the novel is against the claim that Africans are unenterprising. Yet there does not seem to be anything suggesting irony in those passages where the unenterprising claim is made. The contradiction holds—even if the explicit statement is belied by virtually the entire narrative (in a very Lukácsian fashion).

IMPLICATED AUTHORS, THEMATIC ELABORATIONS, AND CONTRADICTION

Again, Stowe's articulation of racist ideology in this case is bound up with her use of a racist model—that Africans are children or are childlike. Statements about the supposedly childlike nature of Africans pervade the novel (see, for example, 33 and 83). They too are almost entirely inconsistent with her actual portrayal of Africans. The general operation of such a contradiction is clear from the case of industriousness. However, there are some significant properties of this particular contradiction that are worth considering.

First, as noted earlier, there are characters who seem to speak, at moments, with the voice of the author. But there are also characters who seem to represent the precise opposite of the author's view, characters that the author is clearly setting out to criticize. Marie St. Clare is one of the most mercilessly lampooned characters in the novel. She is pathologically self-obsessed, incapable of even basic empathy with others, hypocritical, superficial in her judgments, and unaffectionate even to her family—not to mention being hypochondriacal. She is also the one responsible for Tom being sold to Legree. Readers can expect anything coming out of Marie's mouth to be highly suspect. Yet Marie prominently asserts that her slaves are "children" and "childish" (197). This is an astonishing development that I am inclined to read as a highly localized yet sincere self-criticism on Stowe's part. It suggests, in other words, the employment of an implicated author to express a nagging self-doubt on the part of the real author, a doubt of roughly the form "Perhaps even I am not that different from Marie St. Clare."

But this apparent self-criticism is far from the only significant aspect of Stowe's development of this child model for Africans. As noted earlier, an author will sometimes elaborate on an ideological assertion in an attempt to reconcile it with contradictory depictions in the narrative. This is more likely to occur when the conflict is sharp and to some degree evident. The conflict between Stowe's statements about African childlikeness and her depictions of Africans is often quite stark.

For example, Stowe portrays Africans fairly consistently, not as more childish than whites, but as more parental than whites. One instance of this portrayal comes with the St. Clares. When Eva returns home after a long journey with her father, she runs to Marie shouting "Mamma!" However, Marie quickly disengages from her, complaining, "you make my head ache" (186). A moment later, the child spies her half-African nurse. She cries "Mammy!" and runs to the woman. As the narrator explains, "This woman did not tell her that she made her head ache, but, on the contrary, she hugged her, and laughed, and cried" (187). It is clear that Mammy is the motherly figure, not Mamma.

The point is not confined to older black women and young children. It applies to black and white men as well. Thus Tom's relation to Mr. Shelby does put Shelby in the social position of a patriarch. But the personal relation of the two men is the opposite of what one would predict from their social position, despite their relative similarity of age. This contrast is brought out strikingly in one scene. Shelby has sold Tom to Haley. Before Haley takes possession, Shelby tells Tom that, for the interim, "Go wherever you like, boy." Particularly to a modern reader, the "boy" seems gratuitous. However it sounded to the original readers of the novel, it clearly signals the childhood model of Africans. Tom responds by recounting a story. "I was jist eight years old," he explains, "when ole Missis put you into my arms and you wasn't a year old. 'Thar,' says she, 'Tom, that's to be *your* young Mas'r; take good care on him.'" Though Shelby replies "My good boy" (62), the anecdote makes clear that Tom is the real father there, not Shelby.

The sharpness of this contradiction makes it particularly likely that it will be troublesome for the author's receptive response. But the issue here is really why Stowe did not simply do away with the general statements linking Africans with children. Was she so wedded to the dominant racial ideology in this respect? Perhaps in a way she was. But in order to consider this topic more fully, it is necessary to consider the nature of ideology more fully.

As is well known, there are more and less derisive versions of ideology bearing on disprivileged or exploited groups. Indeed, there are commonly positive as well as negative aspects to stereotypes about such groups.[16] Both function generally to preserve social hierarchies. Despite this conservative function, it is sometimes possible to push the positive aspects of stereotypes to the point where they actually threaten the dominant social hierarchy. This is just what Stowe attempts to do with the ideology of African childlikeness.

Before elaborating on this, it is worth pointing out something that the preceding analysis does *not* imply. It does not imply that Stowe has no taint of paternalistic liberalism, no inclination to think of whites as adults and blacks as children. She almost certainly did have such tendencies. These would become dominant in certain contexts and certain moods. But she also undoubtedly had inclinations that contradicted this. The issue is, given that she clearly manifested strong inclinations to think of Africans not as children, but as parents, why did she not choose to eliminate expressions that clearly contradicted this? Part of the reason she did not eliminate these expressions is presumably that she partially accepted them. But, if this were sufficient, then the contradiction itself would presumably not appear so starkly. In other words, the belief would have more strongly affected her representation of blacks. Rather, part of the reason for Stowe's inclusion of the "Africans are children" model is that she was able to use the model counterideologically.

Specifically, Stowe's clear moral orientation in the book is Christian. She begins with the view that what is Christian is good and what goes against Christianity is bad. Moreover, she is envisioning an (implied) Christian readership who will at least potentially be swayed by an appeal to Christian principles. A well-known teaching of Jesus is that "unless you . . . become like little children, you will not enter the kingdom of God" (Matthew 18:3, *New American Bible*). The ideology that made Africans into children must necessarily have cut both ways for Stowe. It deprived Africans of worldly status; yet it also elevated their spiritual status. Even the good white characters lack the fully spiritual elevation of Tom. St. Clare has no religious feeling, and complains that it is "given to children and poor, honest follows, like" Tom. In response, Tom quotes the Biblical passage according to which God has "hidden from the wise" and "revealed unto babes" (343, referring to Luke 10:21). The passage clearly reveals the politically problematic nature of this model, since it excludes Tom from "the wise." But it suggests why Stowe would find a childhood model valuable for her political purposes as well. This complexity is revealed on the next page also, when St. Clare addresses Tom as "foolish boy" (thus the opposite of the wise man), but then goes on to link what Tom is trying to teach about Christianity with what St. Clare's (spiritually idealized) mother taught him.

Moreover, as Ashis Nandy has pointed out, one ideological use of the child model for Africans concerns their "civilizational" status. It is part of a large historical narrative in which the Eastern civilizations rose early in history, but are now old and decrepit. In contrast, African civilization is, according to this model, still in childhood. Only the European is adult, thus rightfully in charge of the superannuated Asian and the infantile African. A clear implication of this model is that European civilization will age and be replaced by Africa. However, this implication seems to have been developed only rarely. Stowe is one of the few writers to have recognized it.[17] Indeed, in what is almost certainly an authorial intrusion, she writes of Africa that "come it must, some time, her turn to figure in the great drama of human improvement." Then, she continues, "the negro race, no longer despised and trodden down, will, perhaps, show forth some of the latest and most magnificent revelations of human life." Indeed, "they will exhibit the highest form of the peculiarly *Christian life*" and God may even make "poor Africa . . . the highest and noblest in that kingdom which he will set up, when every other kingdom has been tried, and failed" (204). The idea is repeated later, ventriloquized through the voice of George Harris, who suggests that the development of African "civilization and Christianity" will be of "a higher type" than what went before (493). The point is perfectly logical in light of the generational model. If Europe superseded the East, then it follows that the child Africa will grow up to supersede an aging Europe.

But, again, this logic does not eliminate either the contradiction or the racist ideology. There is a degree of rationalization in these appeals to the Bible and to a putatively teleological element in history. Here, it is necessary to add yet another consideration, an emotional one. This consideration also does not entirely mitigate the racism of the model. But it helps to explain its rhetorical operation in the context of Stowe's novel. Stowe almost certainly wished to create among her (white) readers a protective attitude toward Africans, even a motherly attitude.[18] She repeatedly appeals directly to the parental feelings of readers, as when she writes, "If it were *your* Harry, mother . . . that were going to be torn from you by a brutal trader, to-morrow morning . . . how fast could *you* walk?" (56).¹⁹ The book presents very few true models for white readers to emulate, since so much of the book is aimed at fostering self-criticism among whites. But one of those characters is Rachel Halliday, who helps Eliza escape and "naturally" calls the escaped African "my daughter" (153). A childhood model of Africans thus had an emotional function for Stowe as an implied author as well: It should help to inspire parental care.

Though the contradictions and problems remain, this analysis suggests some of the political, moral, and emotional complexity of this aspect of the novel. It also leads to the issue of the overarching unity of reasons that give coherence to the implied author. This unity is inseparable from the emotions of parent–child relations and some of the ethical principles connected with those emotions.

THE IMPLIED AUTHORIAL COHERENCE OF *UNCLE TOM'S CABIN*

Clearly, *Uncle Tom's Cabin* is fundamentally an antislavery novel. To understand its implied authorial unity of reasons, then, one needs to begin by considering just what Stowe viewed as the most objectionable aspect of slavery. It was not the physical hardship, the beating, the backbreaking work. She certainly wishes readers to feel badly for the slaves subjected to such treatment. But that is not the central point of her horror at that institution. Her horror focuses rather on what slavery did to the most intimate relations of human life. I take it that Stowe herself is engaging in authorial ventriloquism when one of the characters states that "The most dreadful part of slavery, to my mind, is its outrages on the feelings and affections,—the separating of families, for example" (139). This is why the separations of husbands and wives, parents and children, brothers and sisters are the repeated, heart-rending scenes of the novel. As an affective scientist might put it today, for the implied author of *Uncle Tom's Cabin,* the greatest crime of slavery was its devastation of attachment relations, because they are the only things that can make bearable the physical miseries of slave-owners' brutality. Indeed, without the security of attachment relations, life is unbearable even if one is not subjected to brutality. Due to the nature of slavery, the slave was almost endlessly in a state of attachment deprivation or, at least, attachment vulnerability.

Today, many readers would probably note that spontaneous human empathy should have worked against the operation of slavery, and they might ask just what prevented it from doing so. Stowe in effect asked the same question, though inarticulately, without modern affective science to guide her. In the South, there was clearly some inhibition on empathy, a blocking of spontaneous response, particularly relating to the terrible pain of attachment violation. This blocking is manifest in the repeated statements of Southern whites that Africans simply do not form personal relations in the same way that white people do (see, for example, 197). It might seem, then, that this lack in Southern whites is the sum total of the problem. But Stowe's analysis of the problem is more subtle. She equally criticizes Northerners, not for blocking their empathy, but for feeling disgust at Africans. Ophelia is outraged by slavery and the treatment of slaves, which so prominently includes the violation of their attachment relations. But she is also repulsed to see Eva's attachment relation with an African, manifest in Eva's hugging and kissing Mammy (in fact, it "turned her stomach" [187]).

These points lead to the central ethical and political view of Stowe's implied author. From the beginning to the end of the book, despite the various contradictory ideas and attitudes of the implicated authors, there is a consistent implied authorial view that is both thematic and emotional. Specifically, the implied author holds two emotional/cognitive attitudes to have profound moral and social value. These attitudes are the opposites of the great Southern and Northern faults. The first great virtue is *attachment sensitivity.* This virtue is an ability to recognize attachment bonds, attachment anxieties, attachment needs, wherever they occur, in whatever identity group (here, whatever race). It is also an ability to value those bonds, not merely intellectually, but emotionally. It is the opposite of the empathic insularity that characterizes the emotional lives of so many Southern whites in Stowe's novel. The second great virtue in this work is *attachment openness.* This virtue is the willingness to accept and potentially reciprocate attachment bonds, again independent of the identity group to which the other person belongs. This openness is the opposite of feeling disgust at the thought of any intimacy with members of out-groups, the disgust that characterizes the righteous New Englander, Ophelia.[20] In short, there is implied authorial consistency here along with the implicated authorial inconsistency. Moreover, the consistency and the inconsistency are closely interrelated, both thematically and emotionally.

Profiles of Intentional Coherence, Implied Authorial Misdirection, and Filmic Narrators

The issues of multiplicity and coherence that arise in literature are only intensified and made more complex in film. Again, any given film is likely to have multiple implied authors. The preceding discussion indicates that these implied authors will themselves comprise multiple implicated authors. This multiplication of intentions, so salient in film, suggests a general, theoretical point. Just as each work has a profile of ambiguity, one may say that each work has a "profile of intentional coherence." In the case of film, one prominent part of that profile involves the distribution of productive and receptive intent across different individuals involved in the production process. As in the case of a profile of ambiguity, one can think of this in terms of a graph. In some cases, there will be fairly uniform contributions by many people, perhaps following general craft-based principles. This will give a relatively flat line. One could then say that the director, cinematographer, producer, and others were all contributing in fairly nondistinctive ways to the productive and receptive intent of the work. In contrast, some works could be envisioned as having one sharp peak marking the very distinctive contribution of a director who is perhaps the screenwriter and producer as well, or who greatly influenced the emotional and thematic orientation of the screenplay and the cinematography. There are also possibilities for two or three such peaks.

In addition to this profile across all those involved in the production of a film, there is also a profile of intentional coherence for implicated authors. This is true for both literary works and films. However, a film is shorter than a novel. In other words, a filmmaker can watch a rough cut of his or her film in a couple of hours. A novelist may take several days to read a draft of his or her novel. Put very simply, a filmmaker is less likely to forget details of part one when viewing part three forty-five minutes later (in contrast with a novelist who may read part three two or three days after reading part one). As such, in film, there is less scope for variation in authorial receptive intent. As with literature, different attitudes, models, and so on, arise in different contexts. Sometimes these can vary radically. However, it is perhaps relatively easy for an author to fail to recognize contradictions across a large novel (which, again, may take many hours to read across many days). Such a failure should be more difficult when the span of time is two hours. Indeed, this point holds generally. Thus one would expect less divergence of implicated authors in short stories than in novels and very little in lyric poems. On the other hand, in the case of film, the actual production is very complex and reconciling parts may be very difficult. If an author sees a problem between two scenes in a novel, he or she only needs to rewrite. If a filmmaker sees a problem between scenes in a film, he or she may have to raise money for extra days of shooting. Indeed, if the crew has already dispersed, even money may not suffice. Thus there are complications in the nature of cinematic implicated authorship as well.

Finally, there is another possible level of intentional inconsistency. Richard Maltby has discussed the ways in which some scenes in Hollywood movies project two audiences based on age and moral attitude. One may add that they project different implied or implicated authors as well. Consider, for example, a sequence of scenes in which two people are alone. There is a fade to black. When the image returns, they are lounging in different chairs, jackets removed, collars unbuttoned, and one is leaning back and smoking. In at least some cases, a sequence of this sort has two meanings, thus two implied authors/implied audiences. In one, it suggests sexual relations. In the other, it suggests only informality after some passage of time. Often, this difference may simply be part of the ambiguity of the work. In some cases, however, there may be a "true" alternative, thus a privileged implied author and a privileged implied audience. Brian Richardson has recently explored differences in implied readers, noting that "there is often a distinct hierarchy among these readers" such that "one reader knows both what the other perceives and what it alone can know" ("Singular Text" 263).[21]

Chapter 1 considered the case of someone running for office who wished to conceal his own views. This involves insincerity. But it does not involve any complexity in the implied author. If Sloe wants to project an image of being anticolonial, then the implied author of his speeches is anticolonial even if the real author is not. But now suppose that Sloe wants to appear anticolonial to some voters, but wants other voters to understand his real (colonialist) views. In that case, he projects two audiences and two implied authors. One implied author so to speak *subsumes* or *encompasses* the other. Specifically, the colonialist implied author is the *genuine implied author,* whereas the anticolonialist implied author is a *pseudo-implied author.* Put differently, the work is designed to produce a certain sort of misreading for a particular group. It is designed to lead some people to interpret an ironic narrator as the implied author. One may say that this is a form of implied authorial multiplicity that occurs through *misdirection.*[22]

This sort of misdirection certainly occurs in literature. But it is perhaps more obvious in film, in part because films involve large investments of money and are (in general) more tightly regulated by governments. The financial investment involved in a film often means that real authors have to be much more concerned with the potential financial success of their final product, thus the breadth of audience reception. Regulation by governments means that filmmakers must be very sensitive to the sorts of representation that would be likely to trigger censorship.

The precise operation of misdirection is, of course, bound up with processes of narration. Here, too, there are differences between literature and film. Specifically, as a number of writers have indicated, the primary selection of information given to the film audience is perceptual. As, for example, Scholes and Kellogg note, film "does not present a story directly, without narration, but always through the medium of a controlled point of view, the eye of the camera, which sharpens or blurs focus, closes up or draws off, gives the image its color and shading, and provides, through its synchronous sound track, a continuous commentary of words, music, noise or silence, along with the voices of the dramatis personae" (280). The agency of this selection may be referred to as the "perceptual narrator." As discussed in chapter 2, the perceptual narrator may be distinguished from the verbal narrator. The latter is always the narrator in verbal art.

Gregory Currie has argued against the ubiquity of narration in film. It is worth considering this briefly before continuing. Currie's argument is roughly that the perceptual aspects of the film cannot be the text produced by a narrator. That would be possible only if one assumes that the narrator "has gone to the trouble of recreating" the events "on camera, spending millions of dollars, employing famous actors," and so on (22). First, even if true, this is beside the point. The important thing is that information from the (author-created) storyworld has been selected and organized in the film presentation. The audience is not given some sort of direct and all-encompassing access to the storyworld. That selection and organization are narrator functions. Second, the fiction of film is that we are actually seeing the characters, etc., not that we are seeing actors playing the characters. Whatever we decide is the status of the narrator's "text," it does not involve "employing famous actors." Finally, there is no reason to suppose that the perceptual narrator is confined to real-world filmmaking constraints in presenting images, whether of actors or of characters. Readers accept that a verbal narrator can know peoples' thoughts or recount long stretches of prehistory or be in two places at once. There is no reason to suddenly become strict realists when it comes to perceptual representation.

Despite these theoretical issues, perceptual narration is, in some ways, fairly straightforward. Verbal narration, however, is more obscure in film. In order to understand cinematic verbal narration, it is useful to draw a couple of distinctions. First, one may distinguish the *frame narrator* from the *commentator narrator*. The frame narrator is a (visible) character, voice-over,[23] or text that sets up an embedded story. When that narrator is a character, one is inclined to think that the frame narrator is the narrator of the embedded story. However, he or she is rarely if ever the perceptual narrator (that would be the case only if the story were presented entirely through point-of-view shots). Indeed, often the frame narrator merely serves as a transition to an independent story. If the embedded narrative retains some relation to a personified frame narrator, it is often through focalization. Indeed, the frame narrator often has very little impact on the viewer's ongoing response to an embedded narrative. In contrast, a commentator narrator may repeatedly qualify or explain what the viewer is seeing or hearing, thus modulating his or her perceptual response. This commonly occurs through a voice-over. Often, the two forms of narration are combined and the commentator narrator is identified with the frame narrator. Indeed, where there is a personified frame narrator and a personified commentator narrator, they are almost always the same.

Finally, it is worth noting that there is usually a significant difference between a verbal narrator that is vocal and one that is textual. The textual narrator gives, for example, identifying titles (such as "New York City, September 10, 2001"). In comparison with the vocal narrator, he or she is much more likely to be entirely nonpersonified and omniscient. The vocal narrator may present the same content (i.e., the same words). But the very fact that this content is generated by a distinctive human voice tends to give it an air of personification, even when there is no information about that individual.

By default, viewers tend to assume that nonpersonified narrators—particularly perceptual narrators—are trustworthy. As Margolin writes, "If anonymous," the narrator's "voice is equated with the voice of truth" ("Person" 423) or, as MacCabe puts it, "a visual discourse . . . guarantees truth" (11). Viewers only question the reliability of the perceptual narrator when given reason to do so. Typically, this occurs when the perceptual narrator is in some way personified, as when viewers are informed that they are seeing a character's dream. But there are cases where a nonpersonified narrator may be problematic. Such cases may be involved with the projection of multiple implied authors. Indeed, a problematic nonpersonified narrator is sometimes crucial for the creation of implied authorial misdirection. Kabir Khan's *New York* presents a subtle case of this sort, relying on the interplay of different types of narrator.

Narrators and Implied Authors in Kabir Khan's *New York*

The film begins with panoramic shots of New York behind the titles. The use of perceptual narration is not necessarily consistent in any given film. Moreover, the titles sequence is often visually and aurally separate from the rest of the film. Nonetheless, if this indicates anything about the perceptual narrator,[24] it suggests a sort of godlike omniscience as the viewer is taken through various visual perspectives not ordinarily available to real people. The titles sequence ends with the camera following a yellow taxicab. This begins to hint at surveillance and a sort of "omniscience" that is not associated with God, but with the police. Indeed, this impression is quickly verified when the camera cuts to a second perspective, revealing an FBI helicopter.

Another cut gives a clear POV shot from the helicopter, again tracking the taxi. Now the audience hears words transmitted to the inside of the helicopter, an oral report of the movement of the taxi. The effect here is of a gradual narrowing of the knowledge of the narrator, from the apparently divine omniscience at the start, to the complex of particular, observing and communicating FBI agents. Among other things, this gives the chase both a sinister or foreboding quality (already foreshadowed by the music of the titles sequence) and a possible sense of human fallibility.

Subsequently, the perceptual narrator moves to street level; the black opacity of the limousine following the taxi repeats that of the FBI helicopters. The entire sequence is ambiguous between an Orwellian vision of massive governmental observation and a heroic image of smart and painstaking police work foiling a dangerous plot. This ambiguity, with its associated emotional ambivalence, continues through much of the opening of the film. It is undoubtedly part of the receptive intention of the implied author and it begins to suggest a tacit simulation of distinct implied audiences—one inclined to worries over state terror, the other to worries over nonstate terror.

In a massive show of force, the taxi is surrounded by FBI vehicles. Members of a SWAT team, almost all white, pour out of the vans, training their rifles on the driver. The officer in charge barks orders at the driver, a pudgy Middle Eastern man. In apparent confusion, he asks what he has done. The officer immediately has the trunk of the car opened. It contains weapons. The man protests that they are not his. The officer orders his subordinates, "Get rid of him!"

The scene is fascinating in a number of ways. It suggests a certain sort of temporal complexity to the implied author. Specifically, I suspect that the director's receptive intent here runs along the following lines: Initially, the viewer is uncertain as to the precise nature of this action. Again, some viewers will be inclined to assume a heroic story of police officers foiling crime or terrorism. Others will be inclined to infer the Orwellian tale of massive governmental surveillance. But both will initially take the discovery of weapons to "confirm" the first, heroic reading. Subsequently, however, the audience learns that the FBI has planted the evidence to coerce the cab's owner, Omar, into serving as an FBI spy. In retrospect, it is clear that the driver's protests were sincere. Moreover, the speed with which the officer moves to opening the trunk appears suspicious. How did they know precisely where the weapons would be? Finally, after the detailed treatment of FBI torture later in the film, the officer's order, "Get rid of him!" appears ominous.

This opening sequence suggests the complexity of the perceptual narrator's relation to the implied author, and it indicates that there may be particular sorts of temporal extension for implicated authors. Specifically, the author, on the one hand, simulates the moment-by-moment interpretation and response of a viewer. On the other hand, he or she also simulates such a viewer's recurring revision and reconsideration of earlier inferences and feelings. Those revisions may reflect initial uncertainties or indeterminacies in the meaning or emotional force of the work. In other words, as one views a section of the narrative, one may favor one of the ambiguous possibilities. However, later events may lead one to favor another possibility. That change is part of implied authorial intention. Putting the point technically, one might say that the profile of ambiguity for a work may involve *initial* and *retrospective* implicated authors.

The general idea is hardly a new one. It is widely recognized that viewers and readers come to reinterpret earlier sections of a work in light of later information. The point here is primarily a theoretical one about the nature of that reinterpretation and its relation to local and global implied authorial intentions.

The following scene presents the SWAT team breaking into someone's home and training their laser-guided rifles at his head. Here, too, there is the same ambiguity between efficient crime-prevention and governmental terrorism. The film cuts to FBI headquarters in New York. The audience sees the man who was just arrested, Omar, first through a video surveillance camera. The examining officer, a Hindi/Urdu-speaking Indian, serves at this point as the voice of the implied author explaining that, by the provisions of the PATRIOT Act, Omar has virtually no legal rights. Indeed, he indicates that the usual presumption of innocence is reversed in such cases and the "detainee" is responsible for proving his or her innocence.

The interrogator, Roshan, wants Omar to tell him in particular about his school friend "Sam." Here, there is a sort of teasing ambiguity as well, since Sam could be a European or Jewish American. As it turns out, he too is Muslim—Samir Shaikh.

Roshan's question about Sam leads to an embedded narration frame in which Omar begins to recount his arrival at New York State University. The perceptual narration cuts to the university, presumably seven years earlier. Omar is having his photo taken at a large sign for the university, giving a peace sign. The brief scene suggests Omar's perhaps naïve enthusiasm on his first visit to America.

The embedded story begins with the continuation of the verbal narration, seamlessly moving from frame narrator to commentator narrator. However, when Omar meets the fourth main character, Maya, the commentary stops and the viewer is entirely immersed in the embedded storyworld. Khan marks this in the aural presentation of dialogue. Omar had exchanged a few words with the young woman who took his photograph earlier. But the volume of that dialogue was roughly at the level of the background, suggesting that it was part of the perceptual narration, but not the information explicitly communicated in the dialogue of the frame story. When he begins to speak with Maya, however, the dialogue has the same volume as the narrative commentary, which it replaces, as the nondiegetic music is reduced to the level of background accompaniment. Perhaps even more important than the aural cues, there are several POV shots from Omar's perspective. These partially serve to provide a transition between the commentator narration and the internal focalization[25] on Omar in the embedded storyworld. Techniques of this sort are common in films, signaling shifts in narration, though viewers, it seems, rarely notice them self-consciously.

The next sequence introduces Sam. Sam is involved in an apparently wacky college competition. But it has obvious thematic resonance. There is an annual race to see who can raise the U.S. flag most quickly. Showing great physical prowess, Sam wins. More importantly, the film shows him proudly gesturing toward the flag. The suggestion is that his pride is not only in winning the contest, but in being American. The perceptual narrator not only presents this information. That narrator frames Sam's relation to the flag in a stereotypical posture of a national hero. This is one of moments in the film designed to show that Sam is "all-American" (as he later calls himself).

Subsequent scenes present the developing friendship of Sam, Maya, and Omar, particularly stressing Sam's all-American qualities. In keeping with this, his multicultural and multiracial pals play football on a field with the twin towers prominent in the background. This unobtrusive selection of information serves to highlight that this is before September 11. These scenes generally stress his heroic excellence as well. Omar explains that Sam was good at sports, spoke well, and was a good student. In one sequence, he rescues Maya's purse from a mugger and is wounded in the process. In part because of these virtues, but in part simply because he is sweet and charming, Maya is in love with him. This last point provokes Omar's jealousy. That jealousy is continually suggested as a possible underlying motive for Omar's subsequent cooperation with the FBI. Finally, this entire sequence serves to establish the hopefulness of these young people who anticipate a happy, well-integrated life as Americans in America.

A peculiarity of this part of the film involves the relation between the Indian Americans, on the one hand, and European Americans, on the other. In one rather strange scene, Sam and Omar speak in Hindi while their European American friends join the dialogue speaking English. There are several ways in which one could read this scene. It could be that the viewer is supposed to assume that the whole conversation is in English (even though Sam and Omar are actually speaking Hindi). This would take up a common convention—what allows ancient Greeks to speak English in an American movie about ancient Greece. But this does not fit the fact that the white characters are clearly speaking English. Alternatively, one could assume that the white characters actually understand Hindi. But that seems empirically unlikely and there is no evidence that they ever speak it. Finally, it may suggest that this portrayal of pre–September 11 America is inaccurate, an idealization designed to make a point about what happened in post–September 11 America. More exactly, this may suggest two audiences for the implied author, thus two implied authors (one genuine implied author and one pseudo-implied author). For one audience, this discrepancy is invisible. They should simply accept the utopian vision. For the other audience, this discrepancy serves primarily to prepare the viewer for an untrustworthy epilogue that follows the main action of the film.

After this, Roshan explains that the FBI suspects Sam of operating a terrorist sleeper cell in New York. He also accuses Omar of being part of that cell. However, this already seems highly unlikely, given the attenuated relations between Omar and Sam in the intervening years. Omar shouts that Roshan is framing him. The audience subsequently learns that this is indeed the case.

Generally, the internal focalization on Omar is limited to perception. However, the audience is at this point given fragmentary access to some of his internal thoughts as he remembers Roshan's claims and accusations. This leads to a recollection of Sam's defeat of the mugger and Maya's confession of her love for Sam. The context leads the viewer to assume this is a recollection by Omar. But here something else strange happens. Omar stops seeing Maya and Sam with the excuse that school is about to end and he is packing. As Omar is explaining this to Maya, he hears a scream. They run into a common room on campus and witness many distraught students watching the breaking news about the destruction of the twin towers. The Middle Eastern and South Asian students are as overwhelmed with sorrow as the European students. The scene ends with a transition to frame narration in which Omar is announcing that this day changed everything.

The problem here is no doubt obvious to every reader. The school year (in both the United States and India) ends in early summer. The events of September 11 took place on September 11. It is very difficult not to interpret this as a deliberate challenge to the reliability of Omar's memories. In itself, that is not terribly theoretically interesting. However, it again suggests that the idealization of America prior to this moment of complete change is to some degree problematic. The point has consequences for the ending (which does not involve personified narration of any sort).

In the following scene, Roshan threatens both Omar and his family. He thereby coerces Omar into cooperating with the FBI in an investigation of Sam. Omar soon manages a (seemingly) chance meeting with Maya, who is now married to Sam. They have a young son to whom Sam is a devoted and loving father. Following his FBI cover story as a radicalized militant, Omar convinces Sam that he desires some sort of revenge against America. Sam then introduces Omar to his friends. It turns out that Sam is indeed running a sleeper cell. To test Omar, Sam has him actually kill someone—an act that Omar carries out, with the subsequent approval of his FBI contact.

This leads to Sam's story of the preceding seven years. Before going on to this, however, it is important to mention another character—Zilgai. Maya is working in a law office giving legal aid to people who were detained and tortured following the September 11 events. The audience hears the testimony of Zilgai. He explains the various techniques used by his interrogators. Many of these techniques are familiar to viewers from reports on Abu Ghraib and Guantanamo.

Sam's story in effect corroborates that of Zilgai. The main difference is that Zilgai's story is a testimony spoken into a camera operated by Maya. In contrast, Sam serves as a frame narrator for the perceptual narration of an embedded story. The framing narration is delivered beneath a waving American flag, selected by the perceptual narrator in parallel with the scene where Sam is introduced. He prefaces the story by referring to himself as formerly "all-American" and now a "terrorist," asking, how did the change occur? In the frame, he explains that it was ten days after September 11 and he was taking a train to meet Maya. The film then cuts to the flashback. The perceptual narrator shows Sam looking at the train schedule. A woman approaches and leads him to an empty part of the station where he is hooded and handcuffed. He is subsequently taken to a detention facility, stripped, and chained to a chair. The perceptual narration shows the dogs outside the facility, the barred doors closing, the clothing being cut from his body. The perspective is clearly not that of Samir, since the audience sees these things while his eyes are covered by the hood. However, at least the central images are information inferentially available to Samir as he would have heard the dogs, the clanking of the doors, the slicing of the scissors, just as the audience hears them. In this way the perceptual narrator does not present Samir's optical point of view, but does presumably present his auditory point of view and his (inferential) knowledge of the situation.

Finally, the hood is removed and the interrogation begins. Sam is accused of involvement in the terrorist attacks because he took photographs of the twin towers. Despite his explanation of the photos as work for a class—and despite the more important fact that photos of the towers hardly constitute criminal or even suspicious activity—Sam is still presumed guilty and tortured. The commentator (Samir in a voice-over) explains that he was one of 1,200 people who were subjected to this treatment. Subsequently, the audience is shown the various tortures reported by Zilgai and others—waterboarding (suffocating with water-soaked cloths), hanging by the wrists, sleep deprivation through blaring music and lights, guards urinating on his hooded face and leaving him for the night to choke on the urine. The mutually re-enforcing nature of the perceptual and verbal narrations tends to enhance the viewer's sense of their reliability—not only with respect to the storyworld, but with respect to the real world as well.

The perceptual narration reveals a clear change in Sam. At first, he is defiant and self-confident. By the end, he is weeping and helpless. This is what first makes him susceptible to the suggestion of joining a militant organization. (Another prisoner tells him what he can do if he wishes to take back his "izzat" or honor, precisely what is taken away in humiliation.) When he is finally released after nine months in detention, he is listless and deeply traumatized. The perceptual narration presents what are apparently nightmares derived from the torture and show his clear susceptibility to anxiety and concrete fear. With Maya's support, Sam regains confidence and enters back into life in the world. But his attempt to find a job leads only to further humiliation as employers reject him, perhaps because he is Muslim or perhaps because they have been informed of his detention. He eventually makes the terrorist contact suggested to him in prison.

Omar confronts Roshan with Samir's detention and torture. Roshan admits that Samir was not a terrorist, that no one could remain the same after such an experience, and that following this detention and torture Samir became what he was not previously, a terrorist.[26] Omar then says that such torture and detentions have produced terrorism. For a moment, Roshan is silent. He then gives a speech about how he is Muslim and that he is deeply pained by Muslims leaving the way of peace. Indeed, he goes so far as to say that if one supports Islam, one supports peace. He then explains that only in the United States could he be put in charge of such a sensitive case, even as a Muslim.

The scene is fascinating because it is difficult to say just how it should be read in relation to the implied author. On the one hand, there is some truth to what Roshan is saying. Whatever the U.S. government has done to some innocent people, that does not justify killing other innocent people. At the same time, the ringing support of peace seems, at best, forced. It comes from the mouth of someone whose profession is inseparable from violence. The point is particularly clear in context, since Roshan has just finished telling Omar that it was perfectly fine for him to shoot a man. Moreover, while the United States does provide many opportunities, it is simply false that governments never employ members of a targeted, "enemy" group in their attack on that group. Indeed, employing collaborationists is fairly routine. Moreover, the viewer already knows that his ability to speak Hindi/Urdu is crucial for his work on this case. There is also the obvious fact that there are plenty of countries in the world where Muslims hold such positions—not only Muslim-majority countries, but even countries where they are a discriminated-against minority, such as India.

My own inclination is to read the scene in one of two ways. The first possibility is that this is genuinely dialectical. In other words, there is one implied author and he or she is suggesting the moral complexity of the problem. There is no moral complexity to torture—it is wrong. There is no moral complexity to terrorism—it is wrong. But judgments about individual people are often more difficult than judgments about their acts.

The other possible reading is that there are two implied authors here. One implied author accepts Omar's accusations; the other accepts Roshan's rebuttal. In this case, it is difficult to discern just where the subsuming or encompassing implied author may come out. The viewer can only get a fuller sense of this retrospectively, at the end of the film.

Most of the remaining story concerns the development of Sam's terrorist plot. It turns out that he has managed to have his company hired to clean the FBI building. He explains to Omar that he has no interest in killing random people. His fight is with the FBI, so he is attacking them. The argument is not without plausibility. However wrong, it shows that Sam is, in some ways, morally (or perhaps merely intellectually) superior to his antagonists. He is not striking out at, say, European Christians or at some other identity group, blaming everyone in that group for what he suffered. He is, rather, striking at the institution that tortured him and that subsequently continued those heinous practices.

The climax of the film comes with the attempted bombing of the FBI building. The plot nearly succeeds. Indeed, it is foiled due only to coincidence. This indicates that the apparently ubiquitous FBI surveillance is just as much of a failure at preventing terrorism as is detention and torture. The coincidence is that Maya happens to be in the FBI building. She has agreed to cooperate with the FBI to prevent a terrorist attack. She happens to see Sam outside the building. When Sam is informed of

Maya's presence, he cannot detonate the explosives. He drops the detonator and is immediately shot many, many times by the FBI, although he is no longer a threat. Just before the firing begins, Maya runs toward Sam. She is therefore killed as well. Roshan receives a medal for preventing a terrorist attack, although the FBI created the terrorist and the terrorist himself decided not to detonate the explosives.

The movie is to this point an utterly despairing tragedy. The FBI brutalizes an innocent, and indeed heroic, man. This and broader social isolation lead him to terrorism. The FBI actually fails to learn of an attack he is planning and it is only by chance that he himself decides to call it off. At this point, FBI agents murder him and his wife, orphaning their young child. The final result is that the very agency responsible for this brutality is celebrated.

This leads to the ending. The transition is marked by a single title, a very minimal textual narrator that reports a time lapse, "Six months later." After this, there is only a perceptual narrator. With no personified narrator, it may seem that there could be no discrepancy between the narrator and the implied author. In other words, it may seem that, when not personified, the perceptual narrator could not be untrustworthy. However, the ending of *New York* suggests something else. The final scene begins with Danyal, the son of Maya and Sam, happily playing baseball. Omar has taken over the role of his father and everything seems perfectly fine. Danyal has not changed in any visible way since his parents were murdered. Roshan comes to the baseball game. Initially, Omar is cold. But Roshan delivers another speech about the marvelous opportunities given by this country. He goes so far as to claim that the work of the FBI has enabled a Muslim boy (Danyal) to play on an American team and be celebrated, even though his father was a terrorist. Roshan meets Danyal, who is immediately drawn to this friendly stranger. Danyal invites Roshan to join them for dinner and the three go off together as friends.

The ending takes up some of the uncertainties from earlier in the film. The utopian vision of the United States is here again, though it presents a post- rather than pre-9/11 utopia. As noted earlier, there are hints that this utopian vision may be mistaken with respect to the period before September 11. Is it possible that the implied author really feels that the country has fully overcome those problems—that prejudice against Muslims has really been so eradicated, that there would be no bias against someone known to be the son of a terrorist? Then there is the personal story of Danyal—is it really plausible that he would be so totally unaffected by the murder of both his parents?

Perhaps this is, instead, a case of implied authorial misdirection, thus a dual implied author for a dual implied reader. For one implied author, thus for one audience, this is a perfectly plausible conclusion, one entirely fitting to the situation in the United States after the initial hysteria of September 11 declined. But for another implied author and audience, this is straightforwardly ironic. The personal emotional relations are incredible; the social situation is idealized beyond recognition.

One possible reason for this split is that the subsuming or genuine implied author holds to the position of the second implied author, but has to assuage the sensibilities of precisely the forces that brutalized Sam. Put simply, the first implied author may be understood as implied for the FBI, the CIA, and their supporters in the general population. This possibility actually has a polarizing effect on one's understanding of these two implied authors. Conditions in the United States diverge from the happy communal harmony depicted in the film precisely to the extent that the subsuming implied author fears retribution for his portrayal of the FBI.

The film ends with the more significant introduction of a textual narrator. Again, textual narrators are generally judged highly trustworthy. Given no reason to believe otherwise, one's default response to a textual narrator is to see it as the voice of the (subsuming or genuine) implied author. In this case, the textual narrator explains that more than 1,200 "men of foreign origin" were detained and tortured after September 11. It goes on to state that the government did not find evidence linking any of them to the September 11 attacks. The textual narrator notes that "Eventually, more than a 1000 were released." The statement seems to suggest a sort of reconciliation. However, it also suggests that some 200 of these men—along with many others like them—remained imprisoned at the time of the film's making. Moreover, "To this date, most of [those released] suffer from depression and stress . . . and have not been able to focus enough to hold a job . . ." (ellipsis marks in the original).

These statements arguably make the preceding scene almost entirely implausible. They may even suggest that viewers should disregard the scene, just as they would disregard anything inserted at the insistence of a censor. Of course, one may disagree about whether the textual narrator's challenge to the perceptual narration here is that extreme. However, the point at least suggests that discounting a nonpersonified perceptual narrator is possible, even to the extent of disregarding an entire plot sequence without any replacement. At the very least, this seems to be part of the film's profile of ambiguity. In other words, this profile includes at least the possibility of implied authorial misdirection. Put somewhat simply, the film should lead one audience to infer an implied author who represents a post–September 11 "overreaction" and who now sees that "overreaction" as a historical incident that the nation has overcome. Indeed, for that audience, the implied author is a sort of cheerleader for the United States. However, at the same time, the film suggests another implied author. This second implied author believes that the terrible actions of the U.S. government after September 11 have not been resolved. Moreover, this implied author may even feel that there is enough remaining danger that he must conceal his real views and in effect wrap himself in the American flag.

The film does conclude with a moment of hope. Specifically, the textual narrator reports that "On the 22nd of January 2009, just two days after being sworn in as the new President of the United States of America, Barack Obama signed an order to shut down the infamous symbol of detention and torture, Guantanamo Bay." It seems clear that the (subsuming) implied author did see the possibility of a future that was at least better, if not necessarily utopian. The real author has undoubtedly been deeply disappointed by what has actually been done by the Obama administration since that time.[27]

Conclusion

In sum, both productive and receptive choices by an author are the result of complex *mental causes.* Some of those causes are also narratively, emotionally, or thematically justified—thus reasons. Some implied authorial reasons are *thematized* in that the author is able to articulate them accurately. Many others are *theoretically specifiable.* Thus critics can in principle articulate these reasons by relating patterns in the author's work to abstract knowledge not available to the author.

The unity of a work comes, first of all, from the enduring emotional attitudes and thematic commitments of the textual implied author as these are manifest in his or her final judgment that a work is complete. However, that final authorial response does not necessarily reconcile all authorial receptive responses to the work. An author does not read and evaluate a work in a timeless "now." He or she responds to a work not only globally, but locally as well, not only as a whole, but moment by moment. These local authorial receptions define "implicated authors." The striking feature of implicated authorship is that it entails different sorts of continuity and discontinuity. The highest level of continuity is encompassed in the implied author. But implicated authorial views form various patterns of coherence and contradiction on their own.

The most obvious type of implicated authorial contradiction involves incompatibility between particular developments of story events or character traits, on the one hand, and self-conscious generalizations, on the other. These generalizations are often expressed by authorial intrusions (through the narrator) or authorial ventriloquism (through characters). Contradictions of this sort may operate in any ideological direction. For example, opposition to dominant racist ideology, articulated in authorial intrusions, may be belied by racist portraits. But, by the same token, dominant racist ideology may surface in the overt statements only to be contradicted by the more nuanced and humane depictions of characters. When sensitive to contradictions, authors may elaborate on the self-conscious statements, often producing rationalizations rather than expressing actual justificatory reasons. Contradictions may also arise across different story events or character portraits. These more particular contradictions are often due to changing contexts and the resulting shifts in cognitive models.

Uncle Tom's Cabin manifests contradictions of implicated authorship, particularly between overt statements and depictions. Perhaps the most striking case of such a contradiction concerns the putatively childlike character of Africans. Stowe elaborated on this idea by drawing out the implications of the racist model of Africans as children—including implications that are inconsistent with the ideology of white supremacy. (These implications are made possible in part by the fact that dominant ideologies about exploited groups commonly have both negative and positive versions.) Perhaps most importantly, she used the model of Africans as children to foster parental emotions in her white readers. In doing so, she also sought to foster the two primary virtues that tacitly guided her implied authorial ethics. These are, first, attachment sensitivity, or enhanced empathy toward the attachment vulnerabilities of others, and, second, attachment openness or emotional availability for the formation of attachment relations, particularly attachment relations with members of despised groups.

Film further complicates the issues surrounding implied and implicated authorship. Again, films have many authors. Moreover, any film author shares the local diversity found in implicated literary authors. There are two variables affecting this local diversity. The first is simply length. Shorter works tend to produce less diversity in implicated authorship; thus films will tend to have a higher degree of unified implied authorship than novels. Second, and partially balancing the first variable, some works are more difficult to alter than others. It is much more onerous to reshoot and edit a scene in a film than to rewrite a scene in a novel.

The study of film in this context also gives prominence to several further types of authorial multiplicity. The first is the "profile of intentional coherence." As discussed in the preceding chapter, one cannot simply say that a film has a single implied author. On the other hand, it makes even less sense to claim that every collaborator contributed equally (e.g., the caterer who made the sandwiches for a scene is probably not as interpretively significant an implied author as the screenwriter). Rather, any given film involves a complex set of relations among contributors. In some cases, there will be a fairly broad distribution of intentional coherence. Thus, in some cases, the screenwriter, director, producer, cinematographer, main actors and actresses, and so on, will all be similarly interpretively relevant. In other cases, however, there will be one or two more prominent peaks (often including one for the director). This profile is also affected by the diversity of implicated authorship. Thus, again, the implied director himself or herself manifests multiplicity. Generally, the profile of intentional coherence for a literary work is only of the second sort (i.e., a matter of implicated authorship). Exceptions occur in cases of collaboration or in instances where an editor has made truly extensive changes in a literary work.

Beyond this, there are cases where there may be multiple implied authors in a work. Or, rather, there are cases where the implied author distinguishes two (or more) sets of implied readers. This implied author then may misdirect one group of implied readers to infer a particular (pseudo-)implied author, typically by identifying an ironic nonpersonified narrator as the implied author. He or she then properly directs a second group to understand the implied author quite differently (and correctly), typically while also recognizing that many other readers will infer a very different implied author; in this way, the genuine implied author subsumes or encompasses the pseudo-implied author. This division is most prominent in theme, but occurs also in emotional force and even in storyworld construction. The multiplication of implied authors or the misdirection of implied author inference is not confined to film. However, it may be more prominent in film due to the commercial need to reach a broad audience and due to possibilities for censorship.

Isolating implied authorial misdirection in film is connected with understanding the nature and operation of cinematic narration. First, one needs to distinguish the perceptual narrator, the selector of visual and auditory information. Second, one needs to distinguish different types of verbal narrator. One distinction is between vocal and textual narrators, that is, narrators who speak and narrators who supply text—main titles, intertitles, superimposed identifications (e.g., "Delhi 1947"), and so on. Among speaking narrators, frame narrators may be distinguished from commentators. Frame narrators provide a transition between a frame and an embedded narrative. They are most often personified and explicitly introduced in some frame story. That introduction commonly suggests that they narrate the main story. However, they rarely do. They may become focalizers or commentators. Commentator narrators provide voice-overs or silent-film intertitles at points in the course of a film. These are often personified. But they need not be (thus they may be comparable to nonpersonified verbal narrators in fiction). Still, the mere fact of an individual voice tends to give commentator narrators at least a hint of personification. Different sorts of verbal narrators have different degrees of presumptive authority for viewers. Textual narrators typically have the greatest authority.

In *New York*, Kabir Khan presents a complex interplay of different sorts of perceptual and verbal narration. At some points—prominently, when dealing with the mistreatment of young Muslim men after September 11, 2001—this contributes to a sense of the reliability of the narration. At other points—prominently, when treating the integration of Muslims in U.S. society before September 11—it contributes to a sense of unreliability. This unreliability is not precisely that of the narrator. Rather, there is at least a possibility of unreliability in a pseudo-implied author. This possibility becomes particularly intense with the ending of the film. Specifically, the perceptual narrator presents an apparently true ending, but, in part through textual narration, the film simultaneously provides hints that viewers—or, rather, some viewers—should not take that ending seriously. In other words, the ending of the film suggests implied authorial misdirection bearing on different sorts of implied audiences for the film.

Finally, film makes the temporal process of narration particularly salient. This foregrounds temporal differences in implied authorial meaning, though these occur just as widely in literature as in film. Specifically, the implied authorial profile of ambiguity for a given scene or sequence may shift over the course of a work. In connection with this, it is important to distinguish *initial* from *retrospective* profiles of ambiguity, along with their associated implied and implicated authors and readers.

Chapter 4

Narrative Reliability

Margaret Atwood's *Surfacing*

A S THE PRECEDING chapter begins to suggest, one of the most fundamental interpretive questions about discourse concerns reliability. Indeed, the very distinction between narrator and implied author is in large part motivated by the desire to clarify the difference between reliable and unreliable narrators. Specifically, here as elsewhere, the implied author provides a norm against which one may judge the narrator. Fundamentally, the narrator is unreliable to the extent that he or she diverges from the implied author or "is at virtual odds with the implied author," as Seymour Chatman put it (*Story* 149).

On the other hand, this may not tell very much. As Nünning points out, "Critics who argue that a narrator's unreliability is to be gauged in comparison to the norms of the implied author just shift the burden of determination" ("Reconceptualizing" 91). This is particularly problematic because the very idea of an unreliable narrator, like that of the implied author itself, should serve an explanatory function. As Tamar Yacobi points out, for any given reader facing a particular text, the notion of an unreliable narrator is a "hypothesis" that is "formed in order to resolve textual problems" (110). But this, in turn, raises the need for a "systematic account of the clues to unreliable narration"—in other words, the "textual data" and their relation to "interpretive choices" (Nünning "Reconceptualizing" 105). To begin with, there is a need for a clearer sense of what constitutes unreliability.

What Is Reliability?

People routinely consider real individuals to be unreliable informants. To say that someone is unreliable in ordinary life is, first of all, to say that he or she misinforms one about the real world.[1] In other words, an unreliable informant is someone whose discourse leads one to imagine some aspects of the world incorrectly. The idea of unreliability is fundamentally the same in fiction. A fictional narrator is unreliable to the extent that he or she misrepresents the storyworld, leading one to imagine the storyworld incorrectly. Recognizing unreliability is, then, inseparable from recognizing this incorrectness. As Shen puts it, "A narration is regarded as unreliable precisely because the reader has come to the conclusion that things are not or cannot be as the discourse represents them" ("Story-Discourse" 567).

There is, however, a difficulty here. In the case of real life, there are facts. In real life, if I am told that Jones married Smith, there is a fact about whether she did or did not marry Smith. But when the narrator of *Surfacing* says that she got married, what determines the fact that she did not?

By this point, readers will not be surprised to discover that narratologists do not entirely agree on the topic. Some stress authorial intent. The facts of the storyworld are, in this view, determined by the author. So too are the facts about the narrator, and his or her reliability or unreliability. In contrast with this, there is a "reader-centred ... approach." This posits "an interpretive strategy that naturalises textual anomalies by projecting an unreliable narrator figure" (Nünning "Reliability" 496). But, in order to make a distinction between reliability and unreliability, one needs a norm of some sort. It is difficult to see how a reader's "naturalization" of "an interpretive strategy" constitutes such a norm. Here, again, the different views are at least partially reconciled in the implied author, understood as the receptive or reader-simulating intent of the real author.

But here another problem arises—how is it even possible to recognize unreliability in fiction? In the real world, one discovers unreliability by discovering facts, usually by some means outside the report of the unreliable informant (e.g., by meeting Jones and finding out that she did not marry Smith, despite what one was told by Gallstone). But how does this occur in fiction, since the only source of information is often that unreliable informant?[2]

In order to consider this problem, it may be helpful to distinguish different sorts of unreliability. In fiction, as in real life, an unreliable discourse is likely to have one of three faults. First, it may directly misrepresent the facts of the story. This is "misreporting," in Phelan's terminology (see "Rhetoric/Ethics" 205). Second, an unreliable discourse may leave out information that is crucial for valid inference ("underreporting," in Phelan's terms ["Rhetoric/Ethics" 205]; not being "forthcoming," as Bordwell puts it [60]; limiting communicativeness, as Sternberg would say). Finally, such a discourse may misdirect attention, promoting mistaken inferences.[3]

The first "mode of factual unreliability" is the simplest. Having been given a piece of information (or misinformation), one is most likely to be given a piece of directly contradictory information (or misinformation). In some cases, this involves a narrator's self-contradiction; in other cases, there may be a shift in narrators; in other cases, the contradictory information may be reported by a character in dialogue. In *Surfacing*, the narrator first reports that she was married, and then subsequently reports that she was not. This sort of direct contradiction signals to the reader that the narrator is unreliable in one of those two reports. It thereby requires the reader to infer which report is correct.

The complete withholding of information is usually fairly straightforward as well. In this case, the reader is most often faced with a gap in the Iserian sense. He or she simply cannot figure something out and ultimately realizes that information is lacking. This situation is a bit trickier for the author in that he or she typically must provide enough clues that the reader can infer the withheld information (though some works simply leave the information incomplete, making it part of the profile of ambiguity).

The misdirection of attention is perhaps the most interesting of the three. The direction of attention is one of the main concerns of literary authors and film directors, since readers simply cannot notice everything, as Rabinowitz discusses (*Before* 47–52; on direction of attention in film, see Bordwell *On the History*). One may distinguish two types of attentional misdirection. In the cruder case, some true information is made salient and that information suggests a false inference. This happens all the time in detective fiction, though it may be developed in such a way that the reliability of the narrator is not impugned. For example, suppose Jones has been shot. The reader then learns explicitly (and accurately) that Smith had a fight with Jones the previous day and that he had a rifle. This may lead the reader to infer, falsely as it turns out, that Smith was the killer.

This form of "misdirected foregrounding" is commonly paired with the second sort of unreliable direction of attentional focus—the reduction of salience or "misdirected backgrounding" of information that is crucial to valid inference. Thus, along with the misleading information about Smith, a reader may find himself or herself distracted from information that would lead to valid conclusions. In the case of film, the information may be literally foregrounded or backgrounded. For example, the audience might be shown Smith cleaning a rifle, while in the case of Doe (the real killer) rifles appear in the background on a wall in his home.

Usually, the trick with foregrounding and backgrounding of information is manipulating the relation between spontaneous encoding and processing, on the one hand, and self-conscious inference, on the other. If the reader is explicitly told that Smith went out and bought a rifle after the fight with Jones, that will almost certainly lead to self-conscious reflection on the likelihood that Smith is the murderer. Given the nature of detective fiction, that may actually lead the reader or viewer to reject the inference as too straightforward. On the other hand, simply showing rifles in the background of a shot may not lead to encoding. In other words, the viewer may simply not notice the rifles. In that case, the conclusion of the story—in which Doe is exposed as the murderer—may not produce the required feeling of "retrospective necessity," which is to say, the feeling that, once revealed, it makes perfect sense that Doe is the culprit.

Whether the narrator provides false information, fails to provide necessary, true information, or misdirects attention, his or her unreliability may result from deceit or incompetence, as Chatman notes (*Story* 149). It may also arise from cognitive or emotional bias (e.g., in-group preference). Incompetence—or fallibility—is further divisible into "range and depth of knowledge," as Bordwell explains (*Narration* 60) or, one might add, articulateness. A reader's emotional and cognitive response differs across these types of narrator. One is likely to feel antipathy toward deceitful or biased narrators. In contrast, one may feel a sort of identification with ordinary fallibility and compassion or pity for a cognitive or perceptual disability. In response to deceit, people typically look for motives, particular interests that would guide the narrator's misrepresentations. Understanding these motives may help to correct for the misrepresentation. If the problem is a disability—as in the case of Benjy, a mentally challenged narrator in Faulkner's *The Sound and the Fury*—the reader may try to infer what facts would lead this particular character, with his or her particular disability, to this particular misunderstanding. In any case, one is likely to seek further information, from the same or other narrators.

The topic of emotional response leads to another key issue regarding unreliability—trust. For example, as noted above, a reader or viewer of detective fiction often does not trust the narrator who gives apparently definitive information in a highly salient form. Indeed, trust is arguably the initial basis of readers' and viewers' sense of reliability or unreliability. Talking about unreliability solely in terms of facts may make the process appear too inferential, particularly at the start. Perhaps one's first sense of reliability or unreliability is not an abstract, cognitive relation to ideas, but rather a concrete, affective relation to a person.[4]

Indeed, it seems very likely that, in fiction and in life, emotional trust or mistrust of a person precedes a rational, self-conscious inference regarding the likely validity of particular statements. This is roughly the same process that is found in the well-known experiments testing ventromedial frontal damage. Test subjects are presented with four decks of cards. Unbeknownst to the subjects, the decks are rigged. Normal test subjects develop a spontaneous, emotional aversion to the losing decks and a spontaneous, emotional attraction to the winning decks "before they could consciously articulate the best strategy" (Oatley, Keltner, and Jenkins 136, discussing work by Bechara and colleagues). One may guess that things operate similarly in the case of trust. Indeed, one could construe normal subjects' response to the different stacks of cards as one of trust and mistrust.

There is one possible difference between trusting a stack of cards and trusting a person. It appears that one's default response to strangers is a mild and tentative distrust. People only "build up trust" (or enhance the response of distrust) over the course of personal interactions—or, in some cases, by just seeing the other person repeatedly even without interaction (see Oatley *Emotions* 73). However, there may be an exception to this. It seems likely that people feel a default trust for people placed in positions of institutional authority. The point is suggested by the "Dr. Fox lecture" experiment. In that study, test subjects were presented with an actor playing the role of an academic. Simply because of his stated position as an authority (the participants were not told he was an actor), they accepted what he said and responded positively to this (pseudo-)learning experience, forgoing their usual spontaneous distrust for strangers (see Naftulin, Ware, and Donnelly).

The point about authority is consequential because narratives place narrators in a position of structural authority. Thus, in all likelihood, readers begin with a presumption of narrator reliability and lose trust in a narrator only once they have reason to do so. This leads us to the issue of just how such distrust develops. However, before considering this, we need to address a logically prior issue. Even if an affective relation of trust is primary, it seems clear that distrust is connected with a sense of discrepancy between what the narrator reports and what the facts of the storyworld appear to be. The nature of such facts is fairly straightforward in the case of nonfiction. But the case of fiction is less clear. Thus, before addressing the development of distrust, we need to consider the nature of fictional facts—thus how there can even be anything to distrust a narrator about.

Fiction's Facts

In considering the facts about a fictional world, it is helpful to begin with a broad division between general principles and particular instances. General principles are the patterns that govern physical events, individual actions, group dynamics, and so forth. For example, people generally act in such a way as to further their goals; people generally experience empathy when they witness the face of someone in pain; people generally have five senses. Such principles range from strict laws, such as the law of gravitation, to looser tendencies, such as the idea that empires tend to become overextended and disintegrate. Particular instances are cases of these principles—Smith is a case of a person with five senses, or perhaps four senses, if he is blind or deaf; Imperial Rome is a case of an empire; Jupiter's orbit is a case of the law of gravitation.

People create or understand a fictional story most obviously by constructing or reconstructing particulars. To a great extent, these particulars are explicitly stated in the discourse. Or, rather, the discourse presents enough information so that one may draw on general principles to reconstruct "nondefault" or unique aspects of the story's particularity. Indeed, this is true in nonfictional storytelling as well. In a fictional story, one might read "Jane tripped when running up the stairs. Now she had a prominent, bluish bump on her cheek." Similarly, if this happens to a real person, she may explain her prominent, bluish bump by saying "I tripped on the stairs." In both cases, recipients use general principles about the world to fill in the causal connections. They have, however, been given enough information to know what is unique about the situation, what is not simply part of the world generally.

Most often, the general principles in a work of fiction are those of the real world. As Marie-Laure Ryan has discussed, readers follow a "Principle of Minimal Departure" in their assumptions about the relations between the real and fictional worlds. However, there are exceptions to this continuity of principles. One may distinguish three types or levels of general principle. The first is most easily identified as the level of the real world, but that may not be quite right. It is more accurate to say that it is the level of the real world *as understood by the implied author.* For example, some works may rely on a belief in the miraculous intervention of saints. A reader need not believe that saints really do cure illnesses from beyond the grave in order to recognize that this is a principle presupposed in some narratives (e.g., in the Hindi blockbuster *Amar Akbar Anthony,* where the heroes' mother is cured of blindness after—and presumably because—her son prays at a Sufi shrine).

The second level comprises general principles derived from some category in which the work is located. The obvious case of this is a genre category. In science fiction, for example, one commonly assumes that there are civilizations roughly like one's own on other planets. In this context, "roughly like one's own" means that real-world psychological and sociological principles apply unless we are given other, differentiating information. Categories here also include groupings by culture or discourse mode. For example, when reading Sanskrit literature, one may reasonably expect the appearance of cakravāka birds to anticipate the separation of lovers. This is presumably not a belief that ancient Indians had about the real world. But it is part of the shared literary world of such works.

Finally, there is the level of general principles that are unique to the story at hand. Like particulars, these must be specified in adequate detail. That specification may be explicit or implicit. For example, in Salman Rushdie's novel *Midnight's Children,* people do not generally have supernatural powers. However, each of the children born at the hour of India's independence has some special capacity. This is a straightforward general principle that guides the (implied) reader's understanding of the story.

I speak of these as "levels" because they form a hierarchy. In general, information given in narrower contexts displaces information that applies more broadly. Thus the (conventional) principles of a genre displace any contradictory principles from the real world. Similarly, any principles particular to a story displace principles from a genre or other category. Put differently, in cases of conflict, the more narrowly confined principle is the one that applies.

In addition to principles, particulars enter at all these levels as well. It may seem initially that information from the real world enters only at the level of principles, not at the level of particulars. However, on even brief reflection, it becomes clear that this is not true. Indeed, authors and readers assume extensive particular information in constructing and reconstructing a story. This particular information ranges from the existence of commercial products (e.g., a certain type of chewing gum) to world-changing historical events (e.g., Indian independence).

Needless to say, this does not mean that all potentially relevant particulars of the real world are carried over into the fictional world. Just as the author may change general principles, he or she may change particulars. Here, however, a complication arises. Particulars in the real world are, one might say, "referential." There are real people, real actions, real experiences there. Some particulars include other particulars—thus the Second World War includes particular battles, which include particular troop movements, which include particular individual soldiers, and so on. For any given level of referential particularity, there are certain things that are readily knowable and others that are not. Moreover, there are certain things that are widely known and other things that are not.

For instance, virtually every Russian reader of *War and Peace* would have known the outcome of the battle of Borodino. In contrast, the precise disposition of troops is presumably known by experts, but not by the average reader. Finally, one can assume that no one does or can know the identities or actions of all individual soldiers—even of all individual soldiers who engaged in particularly significant actions.

Such differences regarding historical knowledge have a bearing on the facts of a fictional world and on the reader's response to that fictional world. In a fictional account of the battle of Borodino, an author may create wholly fictional soldiers as he or she likes. At the other end of the spectrum, when there is common knowledge, the reader or viewer automatically assumes that the particulars hold. When watching a film about World War II, treating some event in May 1944, one automatically assumes that the end of the war is one year away, that the end is a triumph for the Allies, and so on. Readers or viewers connect relevant story events with those facts from the real world, even though the events are still an indeterminate future within the story itself. Of course, an author may create a fiction in which the war had a different outcome, as in Philip K. Dick's novel *The Man in the High Castle* where the fascists have won the Second World War. In this case, readers implicitly (or explicitly) recognize that this is a case where fictional information excludes real information. Intermediate cases, however, are less clear. If Tolstoy presents Napoleon as giving certain sorts of order, as having a particular knowledge or lack of knowledge about the battle, one may take this to be a partial fictionalization that further specifies known facts, a complete fictionalization of unknown facts, a counterfactional fiction (i.e., a fictionalization that alters known facts)—or perhaps unreliable narration.

In sum, the facts of a storyworld result from the interaction of quite extensive extratextual information with some minimal textual information. The minimal textual information serves primarily to signal where the storyworld deviates from common knowledge about the real world. That deviation is largely a matter of particulars, but it may include more general principles. There are complications and ambiguities with respect to real-world particulars and principles that are knowable, but not common knowledge. Technically, the role of such particulars and principles for the implied reader may be unclear. The crucial point in each case, however, is that the real and fictional worlds are always tightly interrelated, with the default presumption being one of continuity between the storyworld and the real world rather than discontinuity. This presumption of continuity is often of crucial importance in one's distrust of a narrator.

Distrusting the Narrator

Again, the default attitude toward the narrator appears to be one of trust. Thus one needs some reason to doubt the narrator. Indeed, empirical research suggests such a strong tendency toward trust that, Bortolussi and Dixon explain, "the precise nature of the features in a text that lead the reader to interpret the narrator as unreliable" constitutes a "puzzle" (84). Technically, automatic processing has to be interrupted by some sort of contradiction—or, more precisely, a *felt* contradiction, something one experiences emotionally as a contradiction, something that has a motivational component. That requirement is not as restrictive as it may seem. As already noted, readers or viewers generally have an interest in understanding the storyworld, and if faced with mutually exclusive descriptions, they are likely to want to reconcile them. Of course, one needs to have encoded those descriptions and brought them into connection with one another in order to recognize the contradiction. That is not insignificant. But readers and viewers do this readily with aspects of a work that are salient.

The point is clearer if one recalls that an emotional contradiction need not be a logical contradiction. Indeed, it seems likely that relatively few literary quandaries are logical contradictions. The contradictions that inspire effortful, working-memory-based processing—thus self-conscious interpretive work—are fundamentally *task* contradictions. Readers (including the author as reader) need to imagine some object, explain some event, understand some emotion through imagination. Ordinarily, they accomplish this task automatically. However, sometimes something goes wrong. In Heidegger's terms, something is "broken" and the text, rather than being "ready to hand" for story construction, suddenly faces the reader as something "present at hand." In Iser's term, there is some gap. One tries to fill that gap through self-conscious interpretation.[5]

The judgment of a narrator as unreliable begins with this sort of gap or task contradiction. Clearly, a gap does not imply that the narrator is necessarily unreliable. It may simply mean that one has to draw complex inferences, that one needs to learn something about history or culture that is carried over from the real world to the text, that one needs to familiarize oneself with genre conventions, and so on. (The relation to reality, culture, and genre are commonly recognized in discussions of unreliable narration; see Nünning "Reconceptualizing" 98–99 and Yacobi 110–11.) Moreover, the absence of any sense of contradiction does not mean that the narrator is reliable. For example, I may fail to see that a narrator is unreliable in reporting cultural or historical events from the real world because I myself lack relevant real-world knowledge. Rather, as the preceding example suggests, without a sense that something has inhibited automatic processing, one will never begin to distrust a narrator and thus to engage in effortful inference.

There are different sorts of task contradiction or gap that may arise in connection with constructing a story from discourse. The most obvious is some sort of apparent incompatibility. Again, this need not be a strict logical contradiction. It is more often a matter of unlikelihood or lack of explanation. For example, a reader may learn that a character is opposed to war and then learn that he has joined the army. This is not a logical contradiction. But it is unlikely and requires some particular explanation. As such, it will probably to give rise to effortful thought—to the asking of questions, as Noël Carroll stresses (see "Narrative").

It is important to note here that gaps almost invariably involve real-world principles and/or particulars. Thus they are bound up with the continuity between the storyworld and reality. Some gaps may seem to arise wholly internally to a story. For example, it may seem that an antiwar character joining the army is an anomaly purely internal to the storyworld where it occurs. But, in fact, one cannot even recognize that armies are involved in war unless one incorporates real-world information into the storyworld.

It is also important not to understand gaps too narrowly. The examples just given come fairly close to contradictions. However, gaps may arise due to unexplained coincidences or, more generally, problems of probability. They may arise because, for certain events or characters, reference is vague or identity is unclear (e.g., if the shooting of a scene makes it unclear whether certain actions were performed by one or two characters). In each case, readers or viewers are motivated to understand something further about the story and they find that there is some difficulty in achieving that understanding.

Having identified a problem, one needs to first isolate its source. In technical, narratological terms, the first question concerns whether the source of the gap is the narrator, the implied author, or the real author. One may decide that the gap was produced by the real author, but has gone unnoticed by the implied author. If so, then one is likely to see the gap as a flaw in the narrative, perhaps an important one, perhaps not. Alternatively, one may interpret the gap as occurring in the implied author. In other words, one may view the implied author as, in effect, choosing to make something anomalous. In this case, there is no fact that the implied author is concealing. The anomaly is part of the profile of ambiguity. However, since the implied author is always free to resolve incompatibilities, one must infer some motivation for this gap. It is typically thematic, though it may also be emotional.[6]

Finally, and most importantly for present purposes, one may attribute the gap to the narrator, judging that he or she is unreliable. (In fact, readers or viewers almost certainly try to resolve any anomaly at the level of the narrator before turning to the implied author, and they almost certainly turn to the author only after failing at the level of the implied author.) Again, once one determines that the narrator is unreliable, one undertakes further interpretation. One determines whether the narrator is lacking in knowledge or in good will or is in some way biased. One tries to infer what the fictional facts are in opposition to what the narrator has (unreliably) reported. Perhaps most importantly, one tries to determine the limits of the unreliability, because one generally continues to accept most of what the narrator recounts. The point holds whether the unreliability is motivational or epistemic, though of course one determines the limits of unreliability somewhat differently in the two cases.

How Does One Infer the Fictional Facts?

This leads to the question of how readers or viewers resolve gaps, how they determine just what the fictional facts are, once they have run up against a problem. Here too it is valuable to distinguish two levels of adjudicative processing. One is more automatic; the other is more effortful, but also more general.

The more general and effortful approach is the scientific one. Here, one relies on the usual principles of scientific inference to reach a conclusion. There is nothing magical here; there are no simple solutions. There is, rather, a synthesis of empirical evidence, the generation of hypotheses, evaluation by criteria of logic and simplicity, revision of hypotheses, and so forth. This is more likely to be the province of the literary critic than the ordinary reader.

Before undertaking such a highly effortful process, readers almost certainly begin by relying on some simplified, heuristic procedures. In the case of fictional narratives, these heuristics often involve what might be called *default preference hierarchies*. Drawing on Holland, Holyoak, Nisbett, and Thagard's account of default hierarchies, one may understand these as pragmatic orderings, such that there is a default preference, but alternatives that displace the default when particular circumstances arise. More exactly, readers appear to have default *sources* of information and default *types* of information, with specified alternatives for certain "marked" conditions. The narrator is obviously the primary default for the source of information. The primary trigger for condition marking, thus for a shift from the default, is narrator unreliability, itself made possible by distrust.

The point is in keeping with the general operation of the human mind. The default for a bird is something like a robin. In one's backyard in the American Midwest, the sort of bird one expects is a robin or something similar. However, in the context of the Florida seacoast, one is more likely to expect a gull (cf. Kahneman and Miller 140). One would expect similar processes—of shifting from a default—elsewhere. Indeed, with respect to trust or judgments of reliability, people engage in processes of this sort all the time. I might generally trust Jones's character judgments, but (shifting out of the default) not with respect to his ex-wife (an instance of emotional bias). I may trust police officers with giving directions or dealing with theft, but (shifting out of the default) not with respect to an antiwar demonstration.

Consider a simple literary example. Suppose there is a contradiction between the statements of the narrator and the statements of a character. It seems that, other things being equal, readers are likely to prefer the claim of the narrator, who of course has access to both views (since he or she is presumably the one who has reported the character's statement). However, if one judges the narrator to be unreliable due to a lack of knowledge, one may prefer the character's statement, if it falls into the right epistemic area—as when the narrator is a child who does not understand the topic under consideration (e.g., sex, finances, transcendental Phenomenological reduction). If the narrator is motivationally unreliable, then readers are likely to trust the version that is least in keeping with the speaker's biasing motivations or self-interests.

Of course, these default-replacing alternatives may be overridden also. They may generate their own gaps. Those gaps may, in turn, be resolvable by further alternatives in one or another preference hierarchy, or they may require more effortful hermeneutic work.

Again, this shifting of a default preference hierarchy is intermediate between spontaneous processing and effortful interpretation. In this way, there is a difference from the prototypes governing what sort of bird one expects in what location. Those prototypes operate automatically, with no prior sense of contradiction or gap. In the case of a narrative, one must first come to challenge a source of information or sense a conflict in types of information before one shifts from a default. The shift involves some disruption of normal processing, even if it is not a matter of complex, extended reflection. In this way, the situation with unreliability in narrative information is parallel to first learning of some real person's unreliability, insofar as there is a relevant standard/prototypical alternative for trust in that case. I know that Jones is generally a fair judge of character. However, I come to realize that he is unreliable with respect to his ex-wife. This constraint is easily assimilated to prototypical cases of embittered ex-spouses. I do not have to spend a great deal of hermeneutic effort on the case, though it also does not occur spontaneously. In other cases, I may have to engage in more complex and difficult inferences. This appears to be what happens with shifts from defaults in narratives as well.

Drawing on, but altering, hermeneutic terminology, one may refer to the three types of narrative processing in the following terms. First, the great majority of one's reading is necessarily as simple and straightforward as one's competence in the language allows. This may be called "spontaneous understanding." It is the basis of the other hermeneutic processes, in part because it is necessary to the experience of gaps. For example, readers rely on spontaneous understanding to receive story information that allows for a sense of incompatibility. In this respect, one always has to rely on the narrator to some degree. Once one senses a gap and experiences distrust, however, one shifts from the default through what might be called "interpretive adjustment." Relative to spontaneous understanding, this is an effortful process. However, it is effortful in a limited way, for it operates through a heuristic shift to a preset alternative that is itself largely unquestioned. In contrast, some gaps or some implications of gaps do not have, so to speak, "standard" solutions, particular and ordered alternatives to the default. They require a more diverse, vigorous, and creative exploration of possible solutions. This might be called "critical explication."

As the terms indicate, the first process is undertaken by any reader who makes any sense out of a literary work. The second process is more variable and in many cases requires a reader who has some degree of skill and experience. This does not mean that the reader has to be an academic. Insofar as the default hierarchies rely on genre knowledge, a grammar school youth may be highly competent at interpretive adjustment with respect to, say, the mininarratives of rap songs, and a professor of literary theory may be almost entirely incompetent in that area. Finally, critical explication is the sort of sustained analysis that more typically characterizes criticism than the isolated reading process. Here, too, criticism is not confined to articles published in academic journals. It includes blogs, chat-room discussions, or even conversations among friends, though articles and books do tend to offer the largest scope for expansion and elaboration of critical explication.

Since this is a bit abstract, it is worth giving a brief example before continuing. As will be clear from the following discussion, *Surfacing* faces the reader with several anomalies. The central gaps concern the memories of the narrator—did she marry and have a child, or did she have an affair and an abortion? I have encountered students who fail to recognize the contradiction here and assume that both happened. They have obviously processed the novel at the level of spontaneous understanding, since they recognize the sequences of events. However, they have not noted the contradiction. Some know there is a contradiction, but are not quite sure of the solution. Most, however, sense the gap and the solution. I take it that this is because they recognize the narrator as motivationally and epistemically unreliable, with the particular sort of combined inhibition that results from (psychoanalytic) repression. If her unreliability were solely motivational or solely epistemic, it would be far more difficult to understand. (How could one simply not know that one had an abortion? Alternatively, why would one make up a story about abandoning one's child?) It would require effortful critical explication. In contrast, if the unreliability is a matter of repression then all one needs is some basic psychoanalytic heuristics. One heuristic may be that people are more likely to repress something sexual than nonsexual; another may add that people are more likely to repress something traumatic than nontraumatic. Both heuristics favor the affair/abortion as the repressed content. (There are other heuristic reasons for this choice as well, reasons that do not rely on any knowledge of psychoanalysis. Some of these will be taken up in the following section.)

Of course, even with the psychoanalytic heuristics, critical explication enters. For example, the reader still needs to understand the story told by the narrator as a substitute for the memory of the abortion. A critical explication may explore some of the ways in which the imagery of the novel is consistent with the psychoanalytic heuristics. More significantly, a critical explication may go on to consider a further difficulty. Understanding the story relies on a sort of psychoanalytic schema. But there is a problem with this, because the operation of repression here does not quite fit psychoanalytic principles. Nor is it entirely in keeping with the general understanding of traumatic memory loss, which typically involves an experience that was unexpected, terribly painful, and incomprehensible (for example, Christianson and Lindholm cite "rape and extreme and prolonged acts of violence" [772–73]). This may lead back to the implied author or the real author and the question of whether this discrepancy has an emotional or thematic function or is simply an error.

Before going on to explore *Surfacing* in greater detail, however, it is important to get a more concrete idea of what the usual preference hierarchies are. As already noted, such hierarchies may bear on sources of information or on types of information. In addition, gaps may arise due to different sorts of relation between internal and extratextual information. This may be termed the *epistemic context* of the gap. Thus we may distinguish three varieties of hierarchy—bearing on source, type, and context—which might be briefly considered in turn.

Regarding information source, as already discussed, readers seem to begin with a default, tacit assumption that the narrator is reliable. But there is a complication here, since there are different sorts of narrator. Most importantly, one may distinguish between nonpersonified and personified narrators. This is probably the most basic division that bears on narrator reliability. Specifically, in cases of conflict, we assume that a nonpersonified narrator is to be preferred over any personified figure, either a narrator or a character.

This hierarchy fits with the common view that "If anonymous," the narrative voice "is equated with the voice of truth." In contrast, "In first-person narrative ... the teller is individuated, and his or her vision considered subjective. Such a teller normally has access to their own mind only, and the completeness or reliability of any information or judgment they provide can be questioned" (Margolin "Person" 423; see also Margolin "Authentication" 33, citing Doležel). This appears to overstate the case, however. Nonpersonified narration is not absolutely unquestionable, even in comparison with personified narration (e.g., when one is embedded in the other). At the very least, as Nünning explains, "there is an ongoing debate about whether unreliability is a property of first-person narrators only, or whether it can also be attributed to third-person narrators" ("Reliability" 496). In any case, it seems clear that readers are far more likely to distrust a *person* when faced with some incompatibility. It is both emotionally unlikely and cognitively difficult to question a nonpersonified narrator. When a nonpersonified narrator delivers a particularly secure type of information (e.g., visual perception), then it is almost impossible—almost, because the ending of *New York* indicates that unreliability can arise even in this context.

Among personified figures, one tends to prefer some types to others. It seems likely that, other things being equal, one will first follow the communicative discourse hierarchy of embedding. Thus, after nonpersonified narrators, one will tend to trust the information provided by a personified narrator or a focalizer, then a character who is a topic or protagonist. For example, when, in his role as narrator, Nick directly or indirectly contradicts a statement from Gatsby, we are, it seems, more likely to trust Nick than Gatsby. A rather subtle case of this occurs when Gatsby says, "I suppose Daisy'll call too." The comment expresses a belief that Daisy will call. Nick comments, "He looked at me anxiously, as if he hoped I'd corroborate this" (218), suggesting that the comment is more a desire than an expectation. I suspect that most readers automatically process the passage in such a way as to accept Nick's implication. Note that this involves accepting Nick's view at two levels. First, a reader accepts that Gatsby looks anxious. Second, he or she accepts that Gatsby looks anxious because he doubts whether Daisy will call (he could be anxious about many other things, given the nature of the preceding conversation, and given recent events).

This may be a specifically discourse-related hierarchy, or it may be part of a general heuristic hierarchy of sources whereby one prefers information from those one knows well over information from those one knows less well. The latter is most obvious with two characters who operate as embedded narrators. For example, in book 10, chapter 35 of *War and Peace*, Kutuzov and Wolzogen, the second reporting from Barclay de Tolly, both summarize the Battle of Borodino. Their accounts are radically incompatible, with Kutuzov evaluating the battle positively and Wolzogen/de Tolly evaluating it negatively. The reader is strongly motivated to resolve this incompatibility. Much greater familiarity with Kutuzov seems to be a factor biasing a reader in favor of his account.

This preferential trust in familiar personified figures is precisely what one would expect from research on people's response to familiar and unfamiliar people in real life. This same research suggests that people respond with fear or vigilance to people from out-groups (see Oatley *Emotions* 73; see also Ito and colleagues). Thus one would generally expect an in-group/out-group hierarchy to occur in fiction as well. In the preceding example, the association of Wolzogen and de Tolly with German language and ethnicity could readily contribute to at least a Russian reader's preference in this case. Indeed, this identity-group division is highlighted in this chapter (for Wolzogen) and elsewhere (book 9, chapter 9, and book 10, chapter 25) for de Tolly.

Of course, there is also a potential motivational issue in this case. Even when readers do not have evidence that a particular narrator is unreliable, they have a general preference for information that is contrary to the self-interest of the speaker. In the case of Kutuzov and Wolzogen/de Tolly, this partially favors the latter. Kutuzov, in command of the Russian troops, is motivated to view the results of the battle positively. On the other hand, de Tolly is a rival of Kutuzov, which somewhat taints his version as well. Moreover, Kutuzov does not seem to be interested in any material rewards for success. Rather, his interestedness is a function of his sense of loyalties. In this way, his version is self-interested without being morally faulty. That does not mean it is fully trustworthy. However, it may mean that readers will be less critical of it on motivational grounds.

To some extent, these heuristic preferences share a single emotional basis. Readers have an emotional response of trusting some narrators and not others, some characters (who may contradict narrators) and not others. Spontaneous feelings of trust or distrust arise easily in relation to familiarity/unfamiliarity and in-group/out-group categorization. Decisions about a narrator's self-interest may require somewhat more effortful, self-conscious processing, but they are often relatively simple and spontaneous. Moreover, they certainly bear on one's feelings of trust or distrust.

It is possible to summarize the usual trust hierarchy as a preference hierarchy of the following sort. (A superior item in a preference hierarchy is chosen when all other factors are held constant. Thus the preference rule $a > b$ means that, if everything else is equal, choose a.)

nonpersonified narrator > personified narrator > focalizer > protagonist > other characters

If personified, then

familiar > unfamiliar
in-group > out-group
disinterested > self-interested

As this suggests, there do not seem to be general conditions in which a nonpersonified narrator is distrusted. This can only result from an accumulation of evidence, making it extremely rare.

The second area in which one finds a default preference hierarchy concerns types of evidence. This is in some ways more straightforward than the hierarchy of sources of information. It has a fairly clear relation to everyday experience, and is also closely related to the grammatical operation of evidentials. (Evidentials are grammatical markers indicating, for example, whether one witnessed or was told about the information one is conveying [see Aikhenvald].) Generally, it seems clear that people trust current perception more than they trust memory. Within current perception, people tend to trust vision over hearing (the other senses enter less often). Within memory, people trust current memory more than distant memory. People seem to generally trust memory more than empirical inference. Within empirical inference, people trust empirical inference by experts more than that by nonexperts.[7] For example, the narrator of a crime investigation might be skeptical of the scientific contraptions used in the lab. But, other things being equal, readers are likely to give initial credence to the findings of the lab. Of course, if the narrator is a seasoned detective, the whole point of the story may be to show that the instincts of the seasoned detective are more accurate than those of technicians. But then readers have two types of expertise and this preference hierarchy does not come into play. Finally, below the level of empirical inference, there is something like hearsay—roughly, ideas for which there is no evidence other than someone's assertion.

The hierarchy in types of evidence may be summarized in the following diagram:

perception [visual > auditory] > memory [recent > distant] > empirical inference [by experts > by nonexperts] > hearsay

Of course, like all default hierarchies, this can be overridden in particular circumstances.

The final default preference hierarchy concerns epistemic context. Given certain sorts of contradiction, people give preference to one type of consistency over another. Most fundamentally, in life and in literature, people prefer to preserve logical coherence over any other sort of coherence. This is simply a presupposition of all adjudication of gaps. If people did not seek to preserve the principle of noncontradiction, they would not even recognize gaps. For example, there would be no tension between Jones opposing fascism and joining the Nazi party. Anyone might empirically expect that someone who opposed fascism would not join a fascist party. But, without the principle of noncontradiction, there is no reason to balk even at the statement "He signed a party card and he attended an induction ceremony and he never signed a party card and he never attended an induction ceremony"; there is no reason to determine which alternative is correct or whether they somehow have different meanings.

In real life, below this founding assumption about logic, there are the laws—or at least generalizations—of various sciences or, more generally, modes of knowledge. These include not only the laws of physics, but general principles of psychology, and to some extent sociological or other patterns. For some authors and readers, they may also include supernatural principles, such as divine providence. These too tend to be hierarchized, with physics given preference over biology, which is in turn given preference over the psychological and social sciences, though this subhierarchy rarely has consequences in literature. The relation between natural and supernatural principles is more vexed. Even readers who reject supernatural causality in life must accept that it does often occur in literature. I suspect, however, that when natural and supernatural explanations are both available, authors and readers generally prefer the natural explanations. I suspect that this is the case even for authors and readers who accept supernatural causality in real life.

In literature, another epistemic context intervenes between logic and laws of nature particularly. These are category-specific conventions, such as principles of genre. In cases where the conventions of a genre come into conflict with general laws of physics (drawn from the real world) readers give preference to the former. Indeed, this is usually so automatic that no one is likely to notice. In that sense, it does not give rise to a gap. Particular genre conventions may also complicate the relation between natural and supernatural causality. They can certainly make the invocation of supernatural causality more (or less) likely than usual.

The final epistemic context is that of empirical particulars—not general laws, but specifics of history, culture, biography, and so forth. Of the various epistemic contexts, readers seem most willing to forgo these when reading fiction. On the other hand, these are also likely to prove the most troublesome because this is the level at which most fictional deviation from reality occurs. As already noted, at this level, it is sometimes difficult to tell whether a contradiction with facts is meant to indicate unreliability of the narrator, a fictionalization by the implied author, or an aesthetic or ideological problem deriving from the real author.

The default preference hierarchy for epistemic contexts may be summarized with the following diagram:

logic > principles of genre or other category > natural laws > supernatural principles > particulars of society, history, etc.

Unreliable Narration in *Surfacing*

Margaret Atwood's *Surfacing*, published in 1972, is a prime example of a novel with an unreliable narrator.[8] But, at the same time, it is a novel where it seems fairly clear what the actual story really is. In other words, the narration gives enough information to infer the correct story. Indeed, the narrator herself gives this information as she corrects the story and, in effect, becomes reliable. In this respect, the novel is nicely designed to illustrate the various ways in which readers may judge and limit unreliability, and the ways readers may adjudicate incompatibilities or resolve problems arising through gaps. Put simply, the narrator changes her mind about things. This allows one to consider the question—why do readers (or critics) trust one version and not the other?

It seems likely that most first-time readers of *Surfacing* are unaware that the narrator is unreliable almost until the moment where she herself more or less announces that she has gotten the story wrong. This is in part because the contradictions are largely "unnarrated" (in Prince's sense) until the point where the narrator begins to "denarrate." (Denarration is "the narrator's denial or negation of an event or state of affairs that had earlier been affirmed" [Prince "Disnarrated" 118; see also chapter 3 of Prince *Narrative*].) Moreover, it seems likely that, even then, most readers engage in relatively quick interpretive adjustment, rather than critical explication, more or less automatically assuming that the new statements by the author are reliable—even as they make further interpretive adjustments to allow for her increasing peculiarity of behavior and apparent hallucinations. The following analysis, however, will follow Roland Barthes's "last freedom" of the critic, "that of reading the text as if it had already been read" (15). Thus it will be concerned with how someone who has previously read the novel could critically explicate both the narrator's limited unreliability and the implied reader's adjustment to this.

There are two basic areas of the narrator's unreliability. The following discussion will explore only one of these. The first area of unreliability, outlined briefly above, concerns her memories of her relationship with a lover and their child. Initially she recounts that she and this man were married; they had a child; and the narrator left both the husband and the son. Subsequently, the reader learns that she did not get married. Rather, she had an affair with this man, who was married to someone else. She did become pregnant, but had an abortion.

As she recovers these memories, it becomes clear that she had repressed them and substituted a fantasy, if an ultimately rather unpleasant one. The idea that there is a repressed memory works well with various aspects of the book. For example, in psychoanalytic theory, repressed contents will repeatedly manifest themselves in symptoms, symptomatic acts, ways of speaking, and so on. The repressed ideas or impulses will partially orient one's trains of thought, behavior, and word choice. Thus one's speech and action will often contain hints of those ideas and impulses of which one remains unaware. This is found throughout the narrator's false narration of her marriage.

On the other hand, as already noted, there are important ways in which the narrator's case does not fit psychoanalytic theory. Most importantly, the repressed memories are not infantile. Of course, there are cases of repressed traumas in later life. But these are usually much more limited. Thus it is not impossible that she would suppress some aspects of the abortion—for example, aspects that were particularly physically painful. This might be parallel to a soldier losing memory of certain parts of a battle. But the narrator has repressed the memory of the entire abortion, and the entire pregnancy, and the lover being married. It would require quite severe, pervasive, and probably debilitating psychological problems for someone to have repressed so much of her recent life (cf., for example, the rape victim discussed by Christianson and Lindholm [773]). But, for most of the novel, the narrator exhibits no signs of such severe, pervasive, and debilitating problems. This produces a gap requiring critical explication and suggesting some thematic points of the novel.

Before going on to this, however, it is important to briefly mention the second area of unreliability. This concerns supernatural experiences. At the end of the novel, the narrator sees the spirits of her dead father and mother.[9] This could be understood as the result of a severe psychological disorder, manifest also in the distorted memories. However, it has a simpler explanation. She has taken hallucinogenic mushrooms. She clearly identifies the mushroom in conversation (see 177). The information is presumably included by the implied author to provide an understanding of the narrator's hallucinations. On the other hand, this too is not entirely simple. The mushroom in question was perhaps involved in Ojibway spiritual practices (see Navet). This is particularly germane as the narrator is clearly imitating Native American/First Nations's practices at this point.[10] This too involves a sort of interpretive gap, also with thematic consequences. For example, it bears on whether one reads the end of the novel as hopeful or hopeless (a point of conflict in the criticism[11]). These are obviously important issues for one's understanding of and response to the novel. However, in order to keep the discussion within manageable limits, the following analysis will focus on the narrator's unreliable memories.

Though impossible to tell before reading the novel, the title already suggests the submerged nature of the narrator's memories. It also points, quite literally, to the ways in which they will reappear eventually—when she is below the water. Even before one reads the novel, one knows that "surfacing" suggests something or someone temporarily concealed, then reappearing.

Already, on the first page or two, there are several points at which one could question the narrator's reliability, if one did not have an initial, default trust in her. The narrator and three friends—including her current boyfriend, Joe—are driving to northern Canada, where she grew up. Her father has disappeared and may be dead. They pass "the city." First, she explains that they have not gone through; then she describes its "one main street with a movie theater." Relying on memory, she explains that the movie theater was "the itz, the oyal, red R burned out" (3). The theater was presumably either the Ritz or the Royal, not both. She presents this as if it were a trustworthy memory. But the duplication of the theater's name indicates that it is not entirely trustworthy. She goes on to recount a memory from "before I was born" (3), a memory that also seems dubious. Her brother "got under the table and slid his hands up and down the waitress's legs while she was bringing the food" (3). This simply does not fit with the verb "bringing" (with its suggestion of walking from the kitchen to the table). But even if "bringing" means "serving," it hardly seems likely that the waitress would simply accept this behavior. Then there is a third memory of her and her brother having no shoes in winter (4). The image of them running barefoot through the snow once or twice is plausible enough. But how likely is it that her parents would leave them entirely without shoes in a north Canada winter?

The points are all small and apparently insignificant. However, they suggest that the narrator may not be trustworthy even at the outset. Though a reader may not self-consciously notice any of these small uncertainties, they may provide some preparation for the larger gaps in memory that follow. In other words, few readers will reflectively consider any of these points as genuine contradictions or errors. However, there is something strange about them. Readers may begin to sense at least a "tall tale" element to the narrator's memories, which may unreflectively prepare them for what follows. As a result, her eventual revelation about her memories of marriage and divorce may be surprising, but not incomprehensibly anomalous.

The end of the chapter introduces a peculiar self-consciousness about the narration. Given that there is no narrational frame and no overt narratee, it is strange to find the narrator reflecting on her own practices as a narrator. Specifically, at one point, she refers to something "they" used to do (11). She then corrects herself, saying, "That won't work, I can't call them 'they' as if they were somebody else's family" (12). Again, at least some readers are likely to respond to this with an implicit question about just whom she is addressing and when. It is as if there is narration to an implicit narratee that is interrupted by a shift to the internal consciousness of the narrator. However, without the involvement of some at least moderately motivated task, a reader is unlikely to follow through on such a momentary question, particularly in the context of default trust. The plot thickens when she goes on to suggest that she has an impulse to misrepresent something. The next sentence is "I have to keep myself from telling that story" (12). At the same time, this hint of untrustworthy motives is mitigated by the narrator's stated commitment to *not* being unreliable. Thus, here as elsewhere, the hint might serve to prepare the reader for the narrator's unreliability without yet directly provoking distrust.

In the second chapter, the reader supposedly learns about the narrator's recent past—her marriage and divorce. She recounts that she sent her parents a postcard about the wedding. While certainly not impossible, this is clearly an unusual situation (by real-world standards) and requires clarification. A neighbor of her father's, Paul, seems to know about the marriage, and the narrator explains this by reference to the postcard. This apparently confirms the story (i.e., makes it less anomalous, less likely to appear doubtful). However, she also notes that she is wearing a wedding ring. In retrospect, one may understand that Paul simply inferred the marriage from the ring.

Just after this, the narrator has a sudden memory of the "husband." Its location and time are unclear. She figures that "it must have been before the child" (22). This uncertainty highlights the fallibility of memory (a point stressed in recent memory research; see Schacter). Though not specific to the narrator, such fallibility clearly bears on the degree to which we can trust her recollections. Merely noting this fallibility is unlikely to provoke questions about her reliability. But it probably does help to prepare the reader for what occurs later. The general point is recapitulated—and the preparation enhanced—subsequently, when the narrator thinks about Joe. She makes the strange statement "though I can't reconstruct our first meeting, now I can" (28). The sentence simultaneously reasserts the uncertainty of memory and the subjective conviction that any given reconstruction is correct. It fits with the narrator's apparent confidence in her memories and what we will discover to be their frequent falsity.

Readers are soon given more information about the marriage. She explains that her parents did not understand her marriage and that she herself "didn't understand it." She goes on to state that her son "wasn't really mine" (29). Most of the earlier incompatibilities are probably ignored by first-time readers. But these last points may require some minimal interpretive effort. One can make some sense out of the statement that she did not understand her own marriage by assuming that the marriage was undertaken on the basis of a misconception. But that is not entirely adequate, since the misconception would presumably be about the man or about the reality of married life, not why she married this man at this time. The statement about the child is tougher. Readers may assume that the child has been made into the image of its father. But that would seem to suggest a child who is somewhat older than indicated in the rest of the text. (Later, the narrator says that she got married about nine years earlier. Could the child already be recognizably identical with his father at the age of, say, six or seven, when the narrator would have been contemplating the divorce?)

The chapter ends with a memory of her brother drowning. She explains that "It was before I was born but I can remember it as clearly as if I saw it" (32). People do in effect fabricate memories from things they are told. Her assertion, in that sense, is not precisely untrustworthy, since she indicates that the memory is false. But this does establish that her memories are at least sometimes untrustworthy—and it is far from clear that she will always recognize this fact. Indeed, at this point, a careful reader may be starting to have a fairly strong, if probably still un-self-conscious, sense that the narrator's reported memories are far from reliable. Or, rather, some readers may be starting to feel their trust in the narrator disturbed, even if they could not say precisely why.

Not by coincidence, right after the clause about her memory of her brother drowning, the narrator introduces the idea of "an unborn baby" with "its eyes open" looking out from "the mother's stomach, like a frog in a jar" (32). This is a crucial image because it prepares readers for the "surfacing" of her actual memories of an abortion. Particularly in the psychoanalytic context implied by the text, these become, in retrospect, small, unconscious expressions of the repressed memory. Of course, this sort of rhetorical patterning can occur even outside a psychoanalytic context. Specifically, of all the possible expressions open to a narrator, the implied author may choose just those words and images that serve to prepare the reader for something that is concealed, thus making it more plausible later on.

The beginning of the next chapter offers an explanation of the child not being hers. First, she points out that she "didn't name it before it was born" (34). That is plausible in itself. But, at the same time, it may draw attention to the fact that one never learns any name for the child. Clearly they must have named the child at some point, so why is the reader never told the name? Moreover, if it was a boy, why does she continue to say "it"? This seems very out of keeping with ordinary biological responses to one's offspring.

The rest of the passage presents what was at the time something of a cliché about male domination. The husband uses the wife as a baby machine. (Needless to say, something can be a real and important problem and nonetheless be turned into a cliché.) She particularly complains that "he imposed it on me" (34). It is true that he did impose something on her. But what he imposed on her was the abortion, thus *not* having the child. The point is significant thematically. Perhaps particularly in 1972, the women's movement was deeply concerned with men trying to restrict women's access to abortion. But if women's choice is really the issue, then their freedom to have children should be similarly important.

The next chapter gives further imagistic manifestations of the repressed memory. Thinking about the end of her marriage, the narrator reflects, "A divorce is like an amputation, you survive but there's less of you" (44). That makes sense, certainly. All the lost projects and aspirations, with their foundations in emotional attachment, are aptly analogized to a part of oneself. But it should be clear that the phrase applies at least as clearly to an abortion.

Later in the chapter, her emotional response to her husband "surprise[s]" her. She is angry and resentful, even though "he didn't do anything to me" (50). Clearly, her emotional response is in conflict with her explicit memory here. There does not seem to be a standard hierarchy to resolve this dilemma, so one is left with an ambiguity about which to trust—the emotion or the memory.

She goes on to note that "there aren't any pictures" of the baby (again, referred to as "it") and that she hasn't mentioned him/it to Joe or her other friends (David and Anna). She then reflects on how "the baby . . . was taken away from me, exported, deported" (51). The idea is strange. Her claim up to this point is that she left the child. So it hardly makes sense to say that the child was taken away. The words "exported" and "deported" both suggest a separation across national lines as well. This "nationalization" of her separation may, in turn, serve to associate the "husband" with America. If so, this would relate to her extreme antipathy toward Americans, an antipathy that is almost pathological, even considering the historical context of the Vietnam War. The Americans and Americanism are consistently associated with violence, cruelty, senseless killing—which, in the end, is precisely how the narrator thinks of her abortion.

The following lines recur to the imagery of abortion. She characterizes her separation from her child as "my own flesh canceled" and "my own life, sliced off from me" (51). Here again one sees the narrator choosing images that may be construed as fitting her abandonment of her child. However, they are more fitting manifestations of an unconscious memory. The abortion does slice off her own life and cancel her own flesh in a literal way that abandoning her child does not.

Many of the same issues of memory recur in the following pages. At one point, for example, she thinks how safe she felt in the city. She then immediately tells herself *"That's a lie,"* recalling that she was often "terrified" (82). In this particular case, she reflects on memories and how she has problems discriminating between her own memories and "the memories of other people" that she's been told (82). The passage draws explicit attention to the fallibility of memory and thereby may foster thematic reflection. However, for present purposes, it most importantly continues to prepare readers for the revelation about her own false memories. In other words, it creates a complex of memories and emotional responses in the reader that affect his or her sense of trust in the narrator (just as the events in the experiment with the cards create memories and emotional responses that affect the test subjects' sense of trust in the different stacks).

The narrator's memories of the "birth" are along the same lines. The entire process is associated with being "dead." The doctors are "butchers" who "take the baby out with a fork like a pickle out of a pickle jar" (92). By this point, it is actually becoming difficult not to recognize that this is an abortion rather than a delivery—even though first-time readers probably still do not recognize this. She goes on to explain that "He wasn't there" but "he brought his car to collect me afterward" (92–93). Here, the narrator herself is very close to recognizing that this was not a delivery. The procedure she recalls is what she understands of her abortion. Her departure, apparently immediately afterward, seems to fit with abortion more than a delivery. Finally, and most significantly, she remembers that he collected "me" after the procedure, not "us." The reader still is probably not self-conscious about most of this at this point. For example, he or she is free to imagine "afterward" as referring to a day or so afterward. He or she can imaginatively envision the "husband" picking up the narrator with the child in her arms. In short, the reader need only make slight interpretive adjustments. But Atwood is constructing a set of associations that will make the subsequent change in memory believable and that will encourage readers to judge the abortion memory true and the birth/divorce memories false.

A crucial point comes soon after this. The narrator is supposedly remembering her "wedding." They fill out forms, which prominently include blood type (101). The place smells of "antiseptic" (102). In retrospect, one may realize that this is not the justice of the peace. It is the abortion clinic. The following dialogue makes no sense at a wedding. The man asks if she feels "better" now that "It's over." He consoles her, saying, "it's tough . . . but it's better this way." Her legs shake and she has an ache, presumably in the region of her legs. Crucially outside there is a "fountain" with "dolphins and a cherub with part of the face missing" (102). At least some readers will remember that this is precisely the fountain she sees on her drive, "dolphins and a cherub with part of the face missing" (9).[12] Thus one is presented directly with a memory and a perception. It seems extremely unlikely that both are true. By the usual default hierarchy, the perception is more trustworthy.

Of course, the abortion is more often misremembered as a birth, not a marriage. The links connecting this medical procedure (birth or abortion), the title, and memory are made clear subsequently. She explains that the procedure involved anesthetic that "was like diving, sinking." As a result, "I could remember nothing" (131).

Finally, searching in the water, she sees something, perhaps her father's corpse—readers never know. But it triggers a series of memories. She now in effect explains the strange images that had permeated her (pseudo-)memories up to this point. She did not remember her brother drowning, contrary to her claim (see 32). Moreover, the association of the "unborn baby" with a "frog in a jar" (32) was fabricated. Rather, she had envisioned the aborted fetus in a jar. Indeed, for a moment, she thinks that is a memory. But she corrects herself. Suggesting the image of the baby being removed with a fork, she recalls that the fetus was "scraped . . . into a bucket." It flowed "through the sewers . . . to the sea" (168), from which it was now surfacing as a memory. She goes on to explain why "he" was not there. He had children of his own, and there was a birthday party for one of them (168). She goes on to recall that the fountain "with the dolphins and the cherub" was not there. She recurs to the image of feeling "amputated" (169, cf. 44) and to the smell of "antiseptic" (169, cf. 102).

Again, faced with this contradiction, how does one determine which story is true? At this point, the reader is no longer in the realm of small interpretive adjustments. However, some heuristics do come into play. For example, as already noted, the incompatibility between memory and current perception in the case of the fountain weighs heavily in favor of the perception (i.e., given the unlikelihood that both are correct, there is greater reason to trust the perception than the memory). More importantly, a reader's sense of conviction in the story of the abortion results to a significant extent from the narrator's creation of a network of associations that makes the new story plausible. At the very least, the prior narrative creates a wide range of gaps—tensions, questions, uncertainties, if not outright contradictions—and these, gradually diminishing the reader's trust, prepare readers to find the earlier narration unreliable. Moreover, whatever one may think of psychoanalytic theory, the novel is readily categorized as relying on psychoanalytic ideas. Like principles of genre, the principles connected with this categorization take on an important adjudicative function. Thus repression and the recovery of memories become highly plausible explanatory principles here.

Finally, there is the larger, effortful, critical processing that goes beyond these heuristics. It operates here in the usual fashion, with the usual hierarchies. For example, in the adjudication of theories, people generally prefer the one that provides the more encompassing explanation. Here, readers have been given two accounts of the story—one in which the narrator was married; one in which she had an abortion. As presented, with its implication of a psychoanalytic context, the latter serves to explain the former, but not vice versa. In other words, if one assumes that the narrator's story actually involved an abortion, one is able to explain why she would have the feelings, memories, and conditions (e.g., no baby pictures and no wedding pictures [127]) reported earlier. Put differently, one can infer the nature and limits of her unreliability. One can link the epistemic limitations to her motivations, and circumscribe her motivated distortions to the sexual, traumatic, and guilt-ridden memories. Indeed, the fact that she feels guilt about the abortion ("Whatever it is, part of myself or a separate creature, I killed it" [168]) serves to explain why a sense of guilt seeps into her "screen memories," that is, the apparent memories that both conceal and indirectly reveal a repressed memory (for a concise treatment of the concept of screen memory, see Laplanche and Pontalis 410–11). In contrast, if one assumes that the story of the marriage is true, one is left with a wide range of gaps, unexplained points of irresolution in the story.

Of course, the explanation provided by the abortion story is incomplete. It too leaves some gaps. Again, the novel tacitly invokes psychoanalytic principles of repressing memories connected with sexuality, trauma, and guilt. But, in psychoanalytic theory, it is, first of all, childhood memories that are repressed. This is clearly not a childhood memory, nor assimilated to a childhood memory. In these ways, the novel deviates from psychoanalytic accounts. Nor does it appear to be consistent with what is known about traumatic memory loss in adulthood. This could simply be a mistake on Atwood's part. It seems more likely, however, that this deviation from psychoanalysis has thematic implications.

Specifically, there seem to be three important thematic complexes in Atwood's novel. One is feminist. This is clear in the repeated discussions of the place of women, the sexual relations of men and women, the humiliating treatment to which women are subjected by men, and so on. A second concern is, roughly, nationalist. It is manifest in the repeated discussions of U.S. violence and excess, and the relation of Canada to the United States.[13] The third concern is ecological. It is manifest in the attention to nature and the treatment of animals, among other things. Each of these thematic concerns is partially explicit in the novel. The narrator reflects on feminist, national, and ecological issues; characters discuss them.

The gaps created by discrepancies with psychoanalysis could contribute to any thematic concern. However, the relation of the narrator with her lover and the topic of abortion bear most obviously on feminist issues. The man appears domineering and manipulative. He uses the narrator sexually and belittles her talent as an artist. As noted earlier, the narrator represents him as something of a cliché as a husband—

particularly, as someone forcing her to have a child. This fits well with standard feminist views at the time. Due in part to political activism related to reproductive rights, many feminists rightly saw (many) men as trying to control women's reproduction by outlawing abortion and forcing women to have children. In this standard view, however, one could reasonably argue that another issue had been repressed. A wide range of men would want women to have abortions. It is not really plausible to think that a normally functioning woman would entirely repress an adult memory of an affair, pregnancy, and abortion. But it is quite plausible to see mainstream feminism as metaphorically repressing the story of women who do not want to have an abortion, but are coerced into doing so. Indeed, it is relatively easy to explain why this would happen. Fearful of restrictions on access to abortion, many feminists may have been inclined to avoid stories that lent themselves to anti-abortion use.

This does not mean that Atwood is "anti-abortion" (or "pro-life") in any usual sense. The novel does not seem to take a consistent stand on the status of the fetus. Sometimes, the narrator views the fetus as a baby who perceives the world in much the way an infant does (32). At other times, she insists that a fetus "wasn't a child," though "it could have been one" (168). Perhaps the most plausible interpretation is to see Atwood, at least in this novel, as pro-choice in the fullest sense of the term. In practice, "pro-choice" is used to mean "in favor of access to abortion." But it should mean "in favor of women being able to choose whether to continue a pregnancy to term or not." Thus they should not be forced to have a child when they do not want to—but they also should not be forced to abort a child when they do not want to. When faced with such a statement, I suspect that few if any feminists would disagree. But the suggestion of Atwood's novel is that part of the story of choice has been repressed, and replaced with the single story of women being used as baby machines.

The point may be suggested when the narrator begins to question her own recollections and cautions herself. "I have to be more careful about my memories," she says. "I have to be sure they're my own and not the memories of other people telling me what I felt" (82). Such distortions are most obvious in patriarchal ideology. They turn up in the novel in the narrator's notebooks as a young girl, her imagination of what she should be—"ladies . . . holding up cans of cleanser, knitting, smiling, modeling toeless high heels and nylons with dark seams" (105). But false memories can arise from political correctives to patriarchy as well.

Conclusion

A narrator is unreliable, first of all, to the extent that he or she is untrustworthy regarding the facts of the story. Those facts are defined by the receptive intent of the author. But that receptive intent is not simply a function of what the narrator says. In fact, the readers' and implied author's construction of the story involves the extensive integration of real-world presuppositions with deviations that are marked by the text—that is, the text serves primarily to indicate the points at which the story differs from the real world. The narrator may misrepresent facts, exclude important facts, or divert the reader's attentional focus from some important facts that are presented. In connection with this, the narrator may be unreliable for epistemic reasons (error) or due to some motive, deceitful or emotionally biased (as in the case of outgroup representation).

Readers begin with a default assumption that the narrator is trustworthy—or, more properly, a default sense of trust in the narrator. They tend to retain this sense even as incompatibilities or "gaps" accumulate. These incompatibilities need not be logical contradictions. They are, rather, primarily a matter of what readers experience emotionally as incompatible. Specifically, ordinary textual processing proceeds in a relatively routine way until one encounters a gap. At this point, one needs to resolve the incompatibility. Most often, readers do this with very minimal effort, following heuristic preference hierarchies. One may refer to this as "interpretive adjustment." (Such adjustment temporarily displaces the process of "spontaneous understanding.") Preference hierarchies may be isolated for sources of information (e.g., nonpersonified versus personified), types of information (e.g., direct perception versus memory), and epistemic context (e.g., genre conventions versus real-world laws of nature). However, as gaps accumulate and become more complex, readers may have to engage in more extensive and sustained reasoning of the general sort used in scientific inference. This is the sort of process that a professional critic commonly engages in. But it is also practiced by ordinary readers in conversations about books or films. It is commonly what leads to the clarification of a work's thematic concerns or emotional strategies. This may be referred to as "critical explication."

Atwood's novel shows some of the ways in which narrator unreliability is established through the development of gaps. Specifically, it presents a complex series of limited incompatibilities. These prepare the reader to find the narrator unreliable, to distrust the narrator. However, for the most part these gaps seem to remain below the level of self-conscious awareness. Thus they probably do not provoke a self-conscious response to unreliability before the narrator makes the issue explicit. When the full extent of the unreliability becomes clear, the novel nicely illustrates how readers come to adjudicate between alternative possibilities. In this case, the reader is likely to recognize that the second story line (about an abortion) allows the means for explaining a great deal of both story lines, while the first story line (about a marriage) does not. In keeping with this, the novel also presents a complex case of epistemic and motivational misrepresentation, due to the narrator's repressed memories and un-self-conscious confabulation of a false memory. Finally, it presents a good example of how thematic explication may result from effortful interpretation of gaps that remain even after problems of unreliability have been resolved. In this case, the gap in question bears on a particular aspect of the relation between the story and a theoretical category (psychoanalysis) drawn from the world outside the story.

Chapter 5

Varieties of Multiple Narration (I)

Parallel Narrators in William Faulkner's
The Sound and the Fury and David Lynch's *Mulholland Drive*

WHEN THINKING ABOUT NARRATION, people commonly imagine a single narrator. But many works have multiple narrators. Indeed, multiple narration in some form is found in almost every narrative of any length. This chapter begins by distinguishing three forms of multiple narration—embedded, collective, and parallel. It then explores parallel narration in greater detail, leaving embedded multiple narration for chapter 6.

Multiple Narration

The most common way of having multiple narrators is through embedding. As William Nelles explains, embedding is "the structure by which a character in a narrative text becomes the narrator of a second text framed by the first one." He goes on to comment that "While this might seem a rather specialised topic . . . embedded narrative is ubiquitous in the literature of all cultures and periods" ("Embedding" 134; on some mechanisms of embedding, see, for example, Bal 43–75). Most often, the main embedding involves the insertion of a personified narration into a nonpersonified narration. For example, this is typically the case with trial narratives, where the individual testimonies are included in a larger narrative of the trial that has a nonpersonified narrator. In addition, personified narration itself may embed narratives by other characters. In cases of this sort, the embedding story operates as a frame for the embedded story. The most obvious use of this device is in works such as *The Canterbury Tales,* where the frame presents a context in which multiple speakers tell their tales.

As the preceding examples already suggest, a narrative may have multiple narrators that are not embedded in one another. In some cases, such narrators tell the story *collectively*. (We will consider this case in chapter 6.) More commonly, such narrators are *parallel*. Indeed, the cases mentioned above—testimonies in a trial narrative and the various tales of the Canterbury pilgrims—are themselves parallel to one another, even if embedded in an encompassing narrative. If these parallel narrators are treating the same storyworld—as in a trial narrative—this parallelism may be called *conjunctive*.[1] The different stories are conjunctive in that readers are required to integrate them in inferring the story, thematic concerns, and normative emotions. If these narrators are treating different storyworlds—as in *The Canterbury Tales*—they are *disjunctive*. (The following analysis focuses entirely on conjunctive parallelism. For simplicity of exposition, then, "parallel narration" will be used to refer to specifically conjunctive parallelism, unless otherwise noted.)

The distinction between personified and nonpersonified narrators is important for parallel narration as well as for embedded narration. By far the most common form of parallel narration involves two or more personified narrators. A straightforward, albeit complex, case of parallel personified narration may be found in *The Sound and the Fury*.

The case of nonpersonified narrators is, of course, more complex. Though they are rare, it is possible to discern cases of parallel nonpersonified narration. The most striking instances of this come when a work divides into sections that apparently give different versions of the same events, thus the same storyworld, but these versions have nonpersonified narration. There is a case of this sort in David Lynch's film *Mulholland Drive*. (For a partial, schematic overview of types of multiple narration, see Fig. 5.1.)

Parallel Narration

Again, (conjunctive) parallel narration occurs when there are two or more narrators telling versions of the same story or treating the same storyworld. Such multiple narrations are, in general, of interest to the

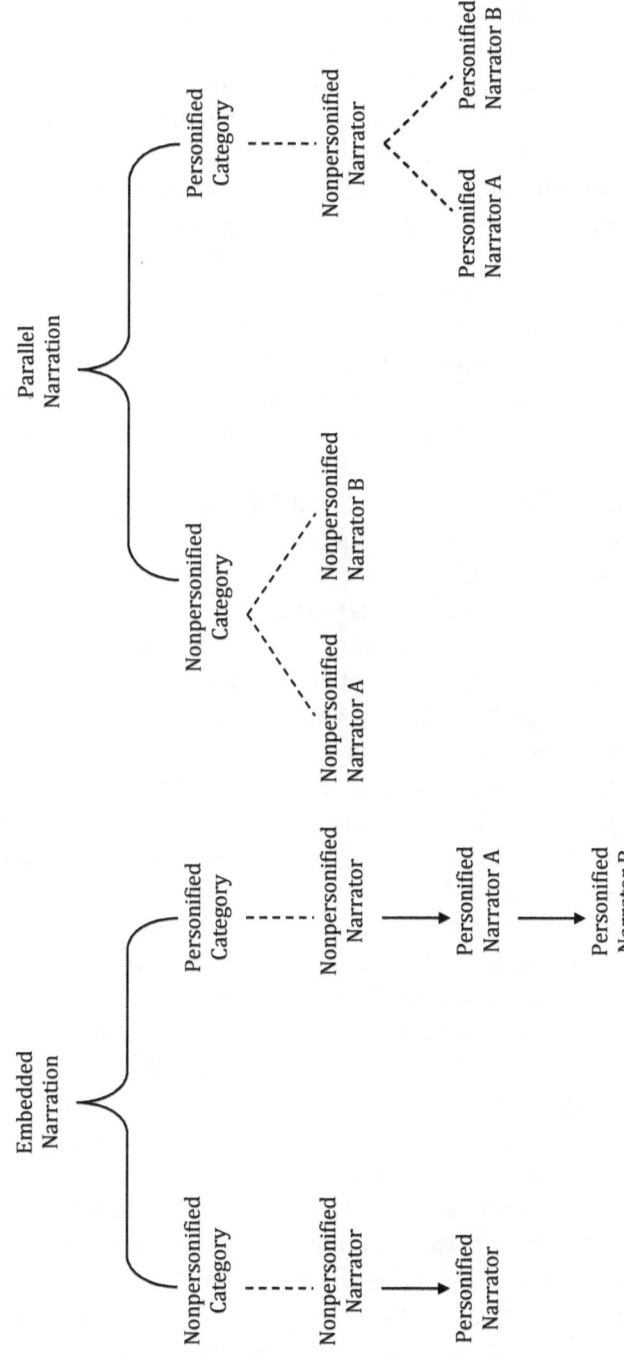

Figure 5.1. The two forms of multiple narration. Embedding is marked by arrows.

degree that they diverge from one another—through contradiction, differences in emphasis, filling in or leaving out different details, and so on. When evaluating diverse narratives of the same story events, readers do what they always do in inferring the story, particularly when faced with an unreliable narrator. The default assumption is that all the narratives have some relation to the facts of the storyworld—through experience, memory, inference, hearsay. However, this relation may be distorted by self-interest or error. In other words, one or more of the narratives may be affected by motivational or epistemic unreliability. When faced with an emotionally consequential tension between two versions—thus, a gap—people first rely on heuristics. When unconnected narrators give the same details, readers tend to assume they are true; when narrators give divergent details, readers tend to accept the ones that do not serve the self-interests of the narrator who reports them. When heuristics fail, readers undertake more effortful explications, trying to formulate the best explanatory account of the narratives.

Even when there are not direct representational contradictions or tensions, readers may see the mere joining of the parallel narratives as constituting a gap that requires interpretive engagement. For example, if there is a series of parallel narrators who treat different aspects of the storyworld (for example, different time periods), the issue arises as to why the parallelism is organized in precisely this way. Thus even in cases where the different parallel narratives create compatible versions of the storyworld, their parallelism alone will probably lead one to think of them together, to look for similarities or contrasts, particularly with an eye on emotional or thematic purposes. Indeed, the same point holds for disjunctive parallelism.

In short, all works with (conjunctive or disjunctive) parallel narrators potentially invite the reader or viewer to relate the individual narratives to one another. This is perhaps the major difference between works of parallel narration and collections (e.g., *Selected Stories by William Faulkner*). Simply put, collections do not presuppose that a reader will read all the works or do so in the order provided. They allow for selective reading. In contrast, works of parallel narration commonly assume *complete* and *directional* reading. More technically, the implied reader of a work understands and responds to a work—including works with parallel narration—as both a particular sequence and as a whole. There is no implied reader for a collection; there are only the implied readers of the individual works. Parallel to this, there is no textual implied author for a collection; there are only the textual implied authors for the individual works and the various levels of cross-textual implied author. There are also no initial and retrospective implicated authors across works in a collection, while these often figure importantly across parallel narrations (e.g., the implied reader's understanding of the first testimony in a trial narrative may alter after the second testimony).

In the case of parallel narration with personified narrators, one may assume a nonpersonified narrator who is constant across the voices of the parallel narrators. This nonpersonified narrator commonly provides hints about the reliability or unreliability of the personified narrators. Obvious cases of this include what the camera reveals about a crime or about suspects in a criminal investigation, separate from embedded testimonies. In addition, all the usual heuristics for personified narrators apply to the embedded, parallel narrators.

In contrast, when a narrative has parallel nonpersonified narrators, many of the usual clues about story correctness are missing. In other words, if the nonpersonified narrators disagree, it is difficult for a reader to discern just what is correct in the storyworld. Here, readers follow the same sequence of experiencing task conflict (a gap), shifting to heuristics and then engaging in effortful explication. However, many heuristics are simply unavailable—for example, that concerning a (personified) narrator's self-interest and that concerning a (personified) narrator's expertise. On the other hand, some heuristics remain in place. For example, the heuristic of overlap would seem to hold. Presumably, whatever is common to the different versions is true in the storyworld. Moreover, the "mimetic" heuristic holds. As discussed in the preceding chapter, fiction may be understood as a specification of difference from the real world. Thus the real world always stands as a default case for the story. When there is no other disambiguating information, readers are likely to choose the version of story events that requires less deviation from the real world. Finally, readers are still able to apply general inferential and evidential processes.

Of course, here as elsewhere, when inferences fail, when one cannot determine the storyworld at one or another point, readers may turn to a functional explanation; readers may consider what emotional or thematic implications this indeterminacy has. Indeed, that is true even for cases where one feels that disambiguation is finally possible. Then too readers may be concerned with the emotional and thematic implications of narrational and other gaps—thus why there is a gap in the first place.

Mentalistic Narration

William Faulkner's *The Sound and the Fury* is one of the most important works employing parallel, personified narration. The novel is divided into four sections, each of which has a different narrator. The first section is narrated by Benjamin "Benjy"—also called "Maury"—Compson, a mentally challenged man of thirty-three. The second is narrated by Benjy's brother, Quentin, a suicidal Harvard student. The third is narrated by another of the Compson siblings, Jason. The final section has a nonpersonified narrator, partially focalized on Jason and the Compson domestic servant, Dilsey. Each section concerns a particular day (given in the chapter title), though many of the events recounted are memories. The first section is April 7, 1928; the second occurs eighteen years earlier; the third occurs on April 6, 1928; and the final section takes place on Easter Sunday, April 8, 1928.

The events recounted by the different narrators are by no means identical. However, they do overlap to some extent. In terms of establishing the story, a reader has several interpretive tasks. He or she needs to establish which events reported by one narrator correspond with which events reported by another narrator. In connection with this, he or she needs to infer what actually happened in the storyworld and what is uncertain or ambiguous. He or she also needs to place various events in temporal and causal relation with one another.

Again, the processes used by a reader in inferring the story are basically the same as those used in works with a single narrator. But there are some partial exceptions. An important and consequential case concerns initial trust of a narrator. Again, the default for judging the particular facts of the storyworld appears to be that the assertions of the narrator are trustworthy unless there is reason to believe otherwise. The point holds to some extent for multiple personified narrations. However, the existence of different points of view on the storyworld tends to foreground the biases, thus unreliabilities, of individual narrators. At the very least, the prospect of multiple versions of the same events makes the possibility of contradiction much more salient. Readers are almost necessarily more aware of that possibility in works of parallel narration. This may not provoke out-and-out skepticism. However, it seems likely to sensitize readers to the cognitive and affective biases of the different narrators, even before conflicts appear.

Indeed, in some cases, multiply narrated works so foreground divergent points of view that they can shift attention away from the events themselves to the psychology of the narrators. In these cases, the events of the storyworld may remain highly ambiguous as readers use the different narratives to draw inferences about and respond emotionally to the narrators themselves. This is particularly likely in works that set out to represent the ongoing mental experience of these narrators.

These points are perhaps particularly clear in a work such as *The Sound and the Fury*. To understand the interpretive complexity of this work, it is useful to begin with some distinctions in what might be called "mentalistic narration." "Mentalistic narration" is any sort of narration that seeks to represent the mental processes of the narrator as he or she represents the storyworld. Of course, this is a relative distinction. All forms of personified narration could be thought of as doing this in some degree. However, some narratives do this much more extensively than others.

The basic and minimal form of mentalistic narration is first-person narration; perhaps the most prototypical form is interior monologue.[2] First-person narration is self-conscious narration in which the personified narrator explicitly formulates his or her representation of events in relation to his or her self-conscious perception, inference, memory, and so on. It may seem that this simply involves the use of the word "I." However, a narration may not be first person and yet may use the first-person singular pronoun. This occurs in interior monologue, which is typically not a form of self-conscious narration. Leopold Bloom (in James Joyce's *Ulysses*) is certainly conscious of himself. But he is not a self-conscious *narrator*.

So, a first important distinction is that between *self-conscious* and *un-self-conscious* or *implicit* narration. First-person narration is self-conscious. Interior monologue is un-self-conscious. This distinction is related to a division between *retrospective* and *ongoing* narration. This is not necessarily a distinction in the use of tense. Retrospective narration in particular may use present tense. However, it gives a sense that the events narrated are complete already and thus understood as a whole by the narrator. In contrast, in ongoing narration, the narrator does not know the outcome of events until those outcomes occur. First-person narration is often retrospective. Interior monologue is ongoing in that it isolates the moment-by-moment thoughts of the narrator.

Another way of putting this is to say that first-person narration always tacitly presupposes a narrating situation. There is always some implied narratee. There is always some context, even if it is wholly implicit. The (often implicit) narratee and context provide principles for selecting and shaping what is told in a first-person narration. Narratees and narrating situations may be embedded in interior monologue (e.g., if a character explicitly reflects on how he or she will recount an event to someone else). But the interior monologue itself is, in principle, removed from such contextual and addressee-oriented selection. In principle, interior monologue gives the character's thoughts as they occur, without choosing those that fit a particular narrative purpose. (Of course, by the account given in chapter 1, interior monologues are shaped by a nonpersonified narrator with the usual implicit, nonpersonified narratee.)

Interior monologue is considerably more significant for representing the mental processes of the narrator than is ordinary first-person narration. Moreover, there are different forms of narration related to interior monologue, with somewhat different properties, highlighting somewhat different cognitive and affective processes. Though not all of them are found in *The Sound and the Fury*, it is important to have a sense of this variety in understanding mentalistic narration.

Interior monologue is a representation of the ongoing sequence of *verbal* thoughts in a character's mind. These thoughts presumably represent events in the storyworld—events that the character perceives, remembers, infers, desires, fears, or whatever. But they also, and often more importantly, manifest the mental processes of the character/narrator—hence the status of interior monologue as prototypical for mentalistic narration.

Given this definition, interior monologue may seem to be relatively straightforward. However, there are several levels at which interior monologue may be, so to speak, "transcribed." The simplest is a direct reporting of subvocalization. People think in sequences of sentences during their ordinary, waking lives. These sentences are referred to as "subvocalizations" because people mentally articulate them without actually opening their mouths and saying them out loud. Joycean interior monologue is, generally, a form of *transcribed subvocalization.*

But there are other ways in which verbal thought may be represented. A slightly extended manner of representing interior monologue involves filling in perceptions, experiences, and so on, that are, so to speak, verbally formulated without being subvocalized. For example, if I see my department head, I recognize him and say hello. That does not mean that I think "There is Wayne" or even "Wayne." But I still in some sense identify him by name and by title. In cognitive terms, one may say that the complex of verbal associations is primed (or partially activated), even if they are not fully activated and brought into subvocalized sentences. Thus one form of interior monologue may represent one or more of the words that are part of a linguistic network associated with experience, even though they are not subvocalized. This may be called *associative reformulation.* In associative reformulation, the nonpersonified narrator supplies words that are part of the character's/narrator's thought, but are not specifically part of subvocalization.

We find associative reformulation in some of Virginia Woolf's work. For example, Septimus Smith is suffering from trauma from the First World War, along with hallucinations. He is out with his wife and hears a sound. Woolf writes, "It is a motor horn, he muttered; but up here it cannoned from rock to rock, divided, met in shocks of sound which rose in smooth columns" (*Mrs. Dalloway* 103). Evidently, "It is a motor horn" is actually vocalized. What follows may be subvocalized. However, the military terms are probably best thought of as primed associations. Septimus experiences the echoing sound and links that to his ongoing preoccupation with the war. This leads to the partial activation of words such as "cannoned," "columns" (which has a military as well as an architectural usage), and "shock" (linked with the unmentioned but clearly primed "shell," as in "shell shock"). It seems that the discourse only returns to something close to strict interior monologue (with minor, third-person rephrasing) in the immediately following parenthetical insertion, "that music should be visible was a discovery" (103).

Stream of consciousness involves a still more inclusive representation of the ongoing experiences of a narrator/character. This potentially includes all such experiences—verbal, perceptual, imaginative, and emotional.[3] Note that there is a, so to speak, "pure" case of interior monologue—the transcription of subvocalization. But there is no pure case for stream of consciousness. First, the representation of ongoing experience is necessarily partial. Second, in literature, that representation is necessarily limited to language, "the unalterable fact . . . that literature uses words," as Dorrit Cohn puts it (109). Thus there is always some degree of *reformulation*—specifically, *verbal encoding*—of nonverbal aspects of stream of consciousness.[4]

This limitation is partially lifted in film, where some aspects of visual and aural stream of consciousness may be represented directly. However, there are complications here. For example, it is very difficult to film point-of-view shots with realistic movement. In this way, there is always some degree of "reformulation" in the cinematic representation of even visual stream of consciousness. The somewhat unnatural quality of attempts at representing visual experience directly may be one reason why extended stream of consciousness is relatively rare in film (as, for example, Chatman has noted [*Story* 194]).[5]

Typically, the implied author chooses a *fully idealized verbalization* in stream-of-consciousness writing. In other words, stream-of-consciousness narration is not typically confined to what the character might have said had he or she articulated the entire stream of consciousness himself or herself. Rather, in stream of consciousness, the implied author—or, rather, the nonpersonified narrator—commonly makes use of all his or her verbal resources to articulate the ongoing mental experience of the character/narrator in its various perceptual, imaginative, and emotional facets.

Consider, for example, Bernard's thoughts about Susan in Woolf's *The Waves*. He follows her across a field, unobserved. She "begins to run with her fists clenched in front of her. Her nails meet in the ball of her pocket-handkerchief. She is making for the beech woods out of the light. She spreads her arms as she comes to them and takes to the shade like a swimmer. But she is blind after the light and trips and flings herself down on the roots under the trees, where the light seems to pant in and out" (14). It seems unlikely that Bernard has explicitly formulated much of this to himself or that the phrasing closely tracks his verbal associations. Rather, he has perceived Susan running and implicitly imagined the trajectory ("making for the beech woods"). Emphasizing the "shade" stresses just what Bernard sees, but also reveals his general sense that Susan is seeking to hide. The choice of words here manifests his emotional and causal understanding rather than his specific, subvocal formulation or his primed verbal associations. The detail of the nails and handkerchief is almost certainly something he cannot see, but something he, perhaps, implicitly experiences by imaginatively mirroring her actions—a spontaneous response (as recent research shows [see, for example, Iacoboni]). Likewise, the image of the light panting in and out may reflect a mirroring response to Susan's labored breath as Bernard tacitly imagines it after her run. The verbalization is, then, idealized in the sense that it reflects Bernard's stream of consciousness in a way that Bernard presumably could not.

The Sound and the Fury

Faulkner's 1929 novel is a paradigmatic case of mentalistic narration. As such, it particularly invites the reader to examine the psychology of its three personified narrators—Benjy, Quentin, and Jason. Put differently, the psychology of those narrators is more important than the story itself for understanding and explaining their various narrations.[6]

Benjy is often spoken of vaguely as mentally challenged. He does not seem to have generalized cognitive disorders. His perception is intact, as is his linguistic capacity. His physical inability to articulate speech sounds does not appear to affect his general capacity for understanding language or thinking linguistically.[7] However, he does have some severe cognitive limitations. These limitations are principally a matter of causal inference.[8]

First, it seems that Benjy is able to attribute causality only very short term and only in perceptually continuous contexts such that the sequence may be understood as a single complex event. The duration of that event is perhaps roughly what would now be characterized as the duration of working memory. Thus he can recognize that Dilsey "lifted me down" and "wiped my face and hands with a warm cloth" (19). But causal connections of any greater extent seem to be beyond him. Even such continuous, but extended, actions as feeding break down into fragmentary moments, separate and apparently unrelated. Thus he reports that "The bowl steamed up to my face, and Versh's hand dipped the spoon in it and the steam tickled into my mouth" (19).

In this particular case, the continuity of the events is complicated by the fact that it involves (unperceived) mental causes—Versh's judgment that the food is hot enough but not too hot, his intention to transport a suitable quantity of food to Benjy's mouth, and so on. Another case of this sort occurs when Dilsey calls to Versh, "Bring his bowl here." Benjy hears and reports this. But he fails to connect it with his next experience, "The bowl went away" (19). All hidden causes are difficult for Benjy. This may be seen, for example, in his understanding of disease as a perceptible object—"*I could smell the sickness. It was a cloth folded on Mother's head*" (47). But Benjy seems particularly inhibited in his ability to infer other people's mental states. On the other hand, even this is not an absolute inhibition.

Cognitive scientists commonly distinguish between two means by which people understand other minds. That understanding is called "theory of mind." One account of theory of mind, called the "theory theory," asserts that a person makes theorylike inferences about other people's mental states. The other account says that a person simulates other people's experiences and then attributes his or her reactions to them. It is increasingly recognized that people do both (see, for example, Doherty

48–49). Suppose I hear that a colleague has been denied tenure, despite receiving the unanimous support of his department. I have to draw some inferences about his state of knowledge—for example, that he does not know yet and is anticipating a positive decision. I am then likely to rely on my own feelings about receiving tenure and my own sense of disappointed expectations in other areas to judge how he will respond when he does hear. There may also be extenuating circumstances (perhaps he has another career) that would lead me, inferentially, to qualify my own emotional response—though, here too, I understand his response to those extenuating circumstances in part by reference to my own feelings. Thus I begin with some theorylike inferences, engage in some simulation based in part on the theorylike inferences, then further qualify the simulations by reference to further theorylike inferences, which themselves lead to another set of simulations.

Despite the usual integration of inference and simulation, one may distinguish two extreme forms of theory of mind response. One extreme is emotion contagion. This is pure simulation without any theoretical inference. As a result, the person experiencing emotion contagion does not even attribute the emotion to the target, but simply feels it himself or herself. For example, suppose little Sally breaks her toy and starts to cry. Little Betty hears Sally and begins to cry. Betty has not inferred anything about Sally's state and has not attributed anything to Sally. Rather, she has simply begun to feel the distress herself. The other extreme theory of mind response is pure inference without empathic simulation. Someone who is successfully cruel (e.g., a torturer) may be able to infer just what will cause pain to a victim. At the same time, he or she may avoid any sort of simulation, which might lead to empathic sharing of that pain.

Benjy seems to be particularly lacking with respect to theoretical inferences in theory of mind. However, he seems to have a greater capacity for nontheoretical simulation. Of course, his simulations are very limited, since they cannot be initiated or guided by theoretical inferences (except perhaps of a very short-term variety). On the other hand, he is very prone to emotion contagion. Indeed, this tendency toward emotion contagion is enhanced by the fact that he largely lacks the inhibitory operation of theoretical inference. In the hypothetical example given above, I was able to modulate my sympathetic simulation of a colleague's distress by a theoretical inference that he had other career opportunities. In many cases this modulation is quite reasonable. In other cases, it is merely a rationalization, a way of avoiding an unpleasant emotional response. In the case of Benjy, the lack of inferential capacity means that he is generally more prone to spontaneous and unmodulated emotion contagion.

As a narrator, this proneness to emotion contagion makes Benjy more reliable than others in certain respects, though of course less reliable in other respects. Specifically, he is more trustworthy in cases where other characters' simulative responses are distorted by rationalization. An instance of this occurs in his response to the events surrounding Damuddy's death. He hears a sound that he apparently does not self-consciously categorize. Nonetheless, he begins to cry (18). Others debate whether it was Mrs. Compson crying or singing. But Benjy's response clearly indicates the emotional valence of his mother's expression—it manifests grief, not joy. This is why other characters attribute a sort of prophetic quality to his responses, as when Quentin thinks, "Benjy knew it when Damuddy died. He cried" (70).

By the same token, however, his responses are less reliable to the degree that spontaneous impulses should be modulated by inferential and elaborative processes. This extends even to simple cases of putting oneself in another person's place when simulating their point of view—their knowledge, inferences, expectations, and so forth. Benjy shows a striking inability of this sort when he grabs the schoolgirl. She screams and he may sense her fear. But he seems unable to recognize what the cause of her fear must be, what terrifying inferences she must be drawing about this enormous, drooling man who has grabbed her.

Benjy's inferential limitations lead to other affective propensities as well. Specifically, some emotions rely on more extensive imagination and inference than others. Some require greater causal elaboration. An emotion such as attachment and the related separation anxiety are quite direct. Separation anxiety requires only the activation of attachment feelings along with the perceptual absence of the attachment object and the correlated inability to engage in any action to end that absence (e.g., by walking into the next room). Benjy's inferential inhibitions make such corrective action almost impossible. Thus he tends simply to moan and weep when separated from his one key attachment figure, Caddy.[9]

The most striking contrast with Benjy is Jason. While Benjy is unable to project intentional causes, Jason overgenerates such inferences.[10] When he fails at the stock market, he infers that he has been cheated by "a bunch of damn eastern jews," who "sit up there in New York and trim the sucker gamblers" (149). Indeed, he conjectures that Western Union telegraph has actually joined in a conspiracy with the New York Jews to sucker country folk out of their money (176, 182). In inferring causes, Jason simply does not accept chance (not to mention bad judgment). In effect, everything is planned, the product of foresight and design.

This comes out clearly when he meets a man from the traveling show and assumes that this man is sheltering his niece, Quentin, and her lover with the red tie. He asks "Where are they?" as if the man would have any idea what he was talking about. Even if the man did know anything about Quentin and her companion, what would allow him to understand that "they" refers to those particular people? The man asks, "Where's who?" (240) and Jason accuses him of lying. The passage is striking for two reasons. First, again, it manifests Jason's tendency to overextend intentional causal explanation. Here, since he has not found Quentin, he infers that this man must be hiding her. Second, it shows that, despite his propensity to generate such inferences, he has some severe theory of mind limitations himself. His theory of mind inferences are often bizarre. In this way, those inferences are highly unreliable.

As the reference to Jews suggests, Jason has a strong propensity toward out-grouping as well. Indeed, he is the most insistently and vehemently racist character in the book, and the most misogynist. Out-grouping tends to severely inhibit empathy. In keeping with this, Jason's empathic responses are limited to nonexistent. Indeed, the inhibitions on Jason's emotional responsiveness are not confined to in-group/out-group relations. He shows an astonishing incapacity to feel any empathy with his sister, Caddy, and his niece, Quentin. He steals their money with no evident qualms, his only worries being a practical matter of whether he will be caught. Of course, both Caddy and Quentin are part of a gender out-group. Jason is very concerned about his status as a man, and he seems particularly humiliated that "the whole world would know that he, Jason Compson, had been robbed by Quentin, his niece, a bitch" (240). Later, he is ashamed "that he had been outwitted by a woman, a girl" (239). Thus perhaps this too can be understood in terms of in-group/out-group divisions. However, his empathic inhibitions are so extensive that in the end it seems as if he forms an in-group of one. Indeed, he is virtually pathological in his absence of empathic response. In other words, while Benjy lacks inferential capacities in theory of mind, Jason seems to lack spontaneous emotion simulation—or, at least, his limited capacities for emotion simulation have been disabled by inhibitory processes. These inhibitory processes include generalized out-grouping.

It seems that Jason's primary emotion is a form of humiliation-based anger. This may be seen most clearly when he responds to Quentin and the man with the red tie. He does not appear particularly worried about Quentin's feelings, future, or safety. Rather, he is angry that she is "letting [her] own uncle be laughed at" by a man who would "come into town and call us all a bunch of hicks" (188).

Jason feels profound shame for his family's actions and his association with them. This results from his inferences regarding what other people might think. For example, when he goes out "without any hat," he worries that other people will infer that "I was crazy too." After all, "a man would naturally think, one of them is crazy and another one drowned himself and the other one was turned out into the street by her husband, what's the reason the rest of them are not crazy too" (180–81).

He is equally ashamed over his related decline in social status. He suffers from the thought that his family is disdained by "town jellybeans." In fact, it seems very likely that he has merely imagined this disdain. In any case, he insists, in his angry and humiliated response, that "my people owned slaves here when you all were running little shirt tail country stores and farming land no nigger would look at on shares" (185).

Jason is perhaps most profoundly affected by his sense of his own failure. He blames that failure on other people, particularly on their moral faults. He is filled with a "sense of injury and impotence feeding on its own sound" leading to a "violent cumulation of . . . self justification and . . . outrage" (235). (These points hold not only in the specific context of the quotation—when he reports being robbed—but generally.) Thus, for Jason, Caddy's promiscuity led to the divorce that cost him a job opportunity through Herbert. Rather than having any sense of his sister's pain, her humiliation, her sorrow at separation from her daughter, he construes her only as a cause of his failure—and as a source of money that may partially compensate for that failure. He characterizes her as "The bitch that cost me a job, the one chance I ever had to get ahead" (236).

He also envisions other people's response to his failure and decline in status as derisive. Indeed, he has a strong inclination to view other people's judgments as mocking and to respond to that supposed mockery with anger. Anger generally tends to inhibit empathic responses. Indeed, a sense of humiliation tends to promote a complementary rather than a parallel response to other people's emotions, thus a response of countering rather than sharing their emotions. (For example, a parallel response to someone else's happiness would be happiness. Complementary responses would include envy, resentment, or indignation.) Thus one would expect an intensified inhibition of empathy in someone who feels mocked by the "town jellybeans."

In short, Jason clearly does not suffer from the same cognitive impairments as Benjy. As such, some of his narration is more reliable than Benjy's because it manifests a more complex ability to infer causes, particularly intentions. But those causal inferences are severely distorted in cases where they bear on his generalized out-grouping or his emotional pathology—particularly his extreme proneness to anger based on shame—which lead to a nearly complete absence of simulative emotion sharing or empathy.

Finally, Quentin provides the most opaque case of the three. In one sense, Quentin's narration is quite straightforward. He records the events of his day and his memories with the usual sorts of causal and intentional inferences. He feels empathy and is able to modulate his emotions—or at least to recognize what modulating those emotions would involve. But there is one striking peculiarity about Quentin's narration. It almost entirely leaves out the central motivating force. His entire day is oriented toward his suicide. But that suicide turns up, for the most part, only indirectly or opaquely in his thoughts.[11] Moreover, there is little in his ongoing narration to suggest depression, anxiety, or another emotion that would underlie and explain that suicide.[12]

The contrast with Jason in particular is striking. Jason fills in the detailed causes of his behavior—for instance, his anger over the lost job and the resulting failure. In contrast, Quentin seems to skirt those causes, hinting at them without naming them. This contrast is presumably related to the cognitive and emotive tendencies that characterize Quentin. These both overlap with Jason's tendencies and contrast with them. Quentin shares with Jason an inclination to overgenerate causal attributions. However, whereas Jason overestimates the causal importance of other people's intentions, Quentin seems to overestimate the causal importance of his own actions. The peculiarity here is that he makes causal attributions in ways that he knows are false. Despite this, he seems to take those causal attributions seriously. The most noteworthy case of this is his insistence that he has committed incest with Caddy, as when he told Mr. Compson, "*Father it was I it was not Dalton Ames*" (62).

In keeping with this tendency to overvalue his own causal role in events, Quentin parallels Jason in his overstatement of blame. In contrast with Jason, however, the most important form of this blame is self-blame or, more properly, guilt. Quentin seems to feel a terrible sense of guilt. This is what allows him to hold to such a false causal attribution.

He, of course, knows that he did not commit incest with Caddy. But he is able to attribute the violation to himself because he feels guilt over Caddy's condition.

Finally, whatever feelings of attachment Jason might have had appear to be undermined by his anger and humiliation, as well as in-group/out-group divisions. In contrast, Quentin shares Benjy's deep attachment bond with Caddy. However, since he understands the nature of Caddy's disappearance and is able to fill in the (not terribly complicated) causal sequence, his emotional response is not so much a matter of mere separation anxiety. It is a rage provoked by jealousy. Of course, jealous rage typically involves three people—the rival, the beloved, and the lover. In keeping with this, Quentin does initially threaten to kill Dalton Ames. He also urges Caddy to agree that he kill her, then kill himself. But this hardly explains the suicide. After all, he does not kill the rival; he does not kill the (betraying) beloved. He only kills himself.

There are at least three possible explanations for Quentin's feeling of guilt here. The first is the simplest. He should have protected his sister from sexual shame and the subsequent public humiliation of rejection by her husband. This is bound up with the standard reading of Quentin in terms of a Southern honor system (see, for example, Singal). But this does not seem very plausible. He proposes claiming that they have committed incest, which would hardly protect his sister from shame or the family from dishonor. As to humiliation, he envisions the benefits of the incest story as including their joint exclusion from society—"*we'll have to go away amid the pointing and the horror*" (115).

A second possibility is that Quentin feels he is somehow responsible for her having sex with other men. There is perhaps a hint of this in the anecdote about Quentin and Natalie. After being chastised for "*kissing . . . some darn town squirt*," Caddy replies "I didn't kiss a dirty girl like Natalie anyway" (104). Caddy is in this way justifying her relations with boys by reference to Quentin's prior relations with girls. But this is peculiar also. It is the sort of argument one might expect from a couple who owe each other sexual fidelity, not from a brother and sister.

This leads to the third, related possibility. It is the least apparently plausible, but it may be closest to the truth. Though it runs contrary to usual moral principles, Quentin's feeling of guilt may have resulted precisely from *not* being the one who impregnated Caddy. In this way, his claim to have impregnated her is not a claim of guilt; it is a denial of guilt. After all, what he wants is a complete unity with her, the two of them fused in a single flame[13] ("if people could only change one another forever that way merge like a flame swirling up for an instant then blown cleanly out along the cool eternal dark" [137]; "*Only you and me then amid the pointing and the horror walled by the clean flame*" [91]), finally away from all society ("Nobody else there but her and me" [62]), if only in the lowest circle of Hell (62). In that fantasy, the ultimate Inferno is a sort of heaven, an ideal of bliss. It is Hell only, it seems, because it violates standard moral principles. In keeping with this, Quentin reflects, "if it were just to hell. . . . Nobody else there but her and me. If we could just have done something so dreadful that they would have fled hell except us. *I have committed incest I said Father it was I it was not Dalton Ames.* . . . If we could have just done something so dreadful and Father said That's sad too, people cannot do anything that dreadful" (62–63).

In any case, it seems clear that Quentin's cognition is strongly oriented toward overgenerating intentional causal attribution, specifically self-blame. In connection with this, his greatest emotional propensity is toward guilt, perhaps particularly guilt based on attachment insecurity. But his inferences are elliptical, his feelings to some extent concealed or misrepresented. As a result, he sometimes seems to blame himself in ways that he knows to be false, but which suggest other forms of self-blame that he presumably takes to be true. In each respect, Quentin is in part resembles and in part differs from his brothers.

Thus Faulkner presents a highly complex set of complementary unreliabilities. The bias of one parallel narrator is matched and perhaps compensated for by the biases of other narrators. This contributes to a nuanced sense of the storyworld. But it does not necessarily resolve ambiguities of that storyworld. Indeed, the different narrations, with their various unreliabilities, often *complicate* the reader's sense of the storyworld. Even more significantly, this narrational complexity serves to place the cognitive and affective psychodynamics of narration at the center of at least many readers' interpretive and responsive interest. In some ways, Faulkner's novel is more about the ways the parallel, personified narrators perceive, understand, and suppress their experiences than about the facts corresponding to those experiences. In a sense, the "real story" of *The Sound and the Fury* is to be found less in the storyworld than in the discourse.

Mulholland Drive

Of course, parallel, personified narration does not necessarily complicate our understanding of the storyworld or turn our attention to the psychology of the narrators. In many cases, the different perspectives complement one another and help to disambiguate the storyworld. Moreover, it is often the case that one can reconcile different narratorial perspectives in an overall interpretation even when the individual narrations contradict one another (as in many trial narratives). In both cases, when inferring the storyworld, readers commonly rely on their comprehension of the narrators as individuals with interests, biases, perceptual and inferential limitations, and so on. However, these standard inferential techniques are unavailable when the narrators are nonpersonified—which leads to David Lynch.

In treating David Lynch's *Mulholland Drive*, it is particularly valuable to focus on the (apparently) *discrete ambiguity* of the work. In a discretely ambiguous work, there are two or more peaks in the profile of ambiguity. These peaks represent interpretations that are mutually exclusive but also plausible within implied authorial intent. Examples would include works that are ambiguous between straight and ironic readings. Works with parallel, nonpersonified narrators may readily involve discrete ambiguity as well, since the alternative interpretations may be paired with the parallel narrations. The presence of discrete ambiguity does not preclude the possibility of arguing for a single, encompassing interpretation. Such an argument remains possible because implied authorial intent can involve both discrete ambiguity and a preference, even a strong preference, for one of the interpretations. For example, the implied author may find the work complete and satisfactory precisely because it points toward a particular interpretation, but discourages one from being fully confident about that interpretation. Alternatively, the implied author may be satisfied with the work because its ambiguities contribute to the overall emotional impact, even if the reader does, ultimately, feel confident about a particular interpretation.

Importantly for present purposes, disambiguating critical explication may have a significant narrational component in these cases. Specifically, when faced with a work that appears to have parallel, nonpersonified narration, readers or viewers often try to explicate—and disambiguate—the work by making its narrators personified and even nonparallel.[14] In other words, attempts to provide a single, encompassing interpretation of such a work frequently rely on an attempt to identify one or more narrators with a personal perspective and to hierarchize the narrators. Such an interpretive procedure involves eliminating the nonpersonified parallelism. This occurs in criticism on *Mulholland Drive*.

Lynch's film has two main parts. The first tells the story of the cheery and successful actress Betty (Naomi Watts), and her amnesiac lover Rita

(Laura Elena Harring). The second tells the story of the struggling and embittered actress Diane (Watts) and her ex-lover, the enormously successful actress Camilla (Harring). One might refer to these as the "optimistic" and "pessimistic" narratives. There are numerous repetitions and overlaps between the two narratives, suggesting that perhaps there is a single storyworld of which these are two versions. The most obvious ways of relating these two narratives, however, are apparently undermined by the nature of these overlaps (e.g., some of them appear to point in different directions as to which story is real). In any case, the two sections at least seem to have two distinct, nonpersonified, perceptual narrators. This is the case most obviously due to the contradictions between the two stories. Such contradiction is a standard feature of parallel narration, familiar, for example, from conflicting testimonies in trial narratives. In addition, and perhaps more significantly, there are systematic differences in the discourse of the two narratives, as we will see.

More exactly, the film begins with a scene of young couples doing the jitterbug. One obvious way of interpreting this sequence is as nondiegetic. Films often begin with a sequence that is not strictly part of the narrative. For example, a Pink Panther detective comedy might begin with cartoons about a pink panther. In this case, the real dancing figures appear against a background that includes silhouettes of dancing figures which themselves include real dancing figures (see Fig. 5.2). The inclusion of reality, shadows, and reality within shadows does seem to have thematic relevance. But it is difficult to say just what that is. The sequence ends with Watts appearing brightly lit and smiling (Fig. 5.3), ultimately along with an older couple, also smiling. It has the feel of an award or celebration.

In the pessimistic narrative, the viewer learns that Diane had won a jitterbug contest back in Deep River, Ontario, and that this sparked her interest in show business. In retrospect, this opening sequence suggests that contest and the subsequent award. The point has been noted by critics.[15] On the other hand, here as elsewhere, the film is not lacking in ambiguity. The bright enthusiasm portrayed by Watts is more in keeping with the Betty character than with Diane. This is compatible with (at least) three interpretations: 1) There are two distinct storyworlds and this scene occurs in the optimistic story (presumably with a less ideal parallel scene in the pessimistic story); 2) The optimistic story is true and fundamental, and this (optimistic) opening scene indicates that it is (i.e., the reference in the pessimistic narrative serves to confirm the validity of the optimistic story); 3) The pessimistic story is true and fun-

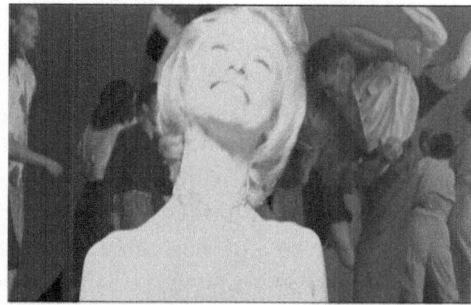

Figure 5.2. Opening jitterbug.

Figure 5.3. Betty/Diane evidently winning the competition.

damental, and this scene shows Diane's naïve and fantasy-bound evaluation of events at the time of the contest (or her distorted, nostalgic memory).

But, again, this segment is part of the opening of the film, a part of the film that is often extradiegetic. The film proper seems to begin with a shot of rose-colored sheets and a tan blanket. The camera moves slowly toward the pillow; the viewer hears breathing. There is a dissolve to black as the camera seems to enter the pillow.

As critics have recognized, this sequence rather strongly suggests that what follows is a dream. In keeping with this, the standard way of interpreting the optimistic part of the film is as a dream, with the pessimistic part being reality (see, for example, McDowell, Shostak, and Ridgway). Thus McDowell refers to "the dream that occupies the first half of the film" (1037). If one follows this interpretation, one collapses the two parallel nonpersonified narrators into a single nonpersonified narrator. In addition, for the first half of the film, one embeds a personified, stream of consciousness (Betty as dreamer) in that nonpersonified narrator.

After the sequence described above, followed by the title, the camera follows a car driving at night. A cut to the inside of the car shows Rita. She says to the driver, "What are you doing? We don't stop here." This scene is intercut with two cars racing along the road, side by side. Back in the first car, the driver points a pistol at Rita and tells her "Get out of the car." Before the men can undertake their obviously nefarious business, one of the racing cars crashes head-on into them. This evidently kills both the men (as well as the people in the other car). A dazed Rita stumbles out of the car and walks down the side of a hill. She ends up outside an apartment complex. The viewer eventually learns that she has amnesia.[16]

Before continuing with this story, it is important to switch to the other narrative. In the pessimistic version (which is, again, presented late in the film), Diane is unhappy, cynical, and unsuccessful. She once had a romantic relationship with Camilla. But Camilla has evidently ended that in favor of a film director. At one point, Camilla has invited Diane to a dinner party and has sent a car for her. The camera follows the car—precisely as in the opening of the optimistic version (as just described). There is a cut to Diane inside the car, and she says, "What are you doing? We don't stop here." In this case, however, Diane leaves the car to meet Camilla, who leads her up a hill to the house of the film director, who is having the party.

The connections between the two scenes are not only clear, but obtrusive. The question is, just what do the connections imply? Again, the viewer may simply understand there to be two storyworlds. Alternatively, he or she may take one storyworld to be real and the other to be derived from that reality. Most obviously, he or she may take one to be a dream and the other to be the experience that becomes a dream. The usual way of interpreting this would be to say that Diane's experience is the real one while Rita's is the dream version. There are difficulties with this, however. The suspicion in Diane's question seems unfounded, whereas Rita's worry is clearly justified. Moreover, the scenario fits a robbery better than a (dreamlike) walk up an unpaved path to the backyard of a home. Both points push the cause/effect (reality/dream) sequence in the opposite direction, suggesting that the optimistic version is reality and the pessimistic version is its derivative dream.

Further complications arise with subsequent events in the optimistic story when Rita falls asleep outside the apartment complex. Indeed, in the first parts of the film, Rita repeatedly sleeps. This calls to mind the opening pillow and reminds the viewer that one possible interpretation of the optimistic story is that of a dream. But here the suggestion is that Rita (or Camilla) is the dreamer, rather than Diane.[17]

In the morning, a woman is leaving her apartment for a trip. The viewer subsequently learns that this woman is Betty's aunt. As she is going back and forth between the apartment and the car, Rita sneaks in and hides.

Subsequently, Betty arrives at the airport, beaming with joy. She is accompanied by the old couple that the viewer may recognize from the jitterbug sequence. She has just met this couple on the flight, but they have become great friends. If one interprets the jitterbug sequence as the contest ending with Diane's receipt of the award, then this sequence seems incompatible with the "real" storyworld. This, in turn, lends support to the idea that the optimistic story is part of a dream. Indeed, the comments made by the old couple seem, in some ways, more appropriate to someone saying goodbye to Diane in her hometown as she leaves for Los Angeles. In other words, the events in this part of the narrative could be understood as actual memories reappropriated for use in a dream. On the other hand, this couple turns up again in the pessimistic story, and they do so in a way that prevents the viewer from seeing that story as a simple perceptual representation of the real storyworld. Specifically, in the pessimistic version, they are tiny, Tom Thumb–like creatures who walk out of a paper bag, then slip under Diane's door to frighten her and drive her to suicide. Again, when faced with conflicting storyworld possibilities, there is a general heuristic preference for the storyworld that is more fully continuous with the real world. The miniaturized versions of the couple in the pessimistic version then would count against accepting that as the storyworld.

Betty eventually arrives at her aunt's apartment. She meets the manager (played by Ann Miller), who says, "Just call me Coco. Everybody else does." In the pessimistic story, at the party of Camilla's film director, Diane meets the director's mother (played by Ann Miller), who says, "Well, just call me Coco. Everybody does." Again, the parallel is obtrusive and suggests a connection between the two events. One option is simply some sort of possible-worlds-type counterpart relation. But, here as elsewhere, the more obvious possibility is that one is reality and the other is a dream based on that reality. In this case, however, the dream/reality derivation could go in either direction. Indeed, the Coco of the optimistic story seems to be more fully developed and to have a more natural place there. Moreover, there is something dreamlike about the director's party—which not only is approached in a strange way (walking up a hill through brush) but includes a somewhat incongruous group of characters.

In the optimistic story, Betty goes into the bedroom in her aunt's apartment and sees a woman's clothes on the floor outside the bathroom. She nonetheless walks into the bathroom, then, hearing someone in the shower, opens the shower door. She is apparently very embarrassed and apologetic on finding Rita there, naked. But the sequence of events is peculiar. Having seen clothing outside the bathroom door, she might have expected someone to be in the bathroom. Having heard someone in the shower, she might have expected the person to be naked. Here there is a point in the optimistic story that seems to suggest that it is a dream and that it presupposes some events of the pessimistic story. Specifically, the confidence with which Betty goes to the shower may suggest the prior sexual relationship between Diane (here, Betty) and Camilla (here, Rita).

The viewer is soon teased by the more overt possibility that the optimistic story is a dream. Specifically, Betty explains to Rita that she is from a small town in Ontario, but "now I'm in this dream place." Of course, "dream place" refers to Los Angeles, as both a place of one's dreams and a place where dreams are made as movies (as in the case of *Mulholland Drive*). But here the nature of the connection with the story-world is not entirely clear. One could take this to be a definitive clue. But one could also take it to be part of implied authorial misdirection.

Moreover, if it is a dream, there is the peculiar fact, already mentioned, that Rita is the one who keeps falling asleep, not Betty, and one might suspect that all this is Rita's dream. Indeed, before the introduction of Betty, there are two events that initially may seem to be dreams of Rita. First two men meet in Winkie's. One of them, Dan, explains that he had two dreams that were "both the same." In retrospect, this comment clearly points toward the two narratives viewers are seeing. The connection would seem to suggest that both narratives are dreams. At the same time, it seems odd for the dream to signal not only that it is a dream, but that something else is a dream also. In any event, Dan's two dreams presented a dangerous figure behind the restaurant. After breakfast, Dan walks to the back of Winkie's. A dark figure lurches out and the man collapses, perhaps from a heart attack.

This sequence is followed immediately by Rita sleeping (see Fig. 5.4). This suggests that it is her dream as well (cf. Thomas 86). That shot of her sleeping is followed by another sequence that the viewer may take to be her dream. On the other hand, it is equally possible to take one or both episodes as real. Indeed, even if one takes some episodes to be part of Rita's dreaming, one cannot take the entire sequence to be part of her dreaming, because the viewer is shown Rita falling asleep and this presumably is not part of her dreaming.

In any case, the second sequence begins with a man in a wheelchair informing someone that "The girl is still missing." The obvious interpretation of this is that he is referring to Rita. Thus one might infer that he has something to do with the threat posed to her by the driver of the car before he was killed in the crash. The man's message is passed on

Figure 5.4. Shot of Rita sleeping, after the Winkie's sequence.

to unseen figures with shots of two telephones. The second telephone (which rings unanswered) sits beside an ashtray and below a red-shaded lamp on a side table.

Despite the suggestion that these episodes are Rita's dreams, both have connections with the pessimistic story. First, Diane goes to that Winkie's. She sees the man who had the two dreams about someone behind the restaurant. More significantly, in this scene, Diane is meeting with a man whom the viewer knows is a murderer. She offers this murderer money, apparently to kill her estranged lover, Camilla. Indeed, at this point in the pessimistic story, Camilla seems to have just announced her engagement to the director, Adam Kesher. Moreover, the pessimistic narrative identifies the second telephone in the episode concerning the "missing" girl. It is Diane's telephone. This suggests that the threat to Camilla was actually Diane's payment of the hired killer. Diane is, therefore, a person who would have an interest in hearing whether "the girl" had been found or not. Indeed, when she meets with the murderer, Diane hands him a photograph of Camilla and says "This is the girl."

Another sequence of events in the optimistic narrative concerns Adam Kesher. He is making a film and is under considerable pressure from some goons to cast "Camilla Rhodes" in the role. The goons keep saying "This is the girl." Moreover, when he sees this actress, he is forced to say, precisely, "This is the girl." The sequence is rather peculiar, with its insistence on the exact phrase. Here, too, there is a connection between the two narratives, given what Camilla says to the hired assassin. But what is that connection? It seems the simplest interpretation is to take Diane's "This is the girl" (from the pessimistic story) as real. Then the repetitions of the phrase in the optimistic story are derived from the pessimistic story, as dream images from life.

But there are still problems. Most obviously, the picture of Camilla in the optimistic story is another woman (i.e., not Harring). Of course, this too has parallels. During the director's party, Camilla (i.e., the Harring character) provocatively kisses another young woman right in front of Diane (see Fig. 5.5). That other young woman is the Camilla Rhodes of the optimistic story. Here, too, one can imagine a unifying interpretation in which the pessimistic story provides a face for a psychoanalytic "displacement" (or shift) in the dream—in this case, a displacement from the real Camilla to this rival.[18] But the staginess of the kiss at the director's party and its gratuitously mean orientation toward Diane (see Fig. 5.6 and Fig. 5.7) are so obtrusive that it is hard to take seriously as a real event. It seems more like Diane's somewhat paranoid fantasy or interpretation. This raises the question of whether either perceptual narrator directly displays the real storyworld. Perhaps both are unreliable, or are representing something other than the real storyworld (e.g., inferences, fantasies, or, again, dreams).

Eventually, in the optimistic narrative, Betty learns that Rita has amnesia. They decide to look in her purse for clues. In the purse, they discover bundles of money and a blue key. The next scene presents the assassin character. The conjunction is important and suggests an association in the narrator's mind. This is fitting, as the entire sequence is apparently explained in the pessimistic narrative when Diane meets with the assassin. In the pessimistic version, after Diane shows the assassin a picture of Camilla, she explains that she has the money to pay for the job, revealing a bundle of bills in her purse. The assassin shows Diane a blue key and tells her "When it's finished, you'll find this where I told you." This seems to add weight to the interpretation that locates the optimistic story in Diane's dream world.

There are, however, still difficulties. Most important, there is a somewhat dreamlike quality to the signal here. We are shown the key on Diane's coffee table, perhaps concealed from Diane's usual line of sight (from her couch) by a large ashtray. We are not given any information as to how or when the key got there. In a later scene, after a neighbor has removed the ashtray, Diane stares at the key almost as if she was not aware of it earlier, thus as if the assassin has had to enter her apartment when she was not there to place it on the table. (We learn that she has been away prior to the scene where the key is revealed.) Moreover, she has a brief imagination of Camilla's return before we see her looking at the key. This does not fit well with the idea that she is aware

Figure 5.5. Camilla kisses another woman before Diane.

Figure 5.6. But before the kiss, they check to make sure Diane is watching.

Figure 5.7. Diane meets their eyes before the kiss.

of the murder at that time. Finally, her intense reaction of guilt after staring at the key seems to suggest that she has only now learned about the murder. On the other hand, detectives have been looking for Diane already, which suggests that that murder took place much earlier—and Diane knows this. In these respects, the putatively real signal and the surrounding events in the pessimistic narrative appear at least to some degree oneiric as well.

Continuing with the optimistic narrative, the viewer finds Betty and Rita trying to figure out a scheme to uncover Rita's identity. Betty explains, "It's just like in the movies. We'll pretend to be someone else." Like references to dreams and the representation of sleep, this seems to suggest that this optimistic story involves a systematic alteration from the real storyworld, with Diane and Camilla pretending to be someone else—Betty and Rita. But, on reflection, one realizes that the idea is equally consistent with Betty being her real name and "Diane" being the pretense.

Subsequently, a strange woman appears at Betty's door. Recalling a mad prophet figure, she insists that someone is in trouble. The ever-friendly Betty introduces herself, saying, "My name's Betty." The woman replies, "No, it's not." This is less equivocal than the previous case. But it still retains a degree of ambiguity, if only because the viewer is uncertain of the extent to which this madwoman is a reliable informant (rather than a means of fostering misdirection). Moreover, to say that this woman is not Betty is not necessarily to say that she is Diane.

Before Betty and Rita can pursue their investigation of Rita's identity, however, Betty must pursue her acting career. She practices a scene with Rita. It begins with Betty asking, "You're still here?" and Rita responding, "I came back. I thought that's what you wanted." The scene ends with Betty threatening to kill Rita—or, rather, Betty's character in the audition dialogue threatening to kill the character read by Rita. Subsequently, Betty reads the same part in an audition. The audition is noteworthy in several respects. First, everyone is extremely nice to her. Second, she acts the part brilliantly, far outshining her own performance in the practice with Rita and, indeed, greatly excelling anything viewers are likely to imagine possible with this vapid script (for an illuminating discussion of this scene, see Toles). She is virtually guaranteed the part. Moreover, a casting agent spies her and takes her to the auditions for Adam's new film. Adam's and Betty's eyes meet and there is immediate interest and chemistry. As already noted, Adam has no choice but to give the role to Camilla. But he is clearly drawn to Betty.

From the perspective of the pessimistic story, the sequence is poignant for several reasons. First, in the optimistic episode, Adam is entranced by Betty (thus Diane), rather than Camilla. Given Betty's/Diane's sexual preferences, it seems clear that this would never come to anything. However, it would help to prevent the loss of Camilla to Adam. Second, Betty's enormous success at the audition contrasts sharply with Diane's admission that directors have not been terribly impressed with her and that she has gotten some roles due primarily to the intervention of Camilla. Third, one of the most pathetic moments of the pessimistic story involves Diane looking across her kitchen at Camilla, who seems to have materialized out of nowhere, and saying "You've come back," recalling the "I came back" from the play script. Finally, the threat of murder written into the scene appears to suggest Diane's attempt to have Camilla murdered.

Here there seems to be a further reason for believing that the optimistic episode presents a dream. The episode involves wish-fulfillment elements, by which the unsuccessful and cynical Diane can be the successful and cheerful Betty, with her beloved and aloof Camilla transformed into the dependent Rita. Rather than being the one who orders Camilla's murder, she is the one who saves Rita; rather than giving the money for the murder, she finds Rita with the money, and so on.

The standard interpretation is further reinforced when Rita remembers the name "Diane Selwyn." Betty and Rita first call Diane's telephone number and hear the message on her answering machine. This too contributes to the oneiric quality of this narration, since the viewer later discovers that this is the answering machine message of Diane in the pessimistic episode. Of course, here too the causality could go in the opposite direction. Even so, the likelihood of the standard interpretation seems further enhanced in what follows. Betty and Rita go to find Diane Selwyn. When they arrive at her apartment, no one answers the door, so Betty climbs through a window and lets Rita in. They hold their noses, suggesting that there is a strong odor. Soon, the source of the odor is revealed. There is a bed with rose-colored sheets. On the bed, there is a woman, lying on her side with her knees bent. She is dead and her body is in an advanced state of decay (see Fig. 5.8). In the pessimistic story, the viewer learns that Diane's sheets are rose. Indeed, the transition between the two narratives comes when Diane wakes up on those rose-colored sheets, rising from almost the exact position of the corpse (see Fig. 5.9). One obvious interpretation is that the dreaming Diane has anticipated her own suicide.

Figure 5.8. The decaying body of Diane Selwyn from the optimistic story.

Figure 5.9. Diane, just before she wakes up in the pessimistic story.

That night the sexual feelings of Betty and Rita finally express themselves. It is worth noting, however, that Betty repeatedly says "I'm in love with you," while Rita does not. In a standard, psychoanalytic dream interpretation, this may be seen as partially restoring the relation of Diane and Camilla, but also as acknowledging its real asymmetry. Thus it combines wish fulfillment on Diane's part and the disturbing recognition that the wish has not really been fulfilled. Indeed, in the middle of the night, the two go to a strange theater called "Silencio" and listen to a woman lip-sync a Spanish version of Roy Orbison's "Crying." The song recounts how the singer cries because her beloved no longer loves her. Both Betty and Rita weep over the song. But it does not seem to have much to do with their story. Rather, it seems to have to do with the story of Diane and Camilla. By this point, the profile of ambiguity seems to strongly favor the standard "optimistic narrative as dream/pessimistic narrative as reality" interpretation—though the early problems still remain.

At the end of this Silencio sequence, Betty finds a blue box in her purse. The box has a lock that clearly recalls the blue key found by Rita in her purse with the money. Here the connection with the putatively real story suddenly becomes opaque. There does not seem to be a realistic source for the blue box in the "real world." Indeed, the appearance of the blue box in the pessimistic story is far less realistic than its appearance in the optimistic story.

Betty and Rita rush home to find the key. But, when Rita gets the key, Betty is suddenly gone. Rita opens the box on her own. The camera descends into the darkness of the open box as it descended into the pillow at the start. Now, there is a transition between the two narrations. The box falls to the carpet. Clearly having heard the box drop, the aunt—once again in her own apartment—enters the bedroom and looks around. Yet now there is nothing on the ground. This is a peculiar scene, as it seems to suggest some sort of reality outside the dream world, a reality that includes the aunt. But it is difficult to say with certainty whether it is reality or not. If it is part of the dream (since it occurs before Diane wakes up), it seems unmotivated. Specifically, its relation to the optimistic narrative is unclear and indeed contradictory (because the aunt is away). If real, it contradicts Diane's assertion that the aunt is dead, perhaps posing a difficulty for the standard interpretation.

Following this, the viewer sees a woman lying on her side, with her legs bent, like the corpse of a few scenes earlier. Indeed, the viewer briefly sees the corpse (in a shot identical with Fig. 5.8), before a change to a living woman (Fig. 5.9). There is insistent knocking. The woman is Diane (known up to now as "Betty"). The knocking wakes her. She goes to the door and finds the neighbor, who has come to pick up some things. The beginning of the dream was signaled by the descent into the pillow. This waking would seem to give the end of the dream.

Yet, this too is not entirely clear. Among other things, it is difficult to say just what the descent into the blue box might mean. If it is a dreamlike aspect of the optimistic narrative, the reappearance of the box in the pessimistic narrative is, if anything, far more dreamlike. Of course, here too the standard interpretation seems to be the most viable. The point is simply that the work's profile of ambiguity is much more complex than a focus on this standard interpretation would suggest, and that ambiguity is fundamentally a matter of narration (i.e., whether there are parallel, nonpersonified narrators or an implicitly personified, embedded, dreaming narrator along with one, encompassing, nonpersonified narrator).

One of the items taken by the neighbor is her ashtray—a distinctive piece in the shape of a piano. Near the ashtray is the blue key. A close-up draws the viewer's attention to the key, though the first-time viewer at this point knows only that it may have some relation to the key in Rita's purse. On a second viewing, however, viewers know that it means Camilla has been killed. In keeping with this—but, as already noted, suggesting that the murder took place some time ago—the neighbor notes that two detectives came by looking for Diane again.

At this point, a series of initially confusing events occurs. Betty looks and sees Camilla (known to the viewer as Rita at this point). She says, "You've come back." The visual narrator cuts from Diane, looking left, to Camilla, looking right, then back to Diane, who gradually expresses extreme anguish. The next cut from Diane should take the viewer to Camilla again, but it presents Diane looking right, as if observing herself, evidently with disgust (see Figs. 5.10–5.13). The sequence is disorienting. On first viewing, viewers are likely to infer that Camilla ended a relationship with Diane and that Diane is wishfully imagining her return or remembering an earlier, temporary return. After learning about the assassination, the viewer might find the sequence even more baffling (except perhaps under the assumption that Diane has not yet seen the key, as already noted). In any case, the narration here is complex. The viewer is presented with what initially seems to be a simple perceptual narration. But on reflection it seems more likely that this is some sort of fantasy, memory, or even hallucination. The scene seems ambiguous among these possibilities—and the possibility that it is part of a dream, thus reversing the standard interpretation.

This shifting from perceptual reality to some sort of inner state indicates that the narrator in the pessimistic narrative has direct perceptual access to the mind of Diane. Moreover, as becomes clear subsequently, this access leads to the nonchronological presentation of causal sequences of story events. Finally, it is connected with the strict focalization on Diane that characterizes almost the entire pessimistic narrative. In all three respects, the narration of the pessimistic narrative differs from that of the optimistic narrative. The latter appears to be entirely chronological and not to involve shifts between perceptual reality, on the one hand, and fantasy, memory, or hallucination, on the other. Moreover, it is obtrusively nonfocalized, shifting among different characters and scenes without apparent constraint. Indeed, these differences are the main discursive reasons to posit parallel narrators here.

Now Diane crosses back to the sofa with her morning coffee. On the other side of the sofa, Camilla is lying down, half naked. Suddenly, Diane is wearing not her robe and nightclothes, but shorts and no top. She is carrying a glass rather than a cup. Most significantly, the neighbor's ashtray still sits on the coffee table and there is no blue key. The interaction is peculiar since Camilla begins by expressing her desire for Diane, but then quickly says that they should end their physical relationship. Diane quickly blames "him" for this change in Camilla's attitude. In terms of realistic plausibility, the scene is odd, hinting at a dream or a combination of memory with fantasy. At least some dream or fantasy element is suggested by the fact that Diane is much prettier in this scene than in the immediately preceding one.

Figure 5.10. Diane turns with delight to the returned Camilla. Cut to Fig. 5.11.

Figure 5.11. Camilla returns Diane's affectionate gaze. Cut to Fig. 5.12.

Figure 5.12. Diane apparently continues to look toward Camilla. However, she becomes increasingly distressed. Cut to Fig. 5.13.

Figure 5.13. Rather than Camilla, we find Diane apparently looking back at Diane.

This is followed by another scene in which Adam is introduced and the developing relationship between Adam and Camilla is indicated. Eventually, the film arrives at the point when Diane attends Adam's party. This is where she has the experience in the car, asks her question ("What are you doing? We don't stop here"), walks up the hill, meets Coco, and so on. Subsequently, she is at Winkie's meeting the assassin, saying "This is the girl," being shown the key, and so forth.

These various events largely fit with the usual dream interpretation. There are, however, some possible problems. The most obvious concerns temporal sequence. The initial narration presumably ends when Diane wakes up. It may at first seem that everything in the second narration occurs after that point. But this is incompatible with the dream interpretation in that the exciting events for the dream (particularly, hiring the assassin) should precede the dream itself, not follow it.

One can largely reconcile this with the standard interpretation once one recognizes the narrational complexity in the second narrative, specifically its integration of perception, memory, and fantasy. At the end of the entire sequence, Diane is sitting alone on her sofa, in the same bathrobe she wore when she woke up. She is staring at the blue key. While the viewer cannot be certain, one possible interpretation is that, after the opening, the entire sequence of events in the pessimistic narrative has been a series of memories and fantasies triggered by Diane's perception of the key. The viewer is prepared for this by the initial indication that the pessimistic narrative will not give any explicit signal that the film is entering a character's thoughts.

Of course, as already pointed out, this is far from definitive. The nonchronological order of presentation and the internal access to Diane's mind (as well as the closely related focalization on Diane) also serve to differentiate the nonpersonified narrator of the pessimistic narrative from that of the optimistic one. In other words, these features also support an analysis of the film in terms of nonpersonified, parallel narration.

Moreover, some further events are more difficult to reconcile with the standard interpretation. First, part of the pessimistic narration includes the monstrous figure behind Winkie's. He or she[19] has the blue box from the optimistic story. If taken as real, this would provide the obvious explanation for the monstrous figure and the blue box in the optimistic narrative/dream. But it is not clear how Diane could have seen this figure and the box or even that they could exist. Of course, these could be merely imagined by Diane. But why would she imagine them? What would give rise to this imagination? Put differently, the existence of the blue box could serve at least as well to support a reversal of the usual interpretation. Betty sees a blue box in the optimistic story. That could serve to explain the blue box in the pessimistic story, if the optimistic story is real and the pessimistic story is a dream. On the other hand, neither Betty nor Diane appears to see the monstrous figure behind Winkie's. That would seem to be information available only to a narrator. This would apparently undermine the interpretation of either narrative as the dream deriving from the other narrative as reality.

Subsequent events seem even more anomalous for the "pessimistic story as reality" view. The monstrous figure has the blue box in a paper bag. Once she sets it aside, two tiny figures walk out of the paper bag—miniature versions of the elderly couple Betty met on the plane and who,

Figure 5.14. Highly unrealistic, highly theatrical scene of Diane's suicide.

in some storyworld, had something to do with her prize in the jitterbug contest. Again, there is knocking at Diane's door. The tiny old couple enters through the space below the door. They assume normal size and pursue Diane. Diane screams, rushes to her bed, reaches for a gun in the side table and kills herself. The knocking recalls the knocking that (apparently) woke Diane that morning. As such, it may suggest that she is asleep again—or that Betty or Rita or maybe even Camilla is asleep—and dreaming this second narration. Other options would include the possibility that Diane is experiencing a hallucination or that the narrator here is not a simple perceptual narrator, but is giving a metaphorical account of Diane's sense of guilt, panic, and despair.

Further difficulties arise due to the representation of the suicide. It is not only unrealistic. It is obtrusively theatrical. The smoke behind the bed recalls a theater effect (see Fig. 5.14) and has no obvious realistic counterpart.

The narrative points of view become—if this is possible—more ambiguous with what follows. First, the film returns briefly to the monstrous figure behind Winkie's, a figure who remains highly obscure. If this is a figure of Diane's imagination, how could he or she survive Diane's death? If he or she is "real" in the storyworld, what does that say about the status of that storyworld?

When Betty/Diane was first introduced at the end of the jitterbug sequence, she was initially presented as an unfocused, cloudy patch of whiteness. This is repeated now. But, instead of being joined with the elderly couple, she is joined with Rita/Camilla. The image connects the narrator of this section with that of the jitterbug sequence. But it also serves to suggest a sort of ghostly presence. It is as if the two characters are now united in spirit. Or, perhaps, it suggests what aspirations for happiness they may have shared, or that Diane (or Betty) may have had for them. The image contributes in a complex way to the profile of ambiguity.

The final shot of the film returns to the Silencio. One woman with strange blue hair sits in the theater and says, simply, "Silencio." Silence suggests, among other things, death. In this way, this final judgment contributes to the sense that there has really been a death, or perhaps two deaths. The silence, then, would be that of both Diane and Camilla. This may seem to define the second narration as a real storyworld. But this is a figure from the first narration, not the second. Her survival beyond the end of the second narration may be taken as suggesting that the first narration defines a real storyworld and that the second is a nightmare preserving the characters seen by Betty in the first narrative (except, again, the monstrous figure). There is then the further complication that the location of the speaker in a dreamlike theater hardly makes her reality status clear.[20]

In sum, Mulholland Drive presents a complex profile of ambiguity. Viewers are accustomed to ambiguity at the level of theme or normative emotion, and to some limited ambiguity in the storyworld. But this work presents quite extensive ambiguity at the level of the storyworld. That ambiguity is inseparable from (the ambiguity of) the work's narration. Specifically, the work may be understood as having two parallel, nonpersonified narrators. There are not many options that allow the viewer to trust both narrators. For example, one might assume that they represent parallel possible worlds in a science-fiction-like sense. Alternatively, one may try to understand them in terms of a single storyworld (thus as conjunctive, rather than disjunctive, parallel narration). Efforts at such interpretation commonly involve establishing some sort of hierarchy and personification of narrators. However, there is apparently contradictory evidence as to what might be "real" and what might be either derived or unreliable. Some of the excitement and effect of this and other postmodern works[21] derives from the ways in which they move viewers to the limits of their ability to resolve ambiguities of both storyworld and narrative voice.

In the case of Mulholland Drive, there is a somewhat unequal profile of ambiguity. Specifically, one common interpretation appears more strongly supported than others. This is the interpretation in which a jealous, humiliated Diane has her ex-lover murdered, but feels deeply guilty for it as well. Her complex emotions and associated memories give rise to the enigmatic dream that constitutes most of the film. The last part of the film brings the viewer into her waking life, where she realizes what she has done, remembers key moments of her relationship with Camilla, then is driven to suicide by her feelings of guilt and shame, as well as terrifying hallucinations. In the end, she seems to have some sort of spiritual connection with the now dead Camilla.

At the same time, this standard account of the film also seems to be undermined by information that supports other interpretations. These other interpretations include reversals of the dream/reality division, as well as pure storyworld parallelism. Perhaps the best way of reconciling these interpretations is to say that both the optimistic and the pessimistic narratives are dreams. That may seem to resolve the contradictions. However, in the end, most of the ambiguities remain. Specifically, in this case the question is not "Is the pessimistic version real, and in what ways does it incorporate fantasy or hallucination?" but "Is the pessimistic version closer to reality, and in what ways does it distort that reality?" Note that, in both cases, we may take parts of the optimistic version as real and parts of the pessimistic version as unreal, though perhaps not precisely the same parts. Moreover, in the two dreams account, we do not know who is dreaming the dreams and if there is one dreamer or there are two. Worse still, there is nothing that prevents the two dreams account from involving parallel nonpersonified narration. To the contrary, all the discourse differences continue suggest this. A final difficulty is that there is no character who is consistently present in the optimistic story, as we would usually expect the dreamer to be present. Indeed, this point counts at least prima facie against the standard interpretation as well.

Whatever interpretation one favors here, it seems clear that even if the profile of ambiguity for the work contains a prominent peak, it does not contain only one peak. Moreover, the possible interpretations and the encompassing pattern of discrete ambiguity are important for viewers' emotional response to the film and for whatever thematic inferences one may wish to draw. In other words, they are a crucial part of the implied author's/implied reader's experience of the work. Finally, the film appears to involve parallel narration for its very different—indeed, contradictory—parts. In its overt presentation, that parallel narration is nonpersonified. In order to overcome the difficulties of parallel nonpersonified narration, critics tend to identify an embedded but implicit narrator who is personified as a character in the story. In other words, they seek to transform an apparently nonpersonified and parallel narration into a covertly personified and embedded narration (or its functional equivalent in dreaming stream of consciousness[22]).

Conclusion

Pre-theoretically, many readers or viewers and critics probably imagine that single narration is the standard case in literature—one story, one narrator. In fact, multiple narration is ubiquitous. Multiple narration can take several forms. The narrators may be embedded in one another, as when Jones tells a story about Smith recounting an incident. Alternatively, narrators may be parallel, as when Jones tells a story and then Smith gives his version of the same events. Finally, some group may be presented as narrating a story.

Typically, parallel narration involves two or more personified narrators who are encompassed by a single nonpersonified narrator. Commonly there are discrepancies between the different narrations, and one main interpretive task for the reader is inferring the facts of the storyworld, the thematic implications, and the normative emotions of the work as a whole. Part of this involves determining just how the different narrators are or are not reliable.

Some narratives are less concerned with exploring the storyworld *per se* than with examining and clarifying the cognitive and affective principles by which a particular narrator transforms the storyworld into the narrated world. Such narratorial transformation is accessible to a reader primarily via contrasts with alternative representations of the storyworld. For this reason, mentalistic narration (which focuses on the mental processes of narrators or focalizers) fits particularly well with parallel, personified narration. The different, personified narrators may diverge in their representations in ways that reflect their underlying cognitive and affective propensities, thus their characteristic epistemic and motivational unreliabilities.

Faulkner's *The Sound and the Fury* is an outstanding example of this. The three parallel narrators manifest distinctive cognitive biases, particularly in their theory of mind inclinations and propensities toward types of causal attribution. Moreover, it is no accident that Faulkner's novel involves interior monologue and related techniques. Mentalistic narration is readily developed in the range of narrational techniques that run from un-self-conscious subvocalization (strict interior monologue), through modifications that incorporate verbal associations, to various forms of "verbal idealization" in which words of an encompassing narrator express a character's perceptual, emotional, and other nonverbal experiences in stream of consciousness.

While personified, parallel narration can pose serious interpretive problems and manifest a high degree of ambiguity, nonpersonified parallel narration is typically far more ambiguous and problematic. Indeed, it may initially seem impossible to have a work with two distinct impersonal narrators. But *Mulholland Drive* suggests that this is possible (as do other works, such as James Joyce's *Ulysses*). That is not because the film definitively is a work of parallel nonpersonified narration. Rather, that is one possible—indeed, highly plausible—interpretation of the work. This plausibility results in part from the story contradictions (a common feature of parallel narration) and in part from the distinct narrational styles of the two narratives, specifically with respect to chronological emplotment, access to internal states, and focalization. Indeed, the nonfocalization of the optimistic narrative—thus the frequent absence of the putative dreamer (Betty, or perhaps Rita) from the events—would seem to count somewhat against interpretations that make the optimistic narrative a dream.

Critical analyses of the film do, however, point to a striking feature of the interpretation of such a work. Despite the resulting anomalies, critics have often set out to reduce the film's apparent nonpersonified narratorial parallelism to a single nonpersonified narrator with an embedded, personified narrator (or functional equivalent). This suggests that viewers are strongly motivated to avoid accepting parallel nonpersonified narration in their interpretations of a work. In the case of *Mulholland Drive*, this avoidance is possible only if one allows a sort of covert personified narration, since the narration of Lynch's film is overtly nonpersonified. The point is in itself theoretically consequential, since it suggests the in principle possibility of covert personification, whatever one concludes about *Mulholland Drive*.

Chapter 6

Varieties of Multiple Narration (II)

Embedded Narration, Focalization, and Collective Voicing in Ngũgĩ Wa Thiong'o's *Petals of Blood* and *Born of the Sun* by Joseph Diescho (with Celeste Wallin)

*A*GAIN, multiple narration may be parallel, embedded, or group-based. This chapter begins with embedded narration and some related issues in focalization. It first considers the topic in general, theoretical terms, then turns to a Kenyan novel that takes up narrational embedding to treat political themes. One central thematic concern of this novel is the unification of diverse individuals into a national or class-based movement. This concern has narrational consequences in that it poses the problem of reconciling individual voices with group expression. This leads to the third form of narrational multiplicity—group narration—as well as group focalization and a Namibian novel in part concerned with discourse, collectivity, and political solidarity.

Embedded Narration

Perhaps the most important distinction in embedded narration is between psychological and rhetorical embedding. Psychological embedding preserves the epistemic and other constraints of both the embedding and embedded narrators. For example, suppose Jones is explaining what Smith said about his (Smith's) experiences on the day of a murder. Jones clearly does not have access to Smith's thoughts. Thus he cannot report those thoughts. This is a limitation of the embedding or "primary" narrator. Conversely, Jones may know about events occurring far away from Smith. However, Jones cannot report those as part of Smith's testimony, because they were unknown to Smith. In psychological embedding, the embedded narration would not include any information unavailable to the embedding or embedded narrator.

Note that there are two sorts of limitation here. One sort comes from the embedding story narrator. The other comes from the embedded story narrator. When the primary narrator is omniscient, however, there is only one sort of limitation. That is the limitation of the embedded narrator. However much the primary narrator knows, that will not affect what the embedded narrator can say, if there is strict psychological embedding. Put simply, Adam's story is the same, with the same limitations, whether Adam is telling it himself or it is being reported by God.

However, not all embedding is psychological, and these constraints are often not preserved. Thus a film may be framed as a recollection by one of the characters involved in the main action. However, in the course of the film, the viewer may be given information that should not have been available to that embedded narrator. Take, for example, James Cameron's *Titanic*. The central narrative of the film is framed as a recollection by Rose. But the viewer is shown a number of scenes in which Jack is alone, doing things that Rose would not have known about. Thus they could not be part of her recollection.

When the embedded narrative is wholly unconstrained by the limitations of the embedded narrator, one may refer to this as "rhetorical embedding." But this is not the usual case. For example, it is not the case in *Titanic*. First, for many scenes where Jack is alone, Rose may have had "factual" knowledge of the events even though she lacked perceptual knowledge. A film does not have to confine embedded narration to a verbal statement, but may show the event to the viewer in its perceptual detail. That is different from showing a scene that would not be known at all to the narrator. In addition, a narrator may draw inferences about events. For example, Rose can infer that Jack had to board the ship at some point, even if she did not see that event or hear Jack recount it. A narrative may present these directly as perceptions. In these and related cases, there is a partial deviation from the constraints of the narrator, but not a complete deviation.

More importantly, perhaps, the embedded narration typically follows the contours of the story that would be told by the embedded narrator, if he or she had all the relevant information and experience. Put differently, it typically follows the embedded narrator's interests. For instance,

Rose has an interest in how a piece of jewelry got into Jack's possession. Even if she does not know how that occurred, it is a topic of importance to her. Thus the narration might convey that information even if it was not available to Rose. In doing so, it is violating many constraints of the embedded narrator, but not all of them. It is still constrained by, so to speak, the story that narrator would like to be able to tell. Put differently, a primary narrator (e.g., the encompassing, nonpersonified narrator of *Titanic*) may freely add information unavailable to the embedded narrator, while following the basic narrative orientation of that embedded narrator. This may be termed *idealized embedded narration*.

More technically, the defining features of a narrator may be divided into two groups—emotional and epistemic. Psychologically embedded narratives are both epistemically constrained and emotionally oriented by the embedded narrator. Purely rhetorically embedded narratives are unaffected by either. Between these extremes, there are, first, embeddings that are partially epistemically constrained; specifically, there are embeddings that are *informationally constrained*, but not *perceptually constrained*. Second, there are *emotionally constrained embeddings*, which is to say, embeddings that are oriented by the emotional interests of the narrator, but not epistemically constrained. Emotionally constrained embeddings commonly appear in the form of idealized embedded narration.

The same situation arises in cases that do not technically involve embedding, but where a nonpersonified narration is oriented by reference to a character, almost as if this character were the narrator. This is, of course, focalization. In parallel with the forms of embedded narration, one may distinguish psychological, informational, and emotional focalization. Psychological focalization is a strict limitation of narration to the knowledge and interests of the focalizer. Informational focalization honors the general informational constraints of the focalizer, but not the precise sources and detail of that information (e.g., inference versus perception). Emotional focalization is constrained only by the emotional orientation and interests of the focalizer. (Focalization does not occur without any constraint from the focalizer. Therefore, there does not appear to be a parallel for rhetorical embedding.)

As this indicates, a focalized narration may present detailed perceptual and other information not available to the focalizer. This may be termed *guided omniscience*, in parallel with idealized embedded narration. Despite great similarity, there are some differences between guided omniscience and idealized embedding. Perhaps most obviously, when reading a work that appears to involve idealized embedding, one may always question whether the excess information—the information that should not be available to the narrator—is evidence of the narrator's potentially unreliable inference or even misrepresentation. That is typically not the case with guided omniscience. There are presumably differences in the reader's emotional response to voice and related matters as well.

Finally, idealized embedding or guided omniscience may suggest another narrative that more narrowly conforms to the constraints of the narrator or focalizer. For example, there may be an actual narrative told by *Titanic*'s Rose. In most cases, this actual narrative will not be something one can reconstruct. However, there are cases where one may at least partially infer its content, and also infer that it in some degree parallels the enhanced embedded narration that is actually given in the text or film. This other narrative may be called an *implicit subtextual template*.

Embedding, Guided Omniscience, and Collective Narration in *Petals of Blood*

Petals of Blood is arguably the most important novel to emerge from Kenya, and one of the major works of Anglophone postcolonial literature. Critics have not always been in agreement on this assessment. Indeed, many critics have greatly undervalued the novel, in part because they have not recognized its narrational subtleties, nor even fully understood its politics.[1] (For a useful overview of the criticism, see McLaren.) As to the former, a few critics have briefly noted the narrational complexity of the novel. For example, Aizenberg points to the work's "multiple voices" (90), including "a plural, communal voice" (92).[2] As to the work's politics, virtually every critic recognizes the anticolonial and anti-neocolonial nature of the work. However, fewer writers have examined the Marxist orientation of the novel (see, for example, Sharma; see also Martini on links with working-class literature), not to mention the complex dialectic that the work establishes between Marxism and nationalism.

Specifically, the novel explores the condition of newly independent Kenya. It focuses on four characters—Munira, a teacher; Wanja, a prostitute (among other things); Abdulla, a bar owner and former revolutionary; and Karega, a teacher then a union leader. There are also important secondary characters, such as Nyakinyua,[3] a small farmer, repository of Gikuyu tradition, and grandmother of Wanja. There is a frame narrative involving a murder investigation. This takes place in the mid-1970s. The main story of the work extends back about a decade earlier, to a period right after independence (in 1963). Further, embedded narratives give stories from various individual and group histories.

Needless to say, *Petals* is as interpretively complex and ambiguous as any work. But it seems clear that the novel centrally involves national allegory, a point only partially explored in criticism on the novel. Perhaps most crucially, Wanja represents the nation. Though underdeveloped, the connection is recognized by some critics. For example, Sharma characterizes her as "the spirit and earth of Kenya, humiliated, exploited and ill-used by the Kimerias, Chuis and Mzigos" (302). Though he does not explore the allegorical status of Wanja, Eustace Palmer does characterize her in such a way as to illuminate that status. As he explains, "Far from wishing to enslave men, Wanja's ruling passion throughout is the need to preserve her independence" (278-79). The point applies at least as straightforwardly to the nation (in contrast with its enslaving leaders) as to an individual. One may extend these general connections first by noting that Wanja allegorically represents both the land and the people of Kenya. As the land, she is a "garden" (34), a woman with "valleys, rivers, streams, hills, ridges, mountains" (315). As the people, she is "myriad selves" (64), someone in whom Karega sees "countless other faces in many other places all over the republic" (294). As the last quotation suggests, she often represents Kenya, though she may also represent the Gikuyu.[4] More precisely, she is either Kenya today or the Gikuyu people today. In keeping with this, her grandmother represents traditional Kenya or traditional Gikuyu society. These alternative interpretations are not mutually exclusive. Traditional Kenya is the collection of Gikuyu, Masai, and other local traditions. Contemporary Kenya is itself manifest in its various modernized ethnicities. Like Wanja, these groups have connections with traditions in the countryside and with the cosmopolitan world of the cities.

As a young girl, Wanja is seduced and abandoned by Hawkins Kimeria, a member of the nascent capitalist class. Kimeria subsequently turns out to have been a collaborationist with the British counterinsurgency forces as well. The affair results in a pregnancy. Wanja gives birth to the child, but abandons it. In national allegories generally, the birth of a child points toward the birth of the nation. The suggestion here is that independent Kenya was the child of the nascent capitalist and collaborationist class. This is in keeping with Ngũgĩ's view of the new nation.

After this, Wanja becomes a prostitute. The allegorical point is, of course, that the new Kenya has to prostitute itself to those with money in order to survive. The idea is elaborated when the reader learns that she initially refused Europeans, but eventually had to succumb. Similarly, "independent" Kenya realized that it had to prostitute itself to foreign investors. For a time, Wanja is able to take refuge in the countryside. There she brews a traditional drink referred to as "[t]he spirit" (210), which is linked with memory of the Gikuyu past and with self-realization (see 209–12). The suggestion is that modern Kenya could for a time retain its integrity by relying on the traditions of the countryside and by fostering a sense of communal spirit bound up with self-realization through historical memory. But eventually capitalist developments—including industries involving Hawkins Kimeria—threaten her traditional land. In addition, the youth of the countryside cannot afford to study. Needing money to preserve traditional lands and to send a talented orphan, Joseph, to school, Wanja is forced to prostitute herself again. Here the point seems to be that, in order to give some minimal protection to cultivators and to give at least a few poor children a chance at education, the prostitution of modern Kenya had to be extended to the traditional countryside.

Ultimately, Wanja is almost killed when three Kenyan capitalists—including Kimeria—are burned in an arson attack on her brothel. She is saved by Abdulla, a former revolutionary who is now a destitute street vendor. At the end of the novel, Wanja is pregnant again. Thus independent Kenya is preparing to give birth to a new nation (a point recognized by several critics; see Stratton 120). But this time, it will not be the child of the capitalists and colonial collaborationists. It will, rather, be the child of the revolutionary poor.[5]

The other two main characters—Karega and Munira—represent a sort of class allegory. Karega is the child of the disenfranchised and dispossessed peasantry, the generation after Nyakinyua. His mother's devotion allows him to earn an education. For a time, this makes him a member of the petite bourgeoisie, as he has a job teaching school in rural Kenya. However, his class origins and ties to the landless peasantry, as well as his experience of unemployment, petty trading, and wage labor, orient his class stance toward the masses and away from the elite. Eventually, he becomes a union organizer. The novel in fact ends, not with Wanja and the new nation, but with Karega and the growing union movement. The workers are coming to recognize their own strength and their possibilities for collective action. Indeed, there is considerable tension between Karega and Wanja. At one point, they are lovers. But he eventually becomes disgusted with her prostitution. The allegorical point would appear to be that the workers' and the peasants' movement is repelled by the prostitution of the modern nation. The novel ends with an unresolved tension between nationalism, on the one hand, and the class-based struggles of the workers and peasants, on the other.

Perhaps surprisingly, the main character in the novel is the final character mentioned above—Godfrey Munira. He is the son of Ezekieli, "a wealthy landowner and a respected elder in the hierarchy of the Presbyterian Church" (13). Like Karega, Munira is educated and becomes a petit bourgeois intellectual. Also like Karega, and the petite bourgeoisie generally, Munira's "class stance" or feeling of class solidarity is malleable (cf. Ngũgĩ on "the vacillating mentality and world outlook of the petite bourgeoisie" [in Sicherman 25]). What is curious is that his class origins do not influence him toward an identification with the wealthy. He is initially a sort of individualist, largely lacking in class solidarity. He does not necessarily pursue his own private gain. But, with some limited exceptions, he does pursue his goals largely in isolation from others.[6] Eventually, he becomes involved in an apocalyptic Christian sect that works to divert the revolutionary energies of the poor away from material struggles (of class or nation) and toward individual spiritual salvation.[7] In this respect, he seems to be a good example of religion as an opiate. The point is connected with petit bourgeois indifference to class, and with the moral intolerance and righteousness often associated with the petite bourgeoisie. Such intolerance and righteousness are found in both Karega and Munira. The result is that they both feel disgust for Wanja. Munira, however, acts. He determines to burn her brothel, first setting fire to the doors and thereby preventing escape (333). The allegory might suggest that the religious obscurantist fraction of the petite bourgeoisie also aims to rid the nation of prostitution, but in a moralistic and misguided way that could potentially destroy the nation itself.

Of course, the reader does not learn about Munira's aims and actions until the end. In good crime-story fashion, the novel begins with a series of arrests. Chapter 1 is short. It comprises five brief sections. Sections one through four recount the police going to Munira, Abdulla, Wanja, and Karega. Section five presents a newspaper account of an apparent case of arson the night before, a case in which three prominent, wealthy Kenyans have been killed.

There are already interesting elements of the discourse here. The nonpersonified narrator is clearly omniscient. The reader has access to different characters' thoughts and feelings. However, this access seems particularly pronounced in the case of Munira. More significantly, the special place of Munira is signaled by the fact that Abdulla, Wanja, and Karega are all named in the first sentence of their sections. However, in the opening section of the novel (treating Munira), the narrator never tells who is being discussed. From the first sentence, then, there is already a presupposed framework, signaling a nonpersonified narratee who is familiar with Munira and with the context. The first sentence reads, "They came for him that Sunday." The reader only learns that this "him" is someone named "Munira" when one of the police officers asks if he is Munira (2).

Other discourse elements enter in the section on Karega, as the reader is given access to the thoughts and feelings of a group of workers. The importance of this is not so much what it tells about the knowledge of the narrator, but what it tells about the interest of both the nonpersonified narrator and the implied author. To a great extent, the novel is thematically concerned with individualist fragmentation and different sorts of group solidarity. It is unsurprising that these concerns would be manifest at the level of the discourse from early on.

The second chapter begins with a flashback to twelve years earlier, when Munira began teaching school in the village of Ilmorog. Munira is the topic of the first part of this chapter. But the focalization is not entirely clear. In the second paragraph, the nonpersonified narrator reports the views of "the elderly folk" of Ilmorog (5). After an intervening paragraph, a peculiar thing happens. The narrator begins to use "we," thereby becoming personified and *collective*, presumably manifesting rather than simply reporting the group's observations and feelings.[8] This collective "we" is contrasted most obviously with Munira, who will (as already noted) turn out to suffer from petit bourgeois individualistic alienation. An obvious reading of the "we" is that it represents a communal mutuality that has been lost in the modern world. Subsequently, Nyakinyua speaks of how "*Our* young men and women have left *us*" (7, emphasis added), which would seem to reinforce this interpretation. But, in fact, the "we," at this point, is exclusionary and closed-minded. The group clearly misunderstands Munira when they think he is "mocking" their traditions (6) and they try to drive him away. Indeed, they show similar collective hostility toward Abdulla (5).

Three pages into the chapter, the focus shifts from Munira to Abdulla, who is introduced apparently by the nonpersonified narrator. But the narrative soon returns to the collective voice, with the group expressing its ambivalence about Abdulla. Again, far from being an admirable expression of solidarity, the collective voice here seems to express primarily suspicion and xenophobia.

Munira is eventually accepted into the village, becoming "one of us" (10). It is worth noting that he is accepted only when he proclaims that "Unity is strength" and refers to working for the new Kenya. This may appear to redeem the collectivity of the group. They only accept an outsider when the outsider demonstrates that he or she is genuinely willing to engage with them in solidarity. But, in fact, this too is undermined. Munira said "Unity is strength," while "not believing it, but noting that the words impressed" those around him (10).

Literary works produced in the context of nation building might be expected to develop group narration in order to overcome individualistic fragmentation. This would be particularly unsurprising in a national allegory, such as *Petals of Blood*. But Ngũgĩ foils expectations. As the preceding points suggest, the traditional group definition of the village society, manifest in collective narration, is highly problematic. Initially, it is clannish and xenophobic; subsequently, it is prone to manipulation. On the other hand, the scope of the collective narration at this point is not entirely clear.[9] There are hints that it may not be village society as a whole but only the village elders, thus a traditional elite. Moreover, in his petit bourgeois opposition to this collective, Munira is often no less closed-minded, as when he characterizes Ilmorogans as "a people opposed to light and progress" (10).

Perhaps more significantly, the representation of the group narrator is by no means invariably critical. For example, though she is the granddaughter of Nyakinyua, Wanja is a stranger to Ilmorog. Thus she needs to be accepted into the group, as did Munira, even if the initial level of distrust is much lower. This acceptance is fairly quick and is signaled by a shift to the collective voice: "Within a week she too had become of us" (31). This seems to involve a reasonable balance of open-mindedness and caution. In this case, moreover, the group appears more encompassing than the group that judged Munira. It now seems to be "the people" generally, and not simply the elders. Consistent with this, the collective voice is associated at this particular point with the song and dance that manifest and recall the cultural traditions of the people. In this section, then, the representation of the "we" is positive. Rather than stressing xenophobia, it emphasizes the shared cultural heritage that unites the villagers.

Returning to Munira's acceptance into the community, we find that, after the shift out of collective narration, the nonpersonified narrator proceeds more or less straightforwardly for another eight pages until a discussion begins about when young people began leaving Ilmorog, which is to say, when the village community began to come apart. Here, rather than an expression of group collectively, there is a series of fragmentary representations of individual views. In other words, the group is represented in a distributed fashion: "The movement away had started after the second Big War . . . No . . . before that . . . No, it was worse after Mau Mau War" (19, ellipses in the original), and so on. Interestingly, this fragmented representation of the village community is explicitly about disintegration. In addition, it is focalized through the alienated, individualistic, petit bourgeois character, Munira. Thus, here again, Ngũgĩ makes thematic use of a discourse technique.

Though it is not a matter of discourse, it is worth pointing out that Ngũgĩ's characterization of Munira stresses his individual isolation relative to the people of Ilmorog. Sitting and observing the Ilmorogans, Munira "would vaguely feel with them" as they were united in work. But he always remained "an outsider to their activities" (20). The phrase "to their activities" is important. In Ngũgĩ's Marxist perspective, it is the shared labor of the people that ultimately unites them—first, in the traditional village, then later in the trade union.

Such story elements are, however, enhanced by discourse techniques. For example, at times the omniscient narrator does very strikingly limit the reader's knowledge to that of Munira. Thus when Wanja is introduced, readers learn as little about her as Munira does. They are not even told that she leaves his home after he goes to the school. They learn this only later when Munira learns it. Of course, this is what one expects with focalization. However, the novel is not consistently focalized. The strictness of constraint here tends to make Munira's isolation more palpable.

Much of the novel is organized around explicitly marked and saliently differentiated embedded narrations by the main characters. Among other things, these narrations fill in character history and provide indirect comments on colonialism, anticolonial struggles, and neocolonialism. Soon after Wanja comes to Ilmorog (in chapter 2), Munira presents the first of these. As discourse structures, these are not particularly noteworthy. The process of embedding in these cases is straightforward, as they are narratives reported by an omniscient, nonpersonified narrator.

Chapter 2 ends after Wanja delivers one of these embedded narratives. Chapter 3 returns from the flashback of chapter 2 to the present—

that is, twelve years later, shortly after the arrests of chapter 1. Munira is trying to "reconstruct" the scene that the reader has just read, now for "a statement to the police" (41). This is revealing because it suggests that there is already an implicit subtextual template here. Clearly, what was given in chapter 2 was not the content of Munira's statement to the police. However, it could very well be a case of omniscience guided by Munira's interests, though not informationally constrained by his inability to recall particulars. Subsequently, an inspector is introduced who provides Munira with pen and paper and asks him to write out his statement treating the events leading up to the murder. The inspector, then, serves as the narratee of this written account. The second section of chapter 3 clearly begins as that account. The opening lines of that section are "How does one tell of murder in a New Town?" This announces that the embedded narrative treats the issue just posed by the inspector. It goes on to stress "God's law" and "God's will," thereby indicating that the narration is by Munira, thus not (directly) by the nonpersonified narrator. Subsequent paragraphs are in first person.

But almost immediately, it is clear that the embedded narration is either psychological but unreliable, idealized or merely rhetorical. It seems most likely that the narration follows Munira's interests and the general structure of his own narration, but draws on the omniscience of the nonpersonified narrator. The first clear indication of this is when Munira claims to remember a lengthy passage from one of Karega's exercise books (46).[10]

In any case, Munira's first-person narration does not continue. Section four shifts to Wanja, who is recovering from the fire. Like Munira, she too is trying to remember the past. Though this section returns to the omniscient nonpersonified narrator, the suggestion is that this omniscient version follows the trajectory of Wanja's recollections. Thus guided omniscience follows idealized embedded narration.

The fourth chapter begins with an unexpected reflection. The narrator explains that anyone would be "overwhelmed and stilled by the sight" of "shimmering moonlit mist" on a particular night. This is not logically incompatible with nonpersonified omniscient narration. But it seems to involve an unusual commitment to a personal emotive response. The second paragraph refers to "recent archaeological finds in Ilmorog." This too is logically consistent with the omniscience of the nonpersonified narrator. But it also seems peculiar. Up to this point, the nonpersonified narrator has not exhibited overt emotions or interests and has been unconcerned with expanses of time outside the experience or attention of the characters. The following paragraph goes further still and personifies the narrator. It is yet a third version of the "we." Specifically, the narrator begins by referring to "our history." This could in principle suggest collective voicing (where a number of people speak together). In context, however, it apparently points toward an individual who, so to speak, instantiates the group. On the other hand, it is not an individual speaking in isolation. It is an individual recounting knowledge that is available to the entire group because it has been preserved by a network of individuals within that group, a network with cultural authority—"poets and players" (67). This is, of course, a network that includes contemporary Kenyan novelists and thus encompasses the author of *Petals of Blood*. The group history has been preserved by poets and players, and is presumably manifest in this novel. However, that does not mean the entire society is familiar with this preserved knowledge. Indeed, there would hardly be any point in having poets, players, and novelists if everyone already did share this knowledge.

This passage, then, extends the range of group narration isolated in the novel. Specifically, the novel suggests three types of group narration: 1) collective (where the group speaks together as "we"), 2) distributed (where individuals present distinct, but interrelated voices from the group), and 3) instantiated (where one speaker is presented as typifying the group). Cross-cutting this division, the novel points toward three ways in which the group may be understood: 1) as the people, 2) as the political elite, and 3) as the cultural experts or bearers of tradition.[11] These represent different ways in which people commonly understand social groups and who is empowered to speak for a group. The suggestions of Ngũgĩ's text are that he celebrates the collective and distributed voices of the people and the instantiated voice of the cultural experts (such as Nyakinyua), but criticizes the collective voice of the political elite (and the purely individual voices of self-seeking politicians).

It is not possible to explore the entire novel in this detail. But by this point, the main discursive techniques used by Ngũgĩ seem clear. To a great extent, the rest of the novel develops these different narrative voices in the complex interactions of their levels of knowledge and trajectories of interest. For example, chapter 5 includes an explicit return to Munira's testimony, again suggesting that much of the novel recapitulates his testimony, but with the omniscience of the nonpersonified narrator adding knowledge.[12] This is true even when the text is in first person. It thus continues to include both guided omniscience and idealized embedded narration, with the suggestion of an implicit subtextual template. Indeed, the nonpersonified narrator's omniscience leads to a presentation that goes beyond what Munira says but could not know (in idealized narration) to what he knows but would not say. Specifically, it includes what passes through his mind in interior monologue, but would undoubtedly not be included in a police statement (see, for example, 101).

A variation of particular thematic significance occurs when omniscience is connected implicitly with tradition. This is in keeping with the partial identification of the nonpersonified omniscient narrator with the cultural experts, the poets and players. However, here it occurs with character narration. Specifically, Nyakinyua recites the history of the place. As such, she functions as "the spirit that guided and held them together. And she talked as if she had been everywhere" (123). The suggestion is that the collective knowledge of tradition, as the product of countless individual points of view, is itself a sort of omniscience. This living, collective tradition is also emotionally unifying, or at least creates an emotional sense of unity. Thus, later, Nyakinyua allows them all to "relive their history" and feel "a oneness" (210, 211). In keeping with both points (regarding knowledge and feeling), it is not surprising that Nyakinyua's significance expands even beyond Kenya. Her representative voice is the result of her being "Nyakinyua, mother of men" (123). Despite the phrasing, this extension may not be intended to encompass all humans. But it is broader than the Gikuyu or even the nation of Kenya. Two pages later, Karega interprets Nyakinyua's story as bearing on "all Africa" (125).

On the other hand, the suggestion of a still more encompassing humanity is not irrelevant here. The trajectory of the rest of the novel suggests widening circles of "we," expansions of the group and the sense of group solidarity. Despite Karega's explanation of Nyakinyua's story as relating to Africa, a larger unification is not excluded by the novel. Karega speaks of the humiliation of Wanja—thus, by allegorical implication, of the entire group—as "a collective humiliation." Of course, that collective humiliation could be ethnic (Gikuyu), national (Kenyan), or racial (pan-African). But he goes on to explain that it is collective because "it has got to do with human beings" (161). This is, of course, in keeping with the Marxist perspective that Karega represents, since Marxism has historically been a force favoring internationalism rather than national, ethnic, or other identities.

In relation to this, it is, again, important that the novel ends, not with Wanja and Abdulla, thus nationalism, but with Karega and the workers movement, including its struggle against "national and regional chauvinism" (305). In keeping with its discursive embedding of voices within other voices, its elaboration of collective narration, and of course its themes of solidarity and division, the novel aptly concludes with Karega thinking about the struggle of the workers and the peasants to bring about a genuine "kingdom of man and woman" (344). In direct opposition to Munira, the other petit bourgeois character, Karega realizes that such a kingdom must be made in this world, not imagined in another. As a result, he is finally able to become part of a collective—or, rather, to help form a new collective based not on false attempts to relive "glorious pasts" of a nation or ethnicity (326), but on work to create a new future. In the last words of the novel, the narrator explains that, finally, Karega "knew he was no longer alone" (345).

In short, Ngũgĩ's novel suggests a number of points about the nature of narrator embedding and group narration. These theoretical implications, in turn, react back on one's understanding of the novel. Specifically, there is a tight interrelation between the discourse structures and processes of the novel, on the one hand, and its thematic points and emotional norms, on the other. This is particularly noteworthy because the novel is not at all thematically or discursively simple. For example, it is critical of petit bourgeois individualism, but its representation of collective voicing is nuanced. Its different forms of group narration suggest different kinds of group formation and modes of group expression, with different values and different faults. This is a version of the profile of ambiguity and the profile of ambivalence. However, Ngũgĩ has integrated thematic and emotional ambiguity with narration in an unusually thorough manner. Moreover, he has done this in a self-consciously dialectical way, so that the different voices can interact with, correct, and complement one another in their real social complexity.

Narrator Knowledge, Collective Experience, and Access to Other Minds

One of the reasons Ngũgĩ's dialectic is important is that group voicing is problematic precisely at the level of difference or diversity. The distributed mode of group narration allows for diversity of thought and feeling within the group. On the other hand, it may make the diversity— even conflict—more salient than group connectedness. This problem is solved by the other versions of group narration. But these, in turn, readily project a degree of uniformity that is often internally oppressive and externally xenophobic, as Ngũgĩ recognized. Moreover, in the real world, groups are not at all so uniform as collective or instantiated voicing implies. In keeping with this, narration suggesting uniformity often raises issues about narrator knowledge and reliability, particularly with respect to personified narrators. As Margolin writes, "Claims about a group's mental states or actions combine uneasily the narrator's own immediate self-knowledge with inferences about the minds of other members" ("Perspective" 423).

Consider the case of an instantiated voice. Here, the first issue is to what extent anyone can reasonably be spoken of as typical of a group, in the sense of manifesting the group's standard properties generally, in the way a sample of gold may be said to manifest the properties of gold generally. The answer is straightforward—groups are not at all like the elements; their properties are not uniform across samples. Of course, one can create a storyworld in which group thoughts are so uniform that this is unproblematic. For example, a science fiction work could include a set of identically programmed robots. But most narratives using an instantiated voice are probably not suggesting that the possibility of such a voice arises only in an unreal world. Indeed, in a case such as *Petals of Blood*, it is crucial to the work's political purposes that there is a close parallel between the instantiated nature of the voice in the fiction and group connectedness in the real world. Similar points hold for the collective narrative voice.

The same issues arise with indirect forms of group narration, when a narrator reports of a group that "they" felt x or thought y. An omniscient narrator may in principle know what everyone in a group is thinking or feeling. However, here again, it usually seems implausible that a group would share a particular understanding or emotion—unless the group is very different from groups in the real world. The problem is only worsened when the narration is rigorously focalized. This is because a focalizer, like a limited narrator, cannot have access to the inner life of group members. Thus, even if there is uniformity, he or she could not know. There are, then, two dilemmas for what might be called the *indirect voicing* of groups by narrators, the same two as found in collective and instantiated narration. First, there is the problem of group uniformity. Second, there is the problem of narrator/focalizer knowledge.

Obviously, these problems are greatest when the group is large and, so to speak, "abstract," as in the cases presented by Ngũgĩ. Judgments about groups become increasingly plausible as the number of people in the group falls, the period of time decreases, and the intensity of interaction among the group members (prominently including the narrator or focalizer) increases. Thus one is or should be highly skeptical of indirect—or collective or instantiated—voicing for a race or nation. But one is or should be more open to the possibility of indirect—or collective or instantiated—voicing for, say, two close friends at a particular moment. This is because their shared experience in the past and present gives significant grounds for inferring at least partially uniform internal states and for an enhanced degree of mutual comprehension.

The point is related to some general issues about omniscience and limitation in narration. Again, there are different kinds of limitation. Consider focalization. As noted earlier, a focalized nonpersonified narrator may be rigorously epistemically restricted to a single character's knowledge. Alternatively, however, such a narrator may be restricted only in interest. In the second case, he or she may have access to a wide range of external facts and internal character states, but may (so to speak) not care to report them. This does not mean, however, that narration is necessarily a matter of either guided, though otherwise complete, omniscience on the one hand or strict focalization on the other. Rather, the narrator may have various sorts and degrees of information not available to the focalizer.

Specifically, there seems to be a rough hierarchy according to which a focalized narrator may have "excess" knowledge. He or she may most readily have general social knowledge not available to the focalizer. An obvious case of this is language. A language may be unfamiliar to the focalizer. However, if the author wishes the reader to know the content of a particular speech, then the narrator must, at the very least, give an accurate transcription of the foreign language. Suppose, for example, that a character says something in Afrikaans, but the focalizer does not speak Afrikaans. If the author wants the content of the speech available to the reader, then the narrator must be able to transcribe the Afrikaans speech, which is something the focalizer would not be able to do.

A focalized narrator may have some knowledge of other minds as well, even when focalization is generally strict and therefore putatively involves confinement to a single perspective. Unsurprisingly, this extension of the focalized narrator's knowledge seems to follow the same general principles that govern one's confidence about inferences to other people's inner states in real life. Observers feel quite confident in attributing a perception to someone else when they are in the same perceptual environment. If Jones and Smith are both at the celebration where a cannon is fired, Jones feels confident that Smith heard the cannon. Observers may also be relatively confident about emotion. Doe witnesses the eliciting conditions of emotion and the expressive and actional outcomes—thus he sees Jones reject Smith's proposal of marriage; Doe then sees Smith break into sobs and run from the room. Doe or any other witness feels quite confident about Smith's inner emotional state. People seem somewhat less confident about someone else's expectations and inferences. Many emotional responses involve relatively automatic processes. But expectations and inferences are less automatic and are therefore more difficult to gauge. Finally, observers appear to have the least confidence about other people's memories and extended plans. Memories require that the observer has shared or otherwise knows about the other person's past experiences and about whether current circumstances are likely to trigger those memories. Plans require a sense of the person's enduring interests, goals, self-understanding, and other matters.

If this hierarchy is roughly correct with respect to people's real-life confidence, and accuracy, in evaluating other people's mental states, one would expect something like it to appear in literature. In keeping with this, it does seem that narrators are often neither omniscient nor strictly focalized with respect to other characters' mental states. Rather, they frequently fall somewhere within an intermediate spectrum, providing some information about the mental states of other characters. What information can be provided by the narrator appears to be broadly guided by the preceding hierarchy.

These points may be further developed by returning to theory of mind issues. Sometimes, one rationally infers someone's inner state; at other times, one has the sense that one just knows what the person is feeling. Similarly, a focalized narrator may infer a state or may present the state as if he or she had direct access to it. In other words, he or she may rely on a theoretically based theory of mind or on simulation (as discussed in chapter 4).

Simulation appears to be particularly prominent in the understanding of other people's emotions (see Doherty 49 and citations). In keeping with this, it is also particularly prominent in the feeling of actually experiencing other people's inner states. In other words, perhaps the most frequent sense of having access to other people's minds comes with the feeling of having a common emotional experience, a feeling that is usually inseparable from simulation. This feeling of common emotional experience is enhanced by the ways in which emotions are actually shared interactively and the various inputs to simulation. When Jones and Doe are laughing and tickling one another and frolicking together in the swaying rye field, they have a strong sense not only of being happy individually but of sharing happiness. Many components of the experience contribute to this. These include joint attention (on a shared object) or mutual attention, mirroring (spontaneous imitation of one another's expressions, gesture, posture, etc. [see Iacoboni]), smooth cooperative activity toward shared goals (including ease of mutual anticipation), and emotion contagion (where one person's emotion expressions, such as laughter, trigger the parallel emotions in the other person; see Hatfield, Cacioppo, and Rapson). The effects of these conditions are further enhanced if there is a relation of attachment between the people involved, since attachment promotes a feeling of intimacy and a tendency for those involved (e.g., lovers) to see themselves as in some sense a single "self" or, more technically, a "cognitive unit" (on the concept of a cognitive unit, see Ortony, Clore, and Collins 77–79).

Since these conditions enhance one's sense of shared emotion in real life, one would expect them to enhance the sense of shared emotion in fiction. In keeping with this, one would expect these conditions to contribute to group voicing in narrative. In fact, much of the group voicing in Ngũgĩ is emotional, whether it is a matter of shared antipathy toward an outsider in the village or cultural pride.

But Ngũgĩ does not provide an ideal instance of this sort, since his narration is omniscient and not strictly focalized. A tighter constraint on the narrator should more clearly highlight the conditions in which group voicing occurs and how it occurs. This leads to *Born of the Sun* by Joseph Diescho (with Celeste Wallin).[13]

Emotion Sharing, Other Minds, and Political Trust in *Born of the Sun*: A Namibian Novel

This 1988 novel concerns a young Kavango villager, Muronga, in South West Africa (Namibia) during the period of South African (Apartheid) administration. Faced with the need to earn money in order to pay taxes, Muronga goes to work in the South African mines. The novel begins with Muronga and his wife, Makena, to whom he is deeply attached. When she has a child, Muronga develops a deep bond with the baby as well. Much of the first part of the novel is concerned with establishing the strong ties of affection that bind Muronga to his family and community. The only dissonant notes in the opening come from colonialism, prominently the South African government's taxation system.

At the end of the first part, Muronga and his good friend, Kaye, decide to leave home in order to secure paid work. Despite his strong feelings for his family, Muronga believes that he must do this, in part for their benefit. The pain of parting is initially softened by the presence of Kaye, with whom Muronga also has strong attachment bonds. However, they too are separated and sent to different regions for work. Thus the first part of the novel establishes a clear conflict between personal attachment and colonial labor.

The very brief second part of the novel traces Muronga's transportation from Namibia through newly independent Botswana to South Africa. Diescho (with Wallin) depicts Muronga's new experiences of colonialism, technology, the diversity of African society, and other matters.

In part three, Muronga learns about work in the mines, about South African racism and exploitation, and about political repression. He begins to attend secret political meetings. When an important African activist is killed in prison, he participates in a strike. (The activist is modeled on Stephen Biko, though the events in the story occur much earlier.) He is arrested, imprisoned, and tortured.

In the final part of the novel, Muronga has been released from prison and returned to the mines. After attending classes, he is now literate. He continues his activism and is arrested again. This time, he is deported. However, in Botswana he and several comrades are placed under the custody of an official who sympathizes with the South West Africa People's Organization (SWAPO, called UPO in the novel), the revolutionary organization struggling for an independent Namibia. This official offers them the opportunity to escape and join SWAPO. After a night of internal conflict, in which he longs for his wife, child, and friends, Muronga decides that he must sacrifice his own personal attachments. The novel ends with Muronga joining his comrades in escape to enter the struggle for his nation's freedom.

As should be clear even from this brief summary, the novel is narratively, thematically, and emotionally concerned with issues of trust, solidarity, shared action, and attachment. As such, it is a novel that addresses a range of concerns that bear on the understanding of other minds. These concerns include both the theory-based inference to other minds and the simulation of other minds that gives a sense of direct access, particularly to the feelings of other people.[14]

Perhaps the most remarkable aspect of the novel is the way it recruits discourse techniques toward these ends. Specifically, the novel has a nonpersonified narrator with focalization on Muronga. This narrator has some general knowledge and skills that Muronga lacks (e.g., he or she has knowledge of several languages unknown to Muronga). Nonetheless, he or she generally does not have access to other minds. There are, however, exceptions to this restriction. The reader is sometimes given inner experiences of characters. In some cases, this is a fairly straightforward matter of the inner experience being easy to infer from perceptual experience that is available to Muronga. These reports of inner states, then, need not be viewed as violating strict focalization.

More importantly, there are cases in which the narration involves an indirect group voicing that is not a matter of simple inference. These cases are marked by precisely the sort of coordination of cooperative activity, commonly enhanced by shared attachment, that gives one the sense of shared emotion in ordinary life. These regulated violations of focalization serve at least three purposes. First, they enhance the emotional effect of Muronga's bonds with family and friends (thus the severing of those bonds due to Apartheid). Second, they extend a parallel relation to the solidarity and trust that occurs between Muronga and his comrades in the struggle against South African colonialism and racism. Third, they highlight the alienation among different groups in Apartheid South Africa, since moments of "shared internality," as one might call it, do not occur across the lines of group division—prominently the division between black and white.[15]

The first chapter begins with Muronga's experiences ("he feels the day breaking" [3]) and thoughts ("It is all fine, he thinks to himself" [3]). These thoughts include an attempt to understand the white priest, Pater Dickmann. It is striking that he does not simulate Dickmann's mind, but rather infers its properties or general tendencies (e.g., it is a "suspicious mind" [4]). He then calculates what the best way is to persuade or pacify the priest. The difference between Muronga's direct subjectivity and Dickmann's objectified, theoretically constructed mind is significant. It suggests already the distance between white and black that is central to the novel, and to life under Apartheid. Indeed, it is in effect the psychological correlate of Apartheid.

Muronga's inner experience may not be presented with precise verbal accuracy. In other words, it may not be strict interior monologue. However, as thought and feeling, it is aptly and convincingly simulated—or, more properly, the apparent monologue gives the reader the cues needed to engage in such simulation. For example, Muronga is thinking about his upcoming conversion and church wedding. He suddenly remembers an added benefit of the church wedding—"Oh, and another good thing is that the priest gives the marrying couples their wedding rings" (5). This memory surprises him, even though he latently had the knowledge all along. This spontaneity and seeming inconsistency in knowledge—both of which characterize real human thought processes—facilitate a reader's simulation of Muronga as a full, subjectively self-experiencing person, in contrast with a calculated understanding of Dickmann.

Muronga's wife, Makena, is pregnant and near to giving birth. Muronga has gone to call the midwife, Mama Rwenge. As he approaches her hut, the narrator seemingly shifts to the perspective of Rwenge. But he or she only reports that Rwenge "hears Muronga's quick footsteps" (6), a perception that is shared by Muronga and readily attributed to Rwenge in the circumstances. In other words, by the preceding hierarchy, it is only the most minimal violation of strict epistemic focalization.

Rwenge goes to Muronga's hut. Muronga is outside, but "His mind . . . is in the hut with Makena" (8). Here, the point is not merely that he is thinking about her. It is that he is trying to understand what her experience is and he is longing to be in physical contact with this object of very strong attachment. Muronga remembers the history of his and Makena's relationship, showing great tenderness. He wishes he was "there to hold Makena's shoulders" (10). This stresses the importance of attachment in the novel. It also suggests the ways in which attachment is bound up with a desire to share the other person's pain and joy, thus with empathic engagement. When the child is born, Muronga shows the same attachment to him as to Makena.

After the birth, there is a sort of intrusion by the narrator, presenting information on Kavango taboos. Clearly, this is information that Muronga has, even if he has no occasion to think about it explicitly. In connection with this, some of the following sections are devoted to establishing the implied author's view of Kavango tradition. Muronga's wise uncle Ndara explains that by their tradition, a chief was supposed to be "like a father" and "rule according to the wishes of his people" or he would be "dethroned by the people" (24). The image of the chief as "like a father" here suggests the devoted attachment of a father to his children rather than the obedience of children to a paternal authority. This is particularly clear since, according to Ndara, the chief could be expelled by the people. This all serves to prepare for Muronga's eventual decision to join SWAPO and fight for the liberation of Namibia from the very nonfatherlike rule of the South African government.

The second chapter takes up some of the same points. For example, Muronga is faced with the clear irrationality of the white priest, and the priest's bizarre assumption that Africans will automatically believe that white angels are good and black angels are bad. He thinks, "The missionaries do not think beyond their long funny hair" (29). The point of the passage is to make readers—perhaps particularly white readers—recognize three things. First, Christian theology is no more rational than that of any other group. Second, European appearance is no more intrinsically beautiful than that of any other group. Finally, whites have historically had a tendency not to think outside their own heads in the sense that they often have made no effort to imagine themselves into the place of nonwhite people, thus no effort to simulate their experience. The remainder of the chapter is replete with instances of resultant misunderstanding.

More in line with the concerns of the present analysis, chapter 3 includes some instances of collective focalization. Muronga and Makena sit "silently." The narrator reports that "Neither of them can forget the hectic ceremony of yesterday" and "they feel as if every villager thinks they are fanatics of Christendom" (60). Readers know that the narrator has access to Muronga's thoughts. But the narrator does not generally have access to Makena's thoughts. Here, however, the narrator's knowledge goes further than usual. At least one reason is that Muronga and Makena are bound by strong mutual attachment and have engaged in shared work together. That attachment and shared work—in this case, work actually bound up with the attachment—enable the mutual simulation that can lead to collective focalization.

Shortly after this, there are scenes of male–male attachment and sharing. For example, one man successfully finishes a proverbial sentence begun by another (63). Two men eat from the same pots and their "fingers touch in the plate" (64). They contrast this sense of interpersonal connection with the loneliness of white people (64). This helps to prepare the reader for further developments of attachment-based mutual simulation—thus collective focalization—particularly among comrades in the struggle against Apartheid. In keeping with the last concern, this chapter also introduces SWAPO, though from the perspective of the white South African government.

SWAPO and taxation are addressed at a large meeting, where an Afrikaans-speaking white man gives a talk that is translated by a self-serving African collaborationist. Here, the narrator evidences general social knowledge beyond Muronga, in this case knowledge of Afrikaans. He or she presents the discrepancies between the original speech and the translation, discrepancies that cannot be available to Muronga. Here, then, there is another violation of strict focalization, but one that readers are unlikely to notice due to its high place in the hierarchy of such violations.

The fourth and fifth chapters continue to stress Muronga's attachment to his wife and child. In the fifth chapter, he and his friend Kaye leave home to go work in South Africa. Just before they leave, the narrator shifts briefly to the perspective of Makena. In keeping with the general principles set out above, however, the narrator gains access to a particular aspect of Makena's mind—her sharing of emotion with Muronga and Kaye. As they are all engaged in separating, she gains a "sense" of their "uncertainty" and "need" for "courage" (107).

At this point, familial attachment bonds are again extended to men who share experiences and solidarity. The reader learns that Muronga and Kaye have "grown closer to each other" through their shared "undertaking." This is not simply familiarity, but also attachment. As the narrator explains, "To be next to each other is one of the things they always wish for" and they "lie quietly side by side" at night (119). The discursive result of this is that they come to be collectively focalized. "Muronga and Kaye are amazed to see.... They are astonished.... They are fascinated.... They have never seen.... they watch," and so on (125). As soon as this mutuality develops, however, they are separated. The oppressive domination of the South African government first led to Muronga's departure from his wife and son. It now leads to his close friend's departure. Thematically, then, Apartheid is genuinely a system of separation, of breaking apart people who should be together. Once Kaye goes off in a bus, Muronga and the narrator no longer have access to Kaye's thoughts or feelings. Thus the narrator must leave the reader, like Muronga, "unsure" about whether Kaye can even see him (129). Once more, the discourse mirrors the thematic and emotional concerns of the work while following the usual hierarchy of simulative access to other minds.

The seventh chapter presents a positive interlude in newly independent Botswana. This points toward the importance of national liberation that becomes central later in the book. It also highlights the brutality of South Africa that immediately follows.

After the men arrive at the mines, group-based inhibitions of simulation appear again in Muronga's relationship with his white supervisor. When Muronga works with a black man—and shares bonds of attachment—they frequently share emotions. This is often signaled in the focalization. But neither the narrator nor Muronga shares the emotions of the white supervisor. Thus Muronga reflects that the supervisor "seems to think that a black man like me does not . . . feel what a white man does" (181). The absence of even ordinary empathy is striking. Subsequently, Muronga generalizes the point. Sharing emotion is a *human* tendency. But "Whites are more 'white' than they are human" (182). They allow their in-group racial definition to inhibit their "heart" (182), thus blocking the ordinary sorts of (simulative) access humans have to one another's emotions. (This is a standard result of in-group/out-group division, as discussed in chapter 5.) The same point applies to black collaborationists. Just as the whites have "a dead heart" (182), these collaborationists "are dead inside" (188). Muronga becomes "more aware than ever that he simply does not understand how these white people think" (189). Inference to emotion is not impossible across races. But it is not a true sharing, based on simulation. Thus Muronga "can see . . . the white man's . . . anger and hatred." But he "does not understand" (236).

In contrast with collaborationist blacks, "Muronga and his friends" may be collectively focalized as they "are stunned" and "do not know what to say or do" (188). Sometimes they are so attuned to one another that they seem to communicate without speaking. Muronga "muses" to himself, wondering why there is "broken glass atop the concrete wall." As if he had uttered the question out loud, he "is surprised when [his fellow-worker] Ndango answers his question" (189).

As he experiences oppression and humiliation at the mines and witnesses the experiences of others, Muronga finds himself drawn to the resistance movement. At a SWAPO meeting, Ndango, one of the activists, explains to Muronga that all the men there are "brothers" (202). This serves to suggest the possibility of a very broad attachment relation among these co-workers. Muronga is initially troubled by his own more local affinities and identifications. However, he prays to the "God of Our Forefathers" to make "us . . . one people" (206). Like Karega at the end of *Petals,* this sense of cooperative group interconnection leads Muronga to "realize that he is not alone" (207).

From here on, Diescho (with Wallin) continues to develop the relation between personal attachment and collective solidarity, as well as collective focalization. Thus, as Muronga sits with a group of comrades, "his mind flashes back and forth between the meeting . . . and his family" (217). When he takes part in a strike, the common aim is for everyone to "speak with one voice" (218). When the strikers come together, the point is recapitulated at the level of discourse. The men, undertaking this joint endeavor, spontaneously share their feelings, without directly communicating them. Moreover, all this is bound up with attachment. As the narrator explains, "There is fear and uncertainty, but no disagreement" regarding the commitment to the strike, a strike that is connected with the well-being of "our own families" (218–19). Due to their emprisonment, Muronga and his comrades sometimes share the same sensations and emotions, narrated collectively ("They are made to feel even more uncomfortable" [244]; "the prisoners are euphoric and fearless" [245]; "all the . . . men feel the same" [248]). This is linked with Muronga's attachment to one comrade in particular, Ndango; thus he "prays repeatedly . . . that he and Ndango will not be split up" (243).

The final chapters further develop the theme of group unity ("we must stand, united, against the whites" [274]). The culmination is marked by the same sorts of individual mental division and union that are seen throughout the novel. For example, Muronga finds that his supervisor does not return his greeting, but this "doesn't tell him much" (279). This is presumably because the stark group oppositions make theory of mind simulation impossible. In addition, Muronga does not have adequate information to draw theoretical inferences. In consequence, he can understand very little from any gesture or expression of the supervisor.

Eventually, Muronga is arrested again and isolated. Once more, his greatest fear is being alone. Once more, Apartheid is represented as dividing those whose bonds of attachment should keep them together. In prison, he tries to remember his wife lying by his side (288). When he is finally released, to be deported, he finds a letter from her. She too is suffering terribly from the separation and begs him to return. The last page of the letter has his child's footprint (293). It seems for a moment as if the crimes of Apartheid might, in a perverse way, cancel each other out. The unjust economic system drove Muronga away from his family. Now the unjust legal system will send him back.

But in fact there is another choice. In Botswana, he learns that he can escape to work with SWAPO, which means abandoning his family. He is with his comrades Ndango and Nakare. If he joins SWAPO, he will escape with them—perhaps only to be separated again. Unsurprisingly, they share each other's emotions; also unsurprisingly, the narrator is able to report this: "Muronga, Ndango and Nakare still do not speak . . . but they hardly need to . . . they can communicate their feelings without words. Each one knows what the others are going through" (300).

The night before the escape, Muronga is tortured by a conflict between love and duty "for his family" and "love and duty to his people and country" (306). Ultimately, he chooses the latter. He leaves with Ndango and Nakare for an uncertain future. Of course, in doing this, Muronga is placing himself in a cognitive unit founded on shared activity and attachment, thus a unit not unlike his family. That is what makes the choice emotionally possible in the context of the novel.

But there is something of a problem here. The ending of the novel points toward an abstract and generalized identification, an identification with Namibia. Muronga's choice is thematically presented as a choice in favor of the nation over more local affiliations. But the discursive development of the novel actually values particularizing trust and practical interaction, as with Ndango. In this way, the alternatives presented in the novel are always local. They are choices among different sorts of attachment bond and their associated forms of concrete shared experience, mirroring, and particularized simulation. At the end, Muronga does not choose abstract allegiance. He in effect chooses a set of local relations of trust, relations based on cooperative work, attachment, and associated empathic simulation—the relations with Ndango and Nakare. This may be the best choice because Muronga's relations with his wife and child may be practically unworkable in a colonialist and Apartheid state. In this sense, Muronga chooses what is best for both sets of attachment relations. But this all remains local. It is never clear that the novel really can support something like national identification, rather than more personalized loyalties with their particular attachment bonds, their mutual mirroring in cooperative activity, and so on. Then again, given the brutal behaviors that are regularly underwritten by national identification, perhaps that is not a bad thing.

Conclusion

There are two prominent types of limitation on embedded narrators—epistemic and emotional. Psychological embedding completely limits the primary narrator to the knowledge and emotional orientation of the embedded narrator. Merely rhetorical embedding involves no limitation of either sort. In intermediate cases, the embedded narrative may include perceptual or other details not available to the embedded narrator. Nonetheless, the embedded narrative may be confined to topics or situations about which the embedded narrator has indirect (reported or inferred) knowledge. In a still more minimal case, the embedded narrative is oriented by the emotional interests of the embedded narrator. When the narration extends beyond the experience of the embedded narrator, but remains guided by (at minimum) that narrator's interests, this may be called "idealized embedded narration." That idealization may be informationally constrained, but not perceptually constrained, or it may simply be emotionally constrained. There are parallel types of focalization. When the narration fills in information not available to an emotionally focalized character, this may be called "guided omniscience." Idealized embedded narration and guided omniscience may point toward an "implicit subtextual template," an actual narrative produced by the embedded narrator or focalizer.

Group narration, the presentation of narrative from some group, in a sense combines singular and multiple narration. It has three basic forms. Instantiated group narration involves an individual speaking as an instantiation of the entire group, either as somehow representative of the group or as allegorically personifying the group. Distributed group narration involves a range of group members speaking as distinct parts of the group. These individual voices may be complementary (thus completing one another) or contradictory (thus challenging one another, perhaps in the service of a social dialectic). Finally, collective voicing presents a group speaking with a single voice (thus it typically involves the use of the pronoun "we," rather than "I"). These different forms of group narration may also express different versions of who defines the group. Here, too, there seem to be three prominent options: 1) the people as a whole, 2) the political elite (i.e., those with social power), and 3) the cultural authorities (i.e., those who have knowledge of the group).

Ngũgĩ's *Petals of Blood* is thematically focused on nationalism, colonialism, and class. For the most part, Ngũgĩ pursues his political project in this novel through story elements, prominently allegory. However, in presenting these story elements, he draws on complex discourse techniques. Some of these may operate primarily to enhance readers' aesthetic engagement with the work. Others have thematic resonances as well. Specifically, he often uses idealized embedded narration or guided omniscience, following the emotional interests and general knowledge of one character. This enhanced narration often suggests a subtextual template. In each case, the technique arguably serves to present adequate information to the reader while simultaneously foregrounding the particularity of those involved in experiencing, enacting, and interpreting the events. Of course, in keeping with his Marxist orientation, Ngũgĩ does not stress particularity only. He also takes up various types of group narration, largely setting them up in parallel with one another. This parallelism is part of Ngũgĩ's attempt to place different groups and ideologies—prominently those bearing on nation and class—in dialectical interaction with one another. Indeed, the group narration and individual narrations themselves point to a further dialectic—of group and individual—that is also thematically central to his novel.

A key issue in the relation of groups and individuals concerns the possibility of genuinely sharing ideas, understandings, and emotions. The cultivation of such sharing—or at least an aspiration toward it—is important for a range of authors trying to create a sense of national or other social unity. The use of group narration is clearly a possible discourse correlate of such shared mentalities. There are, however, two significant problems with "we" narration. First, individuals simply do not have access to other minds in the relevant way. Second, there is rarely if ever profound uniformity in a large group, the sort of uniformity presupposed by most collective and instantiated narration.

On the other hand, there are circumstances in real life where people feel that they are more attuned to other people's thoughts and emotions, not entirely without reason. The most extreme case of this occurs when one has an attachment relation with someone, shares experiences with him or her, and has mirroring responses during a current experience. All this enables simulation. In contrast, one's sense of unity with someone else is most thoroughly blocked by alienating, identity-group divisions (in effect, the opposite of attachment), with distinct or segregated experiences, and no opportunities for mirroring.

Born of the Sun takes up these conditions to explore the ways in which social groups are put in antagonistic relations and the ways in which individuals may begin to share a sense of unity and solidarity. For the most part, the novel is strictly focalized. Nonetheless, it develops a growing sense of black Namibians not merely deciding to join together for practical gains, but actually sharing feelings (and, to a lesser extent, thoughts), due precisely to mutual attachment, common experience, and mirroring. This in turn enables the localized use of collective internal focalization where the encompassing, nonpersonified narrator has access to the mental states shared by two or more characters. The narrational development of this mutuality may help to create a feeling of sharing in the reader as well. The difficulty with this approach—or, from another point of view, a benefit—is that such sharing applies to only a small number of individuals at a time and cannot be extended to a national group.

Afterword

A Note on Implied Readers and Narratees

Mīrābāī's "Even if you break off, beloved, I would not"

*T*HE FIRST CHAPTER concluded with the following schematic representation of the narrational component of discourse:

Real Author [Implied Author, guided by partially "autonomous" imagined agents [Nonpersonified Narrator {Personified Narrator {Focalizer {Topicalizer}} Personified Narratee} Nonpersonified Narratee] Implied Reader/Sahṛdaya] Real Reader/Critic

Subsequent chapters have examined some of the nuances of implied authors, narrators, and the relations among implied authors and narrators, with some treatment of focalization as well. When undertaking this book initially, my plan was to treat all the constituents of narration (leaving aside the real author and real reader/critic, who are not technically part of the discourse). As the writing progressed, I eventually realized that it would not be possible to consider the "receptive" half of narration (narratees and implied readers). Indeed, the current discussion still leaves a great deal to discuss even with respect to implied authors and narrators, not to mention focalizers.

Books on any complex theoretical topic are perhaps necessarily incomplete. Thus, extending the present discussion to other elements of narrational discourse can—and, indeed, should—be put off for future work. However, before concluding, it is worth making a few, very preliminary, comments on narratees and implied readers. When these receptive elements have been mentioned in the preceding pages, they have largely been treated as reflexes of their productive counterparts, narrators and implied authors. To a great extent, that makes sense. However, narratees and implied readers have their own complexities and nuances that merit separate examination.[1] These remaining few pages do not constitute even an introduction to the topic of narrational reception. They are intended simply to suggest some of these complexities and nuances. As a basis for this discussion, I take up a poem attributed to the great sixteenth-century Hindi poet Mīrābāī. With great help from Lalita Pandit Hogan and Philip Lutgendorf, I have translated the poem somewhat freely, trying to capture some of the *dhvani* or suggestiveness of the original, as follows:[2]

> Even if you break off, beloved, I would not;
> Broken off from your love, Kṛṣṇa, with whom could I be joined?
>
> You are the tree, I am the birds.
> You are the lake, I am the fish.
> You are the mountain, I am the pasture.
> You are the moon, I am the partridge thirsty for moonlight.
>
> Even if you break off, beloved, I would not;
> Broken off from your love, Kṛṣṇa, with whom could I be joined?
>
> You Lord are a pearl, we are the ties that bind the necklace.
> You are gold, we are what the jeweler adds to make a wedding band.
> Lord of lady Mīrā [bāī Mīrā], who lives in Brij—
> Listen here cowherd!
> You are my idol, I am your girl in the temple.
>
> Even if you break off, beloved, I would not;
> Broken off from you, Kṛṣṇa, love, with whom could I be joined?

Due to constraints of space, it is not possible to discuss the poem at any length. However, it is probably clear, even on first reading, that the narratee and implied reader are complex and cannot be understood as mirror images of the narrator and implied author. The point is most obvious with the personified narrator and the personified narratee. The former is, roughly, Mīrābāī; the latter is Kṛṣṇa. It may seem initially that the poem more or less collapses the categories of personified and nonpersonified narrator and narratee—and, indeed, implied author, in the former case. In other words, it may seem that the poem presents a personified narrator who is not distinguished from the nonpersonified narrator, who is in turn not distinguished from the implied author. Moreover, it may seem that the personified narratee is not distinguished from the nonpersonified narratee. But, in fact, things are more complex.

The opening line of the poem represents a sort of paradox. Even if Kṛṣṇa separates himself from Mira, the two will remain joined because of Mira's decision. At one level, this suggests simply that Mira will not recognize any ending of the relationship. But, in another way, it suggests that both lovers have control over their union. This relates to the mystical aspect of the poem, for this is not simply a love poem, but a poem of religious devotion as well. It speaks of Mira's romantic love. But it also speaks about the spiritual relation between devotee and God. The line suggests that the devotee and God are not so distinct as the I/you division, the narrator/narratee separation, might initially suggest. The point becomes clearer as the poem develops.

To understand the second line of the poem, one needs to look ahead a bit to the suggestion of later lines that the speaker is a devadāsī, a girl or woman who has been married to a god in a temple and is not free to marry anyone else (see, for example, Srinivasan 1869). At the same time, such women often supported themselves through prostitution (the point is discussed by Srinivasan; see also Bhattacharji 50). In this context, then, the opening stanza comes to have two broad meanings. First, it continues to operate at the level of the romantic and spiritual narratives. At that level, Mira says to Kṛṣṇa that she will never love anyone else, as just noted. But the second meaning is very different. It hints at the speaker's loss of support in the temple and the despairing question of what she could possibly do in response. Here, there are two further implications, derived from different answers to the question and different senses of the word "join." The first sense is "marry," and the answer to the question "with whom could I marry?" is, of course, "no one." The second sense is "physically united." There, the answer might be "anyone who will pay."

The dhvani of these lines alters one's sense of the narrational structure. First, it at least complicates a reader's sense of the narrator as continuous with the implied author. On the one hand, Mira did leave her home to join a group of Kṛṣṇa devotees. However, she was literally married to a Rajput prince, not to a temple deity.[3] Second, the narratee is not precisely Kṛṣṇa, but the icon, the idol of the temple—for the devadāsī, deprived of the temple, would be separated, first of all, from the idol that is localized in space, not the God who is ubiquitous. Or, rather, it now appears that there are two personified narratees. One is the icon. The other is the God represented by the icon. Both are suggested by the culminating line of the poem. I have translated it in such a way as to stress the former meaning—"You are my idol, I am your girl in the temple." But the line equally means "You are my God, I am your devotee."

Indeed, one can go further still and posit yet a third narratee—almost nonpersonified and in effect encompassing the other two. Specifically, the interpretations just considered do not seem easy to reconcile. If the narratee is the beloved, then he is free to break off from the narrator. Thus he may be blamed for the breaking (or, translating differently, the tearing apart). But if the narratee is the idol, then he/it can hardly be responsible for the separation. Indeed, even the personification of God as a lover separating from his beloved is somewhat unclear. Here, it is necessary to make a distinction between the "saguṇa," or "material" form of the deity—either as icon or as incarnation (avatāra)—and the ultimate "nirguṇa," or immaterial and formless deity (see, for example, McDermott 176, 177). The latter is the ultimate source of all the causes or events of the world. As such, whatever happens in the world is the action of Kṛṣṇa. For example, when the devadāsī is separated from her icon, Kṛṣṇa is ultimately responsible. In this way, behind the beloved and the idol is the God. Whatever happens to the narrator—separation from her beloved or loss of her place in the temple—results from the action of God.

The following lines, concerning the tree/birds and the lake/fish, take up the divine quality of Kṛṣṇa, for it makes him into the support for life, as does the final line about the partridge, who, according to legend, survived by drinking moonlight (McGregor 297). The third line, in contrast, appears to make Mira and Kṛṣṇa into complementary aspects of nature. Specifically, Kṛṣṇa is the inanimate aspect of earth, while Mira is the food for animals. This is in keeping with some versions of Hindu mysticism, according to which the ultimate spiritual realization is the unity of the devotee and God, a unity in which they are two sides of one reality. This dualistic unity is sometimes represented as a divine androgyne, in keeping with the common emplotment of the devotee-God relation as driven by romantic love and the desire for physical union. Indeed, it is possible to discern a complementarity in the other lines as well. Mira is given life by Kṛṣṇa. But, in another sense, Kṛṣṇa becomes animate only in Mira. We see this in a limited way in the relation of the tree and the birds. In the case of water/fish and moonlight/partridge, however, the point is striking, as Kṛṣṇa is mere matter that enters into life through Mira. There is a similar relation between the (lifeless) idol that represents Kṛṣṇa and the singing and dancing devotee.

These points complicate the narrator-narratee relation still further by ultimately identifying the two. It thereby makes sense out of Mira's insistence that she would not be separated from Kṛṣṇa even if he separated from her. On the one hand, this means that, even if she loses her place in the temple, thus is separated from her icon, the devadāsī will not lose faith. But, at the same time, it suggests that, even if Kṛṣṇa and Mira appear to be separated, they will not be separated in fact, any more than the two halves of the divine androgyne. They are complementary aspects of a single unity, like the mountain and the pasture. Indeed, the point is extended by their mutual dependency. Mira relies on Kṛṣṇa to stay alive, but Kṛṣṇa depends on Mira to become life. More generally, the relation of Kṛṣṇa and Mira reflects—indeed, is an instance of—the relation between the abstract, nirguṇa deity and the manifestation of that deity, a manifestation that occurs not only in the incarnation of Kṛṣṇa, but in the world generally.

The complications on the side of the narrator are extended further by the fact that the narrator identifies herself not as a single bird or fish, but as birds and multiple fish. This indicates that the narrator is in some sense a collective. Most obviously, she is a group of devadāsīs. But, more broadly, the suggestion is that she is everyone. The cross-textual implied author of Mīrābāī's poems indicates that people all share life in Kṛṣṇa.[4] Of course, not everyone realizes this—and that difference begins to bring in the implied audience for the poem. The implied reader is able to recognize that, in Mīrābāī's understanding, he or she too is birds sheltered by Kṛṣṇa, fish sustained by him. Moreover, the implied reader is implicitly asked to understand himself or herself in relation to the narrator's perseverance in the face of Kṛṣṇa's apparent abandonment. Of course, the understanding and experience of abandonment are not the same for everyone. In connection with this, there are at least two distinct, if related implied audiences for this poem. One is general. The other is specific to devadāsīs.

The fourth stanza intensifies these interrelations. The first and second lines actually shift from "I" to "we." Thus some larger group is again included in Mira's account of her relation to Kṛṣṇa.[5] This extends the plurality of the second stanza. It may or may not count as collective narration. (The narrator may simply be speaking *about* a larger group to which she belongs, rather than speaking *for* that group.) But, either way, the point is that both implied audiences are tacitly included in the scope of the pronoun "we."

Even more significantly, the images once again reverse the usual relation between God and the devotee. Here, God becomes useless without his devotee. A pearl gives the necklace its value. But without the string that binds it into a necklace, the beauty of the pearl would never be seen. Gold is what gives jewelry its worth. But without the chemicals used to form the gold into ornaments, it would never be worn.

The poem began as an apparently pathetic appeal from a lonely and dejected lover, abandoned by her beloved, or by a devadāsī perhaps losing the support of her temple. Over the course of a few lines, it has reversed the relationship. Now the narratee is characterized as dependent on the narrator. Indeed, the narratee is dependent, not only on the narrator, but on the implied reader as well—for the implied reader is part of the "we," without whom the pearls and gold would be invisible. This change in the relation is never arrogant. Mira's tone is familiar when she orders him to listen, but there is still a suggestion of respect.[6] The original here is "Gopāl," a given name that means not only "cowherd," but also "protector of the world" (see Monier-Williams 365). The final line of the fourth stanza reveals the many implications of the narrational discourse presupposed in the preceding analysis. A reader may not think of devadāsīs until this line in the poem—at which point, all the preceding lines alter for the implied reader (in the manner suggested in chapter 3). But, on a second reading, the line can almost become a sort of reassurance to the deity. It is almost as if she were saying—don't worry, though driven away, I will still remain faithful. The final repetition of the refrain may be read in the same way.

Here too there are possible further resonances for the implied audience. Specifically, the early sixteenth century saw the "dawn of the Mughal Empire" (Wolpert 122), "shattering" the Rajput "attempt to stem the tide of Mughal might" (124; Mīrābāī was Rajput). In a period marked by the rise of Islam, the poem appears to orient the implied readership in relation to the then-current politics of religion. Specifically, the poem may be seen as urging loyalty to Kṛṣṇa in the face of temptations to abandon him through conversion. In connection with this, one might even infer a sort of response to Islam in the poem's combination of saguna and nirguna divinity—including the suggestion of idols—and in its close interrelating of the devotee and the deity. The narrator's attitude toward

God has very little to do with submission (central to the meaning of the word *Islam* [see Waines 3]), and her view of temple worship (thus idolatry) does not appear at all negative (in contradiction with Islamic iconoclasm).

If these interpretive points are valid, they are, of course, a matter of the implied author. However, the implied audience is differentiated in terms of its relation to icon worship, its view of Islam, and so on. (Even within Islam, the differentiation may operate by reference to such open and syncretistic developments as Sufism.) Various audiences are situated somewhat differently with respect to the norms of the work. It is important to stress that these are implied audiences and not simply real audiences. A real audience may entirely miss the point of the poem. The implied audience recognizes the point—and relates that point to itself. For instance, devadāsīs would relate the point of the poem to themselves differently from other Kṛṣṇa devotees, who would in turn relate to the norms of the poem differently from recent converts to Islam. Another way of putting this idea is to say that there is a sort of indexical element in the implied authorial meaning of the text. The implied author establishes a norm and in effect asks the reader to take up that norm to reflect, not only on the narrator and narratee, but on himself or herself as well. Of course, it is the real reader who takes up the particular reflection, but the norm of the reflection is defined by the implied author for the implied reader, or at least for the sahṛdaya.

The model for this reflection is not religious per se. Rather, marital relations are the means used by Mīrābāī to represent spiritual relations. Indeed, to a great extent, the emotional impact of the poem is bound up with its romantic and marital associations. The poem continually recurs to the loyalty of a wife to her husband, using that as a model for the loyalty of the devotee. Indeed, this model is developed in a much more complex and subtle way than might at first be apparent—which leads to the sahṛdaya.

The first chapter stressed the emotional attunement of the sahṛdaya. But that attunement is not simply a matter of emotional sensitivity. It is bound up with sensitivity to dhvani, or suggestiveness, as well. Indeed, the Sanskrit theorists emphasized the intertwining of dhvani and rasa.[7] (Rasa is aesthetic and empathic emotion.) For the most part, the marriage relation in the poem is suggested rather than made explicit. Mīrābāī of course did not live in a dating culture. In her social context, the idea of separation from a beloved much more readily brought to mind marriage, making the split more serious. Moreover, as already noted, devadāsīs were married to their deity. These are suggestions that would have been widely available to readers or audience members. Two more subtle hints come in the opening lines of the fourth stanza. The word "dhāgā" means "thread," but in the plural it may refer to "bonds . . . of love" (McGregor 527). I have tried to incorporate that hint in the translation "the ties that bind the necklace." This is the sort of suggestiveness to which a sahṛdaya should be both semantically and emotionally sensitive. A similar point holds for the next line. The word "suhāgā" refers to borax (McGregor 1033), "a superior flux" used "in the refining and soldering of precious metals, especially gold" (Beer 164). However, the closely similar word "suhāga" refers to "the auspicious state of wifehood (as opposed to widowhood)" (McGregor 1033). The wife/widow distinction is marked in part by the presence or absence of jewelry. Thus I translated the word as "what the jeweler adds to make a wedding band" (in this case a necklace, rather than a ring). Here, too, the translation is an attempt to capture the dhvani of the line. Note that, in both cases, the dhvani points toward a marital relation between the narrator and the narratee—and thus, given the preceding analysis, a marital relation between the implied reader and the narratee as well. The point suggests the importance of the implied reader's "wifely" loyalty to Kṛṣṇa, a loyalty that will manifest itself differently for different readers.

Clearly, there is much more to say—not only about receptive discourse in general, but even about narratees and implied readers in this particular poem. However, the preceding comments should be enough to show that the receptive part of narrational discourse is not simply a mirror image of the productive part. It is, rather, a complex, vital, and autonomous component of discourse, a component that requires analysis and appreciation beyond that given to the far more widely discussed productive component.

Notes

Introduction

1. For a concise overview of some work in linguistic discourse analysis treating narrative, see Johnstone.
2. The following analyses will, however, use "discourse" alone when the context makes clear which variety is at issue.
3. For readers unfamiliar with the work, it is available over the Internet—just search using the title—and, being only one page long, it can be read in a few minutes.
4. Here and below, I will often use "literary" as shorthand for "literary and cinematic" or, in some cases, "literary, cinematic, and artistic," when the scope of the intended reference is clear.
5. See Hogan, *The Mind* and *Affective*.
6. Personified narrators are simply narrators that in any way are represented as persons (see chapter 1 for discussion).
7. Joseph Diescho is listed as the author on the cover of the novel, and he is referred to as "the author" on the jacket flap. However, the title page reads "Joseph Diescho with Celeste Wallin," and, on the jacket flap, Wallin is referred to as "the collaborator." In the acknowledgments, Diescho explains that Wallin was his "collaborator . . . who, in the process of typing and editing each draft of the manuscript, contributed her valuable ideas and insights and, as such, co-wrote much of the story" (vii).
8. Normative emotions are, so to speak, the emotions presupposed by the work—more technically, the emotions of the implied reader, the emotions assumed by the implied author (see chapter 1 for these concepts). A given, real reader may or may not feel those emotions. For example, a reader of *Uncle Tom's Cabin* is clearly supposed to grieve for Eva. A reader has interpreted the work badly if he or she fails to recognize this. But a given reader may find Eva's idealization excessive and thus unsympathetic, even while recognizing that the work establishes grief over her death as a norm.

9. Kenneth Newell has argued that meaning and interpretation should be understood probabilistically. Though I cannot make clear sense of the idea of probability in this context, there is a sort of kinship between his idea and the notion of a profile of ambiguity.

Chapter 1

1. "Plot" may seem to suggest only the temporal sequence of events and not, for example, the descriptive elements, whose importance has been stressed by David Herman (see chapter 7 of his *Story*).

2. The "[embedded discourse [embedded story]]" has been added to the usual schema in anticipation of later discussions.

3. The inferred author seems to be what is of central concern to empirical narratologists such as Bortolussi and Dixon. They separate the implied author from the real author because "intentions that seem to be implied by the text need not actually be true of the historical author" (66). But their primary concern is not norms. It is, rather, what readers actually do—hence their reference to "intentions that *seem* to be implied" (thus intentions inferred by readers, whatever the facts may be). They subsequently shift to "the reader's *representation* of the author" (76, italics in the original). When they return to the topic later, they suggest that "most of the time, readers do not clearly distinguish the characteristics and intention of the narrator from that of the implied or historical author" (239). They go on to indicate that, in order to follow through on a narrator/implied author distinction—thus engaging in a relatively professionalized form of interpretation—readers require training (see 250–51).

In a sense, the research of Bortolussi and Dixon is directly complementary to that of the present book. Bortolussi and Dixon examine the real readers with their propensities and inclinations, the readers who infer meanings. The present book examines the norms that may serve to evaluate those inferences.

4. As Peter J. Rabinowitz explains, authors "design their books rhetorically for some more or less *hypothetical* audience" (*Before* 21, emphasis in the original; see also Ong).

5. As is common in narratology, this and the following chapters will refer repeatedly to "storyworlds." As Herman explains, "storyworlds are mental models of who did what to and with whom, when, where, why, and in what fashion" (*Story* 5). Here and below, "storyworld" is used normatively to refer to the storyworld of the implied author, a storyworld to which the storyworlds of other readers may be more or less similar. It is worth noting here that this account of the storyworld allows one to distinguish story from discourse without thereby committing oneself to the idea that the same story can be manifest in different discourses (on the problems with this idea, see, for example, Toolan, and also Herman *Story* 214). Presumably the precise manner in which a narrative is presented—thus the precise discourse—will make a difference to the storyworlds of readers and to the (normative) storyworld of the implied author. It is also important to note that the implied author's storyworld has normative value only for particular interpretive purposes. Readers and critics are free to stipulate different purposes, thereby giving other storyworlds normative value (for discussion, see chapter 1 of Hogan *On Interpretation*). For example, a historical study of a work's impact may aim at isolating the common understanding of the work, even if that contradicts implied authorial intent. In that case, the interpretive norm would be the common

understanding. Similarly, a study of the influence of a work on some author—say, the influence of *Moll Flanders* on James Joyce—may be concerned with Joyce's understanding of *Moll Flanders*, however that is related to the implied authorial norms for that work.

6. I am leaving aside second-person narratives here. Clearly, a full treatment of the narratee would require a discussion of this important, if limited, genre of writing. For a discussion of some key points in second-person narration, see Richardson "Poetics." For my differences from standard views on second-person narration, see the afterword of *How*.

7. This story has received some attention from narratologists, prominently Robert Scholes (*Semiotics* 110–26). For an illuminating discussion of the complex organization of plot in the work—an aspect of discourse not considered here—see Bundgaard and Østergaard. For an application of more recent narrative theories to the story, see Semino. For a broader discussion of the implied reader in Hemingway's fiction, see Zapf.

8. A very nice instance of this duality is discussed by Semino in her treatment of the sentence "Luz would not come home until he had a good job and could come to New York to meet her." As Semino points out, the first "come" has the soldier as the reference point, whereas the second "come" has Luz as the reference point (95–96). On "encoding . . . directionality of movement" through "motion verbs" generally, see Herman (*Story* 282–84). I should note that my use of "dual focalization" here is different from that of Phelan, for whom "dual focalization" refers to the particular case in which "a homodiegetic narrator perceives the perceptions of his or her former self" (Phelan and Booth "Narrative" 372).

9. Obviously, some readers do not draw the distinction at all. I am speaking here only of readers who do distinguish narrators, implied authors, and real authors. Put differently, here as elsewhere I am referring primarily to professional readers or critics.

10. One reader expressed concern about my treatment of sincerity; he claimed that "Authors of fiction are generally presumed *not* to be speaking sincerely, since everything they say in the text is just pretend." I hope that the preceding comments clarify that I am not, first of all, speaking of sincerity with respect to the fictional world. On some issues of implied authorship in relation to fiction versus nonfiction, the reader may wish to consult Phelan's "The Implied Author."

11. Rabinowitz compellingly isolates a series of heuristics that guide interpretation. On the topic of rules and heuristics, it is worth noting that David Herman has sensibly argued for a particular theoretical understanding of such rules, drawing on Jackendoff's idea of "preference rules" (*Story* 28; see also Jackendoff).

12. Several theorists have stressed continuities between the real and fictional worlds. They have pointed out that readers or viewers tend to assume the storyworld is like the real world in, for example, having the same referents for the names of cities ("New York") and historical figures ("Abraham Lincoln"). Perhaps the best articulation of this is Marie-Laure Ryan's treatment of the "Principle of Minimal Departure." These formulations, however, concern the ideas people have about the real world before they read a narrative and whether they extend those ideas to the storyworld or not. The issue under consideration here moves in the opposite direction. It concerns the ideas readers derive from fictional narratives and then potentially extend to the real world.

13. Indeed, the phrase itself is ambiguous enough that its usage may vary considerably even in a single book by a single critic (see Darby 842–43 for a prominent example). It is important to note that such diversity of understandings applies to those who reject the notion of an implied author as well as to those who accept it. For a range of recent

views, see the special, Spring 2011 issue of *Style* (45.1) on the topic, particularly Richardson's valuable "Introduction."

14. The idea is in keeping with other analyses of the creative processes of artists. Thus Locher, drawing on work by Mace and Ward, writes that "As a result of evaluative processes, the artist decides at some point that the work is considered either 'complete' or as non-viable" (132). The point applies even to orature. As Innes explains, regarding Mandinka griots, "a griot in his younger days . . . listens to other griots and borrows . . . repeatedly modifying his own version until eventually he arrives at a version which seems to him the most satisfying" (118).

15. Here, I am connecting the implied author with what I have elsewhere referred to as "aesthetical intent." For the implications of this idea in resolving some problems in aesthetic theory, see chapter 5 of Hogan *On Interpretation*.

16. Consider the famous experiment with young men put on a suspension bridge. They experienced autonomic system arousal due to the swaying of the bridge. However, they (partially) attributed the arousal to their conversation with a young woman and that person's alluring qualities (see Oatley, Keltner, and Jenkins 23, 24).

17. A range of relevant cases may be found in emotion research—for example, in studies where test subjects are not aware of having seen an emotion-provoking image (i.e., information about the image does not enter working memory). However, it has clearly been processed because it has effects on the subjects' subsequent responses within the experiment, effects they cannot explain (see, for example, Öhman and Soares, and Armony and colleagues).

18. This partial opacity of one's own reasons and principles fits well with Booth's view on intention and implied authorship. Specifically, Booth wishes to preserve the insight that "the author's expressed intentions, *outside* the text, could be in total contrast to the intentions finally realized in the finished text" ("Resurrection" 75).

19. This receptive intentional account has some relation to both "actual intentionalism" accounts and "hypothetical intentionalism" accounts (for a lucid discussion of this distinction, see Kindt and Müller). It is a form of actual intentionalism; however, it avoids the intentional fallacy and limits the relevance of biography by specifying the nature of the intention involved. That specification ties the implied author to a form of hypothetical audience understanding. However, it grounds that hypothetical understanding in the author, thereby avoiding the ontological vagueness of hypothetical intentionalism.

20. See chapter 1 of Hogan *How* and "On the Origin."

21. On the operation of memories in the anticipation of future events, see Schacter, Addis, and Buckner.

22. As early as Abhinavagupta, similar points have been made about the role of memories in the response of readers to characters and actions; for a recent treatment of memories and reader response, see Oatley "Emotions" and "Why."

23. On authors' feeling that this is what they are doing, see Keen 125–27 and citations. For a literary representation of this idea, including the possibility of authorial error, see Pirandello.

24. I have drawn the term from Bordwell *Narration*. Some authors use *personalized* (e.g., Margolin "Character" 56).

25. Jacques Lacan famously formulated this distinction as that between the subject (who constitutes) and the ego (that is constituted). (For discussion of Lacan's distinction, see Hogan "Structure.") In Lacanian terms, the distinction between a personified and a nonpersonified narrator is roughly the distinction between a subject and an ego. Cog-

nitive science draws much the same distinction, for instance in developmental studies concerning "self-concept" (Eysenck 284).

26. Theory of mind is generally understood as involving two practices—simulation and theory-based inference. For an outline of the distinction, see Doherty.

27. On literary imagination as simulation, see Oatley "Why" and chapter 1 of Hogan *How*.

28. In exploring the embedding of theory of mind in characters, I am indebted to Lisa Zunshine. Similarly, in stressing the rhetorical purposes, I am indebted to James Phelan.

29. The idea of a nonpersonified narrator that encompasses personified narrators reflects a point made by David Bordwell, though he drew an almost diametrically opposed conclusion. Discussing film and drawing on work by Edward Branigan, Bordwell notes that "personified narrators are invariably swallowed up in the overall narrational process of the film, which they do not produce. So the interesting theoretical problem involves an implicit, nonpersonified narrator" (61). The idea of embedding personified narrators within a nonpersonified narrator also reflects Hayman's idea of a nonpersonified "Arranger" who selects and organizes the details of the various narrations and interior monologues in Joyce's *Ulysses*. In certain respects, the present argument generalizes Hayman's concept, which he characterizes as falling "somewhere between the narrator and the implied author" (122). Dancygier is, to some extent, getting at a similar idea when she treats narration in relation to an encompassing "story-viewpoint space" (chapter 3), though her development of this and related ideas is different from the approach presented here. For a characteristically precise and rigorous treatment of the issue of whether a narrator is ubiquitous, see Margolin "Necessarily."

30. One reader objected to this point on the grounds that we are told he went to Chicago. In fact, we are told only that Luz wrote a letter to Chicago. A number of my students regularly assume that she is writing to the major in Chicago. The point is not that readers cannot figure out it is the soldier. They can figure this out. The point is that standard orientational devices would have introduced the information about his going to Chicago explicitly and early on. Contrast what the narrator tells us: "they agreed that he should go home to get a job," with the more fully orienting alternative, "they agreed that he should go home to Chicago to get a job." The narrator is treating the location of "home" as if it is familiar information, not new information. The same point holds for the reference to Luz's letter to Chicago.

31. The general point is common enough. For example, Chatman writes that "every tale implies a listener or reader, just as it implies a teller" (*Story* 151). The difference here is the extension of a nonpersonified narrator to encompass even works with personified narrators. As Chatman suggests, the generalization of the (in this case, nonpersonified) narrator undermines the traditional distinction between putatively "mimetic" drama and "narrated" stories. Related points have been made by other authors in recent years. For example, Manfred Jahn argues that every drama has a narrator, an "agent who manages the exposition, who decides what is to be told, how it is to be told, . . . and what is to be left out" ("Narrative" 670; see also Richardson "Drama" 151–52). The idea is also consistent with van Peer's isolation of "the perspective through which we are given the story" in Euripides' *Medea*. McIntyre too touches on the topic, though his concern is more with shifting points of view than an encompassing narrative voice.

32. The final point partially agrees with "no-narrator" theory (see Banfield and citations) in that it recognizes the possible collapsing of narrator and (implied) author.

However, the crucial difference from no-narrator theory is that, by the present account, it is always possible for the narrator and the author to be distinguished. In this way, generalizing the narrator is the opposite of "making authors indistinguishable from narrators" (Banfield 396), which Banfield sees as the result of such generalization. In fact, generalizing the narrator means preserving a consistent distinction between narrators and authors—both real and implied.

33. I should note that Jahn allows that a narrator might have an "emotional stance" ("Focalization" 101). But, for Jahn, that is only one of many possibilities. The suggestion of the preceding analysis is that, if one takes seriously the notion of a narrator as a tacitly simulated speaker, one must *always* attribute emotion to the narrator—not sometimes as one possibility among many.

34. Peter Rabinowitz pointed out to me that it seems unlikely Luz wrote that she had never known Italians before. It is, I believe, possible to construe the line as the soldier's inference from some statement in Luz's letter (e.g., "Before, I never got to know the local population very well"). Nonetheless, the point is well taken. This particular sentence is readily interpretable as focalizing Luz. As such, it contributes to the narrational ambiguity of the work. In that ambiguity, there are points such as this that allow an interpretation of the story as having dual affective focalization, though the bulk of the story seems to favor a single affective focalization on the soldier.

35. Such an affective preference is arguably in keeping with some feminist responses to Hemingway, which see his work as not merely patriarchal, but in some cases even misogynistic (see Ferrero and citations)—though I personally do not view this story as either.

36. See, for example, chapter 2 of Hogan *The Mind* and Oatley "Emotions" and "Suggestion."

37. In neurological terms, this sort of processing is commonly triggered when one part of the brain (anterior cingulate cortex) detects some contradiction or conflict in processing elsewhere. This, in turn, activates working memory (including dorsolateral prefrontal cortex), which allows the self-conscious consideration and adjudication of such conflicts. On these processes, see Carter and colleagues, MacDonald and colleagues, Lieberman and Eisenberger, and Kondo and colleagues.

38. One referee worried that I was "underestimat[ing] the resourcefulness of human engagement," since men can imagine what it is like to have a child. My point is not at all that our empathy is confined to nearly identical emotional memories. The point is simply that empathic response involves emotional memories. As such, the presence or absence of intense, approximately parallel emotional memories is likely to enhance empathic response. Of course, I may be wrong about this particular case, and something else may account for the difference in my response to Lahiri's novel.

39. Note that "readers" here include the (implied) author. Indeed, the normative task of critics is commonly one of isolating and explaining features of the text that are experienced, but not self-consciously recognized and understood by the author.

Chapter 2

1. For simplicity, this chapter will use the word "painting" to refer to a range of two-dimensional works of visual art, including, for example, ink drawings.

2. Some writers have treated connections between narratology and painting, primarily by reference to narrative painting. An interesting study that extends beyond

obviously narrative works may be found in Labruda. Peggy Phelan's treatment of action painting and its relation to performance art provides another significant extension.

3. Indeed, film theorists sometimes treat the concepts of *implied author* and *auteur* as equivalent (see Murphet 83).

4. On emotional memories, see LeDoux; on mirroring, see Iacoboni.

5. There are also emotional and thematic consequences of style in both verbal and visual art. However, style requires separate treatment.

6. Instances of narrative paintings range from, for example, representations of Jesus's Passion (see Derbes) to the "patua" scroll painting of Bengal (see Guha-Thakurta 12–13n.3 and 19).

7. See chapter 5 of Hogan *The Mind*.

8. The point was famously emphasized by Lessing, in a different theoretical context. It has recently been addressed by Kafalenos ("Implications"). The practice is not by any means confined to Western art. For example, a great deal of early modern Indian art focused on illustrating key moments from important narratives, such as the great Sanskrit epics (a point attested even by a brief look at the figures in Guha-Thakurta). In fact, the tendency to embed paintings in implicit narratives is so ubiquitous and fundamental that an unclear narrative context can lead to viewer disorientation. Thus Schwabsky explains that, initially, critics responded badly to Manet's paintings. "What was missing, in the eyes of Manet's contemporaries," he explains, "was a coherent story holding together the people and things depicted in the paintings" (32). The point even extends to relatively abstract work. Thus, in a recent newspaper article, Vicenzo Trione characterizes Italian Transavanguardia painters as trying to produce "dream narrations" (26).

9. It is also worth noting that there are many storytelling traditions in which pictures serve a role (see, for example, Mair 5). Of course, after publication technology made possible the mass reproduction of pictures, genres arose that integrate pictures more fully with verbal narrative, as in children's picture books and graphic fiction. Indeed, illustrations extend well beyond these genres. For example, illustrations of narratives were common in British India, as Guha-Thakurta's work shows.

10. On the function of context in interpreting emotion expressions, see Carroll and Russell. See Kafalenos on photographs as "lend[ing] themselves to being interpreted as an event in a number of different stories" ("Photographs" 429).

11. Quoted in Robinson (49).

12. Readers of Rabinowitz will not be surprised at this. See *Reading* 58–65 on the orientational and interpretive function of titles. The disambiguating value of allusions is stressed by Wolf (432).

13. This and subsequent references to plates refer to Robinson.

14. See, for example, the description of the women's quarters in "The Wife's Letter" (208).

15. This is a common approach to Tagore's paintings, particularly in relation to his sister-in-law; see Sen.

16. The value of locating a work in an authorial canon has, of course, been recognized by narratologists. For example, Rabinowitz notes that "The appropriate background group for a given text usually includes the previous works by the same author" (*Reading* 71). Nonetheless, the general idea of a cross-textual implied author is contrary to the usual usage of "implied author" in literary study. For example, Susan Lanser points out that "Narratologists have long maintained that an 'implied' author is the property of a single text, and cannot be extrapolated to a writer's entire oeuvre" (see

also Shen 178). Indeed, in his initial discussion of the implied author, Wayne Booth maintained that "regardless of how sincere an author may try to be, his different works will imply different versions" of himself (*Rhetoric* 71). This is part of the ambiguity of the concept in Booth's work and elsewhere in narratology. In this section of *The Rhetoric of Fiction*, Booth is exploring implied authorship as a sort of authorial self-presentation, an author's creation of an impression on readers. This is an important idea, but one very different from the implied author as an interpretive standard, particularly when this is understood in terms of consistency in receptive intent (as I advocated in chapter 1). In later work, Booth took up this idea of the author's self-presentation, extending it across works, in his notion of a "career-author." The idea may initially seem to have some similarity to the cross-textual implied author. However, Booth's career-author is not the enduring set of cognitive principles that recur in receptive intents across a range of works. Rather, it is a "sustained character" who is "the sum of the invented creators" (*Critical Understanding* 270).

17. In keeping with this idea of pathos, Sen notes that critics such as W. G. Archer and K. G. Subramanyan link the "ovoid face" with "the desolate woman."

18. On Tagore and attachment, see chapter 7 in Hogan *What Literature* and "Reading Tagore."

19. Indeed, there are multiple interrelations between attachment and empathy. For example, Royzman and Rozin point out that sympathetic sorrow tends to foster attachment, while attachment is almost a necessary condition for empathic joy.

20. At a presentation based on this chapter, one audience member objected that this does not mean that the painting constitutes a "pregnant moment" in the way that, for example, the Goya painting does. That is true. A scene constitutes a pregnant moment if it has highly specific and proximate precedents and consequents. In other words, the immediately preceding and following events are well defined. For instance, in the Goya painting, the central figure will be shot and die in the next moment. However, the preceding argument indicates that narrative quality in visual art is not confined to pregnant moments. Rather, narrative quality extends across a range of degrees in precedent/consequent specificity and proximity. Tagore's painting suggests precedents and consequents, but they have relatively low specificity and proximity.

21. The point applies to television narratives as well (see Huisman "Aspects" 156–60).

22. I am grateful to Ben Singer for suggesting this term.

23. Dutt's first film, *Baazi* (1951), already shows some tendency toward interposition, and Murthy was not director of photography for that film. However, he was involved with camera operation, so the assignment of responsibility even in that film remains unclear.

24. See Hogan "On the Meaning."

25. On the necessity of stipulating a guiding intention, see chapter 1 of Hogan *On Interpretation*.

26. After formulating these ideas initially, I came upon Berys Gaut's valuable essay, which happens to use the phrase "minimal auteurism." However, Gaut defines standard auteurism very differently. Thus his notion of minimal auteurism is very different as well.

27. A recurring pattern in an author's canon need not recur in every work. It need only recur sufficiently to distinguish the author from others.

28. Clearly, there are other contexts in which one can locate the film beyond that of the *auteur*. Wendy Doniger presents an analysis of the film in relation to recurring motifs

of doubling and identity. Vijay Mishra locates the play within generic considerations of the "gothic."

29. On some of the many instances of this recurring pattern in national allegory, see Hogan *Understanding Nationalism* 134–36.

30. Guha-Thakurta gives an example of this sort from the visual arts. "The great 'discovery' of the Kalighat *pats* [scroll paintings] as a vibrant and original folk art form" occurred when "the living tradition had become defunct" (23).

31. On this recurring allegorical feature, see Hogan *Understanding Nationalism* 144–47.

32. Actually, there are different accounts of karma in Hindu tradition. Popular accounts tend to stress reward and punishment. However, Vedāntic philosophy stresses the consequences of desire.

33. As one referee pointed out, it is also possible that expectations from across an author's works will mislead an interpreter. Indeed, it is quite possible that there will be contradictions between the textual implied author and the cross-textual implied author. (Presumably, in such cases, we defer to the former.) Moreover, one may isolate cross-textual implied authors for subsets of an author's canon—for instance, certain periods or genres. I have not stressed discontinuities in implied authorship here since that is the topic of the following chapter.

34. One reader worried that I am claiming all pictures tell stories. I hope it is clear that I am not claiming any such thing. The argument here is, rather, that aspects of narrative discourse analysis may help us discuss painting more clearly and that a discussion of painting may enrich narrative discourse analysis. The mutual benefits arise most obviously from the notion of a cross-textual implied author. It is the case that such an implied author will often lead us to locate the moment of a painting in a more or less imprecise sequence of events, thus a sort of minimal story (e.g., longing for a child followed by the birth and death of a child or a failure to conceive). However, not all elements of the cross-textual implied author need be story-related. In any case, it should be clear that a painting is not typically presenting a story itself. Indeed, that is the whole point of requiring that events be filled in from elsewhere.

35. This distinctiveness criterion eliminates the problem of standard techniques or "craft context" as well. Clearly, much of what a director, cinematographer, or other auteur does will be standard in the profession. As such, it will recur across his or her canon, but nondistinctively. This craft context is explicated with particular care in various works by Bordwell (see, for example, Bordwell, Staiger, and Thompson).

Chapter 3

1. The distinction is drawn from Elizabeth Anscombe, though the following discussion will develop it somewhat differently.

2. Unsurprisingly, other authors have noted something along these lines. See, for example, Lanser "The 'I,'" Rader, and Phelan's discussion of "mask narration" in *Living*.

3. As the following discussion will make clear, this unity need not be ideal, which is to say, found at all levels. Indeed, one main point of the present analysis is that the unity will rarely if ever be ideal. Rather, the final receptive intent provides the possibility for isolating patterns across otherwise diverse, local attitudes, themes, and so forth, even when those are contradictory. To anticipate the present argument slightly, a work may shift back and forth in pro- and antiwar attitudes. However, this does not mean

that the only unity is at the level of local, implied—more technically, "implicated"—authors (with one part unified in being prowar and another unified in being antiwar). The encompassing implied author may implicitly unify these different views through a pattern of tacit assimilation to World War II and the Vietnam War respectively. This is far from an ideal unity. But it is a pattern that brings the work together with specifiable consistency. Put differently, there may be profound contradictions in a work. The unity treated here is the consistent pattern that explains the contradictions. Thus the work may be prowar when the model of World War II is activated, but antiwar when the model of the Vietnam War is activated. The alternation of these contexts and models may be perfectly consistent across the work, giving the work unity at that level.

4. For instance, it is well established that people engage in very different cognitive processing strategies depending on mood state (see, for example, Forgas "Introduction" 15–17 and citations).

5. See Holland, Holyoak, Nisbett, and Thagard 313–14.

6. In using "implicated" here, I do not have in mind Grice's idea of implicature. Rather, I am using the term in its more ordinary sense. When people say that someone is implicated in a crime, they usually suggest that he or she had some ancillary role, rather than a main role. Similarly, one may think of the local, implicated authors as ancillary to the larger, encompassing, implied author.

7. This sort of discrepancy in terminology is not unusual. Apparently identical assertions of implied authorial multiplicity may in fact mean something very different from one another. For example, Nelles discusses some "unusual situations," including that in which a reader sees "multiple implied authors" ("Historical" 28). In fact, Nelles means that the work has several inferred real authors, despite one name being given on the cover of the book. This meaning becomes clear when he gives an example of a critic who concluded that "*Jane Eyre* was the product of multiple authors" (29). The point is entirely valid, but completely different from the notion of multiple implicated authors presented above. Similarly, Klaiber talks about "multiple implied authors," but she is concerned with texts by multiple real authors. Somewhat differently, Richardson addresses multiplicity in implied authorship in relation to an author's creation of "different authorial persona[s]" ("Introduction" 6). On the other hand, Richardson's brief example of an apparent contradiction in Chaucer (*Unnatural Voices* 121) does seem to move in the direction of the account presented here.

8. As discussed in chapter 1, people are very bad at explaining their own judgments, even about such simple matters as plural formation in their native language. Again, there is no reason to believe that authors are any more successful characterizing the enormously complex principles that bear on literary narratives.

9. One could also differentiate implicated audiences in terms of themes. For example, the "theme of northern moral complicity in slavery" (Walters 180) obviously has a primarily northern implicated audience.

10. See, for example, Gregg Crane on the legislative impact of the novel.

11. Much of the discussion about the novel concerns the actual, biographical author, rather than one or more implied or implicated authors. This discussion is valuable, but largely irrelevant to the present analysis. For example, there has been much interest in just what Stowe really knew about the South and about slavery (see, for example Otter 17 and Pryse 134; but see also the research of Albion Tourgee cited in Cantave 98–99). Other writers have been concerned about her treatment of real black women, prominently Harriet Jacobs (see Logan 54–55). These are interesting and significant issues. But their relation to the novel is somewhat indirect at best. If they enter at all, they do so in productive rather than receptive intent.

The work of Yuexin Liu seems particularly relevant to cases such as Stowe's in suggesting why such biographical considerations are likely to be irrelevant to the understanding of the implied author. As Shen summarizes Liu's argument, "the real author may be restricted by . . . various social relations, practical interests and pragmatic considerations, which make him or her vulgar and hypocritical. By contrast, in constructing a fictional narrative, the author can transcend . . . the confinement of social relations and pragmatic considerations" ("Booth's" 171). Insofar as one is concerned with the biographical author, it may be that Leslie Fiedler has come closest to identifying those aspects of Stowe's feelings and fantasies that motivated the book. Fiedler writes that Stowe "dreamed only of being able to die well under the extremest persecution, forgiving her persecutors," even "converting them to a redeemed life." "All of this," he continues, "she projects onto Tom, who as her surrogate . . . does not reflect invidiously on Afro-American masculinity" (*What* 173).

12. See Nandy on the general use of childhood as a model for Africans; see chapter 4 of Hogan *Culture* on how particular models are associated with particular political tendencies.

13. See, for example, 402, 405, 409, 423, and 476; for critical discussion, see Donovan's chapter, "Inferno: The Legree Plantation."

14. George's emigration to Liberia has been a point of controversy. A number of critics see this as evidence of Stowe's racist desire to rid the United States of Africans. Ammons characterizes this as "Deportation" (74) to solve "the problem of dealing with demands for racial equality" (74). But this is a curious reading. The novel never advocates rounding up African Americans and shipping them to Liberia against their will ("deportation"). Moreover, Stowe has George indicate that blacks need a nation to defend themselves against the racism of a majority white population. Stowe's attitude here seems more biased against whites than against blacks, since whites seem largely incorrigible (despite a few positive examples, such as Tom Loker [see Gillian Brown 84]).

15. Warhol illuminates some of the ways in which the misunderstanding of Uncle Tom came about (see "'Ain't I'").

16. On the nature and operation of positive and negative stereotypes, and empirical research on these topics, see Hogan *Culture* 129–30 and citations.

17. This is not to say that she is the only person to have asserted African spiritual superiority. As critics have noted, she was drawing in part on lectures by Alexander Kinmont (see Nuernberg 40 and citations).

18. As, for example, Railton stresses, "Stowe had, of course, to write for her readers," who were almost entirely white (104).

19. This sort of appeal has been explored with rigor and insight by Warhol. See her influential essays "Toward a Theory" and "Poetics" and chapter 5 of *Gendered*.

20. An emphasis on the importance of attachment in the novel is broadly consistent with some previous interpretations, particularly Jane Tompkins's important analysis, which stresses the novel's utopian "vision" of "daily living" in "Christian love" as "revealed . . . in motherhood" (141). Understanding the multiplicity of Stowe's implied authorship and locating her emotional orientations in the context of current affective science—particularly work on attachment—do not contradict this observation. Rather, these points extend and deepen Tompkins's insights, particularly in relation to the "enabling contradictions" of the novel, as David Leverenz rightly called them (120).

21. Readers interested in this topic should consult Richardson's essay, which presents a rigorous and wide-ranging treatment.

22. It is important to note that misdirection is not necessarily perfidious, as the preceding example may suggest. It does involve some degree of intentional deception.

However, that intentional deception may be in the service of protecting the real author from persecution (e.g., if he or she holds "heretical" religious views).

23. As the phrasing suggests, the present distinction cuts across that between on-screen and voice-over narration. For a clear summary of some uses of voice-over, see Kozloff.

24. In keeping with the analysis in chapter 1, "narrator" here refers to a potentially unreliable communicator of storyworld information, oriented by epistemic and emotional particularities. This does not mean that the narrator is necessarily a bodily presence at a particular point in space (e.g., a person who takes up the position of the camera). This is the primary sense in which Bordwell, quite rightly, objects to the idea of an invisible observer putatively guiding film narration (see *Narration* 3–15). The following discussion cannot cover all the varieties of film narrator. For an overview of film narration in relation to other standard narratological categories (e.g., homodiegetic or extradiegetic), see Murphet (see also Fulton 115). (For a diagram of some main narratological divisions, see Huisman "Narrative" 26.)

25. Here the internal access is perceptual (e.g., through point-of-view shots). Note that this access is clearly not something that can be communicated in the verbal narration of the frame story. Thus it is available to the viewer, but not to the narratee (i.e., Roshan).

26. The scenario is far from entirely fictional. As Chomsky points out, "There is . . . mounting evidence that Cheney-Rumsfeld torture created terrorists . . . directly," citing the case of Abdallah al-Ajmi (*Hopes* 266). Within the film, the pattern is repeated when Zilgai experiences further humiliation and ends up killing a police officer, then committing suicide. Note that the point here is directly opposed to the view that former detainees "reengage" in terrorism (a widely cited argument against releasing Guantánamo prisoners; see Worthington). The point of the film is precisely that this is not "recidivism." It is, rather, the creation of criminality. The proper response is not continuing to imprison the innocent—or simply abandoning them to the further humiliation faced by Samir—but helping them return to a normal life.

27. For example, his "stunning reversal" on Guantanamo, including a March 7 "executive order formalizing a system of indefinite detention for dozens of the 172 remaining detainees at Guantanamo, all Muslims and . . . the resumption of military trials" ("Abu Ghraib in America" 3).

Chapter 4

1. Along the same lines, Currie points out that "A newspaper article can be unreliable, meaning that it misleads us about what actually happened" (19).

2. A similar general point is made by Dancygier (chapter 3).

3. Readers familiar with Phelan's account in *Living to Tell About It* will recognize that I am confining unreliability here to what Phelan calls "reporting." Phelan has two further categories, "interpreting" and "evaluating." However, interpretive and evaluative views can be reported as true or expressed as opinion (contrast "Smith was deceitful" and "I always felt that Smith was deceitful"). I would reserve the term "unreliability" (or, more precisely, "representational unreliability," as discussed below) for cases where the narrator's information is presented as true (within the storyworld), not as opinion—thus cases where the (mis)information is *reported*.

4. "Trust" here refers to the full spectrum of emotional confidence in the narrator. In other words, here and below, the word "trust" is not confined to "normative unreliability," as found in some writers (see Nünning "Reconceptualizing" 93).

5. As noted in chapter 1, there is neurological research, specifically work on the monitoring of contradiction, that suggests a scenario of this sort.

6. One referee worried that resolving ambiguity here is a matter of understanding rather than motivation. The point is not that understanding is irrelevant to contradiction. It usually is relevant. Indeed, it is usually the means by which we resolve contradictions. The point is that readers experience a contradiction through their engagement with some process. The process in question may be, first of all, a matter of understanding. But it may also be a matter of, for instance, sustaining one's positive view of a hero whom one likes or with whom one identifies. The process in question is always motivated. Without the motivation, we would not engage in the process and we would sense no contradiction—at least no contradiction that would itself motivate our effortful engagement in seeking a resolution.

7. This may seem to refer to a "source" rather than a "type." In fact, one could refer to this entire hierarchy as one of "epistemic source" or "source of justification." The important point is that this is different from the first category, the speaker's location in narrative discourse.

8. Unsurprisingly, critics have noted this basic point about the novel. See, for example, Rigney 39. On the other hand, many critics have arguably underestimated the depth and extent of that unreliability. For example, can one really call the narrator "visionary" (Gray 132) when her "visions" appear to be hallucinations? The hallucinations are related to a spiritual quest, but the situation is at best complicated. More strikingly, can one trust her view that her dead mother left behind a jacket or seeds for her to find? (see Gray 132). It seems, rather, that the implied author views these as saliently unreliable claims.

9. Much of the criticism has been concerned with the narrator's relations with her parents. On the figure of the mother, see, for example, Grace.

10. On the spiritual and shamanic resonances of the work, see, for example, Guédon and Josie Campbell.

11. For a summary of alternative views, see Bouson 59–60. As Bouson points out, "Some readers are optimistic about the fate of Atwood's character," including some critics who focus on her "visions." In contrast, "Other critics . . . are troubled" (59)—sometimes faulting Atwood on this score (60).

12. On some resonances of this image, see Wilson 105–6. Wilson is treating the presence of folklore motifs in the novel. On this topic, see also Baer.

13. Many critics have noted the nationalist themes in the novel. Stein summarizes critical tendencies, noting that "Canadian critics looked at [Atwood's] nationalism; American critics focused on her feminism" (50). As Kapuscinski points out, "a significant proportion" of the criticism on the novel "views the narrative as contributing to the development of a distinctive national identity" (105). Such approaches sometimes simplify the novel's politics. However, as Kapuscinski stresses, the book manifests a "recognition of Canada's ongoing history of violence" (114). Other writers have pointed to complexities in Atwood's relation to nationalism (see, for example, Laura Wright).

There is a similar complexity in Atwood's relation to feminism. It is therefore difficult to accept Bouson's view that *Surfacing* is "A novel premised on the ideology of cultural feminism," that it "rejects the masculinist culture," including its "rationalist" elements, and "idealizes a nature-identified femininity" (40; Bouson also claims that the work "undercuts its own romantic feminism," which makes it difficult to see how it can be viewed as asserting romantic feminism).

Chapter 5

1. As this indicates, conjunctive parallel narrators may treat precisely the same events. In consequence, this use of the term "parallel" should be distinguished from that of writers such as O'Neill (see 368).

2. As Alan Palmer points out, "the formal or theoretical definitions" of *interior monologue* and *stream of consciousness* "vary widely" ("Stream" 570). The intent of the present discussion is to develop theoretically precise descriptive and explanatory ideas. This does not involve any claim that these are somehow the "right" definitions of these particular words. It would make no difference if other labels were attached to the concepts presented here.

3. In this sense, it is not "the 'prespeech' level of consciousness," as Dorrit Cohn puts it (108). Rather, it encompasses the nonverbalized levels of consciousness. There are other important distinctions here as well, most obviously direct versus indirect discourse. (For a rigorous recent discussion of the latter, see Sharvit; for a clear overview of some influential distinctions, see Palmer "Thought.") The set of distinctions in the present discussion of mentalistic narration, like those developed elsewhere in the book, is not meant to be exhaustive.

4. My account of interior monologue and stream of consciousness has obvious connections with that of Lawrence Bowling. However, Bowling does not seem to fully appreciate the operation of verbal encoding by the narrator, as Chatman points out, using different terminology (see *Story* 187–88).

5. András Kovács argues that the cinematic "equivalent" to "stream of consciousness" is "travel [that] takes place . . . in a person's mind" (103). Kovács presents a convincing case that the "mental journey" has a narrative function similar to stream of consciousness. But it does not commonly seem to be an instance of stream of consciousness.

6. As Ross puts it, "Faulkner distorts each brother's narrative in order to explore the depths of the speaker's mind not revealed through his straightforward storytelling." This is possible because "the distortions each brother's narration undergoes are appropriate to his psychological makeup" (169).

7. As this indicates, I see no reason to accept Ross's view that Benjy is not only "physically" but also "mentally incapable of speech" (171). It seems clear that the idealized stream of consciousness incorporates a good deal of Benjy's own subvocalizations. Indeed, it is clear that he is often "trying to say" (see 40) something and is prevented for purely physical reasons. Of course, his comprehension of speech is severely limited by his other cognitive deficits.

8. Some critics have recognized the general point, though they have developed it somewhat differently. For example, Matthews stresses the insularity of distinct moments for Benjy (36). Ross recognizes the limitation most directly by stressing the absence of "because" and "so" in Benjy's speech (172). Some authors have traced peculiarities of the verbal style in this section to Benjy's problems with cause and effect (see Jeffries and McIntyre 6 and citations).

9. Benjy's relation with Caddy has been a focus of much analysis; see, for example, Baum, Page, and Wagner.

10. Critics have, of course, recognized Jason's unreliability. However, they have formulated its reasons differently. For example, Kuminova claims that Jason's bias is "towards oversimplifying and flattening out the complexities of the inner life" of other characters (50).

11. For example, at one point, Quentin thinks, "I can be dead in Harvard Caddy said in the caverns and grottoes of the sea" (136). But this expresses a mere possibility, evidently a metaphorical one, and one articulated by someone else.

12. The reasons for Quentin's suicide have, of course, been of concern to critics. Labatt notes, for example, that the reader is given "several intermittently connected causes" (20), so various as to make the suicide "believable and yet inexplicable" (21). Labatt makes a good point. In terms of the present analysis, acts have, in effect, a profile of causal ambiguity.

13. This desire for unity presumably involves sexual desire. The crucial feature, however, is attachment dependency. Readers interested in the issue of Quentin's sexual desire may consult Irwin or Matthews (48–49).

14. One referee worried that *Mulholland Drive* is "merely nonsensical if its narrations are parallel." I hope the discussion makes clear that parallel narration does not make the work nonsensical in the sense of making the work gibberish. However, it does inhibit the possibilities for developing an encompassing resolution of the ambiguity of the work. At the same time, that lack of resolution may, in turn, serve emotional or thematic purposes that reestablish coherence and "sense" in a different way.

15. See Thomas 83. Critics have noted many of the basic interpretive points considered here. Thomas's essay is particularly well developed and insightful regarding these points.

16. In an interesting interpretation, Bruckner examines the following narrative in terms of Rita's head injury. For reasons of space, the following discussion will leave aside this possibility.

17. A point noted by critics (see Thomas 86).

18. Unsurprisingly, the bulk of interpretations of the film involve at least some psychoanalytic component. Beyond Thomas, McDowell, and Shostak, already mentioned, representative cases would include Schaffner, Restuccia, and Hageman.

19. The character is referred to as a man, but is played by an actress and is not clearly gendered in visual appearance.

20. Moreover, there is a link not only with theater, but with filmmaking, since, as Jean-Marc Lalanne points out, ending with the word *silencio* alludes to the ending of Jean-Luc Godard's *Le Mépris*, which treats filmmaking. Readers interested in the cinematic background to Lynch's film may wish to view Lalanne's lecture, "*Mulholland Drive*, film matrice (2000–2010)," available on the internet at http://www.canal-u.tv/video/cinematheque_francaise/mulholland_drive_film_matrice_2000_2010_conference_de_jean_marc_lalanne.6432 (accessed 15 August 2012).

21. Needless to say, critics have remarked on the postmodernist affiliations of Lynch's film. See, for example, d'Ocarmo.

22. Dreaming stream of consciousness is the equivalent of personified and embedded narration in this context because, in addition to being personified and embedded, the dreaming character's mind becomes the possible source for epistemic or motivational unreliability in the narration. Indeed, to say that something is a dream is, in effect,

to say that it manifests particular sorts of epistemic and motivational unreliability tied to a particular person.

Chapter 6

1. This is not to say that the novel is beyond criticism. For example, there is some truth to the view that "Wanja embodies the features of a number of female stereotypes identified in African literature" (Lovesey 59; see citations 144n.14). Of course, observations such as this must be seriously qualified by a recognition of Wanja's allegorical role. On the other hand, some critics have taken this into account and still found the novel problematic. Stratton offers a particularly compelling argument. However, Stratton seems to overstate her case. It seems clear that Ngũgĩ recognizes and rejects Wanja's sexual exploitation even as he recognizes and rejects that of the nation. Moreover, Wanja's main source of strength and knowledge is her grandmother, Nyakinyua, which hardly suggests that "The trope . . . excludes women from the creative production of the national polity" (122).

2. Some critics have also treated some aspects of narration in other of Ngũgĩ's novels (see, for example, Mwangi on unreliable narration in *Devil on the Cross*).

3. On the significance of this and other names in the novel, see the linguistic glossary in Sicherman.

4. See Treister 268 on Wanja's relation to Gikuyu ethnicity, as manifest in the relation of her name to three daughters of the great Gikuyu ancestor, Muumbi.

5. This seems to be the point where another resonance of Wanja's name enters—its echoing of "Wanjiru," the wife of Mau Mau leader Dedan Kimathi (see Sicherman 187–88 on Wanjiru).

6. The main exception is his participation in a group delegation from the countryside to the capital. But he seems to enter into this more or less by accident (see 114).

7. The role of Christianity in the novel is deep and complex, as critics have noted. See, for example, Sharma and Pagnoulle.

8. There has been relatively little discussion of collective narration by narratologists. An important exception is Margolin's "Collective."

9. Margolin notes that the reference of a narratorial "we" will often "shift in identity, scope, size, and temporal location in the course of the narration" ("Collective" 245).

10. This is one of the most common forms of idealization.

11. After drafting this chapter and deriving these options empirically, I came upon Margolin's "Collective Perspective" essay and found that he reached distinct, but complementary conclusions through logical analysis (see 243). I would urge anyone interested in this topic to read Margolin's insightful and thought-provoking essay.

12. The text also recurs to Munira's testimony on 190, 224, 243, 269, 295, and elsewhere.

13. Though Diescho is a highly respected Namibian public intellectual and political commentator, his novel has generated almost no critical discussion. The *MLA International Bibliography* lists only two works treating Diescho. Both concern his other novel, *Troubled Waters*. Part of the purpose of the present analysis is to foster such discussion and, more generally, attention to *Born of the Sun*.

14. Some readers have seen this as related to Alan Palmer's recent revival of Hegelian idealism, specifically his claim that there is "intermental thought" ("Social Minds"). However, to say that people have a *sense* of direct access to other people's thought is

quite different from saying that people do have such direct access. For a few of the problems with Palmer's views in this area, see Hogan "Palmer's."

15. In the course of the novel, there is one very clear violation of the general pattern just outlined. That is when readers are given the internal thoughts of an Afrikaner minister (170). The passage highlights the inaccessibility of the white man's thoughts to the Africans, and vice versa. This inaccessibility results from the fact that they never share common projects, easy cooperation, mirroring, and so on. However, the fact that the white man's thoughts can be represented in the novel tends to discourage the sort of dehumanization that might have resulted from a complete confinement of interiority to blacks.

Afterword

1. This brief afterword is clearly not the place for an overview of the literature on these topics. There has certainly been valuable research in this area, as illustrated by the pathbreaking work of Prince ("Introduction") and Iser. The standout recent treatment of the implied reader is Brian Richardson's ("Singular Text"), already mentioned in chapter 3. More recent examinations of the narratee would include Phelan's careful treatment of Prince's ideas on the narratee and Rabinowitz's conception of the narrative audience ("Self-Help"). Nonetheless, the relative neglect of the topics is illustrated by the differences between the entries for "Implied Reader" and "Implied Author" (a ratio of roughly one to six) as well as "Narratee" and "Narrator" (a ratio of roughly one to fourteen) in Herman, Jahn, and Ryan.

2. The basis of this translation is the text in Bahadur (44), supplemented by the version in Shantaram.

3. Or, rather, as Hawley and Juergensmeyer explain, this is how legend has it (124–27). Little is known about "the original" Mīrābāī, "if ever indeed she existed at all" (123). The biographical point holds whether the poem was written by Mīrābāī or in her name. The author of a pseudo-Mīrābāī poem would adopt the implied authorial position of a reader reading the poem as authored by Mīrābāī, a point suggested by the reference to "lady Mira."

4. Here, again, the point holds whether the poem was authored by Mīrābāī or written in her name.

5. It is possible to use "we" for "I" in Hindi. However, this does not seem to be the case here, since Mira elsewhere uses "I," and the plurality of "we" is prepared for in the plural images of the second stanza. I should note that Bahadur has "we" already in the moon and partridge line. I have chosen Shantaram's version because it is more internally consistent, confining "we" to a single stanza. (I have also followed Shantaram in repeating the opening lines as a refrain and in a couple of small variants in wording.)

6. This line is not in Bahadur, but is included in Shantaram.

7. See, for example, the references to *rasadhvani* in Ingalls.

Works Cited

Abbott, H. Porter. "Narration." In Herman, Jahn, and Ryan, 339–44.
Abhinavagupta. *The Dhvanyaloka of Ānandavardhana with the Locana of Abhinavagupta.* Ed. Daniel Ingalls. Trans. Daniel Ingalls, Jeffrey Masson, and M. V. Patwardhan. Cambridge, MA: Harvard University Press, 1990.
"Abu Ghraib in America." *The Nation,* 28 March 2011, 3–4.
Aikhenvald, Alexandra. "Evidentiality." In *The Cambridge Encyclopedia of the Language Sciences.* Ed. Patrick Colm Hogan. Cambridge: Cambridge University Press, 2011, 294–95.
Aizenberg, Edna. "The Untruths of the Nation: *Petals of Blood* and Fuentes's *The Death of Artemio Cruz.*" *Research in African Literatures* 21.4 (1990): 85–103.
Althusser, Louis and Etienne Balibar. *Reading Capital.* Trans. Ben Brewster. London: Verso, 1979.
Ammons, Elizabeth. "*Uncle Tom's Cabin,* Empire, and Africa." In Ammons and Belasco, 68–76.
—— and Susan Belasco, eds. *Approaches to Teaching Stowe's "Uncle Tom's Cabin."* New York: Modern Language Association of America, 2000.
Anand, Mulk Raj. *Poet: Painter (Paintings by Rabindranath Tagore; Interpretation by Mulk Raj Anand).* New York: Facet Books, 1985.
Anscombe, G. E. M. *Intention.* 2nd ed. Ithaca, NY: Cornell University Press, 1957.
Armony, Jorge, Vincent Corbo, Marie-Hélène Clément, and Alain Brunet. "Amygdala Response in Patients with Acute PTSD to Masked and Unmasked Emotional Facial Expressions." *American Journal of Psychiatry* 162.10 (2005): 1961–63.
Baer, Elizabeth. "Pilgrimage Inward: Quest and Fairy Tale Motifs in *Surfacing.*" In VanSpanckeren and Castro, 24–34.
Bahadur, Krishna, ed. *Mīrā Bāī and Her Padas.* New Delhi, India: Munshiram Manoharlal, 2002.
Bal, Mieke. *Narratology: Introduction to the Theory of Narrative.* 2nd ed. Toronto, Canada: University of Toronto Press, 1997.

Banfield, Ann. "No-Narrator Theory." In Herman, Jahn, and Ryan, 396–97.
Barloon, Jim. "Very Short Stories: The Miniaturization of War in Hemingway's *In Our Time*." *The Hemingway Review* 24.2 (2005): 5–17.
Barthes, Roland. *S/Z: An Essay*. Trans. Richard Miller. New York: Hill and Wang, 1974.
Baum, Catherine. "The Beautiful One." In Bloom, 39–49.
Bechara, A., H. Damasio, D. Tranel, and A. Damasio. "Deciding Advantageously before Knowing the Advantageous Strategy." *Science* 275 (1997): 1293–95.
Beer, John. Review of *The Tincal Train: A History of Borax* by N. J. Travis and E. J. Cocks. *Isis* 77.1 (1986): 164–65.
Benson, Jackson, ed. *New Critical Approaches to the Short Stories of Ernest Hemingway*. Durham, NC: Duke University Press, 1990.
Bharatamuni. *The Nāṭya Śāstra*. Delhi, India: Sri Satguru Publications, n.d.
Bhattacharji, Sukumari. "Prostitution in Ancient India." *Social Scientist* 15.2 (1987): 32–61.
Blanchard, Margaret. "The Rhetoric of Communion: Voice in *The Sound and the Fury*." *American Literature* 41 (1970): 555–65.
Bloom, Harold, ed. *Caddy Compson*. New York: Chelsea House, 1990.
Booth, Wayne. *Critical Understanding: The Powers and Limits of Pluralism*. Chicago: University of Chicago Press, 1979.
———. "Is There an 'Implied' Author in Every Film?" *College Literature* 29.2 (2002): 124–31.
———. "Resurrection of the Implied Author: Why Bother?" In Phelan and Rabinowitz, 75–88.
———. *The Rhetoric of Fiction*. Chicago: University of Chicago Press, 1961.
Bordwell, David. "Convention, Construction, and Cinematic Vision." In *Post-Theory: Reconstructing Film Studies*. Ed. David Bordwell and Noël Carroll. Madison: University of Wisconsin Press, 1996, 87–107.
———. *Narration in the Fiction Film*. Madison: University of Wisconsin Press, 1985.
———. *On the History of Film Style*. Cambridge, MA: Harvard University Press, 1997.
———, Janet Staiger, and Kristin Thompson. *The Classical Hollywood Cinema: Film Style and Mode of Production to 1960*. New York: Columbia University Press, 1985.
Bortolussi, Marisa and Peter Dixon. *Psychonarratology: Foundations for the Empirical Study of Literary Response*. Cambridge: Cambridge University Press, 2003.
Bouson, J. Brooks. *Brutal Choreographies: Oppositional Strategies and Narrative Design in the Novels of Margaret Atwood*. Amherst: University of Massachusetts Press, 1993.
Bowling, L. E. "What is the Stream of Consciousness Technique?" *PMLA* 65 (1950): 333–45.
Brown, Gillian. "The Problem of Sentimental Possession." In Ammons and Belasco, 111–19.
Bruckner, René. "Lost Time: Blunt Head Trauma and Accident-Driven Cinema." *Discourse: Journal for Theoretical Studies in Media and Culture* 30 (2008): 373–400.
Bundgaard, Peer and Svend Østergaard. "The Story Turned Upside Down: Meaning Effects Linked to Variations on Narrative Structure." *Semiotica* 165 (2007): 263–75.
Cacioppo, John, Penny Visser, and Cynthia Pickett, eds. *Social Neuroscience: People Thinking About Thinking People*. Cambridge, MA: MIT Press, 2006.
Campbell, Josie. "The Woman as Hero in Margaret Atwood's *Surfacing*." In McCombs, 168–79.
Cantave, Sophia. "Who Gets to Create the Lasting Images? The Problem of Black Representation in *Uncle Tom's Cabin*." In Ammons and Belasco, 93–103.
Carroll, James and James Russell. "Do Facial Expressions Signal Specific Emotions? Judging Emotion from the Face in Context." *Journal of Personality and Social Psychology* 70.2 (1996): 205–18.

Carroll, Noël. "Narrative Closure." *Philosophical Studies* 135 (2007): 1–15.
Carter, Cameron S., Todd S. Braver, Deanna M. Barch, Matthew M. Botvinick, Douglas Noll, and Jonathan D. Cohen. "Anterior Cingulate Cortex, Error Detection, and the Online Monitoring of Performance." *Science* 280 (1 May 1998): 747–49.
Chatman, Seymour. *Coming to Terms: The Rhetoric of Narrative in Fiction*. Ithaca, NY: Cornell University Press, 1990.
———. *Story and Discourse: Narrative Structure in Fiction and Film*. Ithaca, NY: Cornell University Press, 1980.
Chomsky, Noam. *Hopes and Prospects*. Chicago, IL: Haymarket Books, 2010.
———. *Knowledge of Language: Its Nature, Origin, and Use*. New York: Praeger, 1986.
Christianson, Sven-Åke, and Torun Lindholm. "The Fate of Traumatic Memories in Childhood and Adulthood." *Development and Psychopathology* 10 (1998): 761–80.
Cohn, Dorrit. "Narrated Monologue: Definition of a Fictional Style." *Comparative Literature* 18 (1966): 97–112.
Crane, Gregg. "Stowe and the Law." In Weinstein *Cambridge*, 154–70.
Culler, Jonathan. "Competence and Performance, Literary." In *The Cambridge Encyclopedia of the Language Sciences*. Ed. Patrick Colm Hogan. Cambridge: Cambridge University Press, 2011, 187–88.
———. *Structuralist Poetics: Structuralism, Linguistics, and the Study of Literature*. Ithaca, NY: Cornell University Press, 1975.
Currie, Gregory. "Unreliability Refigured: Narrative in Literature and Film." *The Journal of Aesthetics and Art Criticism* 53.1 (1995): 19–29.
Dancygier, Barbara. *The Language of Stories: A Cognitive Approach*. Cambridge: Cambridge University Press, 2012.
Darby, David. "Form and Context: An Essay in the History of Narratology." *Poetics Today* 22.4 (2001): 829–52.
Derbes, Anne. *Picturing the Passion in Late Medieval Italy: Narrative Painting, Franciscan Ideologies, and the Levant*. Cambridge: Cambridge University Press, 1996.
Desai, Manmohan, dir. *Amar Akbar Anthony*. Story by J. M. Desai. Screenplay by Prayag Raj. Manmohan Films, 1977.
Diescho, Joseph with Celeste Wallin. *Born of the Sun: A Namibian Novel*. New York: Friendship Press, 1988.
d'Ocarmo, Stephen. "Postmodernist Quietism in Polanski's *Chinatown* and Lynch's *Mulholland Drive*." *Journal of Popular Culture* 42 (2009): 646–62.
Doherty, Martin. *Theory of Mind: How Children Understand Others' Thoughts and Feelings*. New York: Psychology Press, 2009.
Doniger, Wendy. *The Woman Who Pretended to Be Who She Was: Myths of Self-Imitation*. Oxford: Oxford University Press, 2004.
Donovan, Josephine. *"Uncle Tom's Cabin": Evil, Affliction, and Redemptive Love*. Boston, MA: Twayne, 1991.
Dyer, Richard. "Believing in Fairies: The Author and the Homosexual." In *Inside/Out: Lesbian Theories, Gay Theories*. Ed. Diana Fuss. New York: Routledge, 1991, 185–201.
Eagleton, Terry. *Literary Theory: An Introduction*. Minneapolis: University of Minnesota Press, 1983.
Eco, Umberto. *The Limits of Interpretation*. Bloomington: Indiana University Press, 1990.
Eysenck, Michael. "Memory in Childhood." In *Memory*. By Alan Baddeley, Michael Eysenck, and Michael Anderson. New York: Psychology Press, 2009, 267–91.
Faulkner, William. *Light in August*. New York: Random House, 1959.
———. *The Sound and the Fury*. New York: Random House, 1956.

Ferrero, David. "Nikki Adams and the Limits of Gender Criticism." *The Hemingway Review* 17.2 (1998): 18–30.

Fiedler, Leslie. *Love and Death in the American Novel.* New York: Doubleday, 1992.

———. *What Was Literature? Class Culture and Mass Society.* New York: Touchstone, 1982.

Fish, Stanley. *Is There a Text in This Class? The Authority of Interpretive Communities.* Cambridge, MA: Harvard University Press, 1980.

Fitzgerald, F. Scott. *The Great Gatsby.* In *The Fitzgerald Reader.* Ed. Arthur Mizener. New York: Charles Scribner's Sons, 1963.

Forgas, Joseph P., ed. *Feeling and Thinking: The Role of Affect in Social Cognition.* Cambridge: Cambridge University Press and Paris: Editions de la Maison des Sciences de l'Homme, 2000.

———. "Introduction: The Role of Affect in Social Cognition." In Forgas, *Feeling* 1–28.

Frederickson, George. *The Black Image in the White Mind.* New York: Harper Collins, 1971.

Fulton, Helen. "Film Narrative and Visual Cohesion." In Fulton, Huisman, Murphet, and Dunn, 108–22.

———, with Rosemary Huisman, Julian Murphet, and Anne Dunn. *Narrative and Media.* Cambridge: Cambridge University Press, 2005.

Gaut, Berys. "Film Authorship and Collaboration." In *Film Theory and Philosophy.* Ed. Richard Allen and Murray Smith. Oxford: Oxford University Press, 1997, 149–72.

Gerrig, Richard and Deborah Prentice. "Notes on Audience Response." In *Post-Theory: Reconstructing Film Studies.* Ed. David Bordwell and Noël Carroll. Madison: University of Wisconsin Press, 1996, 388–403.

Gilmore, Michael. "*Uncle Tom's Cabin* and the American Renaissance: The Sacramental Aesthetic of Harriet Beecher Stowe." In Weinstein, *Cambridge* 58–76.

Gnoli, Raniero, ed. and trans. *The Aesthetic Experience According to Abhinavagupta.* 2nd ed. Varanasi, India: Chokhamba Sanskrit Series, 1968.

Grace, Sherrill. "In Search of Demeter: The Lost, Silent Mother in *Surfacing.*" In VanSpanckeren and Castro, 35–47.

Gray, Francine du Plessix. "Nature as the Nunnery." In McCombs, 131–34.

Grice, Herbert Paul. "Logic and Conversation." In *Syntax and Semantics,* vol. 3. Ed. P. Cole and J. Morgan. New York: Academic Press, 1975, 41–58.

Guédon, Marie-Françoise. "*Surfacing*: Amerindian Themes and Shamanism." In *Margaret Atwood: Language, Text, and System.* Vancouver, Canada: University of British Columbia Press, 1983, 91–111.

Guha-Thakurta, Tapati. *The Making of a New "Indian" Art: Artists, Aesthetics and Nationalism in Bengal, c. 1850–1920.* Cambridge: Cambridge University Press, 1992.

Hageman, Andrew. "The Uncanny Ecology of *Mulholland Drive.*" *Scope: An Online Journal of Film Studies* 11 (2008).

Harvey, Sylvia. "To Be an Author or Not to Be?" *Journal of Media Practice* 10.1 (2009): 81–85.

Hatfield, Elaine, John Cacioppo, and Richard Rapson. *Emotional Contagion.* Cambridge: Cambridge University Press, 1994.

Hawley, John Stratton and Mark Juergensmeyer. *Songs of the Saints of India.* Oxford, UK: Oxford University Press, 1988.

Hayman, David. *"Ulysses": The Mechanics of Meaning.* Rev. ed. Madison: University of Wisconsin Press, 1982.

Heidegger, Martin. *Being and Time.* Trans. John Macquarrie and Edward Robinson. New York: Harper and Row, 1962.

Herman, David, ed. *The Cambridge Companion to Narrative.* Cambridge: Cambridge University Press, 2007.

———. "Glossary." In Herman, *Cambridge* 274–82.
———. *Story Logic: Problems and Possibilities of Narrative*. Lincoln: University of Nebraska Press, 2002.
———, Manfred Jahn, and Marie-Laure Ryan, eds. *Routledge Encyclopedia of Narrative Theory*. New York: Routledge, 2008.
Hirsch, E. D. *The Aims of Interpretation*. Chicago: University of Chicago Press, 1976.
Hogan, Patrick Colm. *Affective Narratology: The Emotional Structure of Stories*. Lincoln: University of Nebraska Press, 2011.
———. *Cognitive Science, Literature, and the Arts: A Guide for Humanists*. New York: Routledge, 2003.
———. *The Culture of Conformism: Understanding Social Consent*. Durham, NC: Duke University Press, 2001.
———. *How Authors' Minds Make Stories*. Cambridge: Cambridge University Press, forthcoming.
———. *The Mind and Its Stories: Narrative Universals and Human Emotion*. Cambridge: Cambridge University Press and Paris: Editions de la Maison des Sciences de l'Homme, 2003.
———. *On Interpretation: Meaning and Inference in Law, Psychoanalysis, and Literature*. Athens: University of Georgia Press, 2008.
———. "On the Meaning of Visual Style: Cognition, Culture, and Visual Technique in Bimal Roy's *Sujata*." *Projections: The Journal for Movies and Mind* 3.2 (2009): 71–90.
———. "On the Origin of Literary Narrative and Its Relation to Adaptation." In *Arts: A Science Matter*. Ed. Maria Burguete and Lui Lam. Singapore: World Scientific, 2011, 267–92
———. "Palmer's Anti-Cognitivist Challenge." *Style* 45.2 (2011): 244–48.
———. "Reading Tagore Today." In *Tagore's Best Short Stories*. Ed. Malobika Chaudhuri. Kolkata, India: Frontpage Publications, 2011, 1–7.
———. "Structure and Ambiguity in the Symbolic Order: Some Prolegomena to the Understanding and Criticism of Lacan." In *Criticism and Lacan: Essays and Dialogue on Language, Structure, and the Unconscious*. Ed. Patrick Colm Hogan and Lalita Pandit. Athens: University of Georgia Press, 1990, 3–30.
———. *Understanding Nationalism: On Narrative, Cognitive Science, and Identity*. Columbus: The Ohio State University Press, 2009.
———. *What Literature Teaches Us About Emotion*. Cambridge: Cambridge University Press, 2011.
Holland, John, Keith Holyoak, Richard Nisbett, and Paul Thagard. *Induction: Processes of Inference, Learning, and Discovery*. Cambridge, MA: MIT Press, 1986.
Huisman, Rosemary. "Aspects of Narrative in Series and Serials." In Fulton, Huisman, Murphet, and Dunn, 153–71.
———. "Narrative Concepts." In Fulton, Huisman, Murphet, and Dunn, 11–28.
Iacoboni, Marco. *Mirroring People: The New Science of How We Connect with Others*. New York: Farrar, Straus and Giroux, 2008.
Ingalls, Daniel, ed. *The Dhvanyaloka of Ānandavardhana with the Locana of Abhinavagupta*. Trans. Daniel Ingalls, Jeffrey Masson, and M. V. Patwardhan. Cambridge, MA: Harvard University Press, 1990.
Ingarden, Roman. *The Cognition of the Literary Work of Art*. Trans. Ruth Ann Crowley and Kenneth Olson. Evanston, IL: Northwestern University Press, 1973.
———. *The Literary Work of Art: An Investigation on the Borderlines of Ontology, Logic, and the Theory of Literature*. Trans. George Grabowicz. Evanston, IL: Northwestern University Press, 1973.

Innes, G. "Stability and Change in Griots' Narratives." *African Language Studies* 14 (1973): 105–18.
Irwin, John. "Quentin and Caddy." In Bloom, 59–67.
Iser, Wolfgang. *The Implied Reader: Patterns of Communication in Prose Fiction from Bunyan to Beckett.* Baltimore, MD: Johns Hopkins University Press, 1974.
Ito, Tiffany, Geoffrey Urland, Eve Willadsen-Jensen, and Joshua Correll. "The Social Neuroscience of Stereotyping and Prejudice: Using Event-Related Brain Potentials to Study Social Perception." In Cacioppo, Visser, and Pickett, 189–208.
Jackendoff, Ray. "Preference Rules." In *The Cambridge Encyclopedia of the Language Sciences.* Ed. Patrick Colm Hogan. Cambridge: Cambridge University Press, 2011, 659–60.
Jahn, Manfred. "Focalization." In Herman, *Cambridge* 94–108.
———. "Focalization." In Herman, Jahn, and Ryan, 173–77.
———. "Narrative Voice and Agency in Drama: Aspects of a Narratology of Drama." *New Literary History* 32 (2001): 659–79.
Jakobson, Roman. *Language in Literature.* Ed. Krystyna Pomorska and Stephen Rudy. Cambridge, MA: Belknap, 1987.
Jeffries, Lesley and Dan McIntyre. *Stylistics.* Cambridge: Cambridge University Press, 2010.
Johnstone, Barbara. "Discourse Analysis and Narrative." In Schiffrin, Tannen, and Hamilton, *Handbook* 635–49.
Kafalenos, Emma. "Implications of Narrative in Painting and Photography." *New Novel Review* 3 (1996): 54–64.
———. "Photographs." In Herman, Jahn, and Ryan, 428–30.
Kahneman, Daniel and Dale Miller. "Norm Theory: Comparing Reality to Its Alternatives." *Psychological Review* 93.2 (1989): 136–53.
Kapuscinski, Kiley. "Negotiating the Nation: The Reproduction and Reconstruction of the National Imaginary in Margaret Atwood's *Surfacing.*" *ESC: English Studies in Canada* 33.3 (2007): 95–123.
Karcher, Carolyn. "Stowe and the Literature of Social Change." In Weinstein, *Cambridge* 203–18.
Keen, Suzanne. *Empathy and the Novel.* Oxford: Oxford University Press, 2007.
Khan, Kabir, dir. *New York.* Story by Aditya Chopra. Screenplay by Sandeep Srivastava. Yash Raj Films (India), 2009.
Killam, G. D., ed. *Critical Perspectives on Ngugi wa Thiong'o.* Washington, DC: Three Continents, 1984.
Kindt, Tom and Hans-Harald Müller. "Six Ways Not to Save the Implied Author." *Style* 45.1 (2011): 67–79.
Kitzinger, Celia. "Conversation Analysis." In *The Cambridge Encyclopedia of the Language Sciences.* Cambridge: Cambridge University Press, 2011, 225–27.
Klaiber, Isabell. "Multiple Implied Authors: How Many Can a Text Have?" *Style* 45.1 (2011): 138–52.
Knapp, Steven and Walter Benn Michaels. "Against Theory." In *Against Theory: Literary Studies and the New Pragmatism.* Ed. W. J. T. Mitchell. Chicago: University of Chicago Press, 1985, 11–30.
Kondo, Hirohito, Naoyuki Osaka, and Mariko Osaka. "Cooperation of the Anterior Cingulate Cortex and Dorsolateral Prefrontal Cortex for Attention Shifting." *NeuroImage* 23 (2004): 670–79.
Kovács, András Bálint. *Screening Modernism: European Art Cinema, 1950–1980.* Chicago: University of Chicago Press, 2007.
Kozloff, Sarah. "Voice-Over Narration." In Herman, Jahn, and Ryan, 636–37.

Kuminova, Olga. "Faulkner's *The Sound and the Fury* as a Struggle for Ideal Communication." *LIT: Literature Interpretation Theory* 21 (2010): 41–60.
Labatt, Blair. *Faulkner the Storyteller*. Tuscaloosa: University of Alabama Press, 2005.
Labov, William. "Narratives of Personal Experience." In *The Cambridge Encyclopedia of the Language Sciences*. Ed. Patrick Colm Hogan. Cambridge: Cambridge University Press, 2011, 546–48.
Labruda, Adam. "Jan van Eyck, Realist and Narrator: On the Structure and Artistic Sources of the New York *Crucifixion*." *Artibus et Historiae* 14.27 (1993): 9–30.
Lanser, Susan. "(Im)plying the Author." *Narrative* 9.2 (2001). (Online.)
———. "The 'I' of the Beholder: Equivocal Attachments and the Limits of Structuralist Narratology." In *A Companion to Narrative Theory*. Ed. James Phelan and Peter Rabinowitz. Malden, MA: Blackwell, 2005, 206–19.
Laplanche, J. and J.-B. Pontalis. *The Language of Psychoanalysis*. Trans. Donald Nicholson-Smith. New York: W. W. Norton, 1973.
LeDoux, Joseph. *The Emotional Brain: The Mysterious Underpinnings of Emotional Life*. New York: Touchstone, 1996.
Lessing, Gotthold Ephraim. *Laocoön*. Trans. Robert Phillimore. London: Macmillan, 1874.
Leverenz, David. "Alive with Contradictions: Close Reading, Liberal Pluralism, and Nonnarratable Plots in *Uncle Tom's Cabin*." In Ammons and Belasco, 120–31.
Levinson, Stephen. "Pragmatics, Universals in." In *The Cambridge Encyclopedia of the Language Sciences*. Ed. Patrick Colm Hogan. Cambridge: Cambridge University Press, 2011, 654–57.
Lieberman, Matthew D. and Naomi I. Eisenberger. "A Pain by Any Other Name (Rejection, Exclusion, Ostracism) Still Hurts the Same: The Role of Dorsal Anterior Cingulate Cortex in Social and Physical Pain." In *Social Neuroscience: People Thinking About Thinking People*. Ed. John T. Cacioppo, Penny S. Visser, and Cynthia L. Pickett. Cambridge, MA: MIT Press, 2006, 167–87.
Livingston, Paisley. "Cinematic Authorship." In *Film Theory and Philosophy*. Ed. Richard Allen and Murray Smith. Oxford: Oxford University Press, 1997, 132–48.
Locher, Paul. "How Does a Visual Artist Create an Artwork?" In *The Cambridge Handbook of Creativity*. Ed. James Kaufman and Robert Sternberg. Cambridge: Cambridge University Press, 2010, 131–44.
Logan, Lisa. "*Uncle Tom's Cabin* and Conventional Nineteenth-Century Domestic Ideology." In Ammons and Belasco, 46–56.
Lovesey, Oliver. *Ngũgĩ wa Thiong'o*. New York: Twayne, 2000.
Lukács, Georg. *Essays on Realism*. Ed. Rodney Livingstone. Trans. David Fernbach. Cambridge, MA: MIT Press, 1981.
Lynch, David, dir. *Mulholland Drive*. Written by David Lynch. Cinematography by Peter Deming. Canal+, 2001.
MacCabe, Colin. "Theory and Film: Principles of Realism and Pleasure." *Screen* 17.3 (1976): 7–28.
MacDonald, Angus W., Jonathan D. Cohen, V. Andrew Stenger, and Cameron S. Carter. "Dissociating the Role of the Dorsolateral Prefrontal and Anterior Cingulate Cortex in Cognitive Control." *Science* 288.5472 (9 June 2000): 1835–38.
Mace, M. and T. Ward. "Modeling the Creative Process: A Ground Theory Analysis of Creativity in the Domain of Art Making." *Creativity Research Journal* 14 (2002): 179–92.
Macherey, Pierre. *A Theory of Literary Production*. Trans. Geoffrey Wall. New York: Routledge, 2006.

Mair, Victor H. *Tun-huang Popular Narratives.* Cambridge: Cambridge University Press, 1983.
Maltby, Richard. "'A Brief Romantic Interlude': Dick and Jane Go to 3½ Seconds of the Classical Hollywood Cinema." In *Post-Theory: Reconstructing Film Studies.* Ed. David Bordwell and Noël Carroll. Madison: University of Wisconsin Press, 1996, 434–59.
Margolin, Uri. "Authentication." In Herman, Jahn, and Ryan, 32–33.
———. "Character." In Herman, Jahn, and Ryan, 52–57.
———. "Collective Perspective, Individual Perspective, and the Speaker in Between: On 'We' Literary Narratives." In van Peer and Chatman, 241–53.
———. "Necessarily a Narrator or Narrator If Necessary: A Short Note on a Long Subject." *Journal of Literary Semantics* 40 (2011): 43–57.
———. "Person." In Herman, Jahn, and Ryan, 422–23.
Martini, Jürgen. "Ngugi wa Thiong'o: East African Novelist." In Killam, 285–91.
Matthews, John. *"The Sound and the Fury": Faulkner and the Lost Cause.* Boston: Twayne, 1991.
McCombs, Judith, ed. *Critical Essays on Margaret Atwood.* Boston: G. K. Hall, 1988.
McDermott, Rachel Fell. *Singing to the Goddess: Poems to Kālī and Umā from Bengal.* Oxford: Oxford University Press, 2001.
McDowell, Kelly. "Unleashing the Feminine Unconscious: Female Oedipal Desires and Lesbian Sadomasochism in *Mulholland Dr.*" *Journal of Popular Culture* 36 (2005): 1037–49.
McGregor, R. S. *The Oxford Hindi-English Dictionary.* New Delhi, India: Oxford University Press, 1993.
McIntyre, Dan. *Point of View in Plays: A Cognitive Stylistic Approach to Viewpoint in Drama and Other Text-Types.* Amsterdam, Netherlands: John Benjamins, 2006.
McLaren, Joseph. "Ideology and Form: The Critical Reception of *Petals of Blood.*" In Nazareth, 187–202.
McLeod, Peter, Kim Plunkett, and Edmund T. Rolls. *Introduction to Connectionist Modelling of Cognitive Processes.* Oxford: Oxford University Press, 1998.
Mey, Jacob. "Literary Pragmatics." In Schiffrin, Tannen, and Hamilton, *Handbook* 787–97.
Mildorf, Jarmila. "Sociolinguistic Implications of Narratology: Focalization and 'Double Deixis' in Conversational Storytelling." In *The Travelling Concept of Narrative.* Ed. Matti Hyvärinen, Anu Korhonen, and Juri Mykkänen. Helsinki, Finland: Helsinki Collegium for Advanced Studies, 2006, 42–59.
———. "Thought Presentation and Constructed Dialogue in Oral Stories: Limits and Possibilities of a Cross-Disciplinary Narratology." *Partial Answers* 6.2 (2008): 279–300.
Mishra, Vijay. *Bollywood Cinema: Temples of Desire.* New York: Routledge, 2002.
Mitra, Asok. *Four Painters.* Calcutta, India: New Age Publishers, 1965.
Moddelmog, Debra. "The Unifying Consciousness of a Divided Conscience: Nick Adams as Author of *In Our Time.*" In Benson, 17–32.
Monier-Williams, Monier. *A Sanskrit-English Dictionary.* New ed. Delhi, India: Motilal Banarsidass, 1899.
Murphet, Julian. "Narrative Voice." In Fulton, Huisman, Murphet, and Dunn, 73–85.
Mwangi, Evan. "Gender, Unreliable Oral Narration, and the Untranslated Preface in Ngũgĩ wa Thiong'o's *Devil on the Cross.*" *Research in African Literatures* 38.4 (2007): 28–46.
Naftulin, Donald, John Ware, and Frank Donnelly. "The Doctor Fox Lecture: A Paradigm of Educational Seduction." *The Journal of Medical Education* 48 (1973): 630–35.

Nandy, Ashis. *The Intimate Enemy: Loss and Recovery of Self Under Colonialism.* New Delhi, India: Oxford University Press, 1983.
Navet, E. "Les Ojibway et l'Amanite tue-mouche (*Amanita muscaria*). Pour une éthnomycologie des Indiens d'Amérique du Nord." *Journal de la Société des Américanistes* 74 (1988): 163–80.
Nazareth, Peter, ed. *Critical Essays on Ngũgĩ wa Thiong'o.* New York: Twayne, 2000.
Nelles, William. "Embedding." In Herman, Jahn, and Ryan, 134–35.
———. "Historical and Implied Authors and Readers." *Comparative Literature* 45.1 (1993): 22–46.
The New American Bible. N.c.: Catholic Press, 1970.
Newell, Kenneth. *A Theory of Literary Explication: Specifying a Relativistic Foundation in Epistemic Probability, Cognitive Science, and Second-Order Logic.* Beverly Hills, CA: Welleren, 2009.
Ngũgĩ wa Thiong'o. *Petals of Blood.* New York: Penguin, 1977.
Nielsen, Henrik Skov. "The Impersonal Voice in First-Person Narrative Fiction." *Narrative* 12 (2004): 133–50.
Norrick, Neal. "Conversational Storytelling." In Herman *Cambridge*, 127–41.
Notaro, Anna. "Technology in Search of an Artist: Questions of Auteurism/Authorship and the Contemporary Cinematic Experience." *The Velvet Light Trap* 57 (2006): 86–97.
Nuernberg, Susan. "Stowe, the Abolition Movement, and Prevailing Theories of Race in Nineteenth-Century America." In Ammons and Belasco, 37–45.
Nünning, Ansgar. "Implied Author." In Herman, Jahn, and Ryan, 239–40.
———. "Reconceptualizing Unreliable Narration: Synthesizing Cognitive and Rhetorical Approaches." In Phelan and Rabinowitz, 89–107.
——— "Reliability." In Herman, Jahn, and Ryan, 495–97.
Oatley, Keith. *Emotions: A Brief History.* Malden, MA: Blackwell, 2004.
———. "Emotions and the Story Worlds of Fiction." In *Narrative Impact: Social and Cognitive Foundations.* Ed. Melanie Green, Jeffrey Strange, and Timothy Brock. Mahwah, NJ: Erlbaum, 2002, 39–69.
———. "Suggestion Structure." In *The Cambridge Encyclopedia of the Language Sciences.* Ed. Patrick Colm Hogan. New York: Cambridge University Press, 2011, 819–20.
———. "Why Fiction May Be Twice as True as Fact: Fiction as Cognitive and Emotional Simulation." *Review of General Psychology* 3.2 (1999): 101–17.
———, Dacher Keltner, and Jennifer Jenkins. *Understanding Emotions.* 2nd ed. Malden, MA: Blackwell, 2006.
Öhman, Arne and Joaquim Soares. "Emotional Conditioning to Masked Stimuli: Expectancies for Aversive Outcomes Following Nonrecognized Fear-Relevant Stimuli." *Journal of Experimental Psychology: General* 127.1 (1998): 69–82.
O'Neill, Patrick. "Narrative Structure." In Herman, Jahn, and Ryan, 366–70.
Ong, Walter J., S.J. "The Writer's Audience Is Always a Fiction." *Interfaces of the Word: Studies in the Evolution of Consciousness and Culture.* Ithaca, NY: Cornell University Press, 1977, 53–81.
Ortony, Andrew, Gerald Clore, and Allan Collins. *The Cognitive Structure of Emotions.* Cambridge: Cambridge University Press, 1988.
Otter, Samuel. "Stowe and Race." In Weinstein, *Cambridge* 15–38.
Page, Sally. "The Ideal of Motherhood." In Bloom, 50–58.
Pagnoulle, Christine. "Ngũgĩ wa Thiong'o's 'Journey of the Magi': Part 2 of *Petals of Blood*." In Nazareth, 203–12.
Palmer, Alan. "Social Minds in Fiction and Criticism." *Style* 45.2 (2011): 196–240.

———. "Stream of Consciousness and Interior Monologue." In Herman, Jahn, and Ryan, 570–71.
———. "Thought and Consciousness Representation (Literature)." In Herman, Jahn, and Ryan, 602–7.
Palmer, Eustace. "Ngugi's *Petals of Blood*." In Killam, 271–84.
Pandit, B. N. *Specific Principles of Kashmir Śaivism*. New Delhi, India: Munshiram Manoharlal, 1997.
Patañjali. *Yoga Philosophy of Patañjali*. Ed. Hariharānanda Āraṇya. Trans. P. N. Mukerji. Albany: State University of New York Press, 1983.
Phelan, James. "The Implied Author, Deficient Narration, and Nonfiction Narrative: Or, What's Off-Kilter in *The Year of Magical Thinking* and *The Diving Bell and the Butterfly*?" *Style* 45.1 (2011): 119–37.
———. *Living to Tell About It: A Rhetoric and Ethics of Character Narration*. Ithaca, NY: Cornell University Press, 2005.
———. "Rhetoric/Ethics." In Herman, *Cambridge* 203–16.
———. "Self-Help for Narratee and Narrative Audience: How 'I'—and 'You'?—Read 'How.'" *Style* 28.3 (1994): 350–65.
——— and Wayne Booth. "Narrative Techniques." In Herman, Jahn, and Ryan, 370–75.
——— and Wayne Booth. "Narrator." In Herman, Jahn, and Ryan, 388–92.
——— and Peter Rabinowitz. *A Companion to Narrative Theory*. Malden, MA: Blackwell Publishing, 2005.
Phelan, Peggy. "Shards of a History of Performance Art: Pollock and Namuth Through a Glass, Darkly." In Phelan and Rabinowitz, 499–512.
Pirandello, Luigi. "La Tragedia d'un Personaggio." In *Eleven Short Stories: Undici Novelle*. Ed. and trans. Stanley Appelbaum. New York: Dover, 1994, 144–56.
Plantinga, Carl. "The Scene of Empathy and the Human Face on Film." In Plantinga and Smith, 239–55.
——— and Greg Smith, eds. *Passionate Views: Film, Cognition, and Emotion*. Baltimore, MD: Johns Hopkins University Press, 1999.
Prince, Gerald. "The Disnarrated." In Herman, Jahn, and Ryan, 118.
———. "Introduction à l'étude du narrataire." *Poétique* 14 (1973): 178–96.
———. *Narrative as Theme: Studies in French Fiction*. Lincoln: University of Nebraska Press, 1992.
Pryse, Marjorie. "Stowe and Regionalism." In Weinstein, *Cambridge* 131–53.
Rabinowitz, Peter. *Before Reading: Narrative Conventions and the Politics of Interpretation*. Columbus: The Ohio State University Press, 1987.
Rader, Ralph. "The Dramatic Monologue and Related Lyric Forms." *Critical Inquiry* 3.1 (1976): 131–51.
Railton, Stephen. "Black Slaves and White Readers." In Ammons and Belasco, 104–10.
Ray, Satyajit. "Foreword." In Robinson, 12–13.
Restuccia, Frances. "Kristeva's Intimate Revolt and the Thought Specular: Encountering the (Mulholland) Drive." In *Psychoanalysis, Aesthetics, and Politics in the Work of Julia Kristeva*. Ed. Kelly Oliver and S. Keltner. Albany: State University of New York Press, 2009, 65–78.
Richardson, Brian. "Drama and Narrative." In Herman, *Cambridge* 142–55.
———. "Introduction: The Implied Author: Back from the Grave or Simply Dead Again?" *Style* 45.1 (2011): 1–10.
———. "The Poetics and Politics of Second-Person Narrative." *Genre* 24: 309–30.
———. "Singular Text, Multiple Implied Readers." *Style* 413 (2007): 259–74.

———. *Unnatural Voices: Extreme Narration in Modern and Contemporary Fiction.* Columbus: The Ohio State University Press, 2006.
Ridgway, Franklin. "'You Came Back!': or, Mulholland Trieb." *Post Script: Essays in Film and the Humanities* 26 (2006): 43–61.
Rigney, Barbara. *Margaret Atwood.* Totowa, NJ: Barnes and Noble, 1987.
Rimmon-Kenan, Shlomith. *Narrative Fiction: Contemporary Poetics.* London: Methuen, 2002.
Robinson, Andrew. *The Art of Rabindranath Tagore.* London: Andre Deutsch, 1989.
Ross, Stephen. *Fiction's Inexhaustible Voice: Speech and Writing in Faulkner.* Athens: University of Georgia Press, 1989.
Roy, Bimal, dir. *Madhumati.* Story by Ritwik Ghatak. Dialogues by Rajinder Singh Bedi. Cinematography by Dilip Gupta. Editing by Hrishikesh Mukherjee. Bimal Roy Productions (India), 1958.
———, dir. *Prem Patra.* Story by Nitan Bhattacharya. Screenplay by Salil Choudhury and Debobrata Sen Gupta. Dialogues by Rajendra Krishan. Cinematography by Dilip Gupta. Editing by Amit Bose. Bimal Roy Productions (India), 1962.
———, dir. *Sujata.* Story by Subodh Ghosh. Screenplay by Nabendu Ghosh. Dialogues by Paul Mahendra. Cinematography by Kamal Bose. Editing by Amit Bose. Bimal Roy Productions (India), 1959.
Royzman, Edward and Paul Rozin. "Limits of Symhedonia: The Differential Role of Prior Emotional Attachment in Sympathy and Sympathetic Joy." *Emotion* 6.1 (2006): 82–93.
Ryan, M. L. *Possible Worlds, Artificial Intelligence and Narrative Theory.* Bloomington: Indiana University Press, 1991.
Schacter, Daniel. *Searching for Memory: The Brain, the Mind, and the Past.* New York: Basic Books, 1996.
Schacter, D., D. Addis, and R. Buckner. "Remembering the Past to Imagine the Future: The Prospective Brain." *Nature Reviews: Neuroscience* 8 (2007): 657–61.
Schaffner, Anna Katharina. "Fantasmatic Splittings and Destructive Desire: Lynch's *Lost Highway, Mulholland Drive* and *Inland Empire.*" *Forum for Modern Language Studies* 45 (2009): 270–91.
Schiffrin, Deborah, Deborah Tannen, and Heidi Hamilton, eds. *The Handbook of Discourse Analysis.* Malden, MA: Blackwell, 2001.
———. "Introduction." In Schiffrin, Tannen, and Hamilton, *Handbook* 1–10.
Schiller, Friedrich. *On the Aesthetic Education of Man in a Series of Letters.* Trans. Reginald Snell. London: Routledge and Kegan Paul, 1954.
Scholes, Robert. *Semiotics and Interpretation.* New Haven, CT: Yale University Press, 1982.
——— and Robert Kellogg. *The Nature of Narrative.* Oxford: Oxford University Press, 1966.
Schwabsky, Barry. "An Unfinished Tradition." *The Nation,* 20 June 2011, 32–35.
Semino, Elena. "Possible Worlds and Mental Spaces in Hemingway's 'A Very Short Story.'" In *Cognitive Poetics in Practice.* Ed. Joanna Gavins and Gerard Steen. London: Routledge, 2003, 83–98.
Sen, Amrit. "'Beyond Borders': Rabindranath Tagore's Paintings and Visva-Bharati." *Rupkatha Journal on Interdisciplinary Studies in Humanities* 2.1 (2010), http://www.rupkatha.com/tagorepainting.php, accessed 16 May 2010.
Shakespeare, William. *Hamlet.* Ed. Harold Jenkins. London: Methuen, 1982.
Shantaram, V., dir. *Jhanak Jhanak Payal Baaje.* Rajkamal Kalamandir (India), 1955.
Sharma, Govind Narain. "Ngugi's Apocalypse: Marxism, Christianity and African Utopianism in *Petals of Blood.*" In Killam, 292–304.
Sharvit, Yael. "The Puzzle of Free Indirect Discourse." *Linguistics and Philosophy* 31 (2008): 353–95.

Shen, Dan. "Booth's *The Rhetoric of Fiction* and China's Critical Context." *Narrative* 15.2 (2007): 167–86.
———. "Story-Discourse Distinction." In Herman, Jahn, and Ryan, 566–68.
Shostak, Debra. "Dancing in Hollywood's Blue Box: Genre and Screen Memories in *Mulholland Drive*." *Post Script: Essays in Film and the Humanities* 28 (2008): 3–21.
Sicherman, Carol. *Ngugi wa Thiong'o: The Making of a Rebel, A Source Book in Kenyan Literature and Resistance*. London: Hans Zell, 1990.
Silverman, Kaja. "The Female Authorial Voice." In *Film and Authorship*. Ed. Virginia Wright Wexman. New Brunswick, NJ: Rutgers University Press, 2003, 50–75.
Singal, Daniel. *William Faulkner: The Making of a Modernist*. Chapel Hill: University of North Carolina Press, 1997.
Smith, Murray. "Gangsters, Cannibals, Aesthetes, or Apparently Perverse Allegiances." In Plantinga and Smith, 217–38.
Srinivasan, Amrit. "Reform and Revival: The Devadasi and Her Dance." *Economic and Political Weekly* (India) 20.44 (1985): 1869–76.
Stein, Karen. *Margaret Atwood Revisited*. New York: Twayne, 1999.
Sternberg, Meir. *Expositional Modes and Temporal Ordering in Fiction*. Baltimore, MD: Johns Hopkins University Press, 1978.
Stratton, Florence. "'Periodic Embodiments': A Ubiquitous Trope in African Men's Writing." *Research in African Literatures* 21.1 (1990): 111–26.
Surkamp, Carola. "Perspective." In Herman, Jahn, and Ryan, 423–25.
Tagore, Rabindranath. "The Wife's Letter." In *Rabindranath Tagore: Selected Short Stories*. Ed. Sukanta Chaudhuri. New Delhi: Oxford University Press, 2000, 205–18.
Tan, Ed. *Emotion and the Structure of Narrative Film: Film as an Emotion Machine*. Trans. Barbara Fasting. Mahwah, NJ: Lawrence Erlbaum, 1996.
Tao, Liang. "Conversational Repair." In *The Cambridge Encyclopedia of the Language Sciences*. Cambridge: Cambridge University Press, 2011, 225.
Tawil, Ezra. *The Making of Racial Sentiment: Slavery and the Birth of the Frontier Romance*. Cambridge: Cambridge University Press, 2006.
Thomas, Calvin. "'It's No Longer Your Film': Abjection and (the) Mulholland (Death) Drive." *Angelaki* 11 (2006): 81–98.
Toles, George. "Auditioning Betty in *Mulholland Drive*." *Film Quarterly* 58 (2004): 2–13.
Tolstoy, Leo. *War and Peace*. Trans. Louise and Aylmer Maude. Available online at http://en.wikisource.org/wiki/War_and_Peace
Tompkins, Jane. *Sensational Designs: The Cultural Work of American Fiction 1790-1860*. Oxford: Oxford University Press, 1985.
Toolan, Michael. "Story and Discourse." In *The Cambridge Encyclopedia of the Language Sciences*. Ed. Patrick Colm Hogan. Cambridge: Cambridge University Press, 2011, 805–6.
Treister, Cyril. "An Addition to the Genre of the Proletarian Novel." In Killam, 267–70.
Trione, Vicenzo. "Arte, le correnti tornano a sfidarsi." *Corriere della Sera*, 25 July 2011, 26–27.
van Peer, Willie. "Justice in Perspective." In van Peer and Chatman, 325–38.
——— and Seymour Chatman, eds. *New Perspectives on Narrative Perspective*. Albany: State University of New York Press, 2001.
VanSpanckeren, Kathryn and Jan Castro, eds. *Margaret Atwood: Vision and Forms*. Carbondale: Southern Illinois University Press, 1988.
Wagner, Linda. "Language and Act: Caddy Compson." In Bloom, 108–18.
Waines, David. *An Introduction to Islam*. Cambridge: Cambridge University Press, 1995.

Walters, Ronald. "Harriet Beecher Stowe and the American Reform Tradition." In Weinstein, 171–89.
Warhol, Robyn. "'Ain't I De One Everybody Come to See?!': Popular Memories of *Uncle Tom's Cabin*." In *Hop on Pop: The Politics and Pleasures of Popular Culture*. Ed. Henry Jenkins, Tara McPherson, and Jane Shattuc. Durham, NC: Duke University Press, 2002, 650–69.
———. *Gendered Interventions: Narrative Discourse in the Victorian Novel*. New Brunswick, NJ: Rutgers University Press, 1989.
———. "Poetics and Persuasion: *Uncle Tom's Cabin* as a Realist Novel." *Essays in Literature* 13.2 (1986): 283–98.
———. "Toward a Theory of the Engaging Narrator: Earnest Interventions in Gaskell, Stowe, and Eliot." *PMLA* 101.5 (1986): 811–18.
Weinstein, Cindy. *The Cambridge Companion to Harriet Beecher Stowe*. Cambridge: Cambridge University Press, 2004.
———. "Introduction." In Weinstein, *Cambridge* 1–14.
Wexman, Virginia Wright. "Introduction." In *Film and Authorship*. Ed. Virginia Wright Wexman. New Brunswick, NJ: Rutgers University Press, 2003, 1–18.
Wilson, Sharon Rose. *Margaret Atwood's Fairy-Tale Sexual Politics*. Jackson: University Press of Mississippi, 1993.
Wolf, Werner. "Pictorial Narrativity." In Herman, Jahn, and Ryan, 431–35.
Wolpert, Stanley. *A New History of India*. 4th ed. Oxford: Oxford University Press, 1993.
Woolf, Virginia. *Mrs. Dalloway*. New York: Harcourt, Brace and Company, 1925.
———. *The Waves*. New York: Harcourt Brace Jovanovich, 1931.
Worthington, Andy. "The 'Worst of the Worst'?: 9/11, Guantánamo, and the Failures of U.S. Corporate Media." *Extra!* (FAIR) 24.9 (September 2011): 11–12.
Wright, Laura. "National Photographic: Images of Sensibility and the Nation in Margaret Atwood's *Surfacing* and Nadine Gordimer's *July's People*." *Mosaic* 38.1 (2005): 75–92.
Yacobi, Tamar. "Authorial Rhetoric, Narratorial (Un)Reliability, Divergent Readings: Tolstoy's *Kreutzer Sonata*." In Phelan and Rabinowitz, 108–23.
Zapf, Hubert. "Reflection vs. Daydream: Two Types of the Implied Reader in Hemingway's Fiction." In Jackson Benson, 96–111.
Zeki, Semir. *Inner Vision: An Exploration of Art and the Brain*. Oxford: Oxford University Press, 1999.

Index

Abhinavagupta, 56–57
aesthetic effects: example of, 9; as literary effect, 9
ambiguity: audience multiplicity addressed through, 136–37, 138; continuous, 20; interpretation and meaning, 17, 19–20; in *Mulholland Drive*, 20, 201, 210, 213–14, 217–18, 219; narratee, 43; in nonpersonified narration, 221; symbolism for reducing, 71; in Tagore's paintings, 14, 68–74, 75–80, 83, 110; title or story for resolving, 68, 70; in verbal or visual art, 67–68, 70; in Vermeer's paintings, 14; viewer attempt to reduce, 70–71. *See also* profile of ambiguity
Anand, Mulk Raj, 80, 82, 87
art. *See* representational art
associative reformulation: example of, 191; in interior monologue, 190–91
attachment: in *Born of the Sun,* 242–43, 244, 245–46, 247, 249; collective focalization through, 244, 245; empathy and, 266; nature of, 239; openness and sensitivity, 131; relations, 249; *The Sound and the Fury* and, 199–200, 273; in Tagore's work, 82–83, 87; in *Uncle Tom's Cabin,* 130–31, 269

attentional orientation: encoding enabled by, 53–54; examples of, 53–54
Atwood, Margaret, 15, 170. *See also Surfacing*
audience: ambiguity and multiple implied, 136–37, 138; author designing for hypothetical, 260; implicated author in film by, 133; implied author misdirection and, 133–34, 144–46, 148–49, 206; multiple implied authors and multiplicity, 139–40, 145–46. *See also* implied reader
auteur, film: cross-textual implied author relation to, 65, 89, 93–94, 97–98; as director/overseer, 95–97, 111; as implied author in film, 14, 265, 266–67; multiple, 90, 95–96, 111, 148; nature of study of, 89; problems with idea of, 65, 89, 90, 91, 95–96, 110; receptive intent of, 90–91; Roy as, 99–102 107–8, 112
auteurism: classical and revised, principles of, 90, 95, 97; creative control as empirical in, 96–97; film study and, 89; minimal, 97–98, 266. *See also* multiple authorship; technique
author: character creation through cognitive architecture of, 38, 42;

289

character creation through memory of, 38–39, 262; function of, 37; hypothetical audience for, 260; narrator compared to, 39–40, 263–64; nonpersonified narrator from intent of, 45–46; reader imagination divergence from, 38–39; receptive intent explanation by, 36, 262, 268. *See also* implied author; multiple authorship; real author

authorial intent: example of, 114; mental causes of, 114, 146; partial contradictions in, 113; reader response and, 114

authorial self-understanding: limitations of, 113–14; reasons, 114–16

Bal, Mieke, 23, 47
Balzac, Honoré de, 120
Banfield, Ann, 263–64
Barthes, Roland, 170
biographical criticism, 35–36
The Birthday (Chagall), 67
Booth, Wayne, 118, 266
Bordwell, David, 89, 152, 153, 263
Born of the Son (Diescho): attachment in, 242–43, 244, 245–46, 247, 249; collaborator on, 259; description and analysis of, 59, 239–47; emotion sharing and "minds of others" in, 240, 241, 243, 244, 245–47, 249, 274–75; group narration and, 16; informational contradiction in, 58–59; interior monologue of, 241–42; nonpersonified narration and focalization of, 241, 242, 243–44, 245; political activism in, 240, 244, 245, 246–47; thematic concerns of, 240, 241, 242, 244, 246, 247
Bortolussi, Marisa, 260
Bouson, J. Brooks, 271–72
Bowling, Lawrence, 272

Cameron, James, 223
canon. *See specific topics*
The Canterbury Tales (Chaucer), 184
Carroll, Noël, 159

Chagall, Marc, 67
character creation: author cognitive architecture in, 38, 42; author memory in, 38–39, 262; cognitive architecture in, 38, 42; reader versus author imagination in, 39
character imagination, 42–43
Chatman, Seymour, 22, 23, 150, 153, 263
Chitralipi, 75–76
cinema, 15. *See also* film
cognitive architecture: in character creation, 38, 42; implied author multiplicity from, 116–18, 268; partial contradictions in, 113
coherence: defined, 2; as discourse pattern, 2; film containing multiplicity and, 132, 148; implied author and, 14–15, 130–31; in narrative discourse, 3–4. *See also* profile of intentional coherence
Cohn, Dorrit, 191
collections, 186–87
communicative discourse: diagram of, 22, 46, 63; focalizer in relation to, 26; narratology acceptance of, 29–30; narrator and narratee in, 24–25, 37–46; narrator reliability in, 25; real and implied author/reader in, 22–24, 30–36
congruence, 31, 43
constitution, 40
contradiction. *See* narrative contradictions
conversational storytelling, 4
creation, film, 94–95, 111
critic: discourse analysis approach of literary, 3, 5; literary, 9; purpose of, 63, 264; reflection and, 62–63; spontaneous response influenced by, 63
Critical Discourse Analysis: discourse analysis containing, 1; ethico-political evaluation in, 9–10; Foucault in, 10; of Hemingway story, 10; individual works in, 10; linguistic and narrative compared to, 11; political and social structure in, 9; speaker in, 10
critical explication: as hermeneutic narrative processing type, 163, 181;

narrational component to disambiguating, 201
cross-textual implied author: auteur relation to, 65, 89, 93–94, 97–98; in author's or painter's canon, 65, 265–66; continuity sought in, 74–75; craft context in defining, 267; emotional response impacted by, 87; film canon through lens of, 14, 94, 99; film complicating idea of, 98–99; implied compared to, 267; motifs for establishing, 74–75, 82–83, 87, 110; in Tagore's work, 74, 80, 82–83, 85, 87, 94, 112; thematic reflection impacted by, 87; visual art and, 109–10
Currie, Gregory, 134

Dancygier, Barbara, 263
denarration: defined, 170; examples of, 170
devadāsī, 253–54, 255, 256, 257–58
dhvani, 83; defined, 71; of Mīrābāī's work, 252, 253–54, 257–58; rasa, or sentiment, produced by, 71, 257; of Tagore's work, 85, 266
dialectical work, 119
Dick, Philip K., 157–58
Diescho, Joseph, 16, 58–59, 245–46, 274. See also *Born of the Son*
director. See auteur, film
discourse: analysts, 2, 3; communicative and representational parts of, 22; defined, 22; function of, 17; in narratology, 4; story compared to, 22; verbal and visual art compared on basis of, 67; in visual art, 66. See also communicative discourse
discourse analysis: interpretation in, 5; literary critics approach to, 3, 5; literary study uses of, 1; narrative art and, 11–13; nomological part of, 2, 5; politeness in, 2. See also Critical Discourse Analysis; linguistic discourse analysis; narrative discourse analysis
discourse analysts: discourse types distinguished by, 2; narrative and storytelling for, 3
discursive interpretation, 31
divergence: author and reader imagination, 38–39; congruence and, 31, 43; gaps creating, 186; multiple narration, 184, 186, 188–89
divine androgyne, 254–55, 256
Dixon, Peter, 158, 260
Dutt, Guru, 92, 266
Dyer, Richard, 97

embedded narration: diagram of, 185; emotionally constrained, 224; example of, 16, 231–32; focalization compared to, 16, 224–25; idealized, 224–25; implicit subtextual template compared with, 225; informationally constrained, 224; limitations of, 223, 247–48; nature of, 183–84, 223–24; personified, 183–84, 219–20, 221, 273; psychological, 222–23, 224, 247–48; rhetorical, 223, 224, 248; summary of, 247–48
emotion: embedded narration and constrained, 224; of focalizer, 51–52; implied reader, 55; literary narrative and importance of, 12; in narrative discourse, 12–13, 18; in narrator, 49, 51, 264; normative, 259; reader, 55; representative art driven by, 17–18; simulation for understanding, 41, 54–55, 238–39; story distinguished from narrative, 17–18
emotional contradiction: example of, 58, 61; logical and, 159; from real author, 58–59; in real reader, 58
emotional response: appropriate or normal, 57; author sincerity judged in reader, 33; cross-textual consideration impacting, 87; examples of, 56–57, 66; in implied reader, 55–56, 129–30; memory stimulating reader, 55–56, 264; narrator reliability, trust, and, 154, 167, 271; in representational painting, 66
emotion sharing: in *Born of the Sun*, 241, 243, 244, 245–47, 249, 274–75; components of, 239; fiction and, 239;

group narration and, 249; inference versus simulation in, 241
empathy. *See specific topics*
encoding: attentional orientation enabling, 53–54; implied reader and, 54; misdirection, narrator reliability, and, 153; by reader, 53–54
ethico-political effects: example of, 9; as literary effect, 9
ethico-political evaluation, 9–10

facial mirroring, 66
facts: in fiction, 155–58; storyworld intertwined with, 157–58
Faulkner, William, 16, 153–54, 272. *See also The Sound and the Fury*
fiction, 187; emotion sharing in, 239; facts in, 155–58; general principles and particular instances in, 155–56; principle of minimal departure in, 156
Fiedler, Leslie, 121
film: auteurism to study of, 89; coherence and multiplicity issues in, 132, 148; cross-textual canon in, 14, 94, 99; cross-textual implied author complicated by, 98–99; implicated authors in, 132–33, 137, 147–48, 149; intentionalities in, 97; multiple authors for, 90, 95–96, 111, 132–33, 134–36, 148; novel compared to, 90, 132–33; perceptual narration in, 134–35, 136, 144, 270; receptive intent in, 91–92, 132–33; stream of consciousness in, 191–92, 272; techniques for shifts in, 138. *See also* auteur, film; creation, film
film production: creation components of, 94–95, 111; nature of, 94–95
first-person narration: defined, 189; implied narratee in, 189–90; interior monologue compared to, 189–90; self-conscious, 189
focalization: affective orientation in, 51–52; collective, 243, 244, 245–46, 249–50; defined, 47; embedded narration compared to, 16, 224–25; example of, 16, 28–29, 50–52, 138, 140, 214, 231–32, 241, 245, 261, 264; hierarchy for narrator, 237–38; implied author preference through bias in, 28; internal and external, 48, 50–51; Jahn on, 47, 264; knowledge or interest limitation and, 50, 237–38; omniscient/limited narration and, 47–48, 224–25, 237; profile of ambiguity in, 52; psychological, 224; single versus multiple, 52; theory of mind and narrator, 238; types, 47; zero, 48–49
focalizer: communicative discourse in relation to, 26; defined, 26; emotion of, 51–52; focus compared to, 49; narrator compared to, 26, 47; nature of, 26; topicalizer compared to, 49–50
focus, 49
Foucault, Michel, 10
frequency, 100

gaps: critical explication for understanding, 164; divergence created through, 186; emotional versus informational, 61; example of, 60, 61, 163–64, 171, 178, 179–80, 181–82; heuristics for bridging, 164, 178–79, 186; Iser on, 57–58, 59, 159; in multiple narration, 186; narrator reliability and, 159, 160–61, 181; reader resolution of, 161–69; in real world principles or particulars, 160; reflection provoked by, 59; source identification for, 160; in spontaneous processing, 57–58; thematic concerns advanced by, 179–80, 182, 187. *See also* emotional contradiction; informational contradiction
Gaut, Berys, 97, 266
gender. *See specific topics*
general principles: in fiction, 155–56; gaps in, 160; levels of, 156–57; storyworld/real world deviation in, 158
generative principles: in Roy's work, 108–9; in Tagore's work, 109
Genette, Gérard, 47
genre, 169
Gerrig, Richard, 44

Goya, Francisco, 66, 266
The Great Gatsby (Fitzgerald), 49, 165–66
Grice, Paul, 1–2, 268
group ideology, 128
group or collective voice narration: difference or diversity problems for, 235–36; emotion sharing and, 249; example of, 16, 229–31, 232, 233, 234; indirect, issues arising from, 236; instantiated voice in, 236; for large or abstract groups, 236–37; in Mīrābāī's work, 255–56, 275; multiple, 184; in Ngũgĩ's work, 229–31, 232, 233, 234, 235–37, 249, 274; summary of, 248
Guernica (Picasso), 68; emotional response from, 66; as narrative art, 67
guided omniscience, 224–25

Hawaii (Michener), 47
Hayman, David, 263
Heidegger, Martin, 159
Hemingway, Ernest, 50, 60; affective focalization by, 51–52; Critical Discourse Analysis of story by, 10; narrative structure in story of, 6–9. *See also* "A Very Short Story"
Herman, David, 22, 260, 261
hermeneutic narrative processing, 163, 181
heuristics: gaps bridged through, 164, 178–79, 186; interpretation guided by, 261; *Mulholland Drive* understood through, 205; parallel narration engendering, 187; in *Surfacing*, 171, 178–79
Hirschbiegel, Oliver, 61
Hogan, Lalita Pandit, 252
homodiegetic narrator: defined, 25; example of, 49; personification and, 43

implicated authors: ambivalence in, 119; implicated reader bound to, 119; implied distinguished from, 117, 118, 268; Marxist tradition recognizing, 120; narrative contradictions between, 118–19, 120–22, 146–47, 268; race or gender influencing, 120, 121–23; social ideology in conflicts of, 119–20, 121, 122–23; thematized reasons delineating, 118, 146; of *Uncle Tom's Cabin*, 121–30
implicated authors, in film: by audience, 133; initial and retrospective, 137, 149; nature of, 147–48; profile of intentional coherence for, 132–33, 148
implicated reader, 119
implicit subtextual template: embedded narration compared to, 225; example of, 232
implied author: audience and misdirection by, 133–34, 144–46, 148–49, 206; auteur in film as, 14, 265, 266–67; broader application of, 64; in cinema, 15; coherence and, 14–15, 130–31; cross-textual compared with, 267; focalization bias as preference of, 28; implicated distinguished from, 117, 118, 268; implied reader in relation to, 29, 53; inconsistency and, 116–17; interpretation, implicit narrative development, and, 118–19; memory commonality presupposed by, 56; Mīrābāī poem, 257; in narratology, 33–34, 260, 261–62, 265–66; narrator compared to, 26–28, 30–31, 37; narrator reliability in relation to, 150, 151; nature of, 23, 266; nonpersonified narrator congruence with, 46; partial contradictions in intent of, 113; profile of ambiguity and, 13–14, 24; reader reconstruction of, 34; real author insincerity delineating, 30–31, 33, 34, 261; real compared to, 23, 24, 30–36; as receptive intent of real author or auteur, 35, 76, 90–91, 110, 116, 262, 267–68; storyworld of, 260–61; as textual implication, 24, 116. *See also* cross-textual implied author; implied authors, multiple; *specific topics*
implied authors, multiple: audience multiplicity and, 139–40, 145–46; cognitive architecture showing, 116–18, 268; in film, 90, 95–96, 111, 132–33, 134–36, 148; nonpersonified narrator impacted by, 136, 145–46

implied narratee, 189–90
implied painter: painter, reliability, and, 76, 78; in Tagore's work, 64–65. See also cross-textual implied author
implied reader: complexity of, 252, 275; defined, 23; emotion, 55; emotional response, 55–56, 129–30; encoding and, 54; implied author in relation to, 29, 53; for Mīrābāī, 255, 256, 257; narratee compared to, 28–29; nature of, 24, 53; norm provided by, 62; reader resisting, 62–63; real reader compared to, 29; as textual implication, 24
incongruence, 31
inference, 241
information, 39–40
informational contradiction: from real author, 58–59; for real reader, 58; textual versus real world, 59
Inner Vision: An Exploration of Art and the Brain (Zeki), 14
Innes, G., 262
In Our Time (Hemingway), 26
insincerity: guidelines for judging, 32–33; implied versus real author distinction through, 30–31, 33, 34, 261; incongruence and, 31–32; reader emotional response for judging, 33; real knowledge in judging, 33
intent, 23. See also receptive intent
intentional fallacy, 36, 262
interior monologue: associative reformulation in, 190–91; defined, 190, 272; example of, 189, 190, 241–42, 263; first-person narration compared to, 189–90; subvocalizations in, 190, 191, 272
interpretation, 260; ambiguity of meaning and, 17, 19–20; in conversational implicature, 5; defined, 18; in discourse analysis, 5; heuristics guiding, 261; implied author, implicit narrative development, and, 118–19; isolable features open to, 18; as mathematical function model, 19; metaphor and dhvani for painting, 71; multiplicity of, 19; narrative discourse analysis and, 18–19; narrative structure and, 7–8; receptive intent and, 91–93; standards of, 19. See also discursive interpretation; profile of ambiguity; technique; *specific topics*
interpretive adjustment, 163, 181
irony, narrative: defined, 25; example of, 25, 28, 30, 33; in incongruence, 31; in titles, 75
Iser, Wolfgang: gaps for, 57–58, 59, 159; reader terminology of, 57–58

Jahn, Manfred, 47, 264
Joyce, James, 189, 261
junctural moment, 67

karma, 103, 267
Kellogg, Robert, 134
Khan, Kabir: implied authors and narrators in work of, 136–46; narrator reliability in work of, 15, 144, 165. See also *New York*
knowledge. See *specific topics*
Kovács, András, 272
Kṛṣṇa: divine responsibility of, 254; as personified narratee, 252–54

Labov, William, 4, 5–6, 9
Lacan, Jacques, 262–63
Lahiri, Jhumpa, 58
Lalanne, Jean-Marc, 273
Lanser, Susan, 117–18
linguistic discourse analysis: critical and narrative compared to, 11; discourse analysis containing, 1; goals of, 1, 5; narrative and storytelling in, 3, 9
linguists, 63
literary: criticism, 115–16; effects, 9; study, 1
literary narrative: complexity of, 21; emotion importance in, 12; non-literary compared to, 11; political thought and action influenced by, 12
literature, 56–57
Liu, Yuexin, 269
Livingston, Paisley, 97
Locher, Paul, 262

logic, 168–69
logical contradiction, 159
Lukács, Georg, 120
Lutgendorf, Philip, 252
Lynch, David, 16, 183, 221. See also *Mulholland Drive*
lyric poems, 67

MacCabe, Colin, 135–36
Madhumati (Roy), 14, 98; cinematography patterns in, 100–101, 103–4; sound and visual techniques in, 104–5, 106; synopsis of, 101; thematic concerns in, 99–100, 102–3, 104, 105, 107, 109, 267
Maltby, Richard, 133
The Man in the High Castle (Dick), 157–58
Margolin, Uri, 135, 236, 274
Maxim of Relevance, 2
meaning, 260; productive compared to receptive, 34–35; from reader's point of view, 35; textual, 35. See also productive meaning; receptive intent
memory, 45; character creation through author, 38–39, 262; commonality of, 56–57; narrator reliability and, 167–68, 173–74, 176–78, 179, 180, 238; reader emotional response stimulated by, 55–56, 264; visual art inspiring, 66. See also *specific topics*
mental cause: for authorial intent, 114, 146; defined, 114
mentalistic narration: basic form of, 189; defined, 189; summary of, 220–21. See also first-person narration; *The Sound and the Fury*
metaphor, 71
Mey, Jacob, 37
Michener, James, 47, 49
Midnight's Children (Rushdie), 156
Mīrābāī: biographical information on, 275; dhvani of work of, 252, 253–54, 257–58; divine androgyne in work of, 254–55, 256; group or collective narration in work of, 255–56, 275; implied reader for, 255, 256, 257; marital and spiritual relations in work of, 257–58; narrator/narratee complexity in work of, 255, 256; nonpersonified narratee in work of, 254; as personified narrator, 252–53; poem attributed to, 252, 253–54, 275; politics and religion in work of, 256–57
misdirection: audience and implied author, 133–34, 144–46, 148–49, 206; encoding, narrator reliability, and, 153; narration and, 134, 148–49; narrator reliability in attention, 152–53; nature of and reasons for, 269–70; in *New York*, 144–46. See also narrator reliability or unreliability; *Surfacing*
Mitra, Asok, 64–65
"A Modest Proposal" (Swift), 25
morality, 123–24, 128–29
motifs, 74–75, 82–83, 87, 110
Mrs. Dalloway (Woolf), 191
Mulholland Drive (Lynch), 16, 183; description and analysis of, 201–2, 203–8, 210–20, 273; discrete ambiguity of, 20, 201, 210, 213–14, 217–18, 219; dual pessimistic/optimistic narratives in, 202–3, 204, 205–6, 207–8, 210, 211, 212–14, 216–17, 219; focalization in, 214; heuristics in understanding, 205; narrator reliability in, 208, 218; parallel nonpersonified narration of, 202, 203, 214, 216, 218, 219–20, 221, 273; as personified, embedded narration, 219–20, 221, 273; profile of ambiguity of, 212, 213, 218–19; stream of consciousness dreaming in, 273–74
multiple authorship, 97, 132. See also implied authors, multiple
multiple narration: contradiction or gaps in, 186; divergence creating interest in, 184, 186, 188–89; group or collective, 184; narrator psychology in, 188–89; summary of, 220; types of, 15, 183, 222. See also embedded narration; parallel narration
Murthy, V. K., 92, 266

The Namesake (Lahiri), 58
Nandy, Ashis, 129

narratee: ambiguity, 43; in communicative discourse, 24–25, 37–46; complexity of, 252, 255, 275; embedded, 42, 43, 44, 46; heterodiegetic, 28; implied reader compared to, 28–29; inferred, 25–26; narrator and, 25–26, 41; ubiquitous nature of, 46. *See also* nonpersonified narratee; *specific topics*

narration: implicit versus self-conscious, 189; misdirection and, 134, 148–49; profile of ambiguity in, 52; in Tagore's work, 75–80; verbal, 135, 270; in visual art, 66. *See also* denarration; embedded narration; group or collective voice narration; mentalistic narration; multiple narration; omniscient/limited narration; parallel narration; second-person narration

narrative and storytelling: for discourse analysts, 3; hierarchies of power impact on, 11; junctures, 67; linguistic discourse analysis on, 3, 9; pictures in, 67, 265; representational art compared to, 66; story emotion compared to, 17–18

narrative art: discourse analysis and, 11–13; examples of, 67; verbal, 21

narrative contradictions: default preference hierarchy dropped in, 162–63; implicated authors and, 118–19, 120–22, 146–47, 268; in multiple narration, 186; narrator reliability and, 158–59, 271; in Uncle Tom's Cabin, 121–30, 147. *See also* emotional contradiction; task contradiction

narrative discourse: analysts, 3; basic components of, 22–30; diagram of, 22, 46, 63, 251; emotion in, 12–13, 18; story as, 4. *See also* communicative discourse

narrative discourse analysis: coherence in, 3–4; critical and linguistic compared to, 11; discourse analysis containing, 1; interpretation and, 18–19; literary compared to nonliterary, 3, 4–5; narratology and, 4; for painting, 64–88, 267; speaker in, 4; for Tagore's paintings, 110

narrative reconstruction, 67

narrative structure: components of, 5–6; example of, 6–9; interpretation and, 7–8; Labov defining, 5–6, 9; nomological discourse analysis and component isolation of, 6

narratology: advancement of, 11–12; communicative components acceptance in, 29–30; discourse and story in, 4; implied author in, 33–34, 260, 261–62, 265–66; narrative discourse analysis and, 4; narrator approach from, 40; narrator reliability in, 151

narrator: author compared to, 39–40, 263–64; causal inference, 194–96, 198–99, 200, 272; in communicative discourse, 24–25, 37–46; embedded, 15, 16, 42–43, 46; emotion in, 49, 51, 264; focalizer compared to, 26, 47; frame, 149; function and nature of, 37, 39–40, 270; group, 15, 16; heterodiegetic, 25; as humanlike agent, 48, 49; implied author compared to, 26–28, 30–31, 37; multiple narration and psychology of, 188–89; narratee and, 25–26, 41; narratology approach to, 40; out-grouping, 196; painting point of view, 75; parallel nonpersonified, 16; parallel personified, 15–16; perceptual versus verbal, 75; personified compared to nonpersonified, 40–41; perspectival and, 47; stream of consciousness for, 191; topicalizer for, 49; trustworthy versus untrustworthy, 39–40, 144; types of, 24–25, 149; ubiquitous nature of, 46. *See also* homodiegetic narrator; nonpersonified narration; perceptual narration, in film; personified narration; *specific topics*

narrator reliability or unreliability: emotional response, trust, and, 154, 167, 271; examples of, 15, 150, 151, 152, 153–54, 164, 165–67, 170–79, 193, 194–96, 208, 218, 271, 272, 273; familiarity and, 166; gaps or task contradiction pointing to, 159, 160–61, 181; implied author compared for, 150, 151; memory-based, 167–68, 173–74,

176–78, 179, 180, 238; misdirection, encoding, and, 153; misdirection of attention and, 152–53; narrative contradictions and, 158–59, 271; in narrative discourse, 25; in narratology, 151; narrator self-interest in, 166–67; nature of, 151–52, 270; painter reliability compared to, 76, 78; parallel narration, trust, and, 188; personified versus nonpersonified, 165; presumption of, 155; reader response to, 15; sources of, 153–54; summary of, 181–82; supernatural experiences in, 171–72; trust as default, 158, 171, 186; types of, 152–53, 270. *See also* preference hierarchy, default

Nelles, William, 183, 268

Newell, Kenneth, 260

New York (Khan): audience and implied author multiplicity in, 139–40, 145–46; description and analysis of, 136–37, 138, 139–46, 149; focalization in, 140; implied author in, 137, 138, 142–43; misdirection in, 144–46; narrative forms in, 138, 141, 145; narrator reliability in, 15, 144, 165; perceptual narrator in, 136, 137, 141, 144, 270; thematic concerns of, 270

Ngũgĩ, Wa Thiong'o, 16, 239, 248; group narration used by, 229–31, 232, 233, 234, 235–37, 249, 274; Kenya view of, 226; Marxist perspective of, 231, 249; thematic concerns in work of, 229–30, 231, 233, 234, 235, 236. See also *Petals of Blood*

Nielsen, Henrik Skov, 43

nomological discourse: cultural and cross-cultural aspect of, 2–3; politeness in, 2

nomological discourse analysis: example of, 6–7; structural component isolation in, 6

nonliterary narrative, 11

nonpersonified narratee: example of, 229; in Mīrābāī's work, 254; nonpersonified narration and, 40–41, 43–44, 165

nonpersonified narration: ambiguity in, 221; author's intent for, 45–46; example of, 184, 228–29, 230–31, 232–33, 241, 242, 243–44, 245; implied author congruence with, 46; implied author multiplicity for, 136, 145–46; nonpersonified narratee and, 40–41, 43–44, 165; omniscient, 232–33; overhearing to establish, 44–45; personified compared to, 40–41, 43–44, 165, 262–63; reliability and, 165, 167. *See also* parallel narration

norm, 62

Notaro, Anna, 91

novel, 90, 132–33

Nünning, Ansgar, 33, 150, 159, 165

omniscient/limited narration: example of, 231, 232–34, 239; focalization and, 47–48, 224–25, 237; nonpersonified, 232–33

out-grouping, 196

overhearing, 44–45

painter: implied painter, reliability, and, 76, 78; narrator reliability compared with, 76, 78

painting: emotional junctures in, 67, 265; limited time frame, 67–68; lyric poems compared to, 67; narrative, 66, 264–65; narrative discourse analysis for, 64–88, 267; narrator types in, 75; titles for, 75. *See also* representational painting; *specific topics*

Palmer, Alan, 274–75

parallel narration, 16; collections compared to, 186–87; conjunctive, 184, 272; diagram of, 185; disjunctive, 184; heuristics engendered by, 187; narrator reliability and trust in, 188; nonpersonified, disambiguating, 201; nonpersonified examples, 202, 203, 214, 216, 219–20, 221, 273; personified and nonpersonified, 184, 187, 221; personified examples, 183, 184, 188, 192–93, 200–201; reader relating accounts in, 186, 188; sum-

mary of, 220. See also *Mulholland Drive*
particulars: epistemic context in empirical, 169; in fiction, 155–56; gaps in, 160; levels of, 156–57; referential real world, 157; storyworld/real world deviation in, 158
patriarchy, 87
perceptual narration, in film: defense of, 134–35; example of, 136, 137, 141, 144, 270; point of view controlled by, 134; trustworthiness assumed for, 135–36, 144; verbal compared to, 135
personified narration: creation of, 40–41; defined, 259; embedded, 183–84, 219–20, 221, 273; example of, 183, 184, 188, 192–93, 200–201; homodiegetic narrator and, 43; narrator and narratee complexity in, 252–54, 255; nonpersonified compared to, 40–41, 43–44, 165, 262–63; reliability and, 165–66. See also parallel narration; specific topics
perspectival, 49; defined, 47; narrator and, 47
Petals of Blood (Ngũgĩ): under appreciation of, 225, 274; class allegory in, 227–28, 231, 234–35; description and analysis of, 225–35, 274; discourse techniques in, 231, 233–34; embedded narration and focalization in, 16, 231–32; group or collective voice narration of, 229–31, 232, 233, 234; historical preservation and artists' role in, 233; implicit subtextual template in, 232; narrative structure of, 228; national allegory in, 226–28, 230, 234–35; nonpersonified narratee of, 229; nonpersonified narrator of, 228–29, 230–31, 232–33; omniscient narrator in, 231, 232–34, 239; religion in, 228, 274; summary of, 248–49; thematic concerns in narrative form of, 229–30, 231, 235, 236
Phelan, James, 23, 80, 152, 261, 263, 270, 275
Picasso, Pablo, 66
pictures, 67, 265
Pietà (Michelangelo), 68

plot, 260
point of view, in painting, 75
politeness, 2
preference hierarchy, default: contradiction for shifting away from, 162–63; diagrams, 167, 168, 169; epistemic context in, 164–65, 168–69; examples of, 161–62, 165–67, 168; genre, 169; information source, 161, 165–67; logic in, 168–69; nature of, 161, 164–65; for reader resolution, 161–62; type of evidence, 161, 167–68
Prem Patra (Roy), 92–93, 98, 109
Prentice, Deborah, 44
principle of minimal departure, 156
principles of inference, 2
productive meaning: biographical criticism for, 35–36; real author from, 35
profile of ambiguity: all work containing, 19–20, 70; defined, 13–14; discrete ambiguity in, 201; gaps as part of, 160; implied author or painter and, 13–14, 24; in *Mulholland Drive*, 212, 213, 218–19; in narration and focalization, 52; in *New York*, 137; profile of intentional coherence juxtaposed with, 132; in receptive intent, 93; in Tagore's work, 85, 87, 110
profile of ambivalence, 57
profile of intentional coherence: for implicated authors in film, 132–33, 148; profile of ambiguity juxtaposed with, 132
psychoanalytic heuristics: gaps bridged through, 164, 178–79, 186; in *Surfacing*, 171, 178–79

Rabinowitz, Peter, 32, 152, 260, 261, 264
race. See specific topics
racial ideology, 121–30
rasa, or sentiment, 71, 257
Ray, Satyajit, 73, 80, 82
reader: authorial intent and response of, 114; author imagination divergence from, 38–39; default preference hierarchies for, 161–62; effortful versus spontaneous responses by, 57–58, 264; emotion, 55; gaps resolution

by, 161–69; imagination, 54–55; implied author reconstruction by, 34; implied reader resisted by, 62–63; meaning from point of view of, 35; nonpersonified narrator for, 44–45; parallel narration accounts related by, 186, 188; principle of minimal departure for, 156; purposes of fictional narrative, 17–18; for real author, 23–24; sahṛdaya as ideal, 57; as side participant, 44; simulation of response of, 114; tacit encoding by, 53–54. *See also* gaps; implied reader; real reader

real author: defined, 22; emotional or informational contradiction from, 58–59; emotional response in judging sincerity of, 33; implied author in insincerity of, 30–31, 33, 34, 261; implied author in receptive meaning of, 35, 76, 90–91, 110, 116, 262, 267–68; implied compared to, 23, 24, 30–36; productive meaning for, 35; readers for, 23–24; work conception invalid, 34

real reader, 22; emotional contradiction in, 58; implied reader compared to, 29; informational contradiction for, 58; reflection by, 62

real world, 187; gaps in principles/particulars of, 160; informational contradiction between text and, 59; reliability in, 151, 270; storyworld compared to, 31, 261. *See also specific topics*

reasons: in authorial self-understanding, 114–16; defined, 114; literary criticism basis in complexity of, 115–16; thematized and unthematized, 114–15, 118, 146

receptive intent: author's ability to explain, 36, 262, 268; in film, 91–92, 132–33; implied author from, 35, 76, 90–91, 110, 116, 262, 267–68; intentional fallacy filtered out by, 36, 262; interpretation and, 91–93; limitations of, 91; problems with, 91, 92, 110–11; productive compared to, 34–35; profile of ambiguity in, 93

recurrent device, 100–101

reflection: critic and, 62–63; gaps provoking, 59; real reader, 62. *See also* thematic reflection

relevance, 2. *See also* Maxim of Relevance

reliability: defined, 151–52; in real world, 151, 270; types of, 151–52

representational art: emotion driving, 17–18; storytelling compared to, 66

representational painting: emotional response in, 66; as narrative discourse, 65–68; narrative reconstruction in, 67; represented world in, 65–66; thematic reflection in, 66; verbal narrative compared to, 65–66

represented world, 66

Richardson, Brian, 133, 268, 269, 275

Ross, Stephen, 272

Roy, Bimal, 14, 92–93; auteurial features of films of, 99–102, 107–8, 112; background of, 99; cinematography patterns in films of, 98, 100–101, 103–4; generative principles in work of, 108–9; karma in films of, 103; sound and visual techniques in work of, 104–5, 106, 107, 108; Tagore's work compared to that of, 107, 109; thematic patterns in films of, 99–100, 102–3, 104, 105, 107, 109, 267. *See also Madhumati*

rules of conversational implicature: coherence and, 2; example of, 2, 5; Grice's, 1–2, 268; interpretation in, 5

Rushdie, Salman, 156

Ryan, Marie-Laure, 156, 261

sahṛdaya, 62; defined, 56; emotional response by, 56–57; as ideal reader, 57; profile of ambivalence evinced by, 57

Scholes, Robert, 28, 134, 261

second-person narration, 261

Semino, Elena, 261

sentiment. *See* rasa, or sentiment

Shen, Dan, 269

simulation: emotion sharing in inference versus, 241; emotions understood through, 41, 54–55, 238–39; literary

imagination employing, 42–43; of reader response, 114. See also theory of mind
sincerity. See insincerity
Smith, Murray, 28–29
social ideology, 119–20, 121, 122–23
The Sound and the Fury (Faulkner): attachment dependency in, 199–200, 273; description and analysis of, 188, 194–200; guilt in, 198–200; interior monologue in, 190; mentalistic narration in, 220; narrative format of, 188; narrator causal inference in, 194–96, 198–99, 200, 272; narrator reliability in, 153–54, 193, 194–96, 272, 273; parallel personified narration in, 16, 183, 184, 188 192–93, 200; reader interpretive tasks in, 188; shame and failure treatment in, 197–98; suicide and, 198, 273; theory of mind in, 194–95
Southall, Joseph, 68
speaker: in conversational storytelling, 4; in Critical Discourse Analysis, 10; in narrative discourse analysis, 4. See also narrator
speech, 2
spontaneous response: critic influencing, 63; gaps in, 57–58
spontaneous understanding, 163, 181
Sternberg, Meir, 152
story: discourse compared to, 22; narrative compared to emotion of, 17–18; as narrative discourse, 4; in narratology, 4, 22
storytelling. See narrative and storytelling
storyworld, 37, 39; defined, 260; facts intertwined in, 157–58; implied author, 260–61; real world compared to, 31, 261; represented world compared to, 66
Stowe, Harriet Beecher, 15, 55; authorial intent of, 114; biographical interest in, 268–69; implicated authors in work of, 121–30. See also *Uncle Tom's Cabin*
Stratton, Florence, 274
stream of consciousness: dreaming, 273–74; example of, 192; in film, 191–92; 272; fully idealized verbalization in, 192, 272; narrator experience through, 191
subvocalization, 190, 191, 272
Sujata (Roy), 93, 98, 107, 109
Surfacing (Atwood): denarration in, 170; description and analysis of, 170–71, 172, 173–80; gaps in, 163–64, 171, 178, 179–80, 181–82; heuristics in, 171, 178–79; memory in, 173–74, 176–78, 179, 180; narrator reliability in, 15, 151, 152, 164, 170–79, 271; thematic concerns advanced in, 179–80, 271–72
Swift, Jonathan, 25, 30
symbolism, 71

Tagore, Rabindranath, 13; ambiguity in paintings of, 14, 68–74, 75–80, 83, 110; attachment in works of, 82–83, 87; cross-textual implied authorship in works of, 74, 80, 82–83, 85, 87, 94, 112; dhvani in work of, 85, 266; generative principles in work of, 109; implied painter in work of, 64–65; mother and child in works of, 83; narration in work of, 75–80; narrative discourse analysis for paintings of, 110; nondirective orientation in paintings of, 68; patriarchy in works of, 87; profile of ambiguity in work of, 85, 87, 110; Roy's work compared to that of, 107, 109; sentences added to paintings of, 75–76; women's treatment in paintings of, 73–74, 80, 82–83, 87. See also specific topics
Tagore plate 4, 83–84
Tagore plate 9, 68–70, 73, 74
Tagore plate 12, 76–77
Tagore plate 79, 80–82
Tagore plate 145, 83, 86
Tagore plate 151, 78–80
Tagore plate 156: cross-textual interpretation of, 83, 85, 87; description of, 71, 73; illustration of, 72; mutual connection and sorrow in, 73, 74; patriarchy addressed in, 87
Tagore plate 157, 87–88
Tagore plate 162, 83, 85

Tao, Liang, 4
task contradiction, 159
Tawil, Ezra, 121–22
technique: device recurrence for establishing, 100–101; film shift, 138; frequency for establishing, 100. See also specific topics
thematic concerns: of Born of the Sun, 240, 241, 242, 244, 246, 247; gaps advancing, 179–80, 182, 187; of Madhumati, 99–100, 102–3, 104, 105, 107, 109, 267; narrative form for advancing, 229–30, 231, 235, 236; of New York, 270; of Ngũgĩ's work, 229–30, 231, 233, 234, 235, 236. See also specific topics
thematic reflection: cross-textual consideration impact on, 87; in representational painting, 66
theme: defined, 18; as reader purpose, 18. See also specific topics
theory of mind: example of, 194–95; focalized narrator and, 238; forms of, 194; nature of, 193–94, 263
Third of May (Goya): emotional response from, 66; as narrative art, 67
Titanic (Cameron), 223–24, 225
titles: irony in, 75; for paintings, 75
Tolstoy, Leo, 158
topicalization: affective, 52–53; example of, 50, 52–53
topicalizer: focalizer compared to, 49–50; for narrator, 49
trust: emotional response, narrator reliability, and, 154, 167, 271; hierarchy summarized, 167–68, 271; as narrator reliability default, 158, 181, 186; parallel narration, narrator reliability, and, 188; perceptual narration and, 135–36, 144

Ulysses (Joyce), 189, 221, 263
Uncle Tom's Cabin (Stowe), 15; African generational model promoted in, 129; analysis of, 121–30; "child" model for Africans in, 126–30, 269; implicated authors and contradiction in, 119, 121–30, 147; implied authorial coherence in attachment relations, 130–31, 269; implied reader emotion from, 55, 129–30; "industry" and "enterprising" treatment in, 123–26; morality in, 123–24, 128–29; racial ideology in, 121–30
Der Untergang (Hirschbiegel), 62; emotional contradictions elicited in, 61; gaps in, 61

verbal art: ambiguity in, 70; discourse for comparing visual and, 67; narrative, 21; visual art compared to, 65–66, 67–68, 265
Vermeer, Johannes, 14
"A Very Short Story" (Hemingway), 6–9, 10, 13, 261; character imagination in, 42–43; focalization in, 28–29, 50–52, 264; gaps in, 60; implied author compared to narrator in, 26–28; implied compared to real author in, 31–32; narratee and narrator in, 28, 37, 42–43, 46, 50, 263; narrator/narratee personification in, 43–44; topicalization in, 50, 52–53
visual art: ambiguity in, 67–68, 70; cross-textual authorship and, 109–10; discourse and narration in, 66; discourse for comparing verbal and, 67; memory inspired by, 66; text in, 75; verbal compared to, 65–66, 67–68, 265. See also painting; representational art; representational painting
voice, 45–46

War and Peace (Tolstoy), 157, 166–67
The Waves (Woolf), 192
Weinstein, Cindy, 122
women, 73–74, 80, 82–83, 87
Woolf, Virginia, 191, 192
world. See real world; storyworld
Wright Wexman, Virginia, 90

Yacobi, Tamar, 150, 159

Zeki, Semir, 14
Zunshine, Lisa, 263

THEORY AND INTERPRETATION OF NARRATIVE
James Phelan, Peter J. Rabinowitz, and Robyn Warhol, Series Editors

Because the series editors believe that the most significant work in narrative studies today contributes both to our knowledge of specific narratives and to our understanding of narrative in general, studies in the series typically offer interpretations of individual narratives and address significant theoretical issues underlying those interpretations. The series does not privilege one critical perspective but is open to work from any strong theoretical position.

Literary Identification from Charlotte Brontë to Tsitsi Dangarembga
LAURA GREEN

An Aesthetics of Narrative Performance: Transnational Theater, Literature, and Film in Contemporary Germany
CLAUDIA BREGER

Narrative Theory: Core Concepts and Critical Debates
DAVID HERMAN, JAMES PHELAN AND PETER J. RABINOWITZ, BRIAN RICHARDSON, AND ROBYN WARHOL

After Testimony: The Ethics and Aesthetics of Holocaust Narrative for the Future
EDITED BY JAKOB LOTHE, SUSAN RUBIN SULEIMAN, AND JAMES PHELAN

The Vitality of Allegory: Figural Narrative in Modern and Contemporary Fiction
GARY JOHNSON

Narrative Middles: Navigating the Nineteenth-Century British Novel
EDITED BY CAROLINE LEVINE AND MARIO ORTIZ-ROBLES

Fact, Fiction, and Form: Selected Essays
RALPH W. RADER. EDITED BY JAMES PHELAN AND DAVID H. RICHTER

The Real, the True, and the Told: Postmodern Historical Narrative and the Ethics of Representation
ERIC L. BERLATSKY

Franz Kafka: Narration, Rhetoric, and Reading
EDITED BY JAKOB LOTHE, BEATRICE SANDBERG, AND RONALD SPEIRS

Social Minds in the Novel
ALAN PALMER

Narrative Structures and the Language of the Self
MATTHEW CLARK

Imagining Minds: The Neuro-Aesthetics of Austen, Eliot, and Hardy
KAY YOUNG

Postclassical Narratology: Approaches and Analyses
EDITED BY JAN ALBER AND MONIKA FLUDERNIK

Techniques for Living: Fiction and Theory in the Work of Christine Brooke-Rose
KAREN R. LAWRENCE

Towards the Ethics of Form in Fiction: Narratives of Cultural Remission
LEONA TOKER

Tabloid, Inc.: Crimes, Newspapers, Narratives
V. PENELOPE PELIZZON AND NANCY M. WEST

Narrative Means, Lyric Ends: Temporality in the Nineteenth-Century British Long Poem
MONIQUE R. MORGAN

Joseph Conrad: Voice, Sequence, History, Genre
EDITED BY JAKOB LOTHE, JEREMY HAWTHORN, AND JAMES PHELAN

Understanding Nationalism: On Narrative, Cognitive Science, and Identity
PATRICK COLM HOGAN

The Rhetoric of Fictionality: Narrative Theory and the Idea of Fiction
RICHARD WALSH

Experiencing Fiction: Judgments, Progressions, and the Rhetorical Theory of Narrative
JAMES PHELAN

Unnatural Voices: Extreme Narration in Modern and Contemporary Fiction
BRIAN RICHARDSON

Narrative Causalities
EMMA KAFALENOS

Why We Read Fiction: Theory of Mind and the Novel
LISA ZUNSHINE

I Know That You Know That I Know: Narrating Subjects from Moll Flanders *to* Marnie
GEORGE BUTTE

Bloodscripts: Writing the Violent Subject
ELANA GOMEL

Surprised by Shame: Dostoevsky's Liars and Narrative Exposure
DEBORAH A. MARTINSEN

Having a Good Cry: Effeminate Feelings and Pop-Culture Forms
ROBYN R. WARHOL

Politics, Persuasion, and Pragmatism: A Rhetoric of Feminist Utopian Fiction
ELLEN PEEL

Telling Tales: Gender and Narrative Form in Victorian Literature and Culture
ELIZABETH LANGLAND

Narrative Dynamics: Essays on Time, Plot, Closure, and Frames
EDITED BY BRIAN RICHARDSON

Breaking the Frame: Metalepsis and the Construction of the Subject
DEBRA MALINA

Invisible Author: Last Essays
CHRISTINE BROOKE-ROSE

Ordinary Pleasures: Couples, Conversation, and Comedy
KAY YOUNG

Narratologies: New Perspectives on Narrative Analysis
EDITED BY DAVID HERMAN

Before Reading: Narrative Conventions and the Politics of Interpretation
PETER J. RABINOWITZ

Matters of Fact: Reading Nonfiction over the Edge
DANIEL W. LEHMAN

The Progress of Romance: Literary Historiography and the Gothic Novel
DAVID H. RICHTER

A Glance Beyond Doubt: Narration, Representation, Subjectivity
SHLOMITH RIMMON-KENAN

Narrative as Rhetoric: Technique, Audiences, Ethics, Ideology
JAMES PHELAN

Misreading Jane Eyre: *A Postformalist Paradigm*
JEROME BEATY

Psychological Politics of the American Dream: The Commodification of Subjectivity in Twentieth-Century American Literature
LOIS TYSON

Understanding Narrative
EDITED BY JAMES PHELAN AND PETER J. RABINOWITZ

Framing Anna Karenina: *Tolstoy, the Woman Question, and the Victorian Novel*
AMY MANDELKER

Gendered Interventions: Narrative Discourse in the Victorian Novel
ROBYN R. WARHOL

Reading People, Reading Plots: Character, Progression, and the Interpretation of Narrative
JAMES PHELAN

www.ingramcontent.com/pod-product-compliance
Lightning Source LLC
Chambersburg PA
CBHW032001220426
43664CB00005B/102